Cybersecurity Secrets

For Health & Wellness

Black Hat Kathy

ISBN: 978-1-77961-093-4
Imprint: Shush! Daniel

Contents

Introduction

The Importance of Cybersecurity in Health and Wellness

Understanding the Risks of Cyber Attacks in the Health and Wellness Industry

In today's digitally connected world, the health and wellness industry relies heavily on technology to provide efficient and effective services to patients and consumers. However, this reliance on technology also brings with it numerous risks and vulnerabilities, particularly in terms of cybersecurity. Cyber attacks in the health and wellness industry can have far-reaching consequences, not only affecting individuals' personal information but also impacting their overall wellbeing.

One of the main risks of cyber attacks in the health and wellness industry is the potential exposure of sensitive personal health information. This includes medical records, test results, treatment plans, and other confidential data. This information is extremely valuable to cybercriminals, who can use it for various malicious purposes, such as identity theft, insurance fraud, or even blackmail.

Another risk is the potential disruption of critical healthcare services. In a cyber attack scenario, hackers may target the systems and networks that support medical facilities, causing significant disruptions in patient care. For example, access to patient records may be compromised, preventing healthcare providers from delivering accurate and timely care. This can result in delayed treatments, misdiagnoses, or other serious consequences for patients.

Furthermore, cyber attacks can directly impact the physical wellbeing of individuals through the manipulation of medical devices and equipment. With the increasing reliance on Internet of Things (IoT) devices in the health and wellness industry, such as connected wearable devices or remote monitoring systems, there is a greater risk of these devices being hacked. This can lead to unauthorized access or control over these devices, potentially causing harm to the user's health.

Moreover, cyber attacks can also target the reputation and trust of healthcare organizations. In an era where trust and privacy are crucial factors for patients seeking healthcare services, a cybersecurity breach can severely damage the reputation of a healthcare provider. Patients may lose confidence in the organization's ability to protect their personal information and may consequently seek treatment elsewhere. This can have significant financial implications for healthcare providers and can ultimately affect the overall quality of care delivered.

Understanding the risks of cyber attacks in the health and wellness industry is imperative for all individuals, not just healthcare professionals. We live in a digitally interconnected world, where our personal information is constantly at risk. It is crucial to be aware of these risks and take proactive measures to protect ourselves and our information.

In the next sections of this book, we will delve deeper into the various types of cyber threats and attack vectors that pose risks to the health and wellness industry. We will explore the strategies and solutions to mitigate these risks, as well as the legal and ethical considerations surrounding cybersecurity in this industry. By equipping ourselves with knowledge and understanding, we can enhance our overall wellbeing while navigating the digital world safely.

Key Concepts to Remember:

- Cyber attacks in the health and wellness industry can lead to the exposure of sensitive personal health information, disruption of critical healthcare services, manipulation of medical devices, and damage to the reputation of healthcare organizations.
- It is essential for individuals and healthcare professionals to understand the risks associated with cyber attacks and take proactive measures to protect personal information and ensure the security of healthcare systems.
- The next sections of this book will explore various types of cyber threats, strategies to mitigate risks, and the legal and ethical considerations relevant to cybersecurity in the health and wellness industry.

Further Reading:

- Miller, M. R., Massey, A. P., & Levy, M. A. (2019). Cybersecurity for hospitals and healthcare facilities: A guide to detection and prevention. CRC Press.

- Santillana, I., & Haylor, J. (2020). Cybersecurity resilience in healthcare: Securing patient data. Springer.
- Ponemon Institute. (2021). The 2021 State of Healthcare Cybersecurity Report. Retrieved from `https://www.ponemon.org/`

The Impact of Cybersecurity Breaches on Personal Wellbeing

In today's digitally connected world, where personal information is stored and transmitted electronically, the importance of cybersecurity cannot be overstated. Cybersecurity breaches, such as unauthorized access, data breaches, and identity theft, can have a significant impact on individuals' personal wellbeing. In this section, we will explore the various ways in which cybersecurity breaches can affect individuals and discuss the measures one can take to mitigate these risks.

Financial Impact

One of the most immediate and tangible consequences of cybersecurity breaches is the financial impact on individuals. Hackers and cybercriminals target personal information to gain unauthorized access to financial accounts and steal money. For instance, a data breach that compromises credit card information can lead to fraudulent transactions and unauthorized charges. Additionally, identity theft resulting from a cybersecurity breach can result in financial losses, as victims may have to incur expenses to restore their identity and reputation.

To protect personal wellbeing from financial impacts, individuals should regularly monitor their financial accounts for any suspicious activities and report them immediately. It is also essential to use strong and unique passwords for all online accounts, enable two-factor authentication, and be cautious while sharing financial information online.

Emotional and Psychological Stress

Cybersecurity breaches can also have a significant impact on an individual's emotional and psychological wellbeing. Being a victim of a cyber attack can induce feelings of anxiety, stress, and helplessness. The thought of personal information being in the hands of cybercriminals can lead to a loss of trust and feelings of violation.

To cope with the emotional and psychological stress caused by cybersecurity breaches, it is essential to practice self-care and seek support from friends, family, or professionals. Engaging in activities like exercise, meditation, or hobbies can help manage stress levels. It is also important to stay informed about the latest cybersecurity threats and take proactive steps to protect personal information.

Damage to Reputation

When personal information is compromised in a cybersecurity breach, individuals may suffer damage to their reputation. Cybercriminals can use stolen information to impersonate individuals online, ruining their reputation by posting inappropriate content or engaging in fraudulent activities under their name. This can have far-reaching consequences, impacting personal relationships, career opportunities, and overall wellbeing.

To safeguard personal reputation, individuals should regularly monitor their online presence and take steps to remove or report any fraudulent or damaging content. It is important to be cautious while sharing personal information online and to use privacy settings on social media platforms to control who can access personal information.

Health and Wellbeing

While the financial and emotional impacts of cybersecurity breaches are significant, they can also have adverse effects on an individual's health and overall wellbeing. The stress and anxiety resulting from a breach can lead to sleep disturbances, increased blood pressure, and other health-related issues. Additionally, the loss of personal data, such as health records or medical information, can compromise an individual's ability to receive appropriate medical care or make informed healthcare decisions.

To safeguard health and wellbeing, individuals should prioritize self-care practices such as maintaining a healthy lifestyle, seeking support from healthcare professionals, and regularly monitoring and reviewing their medical records for any inaccuracies or unauthorized changes. It is also crucial to be cautious while sharing personal health information online and only use trusted and secure platforms for telehealth or digital health technology.

Social Isolation and Trust Issues

Cybersecurity breaches can create a sense of social isolation and trust issues among individuals. The fear of being a victim of cybercrime may cause individuals to withdraw from digital interactions, leading to a decrease in social connections and a decline in overall wellbeing. Moreover, the loss of trust in digital platforms and online interactions can affect individuals' willingness to engage in e-commerce, online banking, or sharing personal information online.

To combat social isolation and restore trust, individuals should seek support from friends, family, and cybersecurity professionals. Engaging in online communities or support groups can also provide a sense of belonging and empowerment. It is paramount to stay informed about cybersecurity best practices and maintain a cautious yet proactive approach to online interactions.

Societal Implications

Finally, cybersecurity breaches not only impact individuals but also have broader societal implications. Large-scale breaches can lead to compromised infrastructure, government systems, and critical services, affecting the wellbeing of entire communities or even nations. Disruptions in healthcare services, financial institutions, or transportation systems, caused by cyber attacks, can have a lasting impact on individuals' lives and overall societal wellbeing.

To mitigate the societal implications of cybersecurity breaches, governments, organizations, and individuals need to collaborate and prioritize cybersecurity measures. This includes investing in robust cybersecurity infrastructure, promoting awareness and education, and implementing strict regulations and compliance frameworks.

In conclusion, cybersecurity breaches can have a profound impact on individuals' personal wellbeing. The financial, emotional, reputational, and health-related consequences can be significant. By understanding the risks and taking proactive measures to protect personal information, individuals can mitigate the impact of cybersecurity breaches and create a safer and more secure digital world for themselves and others.

Exercise: Think about a scenario where your personal information has been compromised due to a cybersecurity breach. How would you react to this situation? What immediate steps would you take to mitigate the potential impact on your personal wellbeing? Discuss with a partner and share your thoughts.

Additional Resources: - "The Cyber Effect" by Mary Aiken - "Data and Goliath" by Bruce Schneier - "The Art of Invisibility" by Kevin Mitnick

Why Everyone Should Be Concerned About Cybersecurity

Cybersecurity is no longer just a concern for technology experts or IT professionals. In today's digitally connected world, everyone, regardless of their profession or background, should be concerned about cybersecurity. The increasing reliance on technology in our daily lives has made us all potential targets for cyber attacks. This section explores the reasons why cybersecurity should be a top priority for everyone.

Protection of Personal Data

One of the key reasons why everyone should be concerned about cybersecurity is the protection of personal data. In the digital age, our personal information is more vulnerable than ever before. From financial details to medical records, our data is valuable to cybercriminals who can exploit it for financial gain or other malicious purposes.

Imagine the consequences of a cyber attack that compromises your personal information. It can lead to identity theft, financial loss, and even reputational damage. With the increasing prevalence of data breaches and hacking incidents, it is crucial for individuals to take proactive steps to protect their personal data.

Prevention of Financial Loss

Cyber attacks can have severe financial implications. Individuals can become victims of various types of online fraud, such as phishing scams or ransomware attacks. Phishing scams involve tricking individuals into revealing their sensitive information, such as credit card details or login credentials, which can then be used for unauthorized transactions or identity theft.

Ransomware attacks, on the other hand, involve encrypting the victim's data and demanding a ransom for its release. These attacks can paralyze individuals and businesses, causing significant financial loss and disruption to their daily lives.

By being concerned about cybersecurity, individuals can take preventive measures to protect themselves from such financial losses. This includes being cautious when sharing personal information online, regularly updating security software, and being vigilant against suspicious emails or messages.

Preservation of Personal and Professional Reputation

In today's interconnected world, our online reputation can be just as important as our offline reputation. Cyber attacks can severely damage both personal and professional reputations.

For example, if a hacker gains access to an individual's social media account, they can easily post malicious content or engage in cyberbullying. This can tarnish the individual's reputation and even lead to legal consequences.

In a professional context, cyber attacks targeting businesses can result in the leakage of confidential information or the compromise of customer data. Such incidents can lead to a loss of trust from clients and partners, and can even result in legal actions or hefty fines.

By prioritizing cybersecurity, individuals can protect their personal and professional reputations. This includes regularly updating privacy settings on social media platforms, using strong and unique passwords, and being cautious when sharing personal or sensitive information online.

Mitigation of Psychological Impact

Cyber attacks not only have tangible financial and reputational consequences, but they can also cause significant psychological distress. Victims of cyber attacks often experience feelings of violation, helplessness, and anxiety.

Imagine the psychological impact of falling victim to a cyber blackmail scheme or having one's personal photos or videos leaked online. Such experiences can have long-lasting effects on an individual's mental well-being, leading to stress, depression, and even social isolation.

Educating oneself about cybersecurity and implementing preventive measures can help mitigate the psychological impact of cyber attacks. By taking proactive steps to protect personal information and practicing safe online behavior, individuals can reduce their vulnerability to cyber threats and maintain peace of mind.

Safeguarding National Security

Cybersecurity is not only a concern at the individual level, but it also has broader implications for national security. With the increasing digitization of critical infrastructure, such as power grids and transportation systems, the potential for cyber attacks to disrupt essential services and compromise national security has grown significantly.

Nation-states and cybercriminal organizations are targeting governments, businesses, and even individuals to gain access to sensitive information or disrupt critical systems. This poses a significant threat to the stability and security of countries across the globe.

To safeguard national security, individuals need to be aware of the potential risks and take appropriate measures to protect their own digital environments. By doing so, they contribute to a collective effort to strengthen cybersecurity at both the individual and national levels.

Conclusion

Cybersecurity is not a concern that should be limited to a select few. It is a matter that affects everyone in today's digitally connected world. The protection of personal data, prevention of financial loss, preservation of personal and professional reputation, mitigation of psychological impact, and safeguarding of national security are all reasons why everyone should be concerned about cybersecurity.

By understanding the risks and taking proactive measures to protect themselves, individuals can navigate the digital landscape with confidence and contribute to a safer and more secure cyber world for all. Stay informed, stay vigilant, and prioritize cybersecurity in your personal and professional life.

The Intersection of Technology and Health and Wellness

With the rapid advancements in technology, the field of health and wellness has seen a significant transformation. The intersection of technology and health and wellness has not only revolutionized the way we manage our personal well-being but has also brought about new challenges in terms of cybersecurity. In this section, we will explore the various ways in which technology has impacted health and wellness, and how it is crucial to consider cybersecurity in this digital age.

Enhancing Health and Wellness through Technology

Technology has played a pivotal role in improving health and wellness. We now have access to a wide range of digital tools and applications that can help us monitor and manage our physical and mental well-being. For instance, wearable devices such as fitness trackers and smartwatches enable us to track our heart rate, sleep patterns, and physical activity levels. These devices provide real-time feedback, encouraging us to adopt healthier lifestyles and meet our fitness goals.

Furthermore, digital health platforms and mobile applications provide convenient access to healthcare services, even from the comfort of our homes. Telehealth services now allow us to consult healthcare professionals remotely through video conferencing, providing greater accessibility and reducing the need for physical visits to clinics or hospitals.

Technology has also enabled the development of personalized health and wellness interventions. Through data analytics and artificial intelligence (AI), healthcare providers can generate tailored treatment plans based on individual characteristics and medical history. This individualized approach improves the effectiveness of interventions, leading to better health outcomes.

Challenges and Risks

While technology has undoubtedly brought numerous benefits to the field of health and wellness, it has also introduced new risks and challenges. One of the key challenges is the security and privacy of personal health information. With the increasing amount of data being generated and stored digitally, there is a heightened risk of unauthorized access, data breaches, and identity theft.

Healthcare organizations and individuals must be aware of the potential threats and take proactive measures to protect sensitive data. This includes implementing robust cybersecurity measures, ensuring secure storage and transmission of data, and following best practices for data privacy and confidentiality.

Additionally, as technology becomes more integrated into healthcare facilities and practices, there is a growing concern about the vulnerability of these systems to cyberattacks. Hacking attempts, malware infections, and ransomware attacks can disrupt healthcare services and compromise patient safety. It is essential for healthcare organizations to have effective cybersecurity strategies in place to safeguard their infrastructure and protect patient information.

Cybersecurity Considerations

In light of the risks and challenges posed by the intersection of technology and health and wellness, it is crucial to prioritize cybersecurity measures. Healthcare organizations and individuals must adopt a proactive and holistic approach to ensure the confidentiality, integrity, and availability of data, as well as the security of digital systems.

Some key cybersecurity considerations in the health and wellness sector include:

- **Risk assessments:** Regularly assess potential vulnerabilities and risks within digital systems and processes to identify areas that require strengthening.
- **Security policies and procedures:** Develop and enforce comprehensive security policies and procedures that outline clear guidelines for data handling, access control, incident response, and employee training.
- **Secure network infrastructure:** Implement robust network security measures, such as firewalls, intrusion detection systems, and encryption protocols, to protect against unauthorized access and data breaches.
- **Secure software development practices:** Follow secure coding practices and regularly update and patch software to address vulnerabilities and minimize the risk of cyberattacks.

- **User awareness and training:** Educate users, including healthcare professionals and patients, about cybersecurity best practices, such as password hygiene, recognizing phishing attempts, and safe browsing habits.
- **Data encryption and access controls:** Implement encryption techniques to protect sensitive data at rest and in transit. Institute access controls and authentication mechanisms to ensure only authorized individuals can access data.
- **Incident response and disaster recovery:** Develop and test incident response plans to effectively manage and mitigate cyber incidents. Establish robust data backup and recovery strategies to minimize data loss.

The Role of Healthcare Professionals

Healthcare professionals have a vital role to play in ensuring the intersection of technology and health and wellness is secure and beneficial. They must stay updated with the latest technological advancements and cybersecurity practices to safeguard patient information and provide trustworthy advice to patients.

Healthcare professionals should also consider ethical considerations in the use of technology and ensure they adhere to relevant laws and regulations. Patient confidentiality, informed consent, and maintaining the trust of patients should be paramount.

Resources and Further Reading

To delve deeper into the intersection of technology and health and wellness, consider exploring the following resources:

- *Healthcare Information Security and Privacy* by Sean Murphy
- *The Digital Doctor: Hope, Hype, and Harm at the Dawn of Medicine's Computer Age* by Robert Wachter
- *The Fourth Transformation: How Augmented Reality and Artificial Intelligence Will Change Everything* by Robert Scoble and Shel Israel
- The National Institute of Standards and Technology (NIST) cybersecurity framework for healthcare organizations
- The Health Insurance Portability and Accountability Act (HIPAA) Security Rule

Remember, as technology continues to advance, it is imperative to stay informed and proactive in managing the intersection of technology and health and wellness. By prioritizing cybersecurity and implementing appropriate measures, we can ensure the benefits of technology are harnessed while minimizing the associated risks.

Overview of the Book's Structure and Objectives

In this section, we will provide an overview of the structure and objectives of this book, "Cybersecurity Secrets for Health & Wellness: How to Protect Your Personal Information and Stay Safe in a Digitally Connected World While Enhancing Your Overall Wellbeing". By understanding the layout of the book and the goals we aim to achieve, you will be able to make the most out of your reading experience.

The Importance of Cybersecurity in Health and Wellness

We begin by emphasizing the significance of cybersecurity in the health and wellness industry. In this digital age, where technology is deeply integrated into our everyday lives, the protection of personal information has become more crucial than ever. We will explore the risks posed by cyber attacks in the health and wellness sector and their impact on personal wellbeing. By understanding these risks, readers will gain a deeper appreciation for the importance of cybersecurity and the need to prioritize it.

Understanding Basic Cybersecurity Terminology

To ensure that readers can follow along with the book's discussions, we provide an overview of basic cybersecurity terminology. From terms like "phishing" to "advanced persistent threats," we will familiarize you with the language commonly used in the field of cybersecurity. This foundation will help you better understand the content presented in subsequent chapters.

Ethical Considerations in Cybersecurity for Health and Wellness

Ethics play a significant role in the field of cybersecurity, and this section will explore the ethical considerations specific to the health and wellness industry. We will delve into the responsibilities of individuals and organizations when handling personal information and the implications of ethical lapses. By raising awareness of ethical concerns, we aim to promote responsible and conscientious cybersecurity practices.

Overview of Cybersecurity Laws and Regulations in the Health and Wellness Industry

In this section, we provide an overview of the laws and regulations that govern cybersecurity in the health and wellness industry. We will explore the legal framework and compliance requirements that organizations must adhere to when safeguarding personal data. By understanding these laws and regulations, readers will gain insights into the legal obligations and best practices for protecting personal information.

Objectives of the Book

The primary objective of this book is to equip readers with the knowledge and skills necessary to protect their personal information and stay safe in a digitally connected world. By exploring various cybersecurity threats and attack vectors, readers will learn how to identify and mitigate risks effectively.

Additionally, this book aims to provide practical guidance on securing digital devices and networks. From implementing strong passwords and multi-factor authentication to securing home networks and utilizing virtual private networks (VPNs), readers will gain a comprehensive understanding of the technical measures they can take to enhance their cybersecurity.

Furthermore, we emphasize the importance of data privacy and confidentiality in the health and wellness industry. Readers will learn about data privacy regulations, protecting personally identifiable information (PII), secure data storage, and access controls. This knowledge will enable them to handle personal health information responsibly and in compliance with legal requirements.

The book also explores the unique cybersecurity challenges posed by telehealth and digital health technologies. Readers will gain insights into securing telehealth platforms, electronic health records, wearable devices, and the Internet of Medical Things (IoMT). With this understanding, they will be empowered to navigate the evolving landscape of digital health while safeguarding their personal information.

The book also covers secure communication and collaboration. Readers will learn about secure email and messaging systems, social media usage, remote access, virtual meetings, and secure cloud computing. These topics address the common communication channels and platforms used in the health and wellness industry, helping readers enhance their security posture in these areas.

Moreover, the book addresses cybersecurity in healthcare facilities, focusing on securing physical access, surveillance systems, and network security within these environments. By outlining proper security measures and incident response strategies, readers will learn how to protect healthcare facilities from cyber threats effectively.

To ensure comprehensive coverage, this book also emphasizes the importance of cybersecurity training and awareness for both health and wellness professionals and patients. By promoting a culture of security awareness, readers will learn how to educate and empower themselves and others to make informed decisions and adopt secure practices.

Lastly, we will explore emerging technologies and security challenges, such as artificial intelligence, blockchain technology, and genetic data privacy. By delving into these topics, readers will gain insights into the future of cybersecurity in the health and wellness industry and the potential risks and opportunities that come with technological advancements.

How to Make the Most Out of This Book

To maximize your learning experience, we suggest the following strategies:

- Read the book sequentially: The chapters in this book are designed to build upon one another, gradually expanding your knowledge and understanding of cybersecurity in the health and wellness industry. Reading the book sequentially will ensure a comprehensive learning experience.

- Engage with the content actively: Take time to reflect on the concepts presented in each chapter. Consider how the information applies to your personal circumstances and professional responsibilities. Engaging with the content actively will strengthen your understanding and retention of the material.

- Review and revisit: As the field of cybersecurity is continuously evolving, it is essential to review and revisit the book's content periodically. This practice will help you stay up to date with the latest trends, strategies, and best practices in cybersecurity.

- Utilize the resources provided: The book includes additional resources, such as case studies, practical examples, and exercises. Make use of these resources to reinforce your learning and apply the concepts in real-world scenarios.

- Seek further learning opportunities: This book serves as a foundation for your cybersecurity journey, but it is crucial to continue seeking further learning opportunities. Stay curious, explore additional resources, and engage with the broader cybersecurity community to expand your knowledge and expertise.

By approaching this book with an open mind and an eagerness to learn, you will gain valuable insights and practical strategies to protect your personal information and enhance your overall wellbeing in today's digitally connected world.

Now that we have provided an overview of the book's structure and objectives, let us delve into the fundamentals of cybersecurity in the next chapter.

How to Make the Most Out of This Book

In this section, we will discuss how you can effectively utilize this book to enhance your understanding of cybersecurity in the health and wellness industry. By following these guidelines, you will be able to make the most out of the content provided and develop a comprehensive knowledge of the subject matter.

1. **Read Actively:** Approach this book with an active mindset. As you read each chapter, take notes, highlight important information, and jot down any questions or ideas that come to mind. Active reading helps you engage with the material and promotes better retention and comprehension.

2. **Understand the Context:** Before diving into the technical aspects of cybersecurity, it's essential to grasp the broader context of the health and wellness industry. Familiarize yourself with the challenges and risks faced by healthcare organizations, the importance of data privacy, and the impact of cybersecurity breaches on individuals' personal wellbeing. This foundational knowledge will help you appreciate the significance of the topics discussed throughout the book.

3. **Embrace Hands-On Learning:** Cybersecurity is a practical discipline, and hands-on experience is invaluable. Take advantage of the exercises, case studies, and examples provided in this book. They will allow you to apply theoretical concepts to real-world scenarios and develop problem-solving skills essential for cybersecurity professionals.

4. **Engage in Critical Thinking:** Cybersecurity requires critical thinking and a proactive approach. As you progress through the chapters, think critically about the topics covered. Analyze different perspectives, challenge assumptions, and evaluate the effectiveness of various cybersecurity measures. This approach will help you develop a deeper understanding of cybersecurity principles and strategies.

5. **Explore Additional Resources:** This book serves as an excellent starting point, but it's crucial to supplement your learning with additional resources. Consult reputable cybersecurity websites, industry publications, and research papers to stay updated on the latest trends, threats, and best practices. Engage in online forums and communities to connect with fellow learners and industry professionals.

6. **Balance Theory and Practice:** While theoretical knowledge is important, practical application is equally vital in cybersecurity. Seek opportunities to gain

hands-on experience, such as internships, volunteering, or participating in cybersecurity competitions. This combination of theory and practice will enhance your skill set and make you a well-rounded cybersecurity professional.

7. **Networking and Collaboration:** Cybersecurity is a collaborative field, and building a network of like-minded individuals can be highly beneficial. Attend industry events, join professional associations, and engage in networking opportunities. Collaborating with others allows you to share knowledge, exchange ideas, and stay informed about emerging trends.

8. **Continuous Learning:** Cybersecurity is a rapidly evolving field, and continuous learning is essential. Stay updated on the latest advancements, regulations, and threats. Participate in training programs, attend webinars, and pursue relevant certifications to reinforce your knowledge and demonstrate your expertise.

9. **Reflect and Apply:** After completing each chapter, take some time to reflect on what you've learned. Consider how the information can be applied to real-life situations and how it relates to your personal and professional goals. This reflective practice will solidify your understanding and enable you to apply the concepts effectively.

10. **Have Fun:** Cybersecurity, though serious and critical, can also be exciting and intriguing. Embrace the process of learning and exploring the complexities of this field. Approach the content with enthusiasm and a sense of curiosity, and you'll find that cybersecurity becomes an engaging and rewarding journey.

By following these guidelines, you will maximize your learning experience with this book and develop a comprehensive understanding of cybersecurity in the health and wellness industry. Remember, cybersecurity is a continuous journey, and your dedication to ongoing learning and professional growth will ensure your success in this challenging and rewarding field.

Let's embark on this cybersecurity adventure together and equip ourselves with the knowledge and skills necessary to protect personal information and enhance overall wellbeing in our digitally connected world.

Understanding Basic Cybersecurity Terminology

In order to navigate the world of cybersecurity effectively, it is important to have a clear understanding of the basic terminology used in this field. This section will provide an overview of some key terms and concepts that will be referenced throughout the book.

Threats and Attacks

Threat: A potential danger to the security or integrity of a system, network, or computer. Threats can be intentional (e.g., cybercriminals, hackers) or unintentional (e.g., software bugs, system failures).

Attack: An action or series of actions that exploit vulnerabilities in a system or network, aiming to compromise its security or gain unauthorized access to sensitive information.

Exploit: A specific technique or piece of code that takes advantage of a vulnerability in a system to launch an attack.

Zero-day exploit: An exploit targeting a vulnerability that is unknown to the software vendor or has not yet been patched.

Security Controls

Authentication: The process of verifying the identity of a user or system, typically through the use of usernames, passwords, biometrics, or tokens.

Authorization: Granting or denying access rights to resources based on the authenticated identity of the user or system.

Encryption: The process of converting data into a form unreadable by unauthorized users, providing confidentiality and preventing unauthorized access.

Firewall: A security device or software that monitors and controls incoming and outgoing network traffic based on predetermined security rules.

Intrusion Detection System (IDS): A system that monitors network traffic for malicious activity or policy violations and alerts administrators or security personnel.

Intrusion Prevention System (IPS): A system that not only detects and alerts for malicious activity but also takes proactive measures to prevent it.

Vulnerability Assessment: The process of identifying and assessing the vulnerabilities and weaknesses in a system or network to determine the level of risk.

Types of Malicious Software

Malware: A general term referring to any type of malicious software designed to disrupt, damage, or gain unauthorized access to a computer system or network. This includes viruses, worms, Trojans, and ransomware.

Virus: A program that replicates itself by inserting copies into other programs or documents, spreading from one computer to another.

Worm: A standalone program that can self-replicate and spread across a network, often exploiting vulnerabilities in operating systems or applications.

Trojan: A program that disguises itself as legitimate software but contains malicious code or functionality, often allowing unauthorized access to a system.

Ransomware: A type of malware that encrypts a user's files or entire system, demanding a ransom in exchange for the decryption key.

Secure Network Protocols

SSL/TLS: Secure Sockets Layer (SSL) and Transport Layer Security (TLS) are cryptographic protocols that provide secure communication over a network, such as the internet.

HTTPS: Hypertext Transfer Protocol Secure (HTTPS) is the secure version of HTTP, incorporating SSL/TLS encryption for secure web browsing.

SSH: Secure Shell (SSH) is a network protocol that provides secure remote access and secure file transfer capabilities.

Compliance and Privacy

HIPAA: Health Insurance Portability and Accountability Act (HIPAA) is a U.S. law that sets standards for the protection of sensitive patient health information.

GDPR: General Data Protection Regulation (GDPR) is a regulation in the European Union that aims to protect the privacy and personal data of EU citizens.

Cybersecurity Roles and Certifications

CISO: Chief Information Security Officer (CISO) is a senior executive responsible for overseeing the organization's information security strategy and implementation.

CISSP: Certified Information Systems Security Professional (CISSP) is a globally recognized certification that demonstrates expertise in designing, implementing, and managing cybersecurity programs.

CEH: Certified Ethical Hacker (CEH) is a certification that validates skills in identifying vulnerabilities and weaknesses in target systems, simulating real-world hacking techniques.

Ethical Hacking and Penetration Testing

Ethical hacker: An individual authorized to conduct hacking activities within specified boundaries to identify vulnerabilities and weaknesses in a system or network.

Penetration testing: The process of evaluating the security of a system or network by simulating an attack from malicious actors, identifying vulnerabilities, and providing recommendations for improvement.

Risk Management

Risk assessment: The process of identifying, analyzing, and evaluating risks to an organization's information assets and determining appropriate controls to mitigate those risks.

Risk mitigation: The process of reducing or eliminating the impact or probability of a security incident or breach through the implementation of controls and countermeasures.

Business Continuity Planning (BCP): The process of creating a plan to ensure the continued operation of critical business functions in the event of a disruption or disaster.

Key Takeaways

Understanding basic cybersecurity terminology is crucial for navigating the complex world of cybersecurity effectively. Key concepts covered in this section include threats and attacks, security controls, types of malicious software, secure network protocols, compliance and privacy regulations, cybersecurity roles, and risk management. By familiarizing yourself with these terms, you will be better equipped to understand and implement the strategies and practices discussed in this book.

Ethical Considerations in Cybersecurity for Health and Wellness

In the digital world we live in today, where personal information is constantly being exchanged and stored, cybersecurity has become a critical aspect of our lives. This is especially true in the health and wellness industry, where sensitive and personal data is involved. However, apart from the technical and legal aspects of cybersecurity, it is equally important to consider the ethical implications of safeguarding this information.

Ethics is the branch of philosophy that deals with moral principles and values that guide our behavior and decision-making. In the context of cybersecurity for health and wellness, ethical considerations play a crucial role in ensuring the privacy, trust, and overall wellbeing of individuals. Let's explore some of the key ethical considerations in this domain:

Respect for autonomy and informed consent

Respecting the autonomy and informed consent of individuals is fundamental in cybersecurity for health and wellness. Individuals have the right to make their own decisions regarding the collection, use, and storage of their personal information. It is essential to ensure that individuals are fully informed about the risks and benefits associated with sharing their data, and to obtain their consent in a clear and transparent manner.

For example, when a healthcare provider or wellness organization collects personal information from individuals, they should clearly communicate the purpose of the data collection, how it will be used, and any potential risks involved. Individuals should have the opportunity to provide informed consent and make choices about their data, such as opting out of certain data sharing practices.

Privacy and confidentiality

Privacy and confidentiality are crucial ethical considerations in cybersecurity for health and wellness. Safeguarding personal information and maintaining its confidentiality is vital for building trust between individuals, healthcare providers, and wellness organizations. Individuals have the right to expect their personal information to be protected from unauthorized access, use, and disclosure.

Health and wellness organizations should implement robust security measures to protect personal data from cyber threats. This includes encryption of sensitive information, access controls, regular security audits, and training employees on privacy and confidentiality practices. Organizations should also have clear policies and procedures in place for handling and responding to breaches of privacy, ensuring that individuals are promptly informed and supported in such situations.

Equitable access to cybersecurity measures

Ensuring equitable access to cybersecurity measures is another ethical consideration in the health and wellness industry. All individuals, regardless of their socioeconomic status or technological literacy, should have equal access to the necessary tools and resources to protect their personal information.

Healthcare providers and wellness organizations should take proactive steps to educate and empower individuals on cybersecurity best practices. This may involve providing training programs, resources, and support to help individuals understand the risks and take appropriate measures to safeguard their personal information. It is important to bridge the digital divide and promote digital inclusivity, so that everyone can benefit from the advantages of a digitally connected world without compromising their security.

Transparency and accountability

Transparency and accountability are key ethical principles that should guide cybersecurity practices in the health and wellness industry. Organizations should be transparent about their data handling practices and provide individuals with clear information about how their personal information is being used.

Being accountable means taking responsibility for safeguarding personal information and addressing any breaches or incidents promptly and effectively. Organizations should have incident response plans in place and clearly communicate their policies and procedures for handling cybersecurity incidents. This includes conducting thorough investigations, implementing remediation measures, and ensuring that affected individuals are informed and supported throughout the process.

Ethical use of data for research and innovation

In the realm of health and wellness, data plays a crucial role in research and innovation. However, the ethical use of data for these purposes must be carefully considered. Organizations should adhere to ethical guidelines and regulations regarding data use and ensure that individuals' privacy and confidentiality are protected at all times.

When using data for research and innovation, it is important to anonymize or de-identify personal information to protect individuals' privacy. Additionally, obtaining informed consent for the use of data for research purposes is essential. Organizations should engage in responsible data sharing practices, following established protocols and frameworks that prioritize privacy and security.

Ethical hacking and responsible disclosure

Ethical hackers, also known as white-hat hackers, play a crucial role in identifying vulnerabilities and weaknesses in cybersecurity systems. However, ethical considerations apply even in the realm of hacking. Ethical hackers must abide by a code of conduct and ethical guidelines to ensure that their actions align with the principles of privacy, confidentiality, and trust.

Responsible disclosure is an ethical practice that involves reporting identified vulnerabilities to the respective organizations, rather than exploiting them for personal gain. This allows organizations to take necessary actions to address the vulnerabilities and protect their systems and data.

The importance of an ethical culture

Building an ethical culture within the health and wellness industry is essential for promoting cybersecurity and protecting personal information. This involves creating a culture of security awareness, accountability, and continuous learning.

Organizations should prioritize training and educating their employees on cybersecurity best practices and ethical considerations. This includes fostering a sense of responsibility and accountability among employees, encouraging them to be vigilant and proactive in protecting personal information.

In conclusion, ethical considerations are a critical component of cybersecurity in the health and wellness industry. Respecting autonomy, ensuring privacy and confidentiality, promoting equitable access to cybersecurity measures, fostering transparency and accountability, using data ethically for research and innovation, adhering to ethical hacking practices, and building an ethical culture are key principles that guide ethical cybersecurity practices. By integrating these ethical considerations into their cybersecurity strategies, health and wellness organizations can ensure the protection of personal information while enhancing the overall wellbeing of individuals in a digitally connected world.

Overview of Cybersecurity Laws and Regulations in the Health and Wellness Industry

In today's digitally connected world, where personal information is stored and transmitted electronically, cybersecurity has become a critical concern for individuals and organizations across various industries. The health and wellness industry, in particular, holds a wealth of valuable personal information, making it an attractive target for cybercriminals. To protect this sensitive data and ensure the overall well-being of individuals, there are specific laws and regulations in place that govern cybersecurity practices in the health and wellness industry.

The Importance of Cybersecurity Laws and Regulations

Cybersecurity laws and regulations play a vital role in safeguarding the privacy, integrity, and availability of personal health information. They provide a legal framework that outlines the responsibilities, obligations, and standards that organizations must adhere to in order to secure sensitive data and protect individuals' well-being. These laws and regulations are designed to prevent unauthorized access, disclosure, alteration, or destruction of personal health information and mitigate the risks associated with cyber-attacks.

By complying with cybersecurity laws and regulations, individuals and organizations in the health and wellness industry can demonstrate their commitment to protecting personal information, build trust with consumers, and avoid costly penalties and reputational damage resulting from non-compliance.

Key Cybersecurity Laws and Regulations in the Health and Wellness Industry

1. **Health Insurance Portability and Accountability Act (HIPAA):** HIPAA is a federal law that sets national standards for the protection of individuals' health information. It applies to healthcare providers, health plans, and healthcare clearinghouses, as well as their business associates. HIPAA includes the Security Rule, which establishes safeguards to ensure the confidentiality, integrity, and availability of electronic protected health information (ePHI). It also requires covered entities to conduct risk assessments, implement security policies and procedures, and provide employee training on cybersecurity awareness.

2. **Health Information Technology for Economic and Clinical Health Act (HITECH):** HITECH is an extension of HIPAA that focuses on the use of electronic health records (EHR) and the promotion of health information technology. It strengthens the security and privacy requirements of HIPAA by introducing mandatory breach notification requirements and increasing penalties for non-compliance. HITECH also encourages the adoption of certified EHR technology and promotes the meaningful use of electronic health information.

3. **General Data Protection Regulation (GDPR):** Although GDPR is a European Union (EU) regulation, its impact extends to any organization that processes the personal data of EU citizens, even if the organization is located outside the EU. GDPR applies to healthcare organizations that handle the personal data of EU patients. It places stringent requirements on data protection, including the implementation of appropriate technical and organizational measures to ensure the security of personal data. GDPR also grants individuals specific rights, such as the right to access, rectify, and erase their personal data.

4. **California Consumer Privacy Act (CCPA):** CCPA is a state-level privacy law in California that grants consumers certain rights and imposes obligations on businesses that collect, sell, or disclose consumers' personal information. Although not specific to the health and wellness industry, CCPA applies to healthcare providers or businesses that collect personal information through the provision of healthcare services. It requires businesses to implement reasonable security

measures to protect personal information and provides consumers with the right to request disclosure of data collection practices and the deletion of their personal information.

5. **Cybersecurity Act of 2015:** This federal law encourages the sharing of cybersecurity threat information between the private sector and the federal government. It promotes collaboration and information sharing to improve cybersecurity practices and respond effectively to cyber threats. While not exclusively focused on the health and wellness industry, the law is applicable to entities, including healthcare organizations, that possess or control critical infrastructure.

6. **State Data Breach Notification Laws:** Many states have enacted their own data breach notification laws, which require businesses to notify affected individuals in the event of a breach involving their personal information. These laws typically outline the timing, content, and method of notification, as well as penalties for non-compliance. Healthcare organizations need to be aware of and comply with the breach notification laws in the states in which they operate.

Challenges and Compliance Considerations

Complying with cybersecurity laws and regulations in the health and wellness industry can be challenging due to the constantly evolving threat landscape and the complex nature of healthcare operations. Here are some key considerations for organizations:

1. **Risk Assessment and Management:** Organizations need to conduct regular risk assessments to identify vulnerabilities, evaluate threats, and implement appropriate controls and safeguards. Risk management strategies should be tailored to the specific risks faced by the organization and aligned with the requirements of relevant cybersecurity laws and regulations.

2. **Employee Training and Education:** Employees play a crucial role in maintaining cybersecurity. Organizations should provide regular training and education programs to raise awareness about cybersecurity threats, best practices, and compliance requirements. This ensures that employees understand their responsibilities and can actively contribute to the organization's cybersecurity efforts.

3. **Third-Party Management:** Healthcare organizations often work with third-party vendors, such as cloud service providers or IT support companies. It is essential to establish robust contracting and oversight mechanisms to ensure that third parties comply with cybersecurity laws and regulations and adequately protect personal health information.

4. **Incident Response and Reporting:** Organizations should develop and implement an incident response plan that outlines the steps to be taken in the event of a cybersecurity incident. This includes notifying affected individuals, regulators, and, in some cases, law enforcement agencies. Prompt and accurate reporting helps mitigate the impact of a breach and demonstrates compliance with relevant laws and regulations.

5. **Continuous Monitoring and Assessment:** Cybersecurity is an ongoing effort. Organizations should continuously monitor their systems for potential vulnerabilities, conduct regular assessments, and update their security measures to address emerging threats and changing regulatory requirements.

Resources and References

Here are some useful resources and references for further exploration of cybersecurity laws and regulations in the health and wellness industry:

- Department of Health and Human Services (HHS) - Office for Civil Rights (OCR): *HIPAA Security Rule Guidance Material* (`https://www.hhs.gov/hipaa/for-professionals/security/guidance/index.html`)
- European Commission: *General Data Protection Regulation* (`https://ec.europa.eu/info/law/law-topic/data-protection_en`)
- State of California Department of Justice: *California Consumer Privacy Act* (`https://oag.ca.gov/ccpa`)
- National Institute of Standards and Technology (NIST): *Framework for Improving Critical Infrastructure Cybersecurity* (`https://www.nist.gov/cyberframework`)
- Health Information and Management Systems Society (HIMSS): *Cybersecurity, Privacy and Security in Healthcare* (`https://www.himss.org/topics/cybersecurity-privacy-security-healthcare`)

Conclusion

Cybersecurity laws and regulations in the health and wellness industry are essential for protecting personal health information and ensuring the overall well-being of individuals. They provide a legal framework that defines the responsibilities and obligations of organizations and individuals in safeguarding sensitive data.

Compliance with these laws and regulations is crucial to establishing trust, avoiding penalties, and maintaining the integrity and availability of personal health information. By understanding and adhering to these regulations, organizations can play a vital role in creating a secure and resilient healthcare ecosystem.

Cybersecurity Fundamentals

Understanding Cyber Threats and Attack Vectors

Common Types of Cyber Threats

In today's digitally connected world, cyber threats pose a significant risk to the security of personal information in the health and wellness industry. It's essential to understand the common types of threats that individuals and organizations may encounter. By recognizing these threats, individuals can take proactive measures to protect themselves and mitigate the risks involved. In this section, we will explore some of the most prevalent cyber threats in the health and wellness industry and discuss strategies to defend against them.

1. **Phishing Attacks:** Phishing attacks are a form of social engineering that targets individuals through fraudulent emails, text messages, or phone calls. The attackers disguise themselves as trustworthy sources to trick victims into providing sensitive information such as usernames, passwords, or credit card details. In the health and wellness industry, these attacks can be particularly dangerous as they can lead to unauthorized access to personal health records or financial information. To protect against phishing attacks, it is crucial to be cautious when clicking on links or downloading attachments from unknown sources. Verifying the sender's identity and using two-factor authentication can also help mitigate the risk.

2. **Malware and Ransomware Attacks:** Malware refers to malicious software designed to disrupt, damage, or gain unauthorized access to computer systems. Ransomware, a type of malware, encrypts the victim's files and demands a ransom payment in exchange for the decryption key. Healthcare organizations are often targeted by these attacks due to the sensitivity of the data they store. To prevent malware and ransomware attacks, it is essential to install reputable antivirus software, keep systems and applications up to date, and regularly backup critical data. Furthermore, user education and awareness are paramount in preventing

inadvertently downloading and executing malicious files.

3. **Insider Threats:** Insider threats are security risks that originate from within an organization. This can occur when an employee intentionally or inadvertently compromises the confidentiality, integrity, or availability of sensitive information. In the health and wellness industry, insider threats can result in the unauthorized disclosure or modification of patient records, leading to severe consequences. Implementing access controls, conducting background checks, and providing regular employee training on security best practices can help mitigate the risks associated with insider threats.

4. **Denial of Service (DoS) Attacks:** Denial of Service attacks aim to disrupt the availability of a network, system, or service by overwhelming it with a flood of illegitimate traffic. These attacks can cause significant financial losses and negatively impact the delivery of healthcare services. Implementing robust network security measures, such as firewalls and intrusion detection systems, can help detect and mitigate DoS attacks. Developing an incident response plan and establishing communication channels with internet service providers are also essential for minimizing the impact of these attacks.

5. **Advanced Persistent Threats (APTs):** APTs are sophisticated and targeted cyber attacks that aim to gain unauthorized access to systems or networks for a prolonged period. These attacks typically involve a combination of social engineering, zero-day exploits, and malware. The health and wellness industry often faces APTs due to the value of the information stored within their systems. To defend against APTs, organizations need to adopt a multi-layered approach to security, including network segmentation, regular security assessments, and continuous monitoring for suspicious activities.

6. **Supply Chain Attacks:** Supply chain attacks target the vendors or suppliers of an organization to gain unauthorized access to their systems or networks. In the health and wellness industry, these attacks can compromise the integrity and confidentiality of patient data or medical devices. Establishing strong vendor management practices, including conducting regular security audits and assessments, can help mitigate the risks associated with supply chain attacks.

It is important to note that these are just a few examples of the many cyber threats faced by the health and wellness industry. As technology advances, new threats will continue to emerge. Therefore, it is crucial to stay informed about the latest cybersecurity trends and adopt proactive measures to protect personal information and enhance overall well-being.

Example: The Impact of Phishing Attacks on Healthcare

Imagine a scenario where a healthcare organization's employees receive an email that appears to be from the HR department. The email requests them to update their usernames and passwords due to a recent system upgrade. Unaware of the email's fraudulent nature, several employees click on the provided link and enter their login credentials. Unbeknownst to them, they have fallen victim to a phishing attack.

The attacker now has access to the employees' usernames and passwords, which can be used to gain unauthorized access to sensitive patient information. This breach of security can lead to financial loss, reputational damage, and potential harm to patients if their personal and medical information is exposed.

To prevent such attacks, the organization could have implemented a robust email filtering system, educated employees on the importance of verifying the legitimacy of emails, and implemented multi-factor authentication to add an extra layer of security to login credentials.

By understanding the common types of cyber threats and implementing appropriate security measures, individuals and organizations can protect personal information, safeguard systems and networks, and contribute to a safer digital world in the health and wellness industry.

Social Engineering Attacks and Manipulation Techniques

In the realm of cybersecurity, social engineering attacks have proven to be one of the most effective methods for hackers and cybercriminals to gain unauthorized access to systems and sensitive information. Unlike traditional hacking techniques that often rely on technical vulnerabilities in software or hardware, social engineering attacks exploit human psychology and manipulate individuals into divulging confidential information or performing actions that compromise security. This section will explore various types of social engineering attacks and manipulation techniques commonly used by cybercriminals.

Understanding Social Engineering

Social engineering is a technique used to exploit human traits and emotions, such as trust, curiosity, fear, and authority, to deceive individuals into providing sensitive information or performing certain actions. Cybercriminals employ social engineering tactics to bypass security measures and gain unauthorized access to systems or obtain personal information, which can then be used for malicious purposes. Social engineering attacks are often successful because they exploit the weakest link in any security system: humans.

Types of Social Engineering Attacks

There are several common types of social engineering attacks that cybercriminals employ to manipulate individuals and compromise security. Understanding these attack vectors is crucial for both individuals and organizations to protect themselves effectively. Let's explore some of these tactics:

- **Phishing Attacks:** Phishing attacks involve the use of email or electronic communication to deceive individuals into divulging sensitive information or downloading malicious attachments. Cybercriminals commonly impersonate trusted entities, such as banks, government agencies, or well-known companies, to trick individuals into clicking on malicious links or providing personal information. Phishing attacks often utilize urgency or fear to prompt individuals to take immediate action without carefully considering the legitimacy of the request.

- **Pretexting:** Pretexting involves the creation of a false narrative or pretext to manipulate individuals into disclosing sensitive information. Cybercriminals often pose as someone in authority or with a legitimate reason to request information. For example, a hacker might impersonate a company IT technician and contact an employee, requesting their login credentials under the pretense of a system upgrade. By creating a sense of trust and authority, cybercriminals deceive individuals into divulging confidential information.

- **Baiting:** Baiting attacks exploit people's curiosity or desire for something valuable. Cybercriminals often offer enticing incentives, such as a free gift, a prize, or exclusive content, to trick individuals into taking certain actions that compromise security. This may involve clicking on malicious links, downloading infected files, or disclosing personal information. Baiting attacks often use social media platforms, online advertisements, or physical media (e.g., USB drives) to distribute the bait.

- **Quid Pro Quo:** In quid pro quo attacks, cybercriminals offer something of value in exchange for sensitive information or access. This could involve promising a service or favor, such as free software or tech support, in return for login credentials or other confidential information. Quid pro quo attacks exploit people's desire for a reward or benefit, enticing them to provide information that compromises security.

- **Tailgating:** Tailgating, also known as piggybacking, involves unauthorized individuals gaining physical access to restricted areas or systems by following someone with authorized access. Cybercriminals use various techniques to deceive individuals into granting them access, such as pretending to be an employee, delivery personnel, or maintenance personnel. This social engineering technique takes advantage of people's natural inclination to be helpful and polite.

Examples and Real-World Scenarios

To better understand the impact of social engineering attacks, let's explore a few real-world examples:

- **CEO Fraud:** In CEO fraud attacks, a cybercriminal impersonates a high-ranking executive or CEO of a company and requests urgent financial transfers or confidential information from employees. By using the authority and influence associated with the executive position, cybercriminals manipulate employees into complying with their requests, resulting in significant financial losses for organizations.
- **Tech Support Scams:** In tech support scams, cybercriminals pose as technical support personnel from reputable companies and contact individuals, claiming that their computers are infected with malware. They convince the victims to provide remote access to their systems, install malicious software, or pay for unnecessary services. Tech support scams rely on individuals' fear of computer viruses and their trust in legitimate companies.
- **Pharming Attacks:** Pharming attacks involve redirecting users from legitimate websites to malicious ones without their knowledge. Cybercriminals use various techniques, such as DNS cache poisoning or malware, to manipulate DNS (Domain Name System) records or intercept user requests. Pharming attacks can trick individuals into providing sensitive information on counterfeit websites.

Protecting Against Social Engineering Attacks

Protecting against social engineering attacks requires a combination of technical controls, employee training, and organizational policies. Here are some strategies to mitigate the risks:

- **Employee Education and Awareness:** Organizations should provide comprehensive cybersecurity training to employees, regularly updating them on the latest social engineering tactics and how to recognize and respond to potential threats. This includes teaching employees to verify the authenticity of requests, not sharing sensitive information via unsecured channels, and reporting any suspicious activity.

- **Implementing Technical Controls:** Deploying robust technical controls, such as email filters, firewalls, and antivirus software, can help detect and prevent social engineering attacks. Implementing multi-factor authentication, strong passwords, and secure network configurations adds an additional layer of defense against these threats.
- **Regular Security Assessments:** Conducting regular security assessments, including penetration testing and vulnerability scanning, can help identify potential weaknesses and vulnerabilities in an organization's infrastructure and systems. These assessments provide insights into areas that require improvement to mitigate social engineering risks effectively.
- **Adhering to Policies and Procedures:** Establishing clear and well-communicated security policies and procedures is crucial for creating a security-focused culture within an organization. Policies should cover areas such as information sharing, incident reporting, and access controls, and employees should be regularly reminded to adhere to these policies.

Conclusion

Social engineering attacks continue to be a persistent and evolving threat in the cybersecurity landscape. By understanding the various tactics employed by cybercriminals and implementing proactive measures, individuals and organizations can significantly reduce the risks associated with social engineering. A combination of employee education, technical controls, and robust security policies is essential in building a robust defense against these manipulative tactics. Stay vigilant, question suspicious requests, and prioritize cybersecurity to safeguard sensitive information and maintain a secure digital environment.

Phishing and Email Spoofing

Phishing attacks and email spoofing are two common methods used by cybercriminals to deceive individuals and gain unauthorized access to their personal information. In this section, we will explore the concepts of phishing and email spoofing, understand how they work, and learn how to protect ourselves from falling victim to these attacks.

Understanding Phishing Attacks

Phishing is a cyber attack where criminals disguise themselves as legitimate entities, such as banks, online retailers, or government agencies, to trick individuals into revealing sensitive information like passwords, credit card details, or social security numbers. These attacks are typically carried out via email, although they can also occur through other communication channels like SMS or social media.

The key characteristic of a phishing attack is the use of social engineering techniques to manipulate the victim's trust and convince them to take a specific action. This action can range from clicking on a malicious link to downloading an infected attachment or providing personal information on a fake website.

Phishing emails often appear convincing and may use logos, email signatures, and language that mimic legitimate correspondence. They typically create a sense of urgency or fear, urging the recipient to take immediate action to avoid negative consequences. For example, an email might claim that the recipient's bank account has been compromised and prompt them to click on a link to verify their account information.

Recognizing Phishing Emails

To protect ourselves from phishing attacks, it is important to be able to identify and recognize the common signs of a phishing email. Here are some key indicators to look out for:

- **Email address:** Check the sender's email address carefully. Phishing emails often use email addresses that mimic legitimate organizations but may have subtle differences or spelling errors. For example, an email claiming to be from "paypal.com" might have an email address like "noreply@paypa1.com".

- **Urgency and fear tactics:** Phishing emails often create a sense of urgency or fear to prompt quick action. They may claim that your account is about to be closed, or that there has been suspicious activity on your account. Be cautious of emails that pressure you to take immediate action without giving you time to think.

- **Generic greetings:** Phishing emails often use generic greetings like "Dear Customer" instead of addressing you by your name. Legitimate organizations usually personalize their emails by using your name or username.

- **Spelling and grammar mistakes:** Phishing emails often contain spelling and grammar mistakes. While legitimate organizations can make mistakes, it's a red flag if you notice multiple errors in the email.

- **Suspicious links and attachments:** Phishing emails may contain links or attachments that, when clicked or downloaded, can install malware on your device or lead you to a fake website designed to steal your information. Hover over links (without clicking) to check their actual destination, and only download attachments from trusted sources.

Protecting Yourself from Phishing Attacks

Now that we understand what phishing attacks are and how to spot them, let's explore some best practices to protect ourselves:

- **Think before you click:** Be cautious of any unexpected emails or communications that require immediate action. Pause and think critically before clicking on any links or opening attachments. If in doubt, contact the organization directly through their official website or customer service channels to verify the legitimacy of the email.

- **Verify the source:** Always double-check the sender's email address and the URL of any websites you are asked to visit. Legitimate organizations will have official domain names, and their emails and websites should match. If you're unsure, perform a separate search for the organization's official website rather than relying on the information provided in the email.

- **Keep your software up to date:** Ensure that your operating system, antivirus software, and web browsers are always up to date. Software updates often include security patches that can protect you from known vulnerabilities used in phishing attacks.

- **Educate yourself:** Stay informed about the latest phishing techniques and trends. Organizations like the Anti-Phishing Working Group (APWG) and the United States Computer Emergency Readiness Team (US-CERT) provide resources and information on current phishing threats. By educating yourself, you'll be better equipped to recognize and avoid phishing attacks.

- **Enable two-factor authentication (2FA):** When available, enable two-factor authentication for your online accounts. With 2FA, even if cybercriminals manage to obtain your password through a phishing attack, they won't be able to access your account without the second authentication factor, such as a unique code sent to your mobile device.

Case Study: The Google Docs Phishing Attack

One notable example of a widespread phishing attack was the Google Docs incident in 2017. Attackers sent emails appearing to be from someone the victim knew, inviting them to view a Google Doc. The email contained a link that redirected users to a fake Google login page, tricking them into entering their Google account credentials. Once entered, the attackers gained access to the victims' email accounts and contacts, allowing the attack to spread further.

This case demonstrates the importance of verifying the source of any email or communication, even if it appears to come from someone you know. By closely examining the email address, URL, and using caution before entering login credentials, users can avoid falling victim to such phishing attacks.

Conclusion

Phishing attacks and email spoofing continue to be significant cybersecurity threats. By understanding how phishing attacks work, recognizing the signs of a phishing email, and adopting best practices to protect ourselves, we can reduce the risk of falling victim to these scams. Remember to always think before you click, verify the source of emails and links, keep your software updated, educate yourself about phishing techniques, and enable two-factor authentication where possible. With these precautions in place, we can significantly enhance our cybersecurity and keep our personal information safe.

Malware and Ransomware Attacks

In today's digitally connected world, the threat of malware and ransomware attacks has become a critical concern for individuals and organizations alike. Malware refers to malicious software that is designed to infiltrate and damage computer systems, while ransomware is a specific type of malware that encrypts files and demands a ransom for their release. In this section, we will explore the nature of these attacks, their impact, and effective strategies to protect against them.

Understanding Malware

Malware can take many forms and is constantly evolving to bypass security measures. Common types of malware include viruses, worms, trojans, and spyware. Viruses are malicious programs that replicate themselves and spread to other files, often causing damage or disrupting system operations. Worms, on the other hand, are self-replicating programs that spread over computer networks, exploiting vulnerabilities to gain unauthorized access.

Trojans are deceptive programs that appear legitimate but contain hidden malicious code. They typically trick users into installing them unknowingly and can perform various malicious activities, such as stealing sensitive information or granting unauthorized access to the attacker. Spyware is another type of malware that secretly monitors user activities, capturing sensitive information such as login credentials or browsing habits.

Impact of Malware Attacks

Malware attacks can have severe consequences for individuals and organizations. Some of the key impacts include:

- **Data Breaches:** Malware can compromise sensitive data, leading to data breaches and exposing personal or confidential information.
- **Financial Loss:** Malware can be used to steal financial information, such as credit card or banking details, leading to financial losses for individuals and organizations.
- **System Disruption:** Malware can disrupt system operations, causing system crashes, slow performance, or the loss of critical data or files.
- **Identity Theft:** Malware can facilitate identity theft by stealing personal information, such as social security numbers or addresses, which can be used for fraudulent activities.
- **Reputation Damage:** Organizations that experience a malware attack may suffer reputational damage, which can result in loss of trust from customers or stakeholders.

It is important to note that the consequences of a malware attack can vary depending on the type and severity of the attack, as well as the target's cybersecurity measures.

Preventing Malware Attacks

Protecting against malware attacks requires a multi-layered approach that involves both technical measures and user awareness. Here are some effective strategies to prevent malware attacks:

- **Use Reliable Security Software:** Install reputable antivirus and anti-malware software on all devices, keeping them updated with the latest security patches and definitions.

- **Keep Operating Systems and Software Up to Date:** Regularly update operating systems and software to ensure they have the latest security patches, as outdated software can be vulnerable to malware attacks.

- **Exercise Caution with Email Attachments and Links:** Be cautious when opening email attachments or clicking on links, especially if they come from unknown or suspicious sources. Verify the sender's identity before downloading attachments or visiting websites.

- **Enable Automatic Updates:** Enable automatic updates for operating systems, software, and security applications to ensure timely installation of security patches.

- **Use Strong and Unique Passwords:** Create strong, complex passwords and avoid reusing them across different accounts. Consider using a password manager to securely store passwords.

- **Be Wary of Suspicious Websites:** Avoid visiting suspicious websites, especially those offering pirated content or illegal downloads. These websites can host malware or have malicious advertisements.

- **Implement a Firewall:** Enable firewalls on computer systems and networks to monitor and control incoming and outgoing network traffic, protecting against unauthorized access.

- **Regularly Back Up Data:** Regularly back up important files and data to an offline or cloud storage service to mitigate the impact of potential data loss caused by malware attacks.

Responding to Malware Attacks

In the unfortunate event of a malware attack, it is crucial to respond swiftly to minimize the damage. Here are some steps to take in response to a malware attack:

- **Isolate Infected Systems:** Disconnect infected systems from the network to prevent the malware from spreading to other connected devices.
- **Identify and Remove Malware:** Use antivirus or anti-malware software to scan and remove the malware from infected systems. Ensure that the antivirus software is up to date.
- **Restore from Backups:** If data or files were encrypted or compromised by the malware, restore them from secure backups to recover the lost information.
- **Patch Vulnerabilities:** Identify and patch any vulnerabilities that the malware exploited to prevent future attacks.
- **Educate and Train Users:** Provide user education and training to promote awareness of malware risks and best practices for preventing future infections.
- **Report the Incident:** Report the malware attack to the appropriate authorities or IT department for further investigation and assistance.

Real-World Example

In 2017, the ransomware attack known as WannaCry had a significant global impact. The malware exploited a vulnerability in the Microsoft Windows operating system, encrypting files on infected systems and demanding a ransom in Bitcoin for their release. The attack affected organizations across various sectors, including healthcare institutions, causing disruptions, financial losses, and compromising sensitive patient data.

To prevent similar incidents, Microsoft released a security patch to address the vulnerability and urged users to update their systems promptly. The WannaCry attack highlighted the importance of keeping systems up to date with the latest security patches and maintaining robust backup strategies to protect against ransomware attacks.

Additional Resources

To enhance your understanding of malware and ransomware attacks, consider the following resources:

1. Websites:
    - The United States Computer Emergency Readiness Team (US-CERT) website provides guidance on cybersecurity best practices and alerts about the latest threats: `https://www.us-cert.gov/`.
    - The Anti-Phishing Working Group (APWG) website offers resources on phishing attacks and countermeasures: `https://apwg.org/`.
2. Books:
    - "The Art of Deception: Controlling the Human Element of Security" by Kevin D. Mitnick and William L. Simon.
    - "Ransomware: Defending Against Digital Extortion" by Allan Liska and Timothy Gallo.
3. Research Papers:
    - S. A. John et al., "A Comprehensive Study on Different Types of Malware and Cyber Attacks," *International Journal of Computer Applications*, vol. 143, no. 3, pp. 1-6, June 2016.
    - A. G. Itlitye et al., "A Comprehensive Study on Ransomware," *2018 International Conference on Inventive Research in Computing Applications*, Coimbatore, India, 2018, pp. 604-609.

Remember, remaining vigilant and implementing robust cybersecurity practices are key to mitigating the risks of malware and ransomware attacks in today's digital landscape. Stay informed, keep your systems updated, and educate yourself and others to create a safer online environment.

Insider Threats and Employee Security Awareness

In the world of cybersecurity, it is essential to not only protect against external threats but also to address the risks posed by insiders within an organization. Insider threats refer to the potential danger that employees or authorized personnel can pose to the security of an organization's information systems. This section will explore the concept of insider threats, the motivations behind them, and strategies for raising employee awareness about security risks.

Understanding Insider Threats

Insider threats can originate from within the organization, and they can be intentional or unintentional. Intentional insider threats occur when employees use their access privileges with malicious intent, such as stealing sensitive data, sharing confidential information with unauthorized parties, or sabotaging the organization's systems. On the other hand, unintentional insider threats are often the result of negligence or lack of awareness, leading to inadvertent data breaches or system vulnerabilities.

Insiders have access to valuable information and systems, making them potential targets for external attackers seeking to exploit their credentials or coerce them into providing unauthorized access. Therefore, it is crucial for organizations to address insider threats to mitigate the risk of compromise and protect their sensitive data.

Motivations behind Insider Threats

Understanding the motivations behind insider threats can help organizations identify potential indicators and implement effective countermeasures. Some common motivations for insider threats include:

- **Financial gain:** Employees may be tempted to engage in activities that result in personal financial gain, such as selling sensitive company information to competitors or engaging in insider trading.

- **Disgruntlement:** Employees who are dissatisfied with their job, feel undervalued, or have grievances with the organization may be motivated to harm the organization's reputation or disrupt its operations.

- **Espionage:** Insiders with ties to external entities, such as competitors or foreign agencies, may be persuaded or coerced into stealing sensitive information or providing unauthorized access to critical systems.

- **Accidental actions:** Employees may unknowingly compromise organizational security through actions such as falling victim to phishing attacks, downloading malicious software, or inadvertently disclosing sensitive information.

By understanding these motivations, organizations can implement targeted security measures to detect, prevent, and respond to insider threats effectively.

Raising Employee Security Awareness

To address insider threats, organizations must prioritize employee security awareness and foster a culture of cybersecurity. Here are some key strategies for raising employee security awareness:

1. **Training and education:** Develop comprehensive training programs to educate employees about the risks associated with insider threats, common attack vectors, and security best practices. This training should be mandatory for all employees and should be updated regularly to address emerging threats.

2. **Clear security policies and procedures:** Establish clear and concise security policies that outline the acceptable use of organizational resources, access controls, data protection practices, and consequences for policy violations. Communicate these policies effectively to all employees and provide regular reminders to ensure compliance.

3. **Role-based access controls:** Implement a principle of least privilege, where employees are granted access privileges only necessary for their job responsibilities. Regularly review and update access permissions as employees change roles or leave the organization.

4. **Monitoring and detection systems:** Deploy robust monitoring and detection systems to identify suspicious behaviors or activities that could indicate an insider threat. This includes monitoring access logs, network traffic, and endpoint activities to detect unauthorized or abnormal behavior.

5. **Encouraging reporting:** Establish a clear reporting mechanism for employees to report any suspicious activities or security incidents. Create a culture where employees feel comfortable raising concerns and provide an anonymous reporting option if possible.

6. **Regular assessments and audits:** Conduct regular assessments and audits of security controls to identify potential vulnerabilities and address them promptly. These assessments can include testing employee awareness through simulated phishing attacks or social engineering exercises.

7. **Escalation and incident response procedures:** Define clear escalation and incident response procedures to handle suspected insider threats effectively. This includes involving human resources, legal departments, and law enforcement if necessary.

By implementing these strategies, organizations can significantly reduce the risk of insider threats and minimize the potential impact of security incidents.

Real-World Example: The Edward Snowden Case

One notable real-world example of an insider threat is the case of Edward Snowden, a former contractor for the National Security Agency (NSA) in the United States. In 2013, Snowden leaked classified information to the media, exposing widespread global surveillance programs and causing significant damage to the reputation of the U.S. intelligence community.

Snowden's case highlights the importance of employee security awareness and the potential consequences of insider threats. Snowden had privileged access to highly sensitive information within the NSA and was able to exploit his position to leak classified documents. This incident served as a wake-up call for organizations worldwide to reevaluate their security measures and insider threat detection capabilities.

Conclusion

Insider threats pose a significant risk to organizations, making it essential to implement proactive measures to prevent, detect, and respond to such threats effectively. By raising employee security awareness, organizations can foster a culture of cybersecurity and significantly reduce the risk of insider attacks. Training programs, clear security policies, role-based access controls, monitoring systems, and incident response procedures are critical elements in mitigating insider threats. Remember, cybersecurity is everyone's responsibility, and organizations must continuously adapt and evolve their security measures to address the ever-changing threat landscape.

Internet of Things (IoT) Security Risks

With the rapid expansion of connected devices in the health and wellness industry, the Internet of Things (IoT) has become an integral part of our digitally connected world. The IoT refers to the network of physical objects, devices, vehicles, appliances, and other items embedded with sensors, software, and connectivity to exchange data and interact with each other.

While IoT brings numerous benefits and convenience to the health and wellness sector, it also poses significant security risks. The interconnected nature of IoT devices makes them vulnerable to various threats, which can have detrimental effects on personal wellbeing and the security of sensitive information.

In this section, we will explore the security risks associated with the Internet of Things in the health and wellness industry and discuss strategies to mitigate these risks. We will cover common IoT vulnerabilities, such as lack of encryption, weak authentication, and inadequate update mechanisms. Additionally, we will examine specific IoT security challenges within health and wellness, including medical device vulnerabilities, data breaches, and privacy concerns.

Common IoT Vulnerabilities

IoT devices are susceptible to a range of vulnerabilities that can be exploited by malicious actors. Understanding these vulnerabilities is crucial to developing effective security measures. Some common IoT vulnerabilities include:

- **Lack of Encryption:** Many IoT devices transmit data without encryption, making it susceptible to interception and unauthorized access. Without encryption, sensitive information, such as personal health data, can be easily compromised.

- **Weak Authentication:** Inadequate authentication mechanisms in IoT devices can allow unauthorized users to gain access. Weak or default passwords, lack of two-factor authentication, and insufficient access controls can undermine the security of IoT ecosystems.

- **Insecure Firmware and Software:** IoT devices often run outdated firmware or software that may contain known vulnerabilities. Without regular updates and patches, these devices remain exposed to attacks.

- **Inadequate Physical Security:** Physical security measures for IoT devices are often overlooked. Lack of tamper resistance and improper protection against physical attacks can compromise the integrity and confidentiality of the device and its data.

- **Insufficient Network Security:** Weak network security measures, such as poor firewall configurations and lack of proper network segmentation, can expose IoT devices to unauthorized access and data breaches.

Addressing these vulnerabilities requires a holistic approach that encompasses device manufacturers, service providers, and end-users.

Medical Device Vulnerabilities

In the context of health and wellness, medical devices are an integral part of the IoT ecosystem. These devices, such as pacemakers, insulin pumps, and wearable health monitors, are embedded with sensors and can interface with other devices or networks.

However, the use of medical devices also introduces additional security risks. Medical device vulnerabilities can lead to significant harm to patients, compromising their safety and overall wellbeing. Some notable vulnerabilities and security risks associated with medical devices include:

- **Unauthorized Access and Modification:** The connection of medical devices to the IoT increases the risk of unauthorized access and tampering. Malicious actors can potentially exploit vulnerabilities in the device's software or its communication network to compromise its functionality.
- **Privacy Concerns:** Medical devices gather and transmit sensitive health data, which raises concerns over data privacy. Unauthorized access to this data can lead to identity theft, blackmail, and even discrimination.
- **Device Malfunction and Manipulation:** If not adequately secured, medical devices can be vulnerable to malfunction or deliberate manipulation. Malicious actors can remotely modify device settings, resulting in improper operation, incorrect dosage, or even life-threatening conditions for patients.
- **Interoperability Challenges:** With the proliferation of diverse medical devices in the IoT ecosystem, ensuring seamless interoperability becomes critical. Security vulnerabilities introduced by incompatible interfaces or communication protocols can compromise patient care and data integrity.

To mitigate medical device vulnerabilities, manufacturers should prioritize security throughout the device lifecycle, including secure design, rigorous testing, and timely software updates. Healthcare facilities should also establish robust security protocols to safeguard patient safety and privacy.

Data Breaches and Privacy Concerns

One of the gravest consequences of IoT security risks is the potential for data breaches and privacy violations. The interconnectedness of IoT devices means that a compromise in one device can have a domino effect, compromising the security of the entire network.

Data breaches in the health and wellness industry can have profound implications for personal wellbeing. The exposure of sensitive health data can result in identity theft, insurance fraud, and psychological distress for individuals. Moreover, compromised data can be used to manipulate medical treatments, tamper with medical records, or launch targeted attacks on individuals or healthcare providers.

To address data breaches and privacy concerns in the IoT environment, several measures can be implemented:

- **Data Encryption:** Encrypting data both at rest and in transit can help protect sensitive information from unauthorized access. Strong encryption algorithms and secure key management practices are essential to maintaining data confidentiality.

- **Access Control and Authentication:** Implementing robust access control mechanisms ensures that only authorized individuals can access IoT devices and the data they generate. Multi-factor authentication and role-based access control can significantly strengthen security.

- **Privacy by Design:** Incorporating privacy considerations into device design and development processes is crucial. Privacy-enhancing technologies, anonymization techniques, and privacy impact assessments can help minimize the risks to personal privacy.

- **Regulatory Compliance:** Adhering to applicable privacy and security regulations, such as the Health Insurance Portability and Accountability Act (HIPAA) in the United States, helps ensure that organizations handle personal health information responsibly and maintain adequate safeguards.

It is imperative for organizations and individuals within the health and wellness industry to prioritize data security and privacy, adopting comprehensive strategies to protect sensitive information and mitigate the risks associated with IoT.

Case Study: Ransomware Attack on IoT-enabled Hospitals

A notable real-world example highlighting the severity of IoT security risks in the health and wellness industry is the WannaCry ransomware attack in 2017. This widespread attack exploited vulnerabilities in Windows operating systems, affecting hundreds of thousands of computers worldwide.

The consequences of the WannaCry attack were particularly alarming in healthcare facilities. Many hospitals rely on interconnected IoT systems for patient care, including medical devices, electronic health records, and communication infrastructure. The ransomware attack disrupted critical healthcare services, resulting in canceled surgeries, delayed treatments, and compromised patient safety.

This case study illustrates the interconnected nature of IoT ecosystems in healthcare and the devastating consequences that can arise from security vulnerabilities. It underscores the urgent need to address and mitigate IoT security risks to protect patient wellbeing and maintain the continuity of healthcare services.

Resources and Best Practices

Developing robust security measures in the IoT landscape requires a proactive approach and continuous improvement. Organizations and individuals within the health and wellness industry can adopt the following best practices to enhance IoT security:

- Regularly update and patch IoT devices to address known vulnerabilities.
- Implement secure coding practices and perform regular security assessments.
- Employ strong authentication mechanisms, such as two-factor authentication, and avoid default or weak passwords.
- Establish secure communication channels between IoT devices and ensure data encryption.
- Conduct regular security audits and penetration testing to identify vulnerabilities.
- Segment IoT networks to contain systems and limit the impact of breaches.
- Educate employees and end-users about IoT security risks and best practices.
- Stay informed about emerging IoT security technologies and industry standards.
- Collaborate with industry partners and share threat intelligence to strengthen collective defenses.

The health and wellness industry can also benefit from resources and guidelines provided by cybersecurity organizations and regulatory bodies that focus on IoT security. These resources include:

- OWASP Internet of Things Project: Provides guidance and best practices for securing IoT devices and applications.
- NIST Cybersecurity Framework: Offers a framework for managing and reducing cybersecurity risks, applicable to IoT environments.
- IoT Security Foundation: Provides resources, guidance, and certification programs to promote IoT security best practices.
- Manufacturer and industry-specific security guidelines and certifications, such as UL 2900 for medical devices.

By following these resources and adopting best practices, stakeholders in the health and wellness industry can proactively address IoT security risks and enhance the overall security of IoT-enabled systems.

Conclusion

As the health and wellness industry embraces the Internet of Things, it is essential to recognize and address the security risks associated with interconnected devices. IoT security vulnerabilities, medical device vulnerabilities, data breaches, and privacy concerns necessitate a comprehensive approach to safeguard personal wellbeing and protect sensitive information.

By understanding common IoT vulnerabilities, implementing robust security measures, and staying informed about emerging threats and best practices, organizations and individuals within the health and wellness industry can enhance the security posture of IoT ecosystems. Prioritizing security in the design, development, and deployment of IoT devices and systems is critical to building a safe and secure digital environment for health and wellness in our digitally connected world.

Key Takeaways:

- IoT devices in the health and wellness industry are prone to several vulnerabilities, such as lack of encryption, weak authentication, and insecure firmware and software.
- Medical device vulnerabilities pose significant risks to patient safety and privacy, requiring robust security measures and interoperability standards.
- Data breaches and privacy concerns associated with IoT devices highlight the need for data encryption, access control, privacy by design, and compliance with regulations.

- The WannaCry ransomware attack on IoT-enabled hospitals serves as a case study emphasizing the consequences of IoT security risks.
- Best practices include regular updates and patching, strong authentication, secure communication channels, security audits, and employee education.
- Resources and guidelines from organizations like OWASP, NIST, and IoT Security Foundation can aid in building IoT security resilience.

Denial of Service (DoS) Attacks and Distributed Denial of Service (DDoS) Attacks

In this section, we will explore the concept of Denial of Service (DoS) attacks and Distributed Denial of Service (DDoS) attacks, two common cyber threats that can greatly impact the availability and functionality of digital systems. We will discuss the methods used in these attacks, their potential consequences, and the measures that can be taken to mitigate the risks associated with them.

Understanding DoS Attacks

A Denial of Service (DoS) attack is a malicious attempt to disrupt the normal functioning of a computer system, network, or website by overwhelming it with a flood of illegitimate requests or by exploiting vulnerabilities in the system. The goal of a DoS attack is to exhaust the targeted system's resources, such as bandwidth, memory, or processing power, making it incapable of responding to legitimate user requests.

DoS attacks can take various forms, including:

- **Flooding attacks:** These attacks involve sending an excessive amount of traffic or requests to the targeted system, overwhelming its resources. This can be achieved by sending a large number of emails, initiating multiple connection requests, or flooding a network with data packets.
- **Service abuse:** In this type of attack, the attacker exploits vulnerabilities in the targeted system's software or configuration to consume excessive resources. For example, an attacker might send specially crafted requests that require the system to perform resource-intensive operations, leading to a DoS condition.
- **Application layer attacks:** These attacks target specific applications or services running on the targeted system. They exploit weaknesses in the

application code or infrastructure to exhaust system resources or cause instability. Examples include HTTP floods and Slowloris attacks.

The consequences of a successful DoS attack can range from temporary inconvenience to significant financial loss, reputational damage, and legal liabilities. In healthcare and wellness environments, DoS attacks can disrupt critical systems, such as electronic health records (EHR) or telehealth platforms, potentially compromising patient care and privacy.

Understanding DDoS Attacks

A Distributed Denial of Service (DDoS) attack is an evolution of the traditional DoS attack. In a DDoS attack, multiple compromised computers, known as bots or zombies, are used to orchestrate the attack simultaneously. These compromised systems are usually part of a larger network of infected computers, referred to as a botnet.

The major difference between a DoS attack and a DDoS attack is the scale and distributed nature of the latter. By leveraging a botnet, attackers can generate a massive volume of traffic or requests from various sources, making it harder to mitigate the attack by simply blocking specific IP addresses.

DDoS attacks can be categorized based on the techniques used:

- **Volumetric attacks:** These attacks aim to saturate the targeted system's bandwidth by flooding it with a high volume of traffic. Attackers may utilize botnets composed of thousands or even millions of compromised devices to generate this massive amount of traffic.

- **TCP/IP protocol attacks:** These attacks exploit vulnerabilities in the TCP/IP protocol stack to consume system resources, such as the server's CPU or memory. Examples include SYN flood attacks, which overload the server with half-open TCP connections, and ICMP floods, which flood the network with ICMP packets.

- **Application layer attacks:** Similar to application layer DoS attacks, DDoS attacks can target the application layer, overwhelming the targeted system's resources or exploiting application-level vulnerabilities. These attacks are often more sophisticated and harder to detect than volumetric or protocol-based attacks.

DDoS attacks pose a significant threat to healthcare and wellness organizations, as they can result in prolonged service disruptions, financial losses, damage to reputation, and potential legal implications. Therefore, it is crucial to implement effective defensive measures to protect against such attacks.

Defending Against DoS and DDoS Attacks

Mitigating the risks associated with DoS and DDoS attacks requires a multi-layered approach that combines proactive preventive measures and responsive strategies. Some key strategies for defending against these attacks include:

- **Network traffic monitoring:** Implementing network monitoring tools and intrusion detection systems (IDS) can help detect and mitigate DoS and DDoS attacks in their early stages. These systems can analyze network traffic patterns and alert administrators when abnormal traffic spikes or anomalies are detected.

- **Firewalls and rate limiting:** Configuring firewalls to filter and block traffic from suspicious or blacklisted IP addresses can help prevent some DoS and DDoS attacks. Rate limiting techniques can also be applied to limit the number of requests allowed from a single IP address within a specified time frame.

- **Load balancing and scalability:** Distributing the workload across multiple servers or using load balancing techniques can help mitigate the impact of DoS and DDoS attacks. By spreading the traffic load, systems can maintain availability and handle a larger volume of requests.

- **Content Delivery Network (CDN):** Implementing a CDN can help mitigate the impact of DDoS attacks by distributing content across multiple geographically dispersed servers. This helps absorb the attack traffic and minimize the impact on the origin server.

- **Intrusion prevention systems (IPS):** IPS systems can analyze traffic in real-time and detect and block malicious traffic associated with DoS and DDoS attacks. These systems can also detect various attack patterns and apply rule-based mitigation techniques.

- **Redundancy and backup systems:** Maintaining backup systems and data redundancy can help ensure business continuity during and after DoS or DDoS attacks. Regularly backing up critical data and having alternative communication channels can minimize the impact of an attack.

It is important to note that no defense mechanism can provide absolute protection against DoS and DDoS attacks. Attack techniques constantly evolve, and attackers continuously find new ways to bypass security measures. Therefore, organizations should regularly assess their risk posture, deploy appropriate defenses, and update their incident response plans to address emerging threats.

Exercise

Imagine you are the cybersecurity manager of a telehealth company that has recently experienced a DDoS attack, resulting in a significant disruption in service availability. As part of your incident response plan, outline the steps you would take to mitigate the attack and minimize its impact on the organization.

Hint: Consider implementing network traffic analysis, leveraging cloud-based DDoS protection services, and collaborating with your internet service provider (ISP) to implement traffic filtering capabilities.

Additional Resources

To further enhance your understanding of DoS and DDoS attacks, and their implications in the health and wellness industry, we recommend the following resources:

1. Moore, T., Tipper, D., & Karygiannis, T. (2014). *Cybersecurity for industrial control systems: SCADA, DCS, PLC, HMI, and SIS*. Auerbach Publications.

2. Knapp, E. D. (2014). *Industrial network security: Securing critical infrastructure networks for smart grid, SCADA, and other industrial control systems*. Syngress.

3. CERT Division, Software Engineering Institute, Carnegie Mellon University. Distributed Denial of Service (DDoS) Attacks. Retrieved from `https://www.cert.org/ddos/`.

By exploring these resources, you will gain deeper insights into the technical aspects, best practices, and real-world case studies related to DoS and DDoS attacks. Remember that staying current with the evolving threat landscape is crucial to effectively protect your organization against these cyber threats.

Advanced Persistent Threats (APTs)

In today's digital landscape, cyber threats have become increasingly sophisticated and persistent. One such threat is the Advanced Persistent Threat (APT), which poses significant risks to organizations and individuals alike. In this section, we will explore the nature of APTs, their characteristics, and strategies to mitigate their impact.

Understanding APTs

An Advanced Persistent Threat refers to a long-term, targeted cyber attack conducted by highly skilled attackers. Unlike traditional cyber attacks, APTs are not opportunistic, but rather carefully orchestrated with the aim of gaining unauthorized access to sensitive information or systems. APT actors are typically well-funded, patient, and possess advanced technical capabilities.

The main objective of APTs is to infiltrate an organization's infrastructure, remain undetected for an extended period, and continually exfiltrate data or carry out covert operations. APT attackers are often nation-state-sponsored or affiliated with organized crime groups, making them highly resourceful and motivated.

Characteristics of APTs

APTs possess several distinctive characteristics that distinguish them from other cyber threats. Understanding these characteristics is crucial for developing effective countermeasures:

- **Stealth and Persistence:** APTs utilize sophisticated techniques to evade detection and maintain access to targeted systems for an extended period, sometimes years. They employ various obfuscation techniques, such as rootkits and encrypted communication channels, to remain undetected by security defenses.

- **Targeted Approach:** APTs focus on specific organizations or individuals, tailoring their attacks to exploit specific vulnerabilities and gain access to valuable data or systems. They conduct extensive reconnaissance, gathering information about the target to craft customized attack vectors.

- **Multifaceted Attacks:** APTs employ a combination of attack vectors, including social engineering, zero-day exploits, malware propagation, and lateral movement within the target's network. They constantly adapt their tactics to bypass security measures, making detection and mitigation challenging.

- **Long-term Objective:** APTs operate with a long-term strategic goal, continuously exfiltrating data, establishing backdoors, or conducting espionage activities. The attackers may patiently explore the victim's environment to find valuable assets and exploit them over an extended period.

Mitigating APTs

Fighting against APTs requires a multi-layered approach that combines technical measures, user education, and proactive defense strategies:

- **Endpoint Security:** Implement robust endpoint security measures, including advanced anti-malware tools, host intrusion prevention systems, and secure configuration management. Regularly update and patch software to address known vulnerabilities exploited by APTs.

- **Network Security:** Deploy an effective network security infrastructure that includes firewalls, intrusion detection and prevention systems, web content filtering, and secure email gateways. Implement network segmentation to restrict lateral movement and limit the impact of potential APT attacks.

- **Employee Awareness:** Educate employees about APTs, their characteristics, and the risks they pose. Conduct regular security awareness training sessions to teach employees how to identify and report suspicious activities, such as phishing emails or social engineering attempts.

- **Threat Intelligence:** Establish relationships with trusted threat intelligence providers to stay informed about emerging APT campaigns and evolving tactics. Leverage threat intelligence feeds to enhance detection and response capabilities within your organization.

- **Incident Response Planning:** Develop an incident response plan specifically tailored to address APTs. Define roles, responsibilities, and escalation procedures. Regularly test the plan through simulated exercises to identify and address any gaps or weaknesses.

Case Study: The APT1 Threat

One notable example of an APT is the APT1 threat, also known as "Comment Crew." APT1 is a Chinese-based cyber espionage group responsible for numerous high-profile attacks on global organizations.

APT1's modus operandi involved carefully targeted spear-phishing campaigns combined with custom malware, allowing them to gain persistent access to compromised networks. Over a span of several years, APT1 successfully stole vast amounts of intellectual property and sensitive information from targeted entities.

Understanding the tactics and techniques employed by APT1 and similar groups underscores the importance of proactive defenses against APTs.

Resources for Further Study

To dive deeper into the world of APTs, consider exploring the following resources:

- *Advanced Persistent Threats: Understanding the Danger and How to Protect Your Organization* by Eric Cole
- *Countdown to Zero Day: Stuxnet and the Launch of the World's First Digital Weapon* by Kim Zetter
- *The Cuckoo's Egg: Tracking a Spy Through the Maze of Computer Espionage* by Clifford Stoll
- *Cybersecurity and Cyberwar: What Everyone Needs to Know* by Peter W. Singer and Allan Friedman
- Web resources such as the MITRE ATT&CK framework and reports from cybersecurity firms like FireEye and CrowdStrike

Conclusion

Advanced Persistent Threats present significant challenges for organizations and individuals alike. By understanding the nature of APTs, their characteristics, and implementing appropriate defensive measures, we can mitigate the risks and protect our valuable assets. Vigilance, continuous education, and a proactive cybersecurity stance are key in safeguarding against these persistent and determined adversaries.

Supply Chain Attacks in the Health and Wellness Industry

Supply chain attacks are a growing concern in the field of cybersecurity. These attacks occur when an attacker targets a less secure component or vendor and uses it as a gateway to gain unauthorized access to a more secure target. In the health and wellness industry, supply chain attacks can have serious consequences, as they can compromise the integrity of medical devices, electronic health records, and other critical systems.

Understanding the Threat

Supply chain attacks in the health and wellness industry can take various forms. For example, attackers may compromise the software or hardware during the manufacturing process, inserting malicious code or backdoors. They may also target vendors providing services such as cloud storage, telehealth platforms, or medical device manufacturers. By targeting these vendors, attackers can gain unauthorized access to sensitive data or disrupt critical operations.

Example: Compromised Medical Device Consider a scenario where a manufacturing company that produces medical devices is compromised during the supply chain process. The attacker may inject malicious code into the firmware or software of the devices, allowing them to remotely control or manipulate the devices. This could have severe consequences, such as altering dosage levels, tampering with vital signs monitoring, or even causing harm to patients.

Preventing and Mitigating Supply Chain Attacks

Preventing and mitigating supply chain attacks requires a multi-faceted approach, involving collaboration between manufacturers, vendors, and healthcare organizations. Here are some key steps that can be taken:

1. **Vendor Risk Management** Healthcare organizations should conduct thorough risk assessments of their vendors, especially those involved in critical areas such as medical device manufacturing, software development, or data storage. Vendors should be evaluated based on their security practices, compliance with industry standards, and track record of security incidents. Regular vendor audits can help ensure that security measures are being implemented effectively.

2. **Software and Firmware Verification** Healthcare organizations should implement a robust software and firmware verification process to ensure that all components and devices are free from malicious code. This includes conducting code reviews, using static and dynamic analysis tools, and performing penetration testing. Regular software updates and patch management are also crucial for addressing vulnerabilities and reducing the risk of supply chain attacks.

3. **Secure Communication and Authentication** To mitigate the risk of supply chain attacks, secure communication channels and strong authentication mechanisms should be implemented. This includes establishing secure connections

with vendors, using encryption for data transmission, and implementing multi-factor authentication for system access. Secure protocols such as Transport Layer Security (TLS) should be employed to ensure the confidentiality and integrity of data exchanged in the supply chain.

4. **Continuous Monitoring and Intrusion Detection** Healthcare organizations should implement robust monitoring and intrusion detection systems to detect any suspicious activities or anomalies within the supply chain. This includes monitoring network traffic, system logs, and access controls. Intrusion detection systems can help identify and mitigate potential supply chain attacks in real-time, minimizing the impact on critical systems.

5. **Incident Response and Business Continuity Planning** Healthcare organizations should have well-defined incident response plans and business continuity plans in place to effectively respond to and recover from supply chain attacks. This includes establishing roles and responsibilities, defining communication protocols, and conducting regular drills and simulations. Backups of critical data and systems should be regularly performed and tested, ensuring data recovery in the event of an attack.

Ethical Considerations

When addressing the issue of supply chain attacks in the health and wellness industry, ethical considerations play a significant role. Healthcare organizations have an ethical obligation to protect the privacy and security of their patients' information and maintain the integrity and availability of their services. Ethical responsibilities include:

1. **Transparency and Disclosure** Healthcare organizations have a responsibility to be transparent about their security practices and the measures they have in place to prevent and respond to supply chain attacks. This includes informing patients and employees about any potential risks and vulnerabilities associated with the use of certain medical devices or services.

2. **Ethical Vendor Selection** Healthcare organizations should prioritize working with vendors who adhere to ethical practices and prioritize security in their supply chain. This includes conducting due diligence to ensure vendors have appropriate security measures in place and regularly reassessing their security posture.

3. **Patient Consent and Ownership of Data** Healthcare organizations must obtain informed consent from patients regarding the collection, use, and storage of their data. Patients should be aware of the risks associated with supply chain attacks and have control over their personal health information. Organizations should also consider patient rights to access, amend, or delete their data in the event of a supply chain attack.

In conclusion, supply chain attacks pose a significant threat to the health and wellness industry. To mitigate these risks, healthcare organizations must prioritize vendor risk management, implement software and firmware verification processes, establish secure communication channels, continuously monitor for suspicious activities, and have well-defined incident response plans in place. Ethical considerations, including transparency, ethical vendor selection, and patient consent, are vital in safeguarding the privacy and security of patient data in the face of supply chain attacks.

Securing Digital Devices and Networks

Implementing Strong Passwords and Multi-Factor Authentication

In today's digitally connected world, passwords play a crucial role in protecting our personal information and online accounts. However, many people still use weak and easily guessable passwords, making themselves vulnerable to cyber attacks. Implementing strong passwords and using multi-factor authentication (MFA) are essential steps in enhancing cybersecurity and safeguarding our digital identities.

The Importance of Strong Passwords

A strong password is the first line of defense against unauthorized access to our accounts. It should be unique, complex, and difficult for others to guess. Here are some key principles to keep in mind when creating strong passwords:

- **Length:** Longer passwords are generally more secure. Aim for a minimum of 12 characters.
- **Variety:** Use a mix of uppercase and lowercase letters, numbers, and special characters.
- **Avoid common patterns:** Avoid using easily guessable patterns like consecutive numbers or letters on the keyboard.

- **Avoid personal information:** Do not include personal information such as your name, birthdate, or address in your password.

- **Avoid dictionary words:** Avoid using common dictionary words, as these can be easily cracked by attackers.

- **Avoid password reuse:** Never reuse passwords across different accounts; if one account is compromised, others will remain secure.

Secure Password Management

With the increasing number of online accounts we have, it can be challenging to remember strong and unique passwords for each one. To simplify password management, consider using a password manager. A password manager securely stores your passwords and generates strong, random passwords for you. It also offers the convenience of automatically filling in passwords when you visit websites or use applications.

When choosing a password manager, look for one that encrypts your password database with strong encryption algorithms. Additionally, opt for a password manager that supports multi-factor authentication for an added layer of security.

Multi-Factor Authentication (MFA)

While strong passwords are crucial, they can still be compromised. Multi-factor authentication (MFA) provides an additional layer of security by requiring multiple forms of verification to access an account. In addition to something you know (such as a password), it also involves something you have or something you are.

Common types of MFA include:

- **One-time Passwords (OTP):** OTPs are typically generated by an authenticator app or sent via SMS to your registered mobile device. They provide a temporary code that you must enter along with your password.

- **Biometrics:** Biometric authentication uses unique physical characteristics to verify your identity, such as fingerprint or facial recognition.

- **Hardware Tokens:** Hardware tokens, like USB security keys or smart cards, generate time-based or challenge-response codes for authentication.

Enabling MFA significantly reduces the risk of unauthorized access to your accounts, even if your password is compromised. It adds an extra layer of protection, as an attacker would need to possess not only your password but also the additional factor to gain access.

Best Practices for Passwords and MFA

Here are some best practices to follow when implementing strong passwords and MFA:

- **Regular password updates:** Change your passwords at regular intervals, especially for critical accounts. This helps prevent unauthorized access in case of a breach.
- **Avoid sharing passwords:** Never share your passwords with anyone, even with close friends or family members.
- **Use unique passwords:** Use a different password for each online account to prevent credential reuse attacks.
- **Regularly review account activity:** Regularly review your account activity and watch for any suspicious behavior or unauthorized access attempts.
- **Keep software and devices updated:** Regularly update your operating systems, applications, and devices to protect against known vulnerabilities that attackers may exploit.

Remember, cybersecurity is a continuous effort. Implementing strong passwords and MFA is just one step towards protecting your digital identity. Stay vigilant, keep your software up to date, and follow best practices to stay one step ahead of cyber threats.

Real-World Example: Password Security Breach

In 2019, a well-known social media platform experienced a massive data breach that exposed the passwords of millions of its users. The breach occurred due to weak password security practices within the platform's infrastructure. As a result, cybercriminals were able to gain unauthorized access to user accounts, potentially compromising personal and sensitive information.

This incident highlights the importance of implementing strong passwords to protect against such breaches. By using unique, complex passwords and enabling MFA, users can significantly reduce the risk of their accounts being compromised, even in the event of a data breach.

Resources for Strong Passwords and MFA

Here are some resources that can help you create and manage strong passwords and enable multi-factor authentication:

- LastPass (`https://www.lastpass.com/`)
- 1Password (`https://1password.com/`)
- Google Authenticator (`https://support.google.com/accounts/answer/1066447`)
- Microsoft Authenticator (`https://www.microsoft.com/en-us/account/authenticator`)

Take advantage of these tools and resources to enhance your password security and enable multi-factor authentication for your accounts.

Key Takeaways

- Strong passwords are essential for protecting your accounts from unauthorized access. Use a mix of uppercase and lowercase letters, numbers, and special characters, and avoid common patterns or personal information.
- Consider using a password manager to securely store and generate strong passwords for your accounts.
- Multi-factor authentication (MFA) adds an extra layer of security by requiring multiple forms of verification to access an account.
- Implementing MFA significantly reduces the risk of unauthorized access, even if your password is compromised.
- Regularly update your passwords, review account activity, and keep your software and devices up to date to maintain strong security practices.

With strong passwords and multi-factor authentication, you can significantly enhance the security of your personal information and stay one step ahead of cyber threats. Keep these practices in mind to protect your digital identity and maintain a safer online presence.

Keeping Operating Systems and Software Up to Date

In order to maintain a secure digital environment, it is crucial to regularly update and patch operating systems and software. This section will discuss the importance of keeping your systems up to date, explain the risks and consequences of outdated software, and provide guidelines for effective updating.

The Importance of Software Updates

Software updates are released by vendors to address security vulnerabilities, fix bugs, and improve overall system performance. Ignoring these updates can leave your system susceptible to attacks and compromises. Updating your operating system and software is essential to ensure the integrity and security of your digital environment.

Risks and Consequences of Outdated Software

Using outdated operating systems and software exposes your system to various risks and consequences, including:

- **Security Vulnerabilities:** Hackers are constantly exploring and exploiting vulnerabilities in software. By not updating your systems, you are leaving known vulnerabilities unpatched, making it easier for attackers to gain unauthorized access.

- **Malware Infections:** Outdated software often lacks necessary security measures to defend against malware. Cybercriminals can exploit these weaknesses to inject malicious code into your system, leading to data breaches, ransomware attacks, or other forms of compromise.

- **Data Loss:** Outdated software may have compatibility issues with new hardware or file formats, which can result in data corruption or loss. Without updates, you may encounter difficulties in accessing or recovering your important files and documents.

- **Incompatibility with New Technologies:** As technology advances, software vendors release updates to ensure compatibility with new hardware, protocols, or standards. Failure to update your software may hinder your ability to take advantage of new features and advancements.

- **Decreased Performance:** Outdated software often suffers from performance issues and inefficiencies. Updates often include optimizations and bug fixes, leading to improved stability and speed.

Effective Software Updating Practices

To ensure that your operating systems and software remain secure and up to date, consider implementing the following practices:

1. **Enable Automatic Updates:** Most operating systems and software offer automatic update options. Enabling this feature allows the system to download and install updates seamlessly, reducing the risk of human negligence or forgetfulness.

2. **Regularly Check for Updates:** For software that does not support automatic updates, manually checking for updates is essential. Visit the vendor's website or use built-in update tools to verify if any updates are available.

3. **Prioritize Critical Updates:** Not all updates are created equal. Focus on installing critical security updates and patches first, as they address known vulnerabilities that attackers may exploit. Non-critical updates, such as feature enhancements, can be deferred until a more convenient time.

4. **Beware of Fake Updates:** Cybercriminals may disguise malware as software updates. It is important to download updates only from official vendor websites or trusted sources. Avoid clicking on suspicious pop-ups or links claiming to provide updates.

5. **Keep a Record of Installed Software and Versions:** Maintaining a comprehensive list of installed software, along with their versions, makes it easier to track and ensure that all applications are up to date. This also aids in identifying any legacy software that may require replacement or updates.

6. **Test Updates in a Controlled Environment:** Before deploying updates on critical systems, it is advisable to test them in a controlled environment. This helps identify any compatibility issues or conflicts with other software before rolling out the updates system-wide.

7. **Educate Users on the Importance of Updating:** Staff members should be trained on the significance of software updates and their role in maintaining security. They should understand the potentially severe consequences of ignoring updates and be encouraged to promptly install them.

Example Scenario: Updating Operating System and Software

Consider a scenario where a health and wellness clinic relies on a legacy electronic health records (EHR) system to manage patient data. The clinic has recently experienced a security breach due to outdated software. To mitigate the risk, the clinic decides to implement an effective software updating process.

First, the clinic establishes a list of all software applications used, including the EHR system and supporting software. They identify the version numbers and check the vendor websites to determine any available updates.

The clinic enables automatic updates for the operating system, ensuring critical security patches are automatically installed. For the EHR system and other software that lack automatic update features, a designated IT staff member is assigned to regularly check for updates and apply them promptly.

To avoid the risk of fake updates, the clinic educates its staff on the importance of downloading updates from trusted sources. They emphasize the need for caution when encountering pop-ups or links claiming to provide updates.

The IT staff also sets up a test environment to validate updates before deploying them to patient-facing systems. This allows them to identify any compatibility issues or conflicts with other software before applying updates clinic-wide.

Through these practices, the health and wellness clinic establishes a reliable software updating process, ensuring the security and performance of their digital infrastructure.

Additional Resources and Tools

Staying informed about software updates and their impact on cybersecurity is crucial. Consider the following resources and tools for further learning:

- The National Vulnerability Database (NVD): A comprehensive database of vulnerabilities, providing information and links to relevant patches and updates.
- Vendor Websites: Visit the official websites of software vendors to access documentation, release notes, and download updates.
- Vulnerability Scanners: Tools such as Nessus, OpenVAS, or Qualys can scan your system for vulnerabilities and suggest updates.
- Software Update Managers: Applications like Chocolatey or Patch My PC can help automate and manage software updates for multiple applications.
- Cybersecurity Blogs and News Sites: Stay informed about the latest cybersecurity threats and the importance of software updates through reputable blogs and news sites.

Key Takeaways

Regularly updating operating systems and software is essential for maintaining a secure digital environment. Failing to update software can lead to security vulnerabilities, malware infections, data loss, and decreased performance. Implementing effective software updating practices, such as enabling automatic updates, regularly checking for updates, and prioritizing critical updates, helps ensure the integrity and security of your systems. It is also crucial to educate users on the importance of updates and the risks associated with outdated software. By following these guidelines and utilizing available resources, you can enhance the security and performance of your digital infrastructure.

Securing Mobile Devices and BYOD Policies

Mobile devices, such as smartphones and tablets, have become an integral part of our personal and professional lives. They provide us with convenience and productivity, allowing us to stay connected and access information on the go. However, with the increasing use of mobile devices in the health and wellness industry, there is a growing need to ensure their security to protect sensitive data and maintain the confidentiality of patient information. This section will cover the best practices for securing mobile devices and implementing Bring Your Own Device (BYOD) policies in the health and wellness industry.

Understanding Mobile Device Security Risks

Mobile devices are susceptible to a wide range of security risks, including:

- **Lost or stolen devices:** Mobile devices are easy targets for theft, and if they contain sensitive data, it can lead to a data breach.
- **Malware and app vulnerabilities:** Mobile devices can be infected with malware through malicious apps or vulnerabilities in the operating system. This can result in unauthorized access to sensitive information.
- **Unsecured Wi-Fi networks:** Connecting to unsecured Wi-Fi networks can expose mobile devices to various security threats, including eavesdropping and man-in-the-middle attacks.
- **Physical security weaknesses:** Mobile devices can be physically accessed by unauthorized individuals, compromising the security of stored data.

To mitigate these risks, it is crucial to implement security measures and establish policies that ensure the safe use of mobile devices in the health and wellness industry.

Implementing Mobile Device Security Measures

To secure mobile devices in the health and wellness industry, consider the following measures:

1. **Device encryption:** Enforce device encryption to protect data stored on mobile devices. This ensures that even if the device is lost or stolen, the data remains unreadable without the encryption key.

2. **Strong passwords and biometric authentication:** Require users to set strong passwords and enable biometric authentication, such as fingerprint or facial recognition. This adds an extra layer of security to prevent unauthorized access.

3. **Remote wipe and device tracking:** Enable remote wipe functionality so that if a device is lost or stolen, it can be remotely erased to protect sensitive data. Similarly, device tracking enables the location of a lost or stolen device to facilitate its recovery.

4. **App vetting and updates:** Regularly vet the apps installed on mobile devices to ensure they come from trusted sources and have the necessary security measures in place. Additionally, keep the operating system and apps up to date to protect against known vulnerabilities.

5. **Secure app development practices:** If developing custom apps for use in the health and wellness industry, implement secure coding practices to prevent vulnerabilities that could be exploited by attackers.

6. **Mobile device management (MDM) solutions:** Implement MDM solutions to centrally manage and enforce security policies on mobile devices. This allows for remote configuration, monitoring, and enforcement of security controls.

7. **Containerization and data segregation:** Use containerization technologies to separate personal and business data on mobile devices. This helps protect sensitive business data without compromising the privacy and usability of personal apps and information.

8. **Secure Wi-Fi connectivity:** Encourage the use of secure Wi-Fi networks, such as those with WPA2 encryption, to minimize the risk of eavesdropping and data interception. Avoid connecting to public or unsecured networks whenever possible.

By implementing these security measures, organizations can significantly enhance the security posture of their mobile devices and protect sensitive data from unauthorized access.

Bring Your Own Device (BYOD) Policies

Bring Your Own Device (BYOD) policies allow employees to use their personal mobile devices for work purposes. While BYOD can improve productivity and cost-effectiveness, it also introduces security challenges. To address these challenges, organizations should develop comprehensive BYOD policies that consider the following:

1. **Device registration and management:** Require employees to register their devices with the organization's MDM solution, enabling the management and enforcement of security policies on BYOD devices.

2. **Separation of personal and work data:** Implement containerization or virtualization techniques to segregate personal and work data on BYOD devices. This ensures that only work-related data is subject to organizational security policies.

3. **Acceptable use and security awareness training:** Educate employees about the acceptable use of their personal devices for work, including the potential security risks. Provide regular security awareness training to help employees recognize and avoid common threats.

4. **Access control and authentication:** Implement strong authentication mechanisms, such as two-factor authentication, to ensure that only authorized users can access work-related data.

5. **Data backup and remote wipe:** Require employees to perform regular backups of work-related data on their BYOD devices. In case of loss or theft, the organization should have the capability to remotely wipe work-related data from the device.

6. **Compliance with data privacy regulations:** Ensure that BYOD policies align with data privacy regulations, such as the General Data Protection Regulation (GDPR). This includes obtaining explicit user consent for the collection and processing of personal data on BYOD devices.

7. **Monitoring and incident response:** Define monitoring practices to detect and respond to security incidents involving BYOD devices. Establish procedures for reporting and investigating potential security breaches.

A well-defined BYOD policy helps strike a balance between employee productivity and data security, enabling organizations in the health and wellness industry to leverage mobile devices while minimizing the associated risks.

Case Study: Securing Mobile Devices in a Telehealth Organization

As an example, let's consider a telehealth organization that provides remote healthcare services to patients through mobile devices. To ensure the security of their mobile devices, the organization has implemented the following measures:

- All mobile devices used by healthcare professionals are equipped with full-disk encryption and require strong passwords for device access. Additionally, biometric authentication, such as fingerprint or facial recognition, is enabled to enhance security.

- The organization has implemented a mobile device management (MDM) solution that allows for centralized management and enforcement of security policies. This includes app vetting, remote wipe capability, and device tracking in case of loss or theft.

- Healthcare professionals are required to only install apps from trusted sources and regularly update the operating system and apps to protect against known vulnerabilities.

- Personal and work-related data on mobile devices are segregated using containerization techniques. This ensures that sensitive patient information is protected without compromising the privacy of personal apps and data.

- Secure Wi-Fi networks with WPA2 encryption are used whenever possible to establish a secure communication channel between healthcare professionals and patients. Employees are trained to avoid connecting to unsecured or public Wi-Fi networks.

- The organization has developed a comprehensive BYOD policy that outlines the acceptable use of personal devices for work purposes. It includes guidelines on device registration, data segregation, access control, and incident reporting.

By implementing these security measures and adhering to the BYOD policy, the telehealth organization can provide healthcare services securely, protecting patient data and maintaining compliance with regulatory requirements.

Key Takeaways

Securing mobile devices in the health and wellness industry is crucial to protect sensitive data and maintain the confidentiality of patient information. Key takeaways from this section include:

- Mobile devices are susceptible to various security risks, such as loss or theft, malware infections, unsecured Wi-Fi networks, and physical security weaknesses.

- Implement security measures like device encryption, strong passwords, remote wipe capability, and secure Wi-Fi connectivity to mitigate mobile device security risks.

- BYOD policies should address device registration, data segregation, acceptable use, access control, and compliance with data privacy regulations.

- Case studies provide real-world examples of how organizations can secure mobile devices in the health and wellness industry.

By following these best practices, organizations can establish a secure mobile device environment, ensuring the privacy and security of patient information in the digital age.

Securing Home Networks and Wi-Fi Connections

In today's digitally connected world, where almost every aspect of our lives depends on the internet, securing our home networks and Wi-Fi connections has become more important than ever. This section will explore the fundamental principles and best practices for protecting our home networks and ensuring the security of our Wi-Fi connections.

The Importance of Securing Home Networks

Home networks serve as the gateway to our digital lives, connecting our computers, smartphones, smart TVs, and other devices to the internet. Any vulnerabilities in our home networks can leave us exposed to various cyber threats, such as unauthorized access to our personal information, hacking attempts, and malware infections.

By implementing effective security measures, we can significantly reduce the risk of cyber attacks and protect the privacy and integrity of our personal data. Securing our home networks also ensures that our Wi-Fi connections are not misused by unauthorized individuals, preventing them from accessing sensitive information or engaging in illegal activities using our network.

Understanding Wi-Fi Security Protocols

Wi-Fi security protocols are designed to encrypt the data transmitted between our devices and the wireless router, ensuring that only authorized users can access the network. There are several commonly used protocols, each with different levels of security:

- **Wired Equivalent Privacy (WEP):** WEP was the first widely adopted Wi-Fi security protocol. However, it is now considered insecure due to its vulnerabilities. It is recommended to avoid using WEP and opt for more secure protocols.

- **Wi-Fi Protected Access (WPA2):** WPA2 is currently the most secure protocol for home Wi-Fi networks. It uses the Advanced Encryption Standard (AES) to encrypt data and provides stronger security compared to WEP. It is strongly recommended to configure WPA2 security for home networks.

- **Wi-Fi Protected Access 3 (WPA3):** WPA3 is the latest generation of Wi-Fi security protocol. It further enhances the security provided by WPA2, offering stronger encryption and more robust authentication mechanisms. Although not widely supported by devices at the time of writing, transitioning to WPA3 is recommended when feasible.

Setting Up a Secure Wi-Fi Network

To ensure the security of our home Wi-Fi network, we need to follow some key practices during the setup and configuration process.

1. **Change Default Network Credentials** By default, Wi-Fi routers and access points come with preconfigured usernames and passwords. It's crucial to change these default credentials to a unique, strong password. Avoid using easily guessable or common passwords, and consider using a password manager to securely store and manage your passwords.

2. **Enable Network Encryption** As mentioned earlier, WPA2 or WPA3 should be selected as the encryption protocol for the Wi-Fi network. This ensures that data transmitted between devices and the router is encrypted and cannot be easily intercepted by malicious actors.

3. **Implement a Strong Wi-Fi Password** In addition to changing the default credentials, it's essential to set a strong password for your Wi-Fi network. A strong password consists of a combination of upper and lowercase letters, numbers, and special characters. Remember to avoid using personal information or easily guessable patterns.

4. **Disable SSID Broadcast** The Service Set Identifier (SSID) is the name of your Wi-Fi network. By default, routers broadcast the SSID, making it visible to nearby devices. It is recommended to disable SSID broadcast so that the network does not appear in the list of available networks. This adds an extra layer of security, as it makes it more difficult for potential attackers to target your network.

5. **Set Up a Guest Network** If your router supports it, consider setting up a guest network for visitors. This separate network allows guests to connect to the internet without compromising the security of your main network. Be sure to set a separate password for the guest network and restrict access to other devices on the main network.

Additional Security Measures

In addition to the Wi-Fi network setup, there are other important security measures to consider for securing home networks:

1. **Keep Router Firmware Up to Date** Regularly check for firmware updates provided by the manufacturer and apply them as soon as they become available. Firmware updates often include security patches that address vulnerabilities and improve the overall security of the router.

2. **Enable a Firewall** Most routers come with built-in firewalls that provide a basic level of protection. Ensure that the firewall is enabled to filter incoming and outgoing traffic, preventing unauthorized access to your network.

3. **Disable Remote Management** Remote management allows the router to be accessed and configured from outside the local network. Disable this feature unless absolutely necessary, as it can be exploited by attackers to gain control of the router.

4. **Use MAC Address Filtering** Media Access Control (MAC) address filtering allows you to specify which devices can connect to the network based on their unique MAC addresses. By enabling MAC address filtering, you can prevent unauthorized devices from connecting to your network even if they have the Wi-Fi password.

5. **Regularly Check Connected Devices** Periodically review the list of devices connected to your network and ensure that only authorized devices are present. If you notice any unfamiliar devices, investigate immediately as it could be an indication of unauthorized access.

Conclusion

Securing home networks and Wi-Fi connections is essential for protecting our personal information and ensuring the overall security of our digital lives. By following the best practices outlined in this section, such as using strong Wi-Fi passwords, enabling network encryption, and keeping router firmware up to date, we can significantly reduce the risk of cyber attacks and maintain a secure home network environment. Remember, a secure home network is the foundation for a safe and connected digital experience. Stay vigilant and prioritize the security of your home network to enjoy the benefits of the digital world while safeguarding your personal information.

Firewalls and Intrusion Detection Systems

In today's digitally connected world, where cyber threats are constantly evolving, it is crucial to implement effective security measures to protect sensitive data and systems. Two key components of a robust cybersecurity strategy are firewalls and intrusion detection systems (IDS). In this section, we will explore the concepts, principles, and best practices of firewalls and IDS, and how they contribute to the overall security of health and wellness systems.

Firewalls

Firewalls act as a first line of defense against unauthorized access and malicious activities by filtering network traffic based on a set of predefined rules. They are essentially a barrier between trusted internal networks and untrusted external networks, such as the internet. Firewalls can be implemented using both hardware and software, and they analyze incoming and outgoing packets to determine whether they should be allowed or blocked.

There are several types of firewalls, including packet-filtering firewalls, stateful firewalls, and next-generation firewalls. Packet-filtering firewalls examine the header information of each packet to make decisions. Stateful firewalls, on the other hand, keep track of the state of connections and make decisions based on the context of the packets. Next-generation firewalls combine traditional firewall capabilities with additional features like intrusion prevention systems and application control.

To effectively configure and deploy firewalls, it is essential to follow some best practices:

- Define a well-thought-out firewall policy: Clearly define the rules and policies governing traffic flow and access control.
- Regularly update firewall rules: Stay up to date with emerging threats and modify firewall rules accordingly.
- Use default-deny rule sets: Deny all traffic by default and only allow specific traffic that is necessary for business operations.
- Separate internal and external networks: Place firewalls strategically to isolate internal networks from untrusted external networks.
- Implement network address translation (NAT): Use NAT techniques to hide internal IP addresses and enhance privacy.

- Regularly monitor and review firewall logs: Keep a close eye on firewall logs to identify potential security incidents and anomalies.

Firewalls are an integral part of network security, but they are not foolproof. It is important to complement them with other security measures like IDS, which we will discuss next.

Intrusion Detection Systems (IDS)

While firewalls act as a preventative measure, IDS play a complementary role by detecting and responding to potential security breaches. IDS monitor network traffic, system logs, and events in real-time to identify any suspicious activity or potential threats.

There are two types of IDS: network-based IDS (NIDS) and host-based IDS (HIDS). NIDS monitor network traffic, analyzing packets to detect known attack signatures or abnormal patterns. HIDS, on the other hand, reside on individual hosts or servers, analyzing system logs and file integrity to detect any signs of compromise.

The key benefits of IDS include:

- Early detection of attacks: IDS can identify malicious activities at an early stage, allowing for prompt response and mitigation.
- Real-time monitoring: By continuously monitoring network traffic and system logs, IDS can provide real-time alerts and notifications.
- Compliance with regulations: IDS solutions can help organizations meet regulatory requirements and standards related to cybersecurity.
- Incident response and forensic analysis: IDS logs provide valuable information for incident response and forensic investigations.

To implement IDS effectively, consider the following best practices:

- Define a comprehensive IDS policy: Clearly define the scope, objectives, and rules for IDS deployment.
- Configure IDS according to network topology: Ensure IDS sensors are strategically placed to monitor critical network segments.
- Regularly update IDS signatures: Keep IDS signatures up to date to detect the latest threats and attack patterns.

- Consolidate and centralize IDS logs: Collect and analyze IDS logs in a central location to facilitate correlation and analysis.
- Integrate IDS with incident response procedures: Develop incident response plans that incorporate IDS alerts and notifications.
- Regularly review and analyze IDS logs: Identify and investigate any anomalies or potential security incidents.

It is important to note that firewalls and IDS are not standalone solutions but rather integral components of a comprehensive cybersecurity strategy. They work hand in hand to protect critical assets and systems from a variety of cyber threats.

Case Study: Detecting and Preventing Network Intrusions

Let's take a look at a real-world scenario where the combination of firewalls and IDS helped detect and prevent network intrusions in a health and wellness facility.

ABC Medical Clinic, which handles sensitive patient information and medical records, implemented a robust cybersecurity strategy that included firewalls and IDS. One day, the IDS alerted the clinic's IT team about a series of suspicious activities originating from an internal computer. The firewall logs also indicated a high volume of data being transferred to an unknown external IP address.

Upon receiving the alert, the IT team quickly investigated the issue. They discovered that an employee's computer had been compromised by a malware infection, which allowed an external attacker to gain unauthorized access to patient records.

Using the IDS logs and firewall data, the IT team was able to trace the attacker's IP address and take immediate action to block any further communication. They also isolated the compromised computer and conducted a thorough forensic analysis to determine the extent of the breach.

Thanks to the proactive implementation of firewalls and IDS, ABC Medical Clinic was able to detect and respond to the network intrusion swiftly, minimizing the potential impact on patient data and overall operations.

Resources and Further Reading

If you are interested in learning more about firewalls, IDS, and network security, here are some recommended resources:

- Anderson, K. (2012). *Security Engineering: A Guide to Building Dependable Distributed Systems.*

- Cheswick, W. R., Bellovin, S. M., & Rubin, A. D. (2003). *Firewalls and Internet Security: Repelling the Wily Hacker.*
- Northcutt, S. (2002). *Network Intrusion Detection: An Analyst's Handbook.*
- Scarfone, K., & Mell, P. (2007). *Guide to Intrusion Detection and Prevention Systems (IDPS).*

In addition to these resources, it is always recommended to stay updated with the latest security advisories and guidelines from reputable cybersecurity organizations.

Key Takeaways

- Firewalls act as a barrier between trusted internal networks and untrusted external networks, filtering network traffic based on predefined rules.
- Intrusion Detection Systems (IDS) monitor network traffic and system logs in real-time to detect and respond to potential security breaches.
- Firewalls and IDS are essential components of a comprehensive cybersecurity strategy, working together to protect sensitive data and systems.
- Best practices for firewalls include defining a firewall policy, regularly updating firewall rules, and monitoring firewall logs.
- Best practices for IDS include defining an IDS policy, strategically placing IDS sensors, and regularly updating IDS signatures.
- Firewalls and IDS are not standalone solutions – they should be complemented with other security measures to ensure comprehensive protection.

In the next section, we will explore data privacy and confidentiality in the context of cybersecurity for health and wellness.

Virtual Private Networks (VPNs) for Secure Remote Access

In today's digitally connected world, where remote work is becoming increasingly prevalent, ensuring secure remote access to networks and sensitive data is of utmost importance. Virtual Private Networks (VPNs) are a crucial tool in achieving secure remote access for individuals and organizations. In this section, we will explore the fundamentals of VPNs, their benefits, and how they can be used to protect data during remote access.

Understanding the Basics of VPNs

A VPN is a network technology that provides a secure and encrypted connection between a remote user and their organization's network. It creates a private tunnel through a public network, such as the internet, allowing remote users to access the organization's resources securely. This tunnel encrypts the data transmitted between the remote user's device and the organization's network, preventing unauthorized access and ensuring data confidentiality.

Key Features and Benefits of VPNs

VPNs offer several key features and benefits that make them an essential tool for secure remote access. Let's explore some of these features:

- **Data Encryption:** VPNs use strong encryption algorithms to protect the data transmitted over the network. This ensures that even if the data is intercepted, it remains secure and unreadable to unauthorized users.

- **Secure Authentication:** To establish a VPN connection, users are required to authenticate themselves using credentials provided by the organization. This ensures that only authorized individuals can access the network resources.

- **Anonymity and Privacy:** VPNs allow users to browse the internet and access resources anonymously. They mask the user's IP address, making it difficult for third parties to track their online activities.

- **Geo-Spoofing:** VPNs enable users to bypass geographical restrictions, allowing them to access region-restricted content and services. This is particularly useful for remote workers who may need to access resources that are only available in their organization's physical location.

- **Secure Remote Networking:** VPNs provide a secure method for connecting remote offices or branch locations to the organization's main network. This allows employees in different locations to access shared resources as if they were on the same local network.

- **Protection on Public Wi-Fi:** When connecting to a public Wi-Fi network, such as those found in coffee shops or airports, VPNs provide an extra layer of security. They encrypt the data transmitted over the network, protecting it from potential eavesdroppers.

Types of VPNs

There are various types of VPNs that can be used for secure remote access. Let's explore some common ones:

- **Remote Access VPN:** This type of VPN allows individual users to connect securely to the organization's network from remote locations. It enables employees to access their work resources and applications as if they were physically present in the office.
- **Site-to-Site VPN:** Site-to-Site VPNs, also known as router-to-router VPNs, establish encrypted connections between two or more networks. This is useful for connecting remote offices or branch locations to the organization's main network. It allows for seamless communication and resource sharing between the sites.
- **Mobile VPN:** Mobile VPNs are designed for mobile devices, such as smartphones and tablets. They provide secure access to the organization's network while users are on the move, ensuring that sensitive data remains protected even when connecting via public networks.
- **Client-to-Site VPN:** Client-to-Site VPNs, also known as user-to-network VPNs, allow individual users to connect securely to a specific network or server. This is commonly used for remote access to resources such as company intranets or file servers.

Implementing VPNs for Secure Remote Access

To implement VPNs effectively for secure remote access, organizations should follow some key best practices:

- **Robust Authentication:** Use strong authentication methods, such as two-factor authentication (2FA), to ensure only authorized users can establish VPN connections.
- **Proper Configuration:** Configure VPNs correctly to ensure that encryption is properly implemented and all security features are enabled. This includes using up-to-date encryption protocols and strong encryption keys.
- **Regularly Update VPN Software:** Keep VPN software up to date with the latest security patches and updates. This helps protect against known vulnerabilities and ensures the VPN remains secure.

- **Network Segmentation:** Segment the network to restrict VPN access to only the necessary resources. This limits potential exposure in case of a breach and helps protect sensitive data.
- **Monitoring and Logging:** Implement monitoring and logging mechanisms to track VPN usage and detect any suspicious activities. This can help identify potential security incidents and aid in incident response.
- **User Education and Awareness:** Train and educate users on the proper use of VPNs and the importance of following security practices. This includes recognizing phishing attempts, avoiding suspicious websites, and protecting their VPN credentials.

Real-World Example: VPNs in the Healthcare Industry

In the healthcare industry, the use of VPNs is essential for secure remote access to patient records and other sensitive data. Healthcare professionals often need to access patient information from outside the hospital or clinic, whether they are working remotely or on the go. VPNs provide a secure and encrypted connection, ensuring that patient data remains protected during transmission.

For example, a doctor working from home can connect to the hospital's network using a VPN. They can securely access electronic health records (EHRs) and collaborate with other healthcare professionals without compromising data confidentiality. The VPN encrypts the data transmitted between the doctor's device and the hospital's network, preventing unauthorized access and ensuring patient privacy.

Additional Resources and Further Reading

To learn more about VPNs and their role in secure remote access, the following resources are recommended:

- *Virtual Private Networks (VPNs) - National Institute of Standards and Technology (NIST)*: Available at: `https://nvlpubs.nist.gov/nistpubs/SpecialPublications/NIST.SP.800-77r1.pdf`

  This publication by NIST provides a comprehensive guide to VPN technologies, deployment best practices, and security considerations.

- *Virtual Private Networks (VPNs) - Cisco*: Available at: `https://www.cisco.com/c/en/us/products/security/vpn-endpoint-security-clients/index.html`

Cisco offers a range of VPN solutions for secure remote access. Their website provides valuable information on VPN technologies and their implementation.

- *VPN Comparison Chart - That One Privacy Guy*: Available at: `https://thatoneprivacysite.net/vpn-comparison-chart/`

  This comparison chart provides an overview of various VPN services, helping users choose the right VPN provider based on their specific needs and requirements.

Exercises

To reinforce your understanding of VPNs for secure remote access, consider the following exercises:

1. Research and compare different VPN protocols (e.g., OpenVPN, IPsec, WireGuard) and their strengths and weaknesses. Discuss which protocol you would recommend for secure remote access and justify your choice.

2. Investigate recent cybersecurity incidents where remote access to networks was compromised. Explore how implementing VPNs could have mitigated or prevented those incidents.

3. Set up a VPN connection on your personal device and configure it to connect to a simulated organization's network. Verify the secure connection by accessing network resources and confirming that the data is encrypted.

Remember, VPNs are just one piece of the cybersecurity puzzle. It is crucial to employ a holistic approach to cybersecurity, including other measures such as strong passwords, regular software updates, and employee training, to ensure comprehensive protection against cyber threats.

Encrypting Data at Rest and in Transit

In today's digitally connected world, data breaches and unauthorized access to personal information have become a major concern. Whether it is your financial data, medical records, or any other sensitive information, securing it is vital to maintaining your privacy and protecting your overall wellbeing. In this section, we will explore the importance of encrypting data at rest and in transit, and how it can enhance cybersecurity in the health and wellness industry.

Understanding Data Encryption

Data encryption is the process of converting readable data into an unreadable form, called ciphertext, to prevent unauthorized access. Encryption ensures that even if someone gains access to your data, they will not be able to understand its contents without the decryption key. There are two main types of encryption algorithms: symmetric encryption and asymmetric encryption.

Symmetric Encryption: Symmetric encryption uses a single key to both encrypt and decrypt the data. This means that the same key used to encrypt the data is also used to decrypt it. The key must be kept secret, as anyone with knowledge of the key can decrypt the data. Symmetric encryption is fast and efficient for encrypting large amounts of data, making it ideal for encrypting data at rest.

Asymmetric Encryption: Asymmetric encryption, also known as public-key encryption, involves the use of two different keys: a public key and a private key. The public key is used to encrypt the data, while the private key is used to decrypt it. The public key can be freely shared with others, allowing them to encrypt data that only you can decrypt with your private key. Asymmetric encryption is widely used for securing communication channels and encrypting data in transit.

Encrypting Data at Rest

Data at rest refers to data that is stored on physical or digital storage devices, such as hard drives, databases, or cloud servers. Encrypting data at rest ensures that even if the storage medium is compromised, the data remains protected and unreadable. Here are some key considerations for encrypting data at rest in the health and wellness industry:

1. **Full Disk Encryption (FDE):** FDE encrypts the entire storage medium, such as a hard drive or solid-state drive, at the sector level. It provides a high level of security as all data, including the operating system and applications, is encrypted. FDE is commonly used for encrypting laptops, desktop computers, and mobile devices used in the health and wellness industry.

2. **File and Folder Encryption:** File and folder encryption allows for selective encryption of specific files or folders. This method is useful when you want to encrypt only certain sensitive files or when sharing encrypted files with others. Encrypted files and folders can only be accessed with the appropriate encryption key or passphrase.

3. **Database Encryption:** Database encryption involves encrypting specific fields or entire databases to protect sensitive information, such as personal

health records or financial data. Database encryption can be implemented at different levels, such as column-level encryption, where only specific columns are encrypted, or full database encryption, where the entire database is encrypted.

4. **Cloud Storage Encryption:** When storing data in the cloud, it is important to ensure that the data is encrypted both at rest and in transit. Many cloud service providers offer built-in encryption options that encrypt the data before it is stored in their infrastructure. Additionally, you can choose to encrypt the data before uploading it to the cloud using client-side encryption.

It is worth noting that encryption alone is not enough to secure data at rest. Proper key management, secure storage of encryption keys, and access control mechanisms must also be implemented to ensure the integrity and confidentiality of the encrypted data.

Encrypting Data in Transit

Data in transit refers to data that is being transmitted over a network between devices or systems. Encrypting data in transit protects it from interception and unauthorized access while it is being transmitted. Here are some common encryption mechanisms used for securing data in transit:

1. **Transport Layer Security (TLS)/Secure Sockets Layer (SSL):** TLS and its predecessor SSL are cryptographic protocols that provide secure communication over a network. These protocols use a combination of symmetric and asymmetric encryption to encrypt data between a client (e.g., web browser) and a server (e.g., web server). TLS/SSL ensures that the data exchanged between the client and server is encrypted and remains confidential.

2. **Virtual Private Networks (VPNs):** VPNs create a secure and encrypted connection, often over the internet, between a client device and a private network. By encrypting the data transmitted between the client and the VPN server, VPNs ensure the confidentiality and integrity of the data. VPNs are commonly used by remote workers and can provide a secure connection for accessing sensitive information within the health and wellness industry.

3. **Secure File Transfer Protocols:** Secure file transfer protocols, such as Secure File Transfer Protocol (SFTP) and Secure Shell (SSH) File

Transfer Protocol (SCP), use encryption to protect files transferred over a network. These protocols ensure that files exchanged between systems are encrypted, preventing unauthorized access or tampering.

4. **Email Encryption:** Email encryption allows for the secure exchange of sensitive information via email. Encryption can be implemented using various methods, such as symmetric encryption, asymmetric encryption, or digital signatures. Email encryption ensures that the content of the email and any attachments are only accessible to authorized recipients.

Implementing strong encryption protocols and ensuring their proper configuration is essential for protecting data during transmission. It is important to regularly update encryption protocols to mitigate vulnerabilities and stay ahead of emerging threats.

Caveats and Challenges

While encrypting data at rest and in transit provides significant security benefits, there are some considerations and challenges to keep in mind:

- **Key Management:** Proper key management is crucial for the security of encrypted data. Keys must be kept confidential and secure to prevent unauthorized access to the encrypted information. Regularly rotating encryption keys and using strong key management practices are essential.

- **Performance Impact:** Encryption and decryption processes introduce additional computation overhead, which can impact system performance, especially for resource-constrained devices. Careful consideration should be given to balancing security requirements with the performance needs of the health and wellness industry.

- **Interoperability:** Ensuring interoperability between different systems and devices that use encryption is essential. Standardized encryption algorithms and protocols facilitate secure communication and data exchange across diverse platforms.

- **User Experience:** Encryption should not hinder user experience or impede workflow efficiency. It is crucial to strike a balance between security measures and practical usability to encourage adoption and compliance with encryption practices.

Real-World Example: Securing Electronic Health Records

One of the critical applications of encrypting data at rest and in transit is securing electronic health records (EHRs). Electronic health records contain sensitive patient information, including medical history, diagnoses, and treatment information. Encrypting EHRs ensures the confidentiality and integrity of this information, reducing the risk of unauthorized access or tampering.

For example, a healthcare provider can implement full disk encryption on their computer systems to protect EHRs stored on local hard drives. Additionally, using TLS encryption when transmitting EHRs between healthcare providers and integrating secure file transfer protocols for exchanging EHRs with external entities further enhances security.

By encrypting EHRs at rest and in transit, healthcare providers can meet data protection requirements mandated by privacy laws and regulations, such as the Health Insurance Portability and Accountability Act (HIPAA) in the United States. It also helps build trust among patients, knowing that their sensitive medical information is appropriately safeguarded.

Conclusion

Encrypting data at rest and in transit is a fundamental cybersecurity practice that helps protect personal information and enhance overall wellbeing. Whether it is securing data stored on physical or digital storage devices or protecting data during transmission, encryption plays a vital role in safeguarding sensitive information in the health and wellness industry. By implementing proper encryption mechanisms, addressing key management challenges, and ensuring interoperability and user experience, organizations can establish a strong foundation for data security and privacy.

Secure Web Browsing and Avoiding Malicious Websites

In today's digitally connected world, web browsing has become an integral part of our daily lives. Whether we are conducting research, shopping online, or accessing our personal accounts, it is crucial to prioritize security and protect ourselves from the various threats lurking on the internet. This section will explore the fundamentals of secure web browsing and provide practical tips on how to avoid malicious websites.

Understanding the Risks

When we browse the internet, we expose ourselves to several risks, including malware infections, phishing attacks, and data breaches. Malicious websites are designed to exploit vulnerabilities in our web browsers and operating systems, aiming to compromise our personal information or gain unauthorized access to our devices. Understanding these risks is the first step towards secure web browsing.

Keeping Your Browser Up to Date

Web browsers regularly release updates that address security vulnerabilities and enhance overall browsing experience. It is crucial to keep your browser up to date to protect yourself from known security threats. Enable automatic updates or regularly check for updates manually to ensure you are running the latest version of your browser.

Enabling Browser Security Features

Modern web browsers offer various security features to protect users from malicious websites. Take advantage of these features to enhance your browsing security. Enable browser warnings for known malicious sites and enable the "Safe Browsing" feature, which can detect and warn you about dangerous websites. You can typically find these settings in your browser's security or privacy settings.

Verifying Website Security

Before interacting with a website, it is essential to verify its security. Look for the padlock icon in the address bar, indicating that the website has a valid SSL/TLS certificate and is using HTTPS encryption. Avoid entering personal information or providing sensitive data on websites without this security indicator.

Avoiding Suspicious Links and Downloads

Exercise caution when clicking on links or downloading files from unknown sources. Malicious websites often use deceptive techniques to lure users into clicking on links that lead to malware-infected pages. Be particularly wary of unsolicited emails, pop-up ads, or social media posts that contain suspicious links. Instead of clicking directly, hover over the link to view the target URL, and if it appears suspicious, avoid clicking on it.

Using Ad and Script Blockers

Ad and script blockers are browser extensions that can provide an additional layer of protection by blocking potentially malicious ads and scripts. These tools can prevent drive-by downloads and block pop-ups, reducing the risk of encountering malicious content. Install a reputable ad and script blocker extension for your browser and keep it up to date.

Implementing Web Filtering

Web filtering solutions can help prevent access to malicious websites by blocking or warning users about potentially dangerous content. These solutions can be implemented at the network level, such as through a router or firewall, or at the individual device level using specialized software. Consider implementing a web filtering solution to protect yourself and your family from accessing malicious websites.

Educating Yourself and Practicing Vigilance

The most effective defense against malicious websites is to educate yourself about common threats and practice vigilance while browsing the internet. Stay informed about the latest phishing techniques, scams, and malware trends. Be cautious of unexpected prompts to download software or enter personal information. If a website looks suspicious or too good to be true, trust your instincts and navigate away from it.

Conducting Routine Security Audits

Performing routine security audits can help identify any potential vulnerabilities in your web browsing habits. Periodically review your browser extensions and remove any unnecessary or outdated ones. Check your browser's settings and ensure that privacy and security features are enabled and appropriately configured. By conducting regular audits, you can stay proactive in maintaining a secure browsing environment.

Summary

Secure web browsing is a critical aspect of maintaining personal cybersecurity. By understanding the risks, keeping your browser up to date, enabling security features, verifying website security, avoiding suspicious links and downloads, using ad and script blockers, implementing web filtering, educating yourself, practicing vigilance, and conducting routine security audits, you can significantly reduce your exposure to malicious websites. Remember, staying informed and proactive is key to a safe browsing experience.

Managing Software and Hardware Vulnerabilities

In order to maintain a secure cyber environment in the health and wellness industry, it is crucial to effectively manage software and hardware vulnerabilities. Vulnerabilities are weaknesses in software or hardware systems that can be exploited by attackers to gain unauthorized access or cause harm to the system. By proactively identifying and mitigating these vulnerabilities, organizations can significantly reduce the risk of cyber attacks and protect the personal information of individuals.

The Importance of Vulnerability Management

Vulnerability management is the process of identifying, evaluating, and addressing vulnerabilities in software and hardware systems. It is a critical component of cybersecurity as it allows organizations to stay ahead of potential threats and minimize the impact of cybersecurity incidents. By effectively managing vulnerabilities, organizations can:

- Enhance the overall security posture: By regularly identifying and patching vulnerabilities, organizations can strengthen their security infrastructure and minimize the risk of unauthorized access to sensitive data.

- Protect against known vulnerabilities: Many cyber attacks exploit well-known vulnerabilities in software and hardware. By actively managing vulnerabilities, organizations can ensure that their system is protected against these common attack vectors.

- Comply with industry regulations: Many industries, including the health and wellness sector, have specific regulations and compliance requirements related to vulnerability management. By implementing effective vulnerability management practices, organizations can ensure compliance with these regulations and avoid potential penalties.

- Reduce the likelihood of successful attacks: By promptly addressing vulnerabilities, organizations can minimize the window of opportunity for attackers, making it harder for them to exploit vulnerabilities and gain unauthorized access.

Identifying and Assessing Vulnerabilities

To effectively manage vulnerabilities, organizations should have a systematic approach to identify and assess vulnerabilities in software and hardware systems. The following steps can be followed:

1. **Asset Inventory:** Create an inventory of all software and hardware assets within the organization. This includes servers, endpoints, applications, and network devices. It is important to have a comprehensive understanding of the organization's IT infrastructure to effectively assess vulnerabilities.

2. **Vulnerability Scanning:** Conduct regular vulnerability scans using automated tools to identify potential vulnerabilities in software and hardware. Vulnerability scanning tools can detect common weaknesses, misconfigurations, and outdated software versions.

3. **Vulnerability Assessment:** After the initial scan, perform a detailed assessment of identified vulnerabilities. This involves evaluating the severity of each vulnerability, understanding the potential impact on the system, and prioritizing remediation efforts based on the risk level.

4. **Patch Management:** Develop a patch management process to apply necessary updates and patches to mitigate known vulnerabilities. It is crucial to stay informed about security patches provided by software and hardware vendors and promptly apply them to the affected systems.

5. **Risk Analysis:** Perform a risk analysis to determine the potential impact of unpatched vulnerabilities on the organization's operations. This involves considering the likelihood of exploitation, the potential consequences of an attack, and the value of the assets at risk.

Mitigating and Remediating Vulnerabilities

Once vulnerabilities have been identified and assessed, organizations should take appropriate actions to mitigate and remediate these vulnerabilities. The following strategies can be employed:

- **Apply Security Patches:** Install and apply security patches provided by software and hardware vendors to address known vulnerabilities. Regularly update systems and ensure that patches are applied promptly to minimize the exposure window.

- **Software and Firmware Updates:** Keep all software and firmware up to date to ensure that known vulnerabilities are patched. This includes operating systems, applications, and network devices. Regularly check for updates from vendors and apply them as soon as they become available.

- **Secure Configuration:** Configure software and hardware systems securely by following industry best practices and hardening guidelines. This includes disabling unnecessary services, changing default credentials, and implementing strong access controls.

- **Vulnerability Remediation Plan:** Develop a remediation plan that outlines the steps to be taken to address each vulnerability. Prioritize the most critical vulnerabilities and establish timelines for remediation based on the risk level and potential impact.

- **Continuous Monitoring:** Implement continuous monitoring of software and hardware systems to detect and respond to new vulnerabilities. This can include automated vulnerability scanning, intrusion detection systems, and real-time threat intelligence feeds.

- **Vendor Management:** Maintain a strong relationship with software and hardware vendors to stay informed about any new vulnerabilities or patches. Regularly review vendor security advisories and collaborate with vendors to address vulnerabilities in a timely manner.

Challenges and Considerations

Managing software and hardware vulnerabilities can be a complex task due to various challenges and considerations. It is important to be aware of these challenges and proactively address them:

- **Patch Management Complexity:** With a large number of software and hardware assets, managing and applying security patches can be challenging. Organizations need to establish a robust patch management process to ensure timely and accurate patch deployment.

- **Legacy Systems and End-of-Life Products:** Legacy systems and end-of-life products may no longer receive security patches and updates from vendors, making them more vulnerable to attacks. Organizations should develop a plan to migrate or replace these systems to maintain a secure environment.

- **Vulnerability Prioritization:** When faced with a large number of vulnerabilities, it can be challenging to prioritize remediation efforts. Organizations should consider the risk level, potential impact, and likelihood of exploitation when prioritizing vulnerabilities for remediation.

- **Third-Party Software and Vendor Dependencies:** Organizations often rely on third-party software and vendors for critical business operations. It is important to assess the security practices and vulnerability management processes of these third parties to ensure that they do not introduce additional risks.

- **Limited Resources:** Adequate resources, both in terms of personnel and technology, are essential for effective vulnerability management. Organizations should allocate sufficient resources to identify, assess, and remediate vulnerabilities in a timely manner.

Conclusion

Managing software and hardware vulnerabilities is an integral part of maintaining a secure cyber environment in the health and wellness industry. By following a systematic approach to identify, assess, and remediate vulnerabilities, organizations can significantly reduce the risk of cyber attacks and protect sensitive information. However, it is important to consider the challenges and limitations associated with vulnerability management and allocate resources accordingly. By prioritizing vulnerability management and staying proactive in addressing vulnerabilities, organizations can enhance their security posture and safeguard the wellbeing of individuals in a digitally connected world.

Resources and Further Reading

- CISA. (2021). *Vulnerability Management.* Retrieved from https://www.cisa.gov/vulnerability-management

- National Institute of Standards and Technology. (2018). *Guide to Vulnerability Management.* Retrieved from https://nvlpubs.nist.gov/nistpubs/CSWP/NIST.CSWP.04182018.pdf

- SANS Institute. (2021). *Critical Security Controls.* Retrieved from https://www.sans.org/critical-security-controls/

Data Privacy and Confidentiality

Understanding Data Privacy Regulations in the Health and Wellness Industry

Data privacy is a critical concern in the health and wellness industry, where the protection of sensitive personal information is of utmost importance. With the increasing digitization of healthcare, there has been a growing need for regulations to safeguard patient data from unauthorized access, use, or disclosure. In this section, we will explore the key data privacy regulations in the health and wellness industry and understand their implications for healthcare organizations and individuals.

Health Insurance Portability and Accountability Act (HIPAA)

One of the most significant data privacy regulations in the United States healthcare system is the Health Insurance Portability and Accountability Act (HIPAA) of 1996. HIPAA provides a comprehensive framework for protecting individuals' medical records and other personal health information (PHI). It applies to covered entities, including healthcare providers, health plans, and healthcare clearinghouses, as well as their business associates.

Under HIPAA, covered entities must ensure the confidentiality, integrity, and availability of PHI. They are required to implement physical, technical, and administrative safeguards to protect PHI and prevent unauthorized access or disclosure. This includes implementing access controls, conducting risk assessments, and maintaining audit logs of system activity.

HIPAA also grants individuals certain rights over their PHI, such as the right to access their own medical records and request corrections to any inaccuracies. Covered entities must comply with these individual rights and provide patients with notice of their HIPAA privacy practices.

Non-compliance with HIPAA can result in severe penalties, including substantial fines and criminal charges. Therefore, healthcare organizations must have robust policies and procedures in place to adhere to HIPAA requirements and ensure the privacy and security of patient data.

General Data Protection Regulation (GDPR)

While HIPAA is specific to the United States, the General Data Protection Regulation (GDPR) is a European Union (EU) regulation that has a global impact on data privacy. The GDPR, which came into effect in 2018, aims to protect the personal data of EU citizens and residents and harmonize data protection laws across the EU member states.

The GDPR applies to any organization, regardless of its location, that processes personal data of individuals who are in the EU. This means that healthcare organizations outside the EU may need to comply with the GDPR if they collect or process personal data of EU residents.

The GDPR introduces several key principles for data protection, including lawfulness, fairness, and transparency in data processing. It also grants individuals enhanced rights, such as the right to be informed, the right to access personal data, the right to rectify inaccuracies, and the right to erasure (or "right to be forgotten").

Healthcare organizations subject to the GDPR must implement appropriate technical and organizational measures to ensure the security of personal data and demonstrate compliance with the regulation. This includes conducting data protection impact assessments, appointing a data protection officer (DPO), and notifying supervisory authorities of data breaches within specified timeframes.

Failure to comply with the GDPR can result in significant penalties, with fines of up to 4

California Consumer Privacy Act (CCPA)

In an effort to strengthen data privacy rights for California residents, the California Consumer Privacy Act (CCPA) was enacted in 2018 and went into effect on January 1, 2020. The CCPA provides consumers with greater control over their personal information and imposes obligations on businesses that collect or sell consumers' personal data.

Under the CCPA, consumers have the right to know what personal information is being collected about them, the right to opt-out of the sale of their personal information, and the right to request deletion of their personal information. Businesses covered by the CCPA are required to disclose their data collection and sharing practices, provide mechanisms for consumers to exercise their rights, and implement reasonable security measures.

The CCPA applies to businesses that meet certain criteria, including those with annual gross revenues exceeding $25 million, those that buy, sell, or share personal information of at least 50,000 California consumers, and those that derive 50

Non-compliance with the CCPA can result in significant penalties, including fines of up to $7,500 per violation. Therefore, healthcare organizations that collect personal information from California residents must ensure that they comply with the CCPA and respect consumers' privacy rights.

Implications and Challenges

Understanding and complying with data privacy regulations in the health and wellness industry is crucial for healthcare organizations to protect patient privacy and maintain trust. However, achieving compliance can be challenging due to the evolving nature of technology and the increasing sophistication of cyber threats.

Healthcare organizations need to implement suitable technical and organizational measures to protect personal data, including robust security systems, data encryption, and access controls. Regular staff training and awareness programs are essential to foster a culture of privacy and security.

Compliance with data privacy regulations also requires continuous monitoring of the changing legal landscape and staying up to date with evolving industry standards. Healthcare organizations should periodically assess their privacy practices, conduct audits, and address any identified vulnerabilities or non-compliance issues.

Moreover, healthcare organizations must adopt a risk-based approach to data privacy, considering the potential impact of data breaches and the sensitivity of the information involved. This involves conducting thorough risk assessments, prioritizing security investments, and developing incident response plans to mitigate the consequences of a data breach.

In summary, understanding data privacy regulations, such as HIPAA, GDPR, and the CCPA, is essential for healthcare organizations to protect patient information and stay compliant. Compliance requires a comprehensive approach involving technical, organizational, and legal measures, as well as a commitment to ongoing training and awareness. By prioritizing data privacy, healthcare organizations can enhance trust, reduce the risk of data breaches, and safeguard the wellbeing of individuals in the digital age.

Key Takeaways

- Data privacy regulations, such as HIPAA, GDPR, and the CCPA, play a crucial role in protecting personal information in the health and wellness industry.

- HIPAA sets the standard for protecting PHI in the United States healthcare system and applies to covered entities and their business associates.
- The GDPR harmonizes data protection laws across the EU and applies to organizations worldwide that collect or process personal data of EU residents.
- The CCPA grants California residents enhanced rights over their personal information and imposes obligations on businesses that collect or sell personal data.
- Healthcare organizations must implement technical and organizational measures to comply with data privacy regulations, conduct regular risk assessments, and prioritize data security investments.

Exercises

1. Research and analyze a recent data breach incident in the health and wellness industry. Identify the potential violations of data privacy regulations and discuss the implications for the affected individuals and the organization involved.
2. Conduct a risk assessment exercise for a fictional healthcare organization to identify potential vulnerabilities and recommend appropriate security measures to ensure compliance with data privacy regulations.

Additional Resources

1. United States Department of Health and Human Services - HIPAA: `https://www.hhs.gov/hipaa/index.html`
2. European Commission - General Data Protection Regulation (GDPR): `https://ec.europa.eu/info/law/law-topic/data-protection_en`
3. State of California Department of Justice - California Consumer Privacy Act (CCPA): `https://oag.ca.gov/privacy/ccpa`

Conclusion

Data privacy regulations are essential for protecting personal information in the health and wellness industry. Healthcare organizations must understand and comply with regulations such as HIPAA, GDPR, and the CCPA to safeguard patient privacy, maintain trust, and mitigate the risks of data breaches. By implementing robust technical and organizational measures, conducting regular risk assessments, and prioritizing data security, healthcare organizations can navigate the challenges of data privacy in the digital age.

Protecting Personal Identifiable Information (PII)

In today's digitally connected world, the protection of personal identifiable information (PII) is of utmost importance. PII refers to any information that can be used to identify an individual, such as their name, address, Social Security number, or medical records. This section will discuss the significance of protecting PII in the health and wellness industry and provide guidelines on how to safeguard this sensitive information.

The Significance of Protecting PII in Health and Wellness

The health and wellness industry handles vast amounts of PII, including medical records, insurance information, and personal health data. This information, if compromised, can lead to severe consequences for individuals, ranging from identity theft to medical fraud. It is crucial to recognize the potential risks associated with PII breaches and take appropriate measures to protect this sensitive data.

Regulatory Framework for PII Protection

Various laws and regulations govern the protection of PII in the health and wellness industry. The most notable ones include the Health Insurance Portability and Accountability Act (HIPAA) in the United States and the General Data Protection Regulation (GDPR) in the European Union. These regulations define the standards for data privacy and security and impose legal obligations on organizations to safeguard PII.

Compliance with these regulations requires implementing appropriate technical and organizational security measures to protect PII. Failure to adhere to these requirements can result in severe penalties and reputational damage for organizations.

Best Practices for Protecting PII

To effectively protect PII, organizations need to implement a robust set of security practices. The following best practices can help mitigate the risks associated with

PII breaches:

1. **Data Classification:** Classify PII based on its sensitivity and importance. This classification will aid in implementing appropriate security controls and allocating resources accordingly.

2. **Access Control and Authentication:** Implement strict access controls to ensure that only authorized individuals can access PII. This includes utilizing strong passwords, multi-factor authentication, and role-based access control mechanisms.

3. **Encryption:** Encrypt PII both at rest and in transit. Encryption transforms the data into an unreadable format, making it useless to unauthorized individuals even if they gain access to it.

4. **Secure Data Storage:** Store PII in secure and monitored environments. This includes using encrypted databases, secure cloud storage, and regularly patching and updating the storage systems.

5. **Data Minimization and Retention:** Minimize the collection and retention of PII to the necessary minimum. Ensuring appropriate data retention policies will limit the exposure of PII and reduce the risk of unauthorized access.

6. **Employee Training and Awareness:** Provide comprehensive training programs for employees on the importance of protecting PII and the best practices to follow. Regular awareness campaigns can help instill a culture of security within the organization.

7. **Vendor Management:** Evaluate the security practices of third-party vendors who have access to PII. Ensure that proper security measures are in place when sharing PII with external partners.

8. **Incident Response and Notification:** Develop an incident response plan to promptly respond to any PII breaches. Establish a procedure for notifying affected individuals and regulatory authorities in accordance with the applicable laws and regulations.

Case Study: Healthcare Data Breach

To understand the real-world implications of PII breaches, let's consider a case study of a healthcare data breach:

A large healthcare organization suffered a cyber-attack, resulting in the exposure of PII of thousands of patients. The compromised data included names, addresses, social security numbers, and medical records. The consequences of this breach were significant, including financial losses due to identity theft, reputational damage to the organization, and increased risk of medical fraud for affected individuals.

This case highlights the importance of implementing robust security measures to protect PII and the severe impact that breaches can have on both individuals and organizations.

Resources for Protecting PII

Staying up to date with the evolving landscape of PII protection is crucial. Here are some resources to support your efforts in protecting PII:

- **National Institute of Standards and Technology** (NIST) provides comprehensive guidelines and frameworks for protecting sensitive information.

- **International Association of Privacy Professionals** (IAPP) offers training and resources related to privacy and data protection.

- **Healthcare Information and Management Systems Society** (HIMSS) provides industry insights and best practices for securing PII in the healthcare sector.

- **Data Protection Authorities** (DPAs) in each jurisdiction provide guidance and enforcement of data protection laws. Familiarize yourself with the DPA relevant to your location.

Conclusion

Protecting PII is of utmost importance in the health and wellness industry. Strict adherence to regulations, implementation of best practices, and continuous employee training are essential in safeguarding this sensitive information. By taking proactive measures and staying informed about emerging threats and technologies, organizations can effectively protect PII and maintain the trust of their customers and patients.

Remember, the responsibility to protect PII extends beyond organizational boundaries. Individuals should also be vigilant and practice safe online habits to minimize the risk of their personal information falling into the wrong hands.

Together, we can create a safer and more secure digital landscape for health and wellness.

Secure Data Storage and Retention Policies

Data storage and retention policies play a crucial role in ensuring the security and privacy of sensitive information in the health and wellness industry. These policies define how data should be stored, accessed, and retained to minimize the risk of unauthorized access, data breaches, and compliance violations. In this section, we will explore the key principles and best practices for secure data storage and retention in the context of cybersecurity in health and wellness.

Understanding Data Storage Requirements

Before implementing secure data storage and retention policies, it is essential to have a clear understanding of the data storage requirements. Different types of data have varying levels of sensitivity and legal obligations for retention. Here are some key considerations:

- **Data Classification:** Classify your data based on its sensitivity, such as personally identifiable information (PII), protected health information (PHI), or financial data. This classification helps determine the level of security controls and retention periods required for each type of data.

- **Legal and Regulatory Requirements:** Identify the applicable legal and regulatory requirements for data storage and retention in the health and wellness industry. This includes laws such as the Health Insurance Portability and Accountability Act (HIPAA) and the General Data Protection Regulation (GDPR). Ensure that your data storage and retention policies are in compliance with these regulations.

- **Business Purposes:** Consider the business purposes for data storage and retention. Determine how long you need to retain data to meet operational, research, or legal requirements. It is important to balance data retention with privacy and security considerations.

Secure Data Storage Practices

Implementing secure data storage practices helps protect data from unauthorized access, modification, or loss. Here are some important practices to consider:

- **Encryption:** Apply encryption to sensitive data both at rest and in transit. Encryption ensures that even if attackers gain unauthorized access to the data, they cannot decipher it without the encryption keys. Use strong encryption algorithms and keep the encryption keys secure.

- **Access Controls:** Implement strict access controls to limit data access only to authorized individuals. This includes user authentication mechanisms, role-based access control, and strong password policies. Restrict access to sensitive data on a need-to-know basis.

- **Data Segmentation:** Separate data into logical or physical segments based on sensitivity. This helps minimize the impact of a data breach as attackers would have limited access within a segmented environment. For example, store highly sensitive health records separately from less sensitive administrative data.

- **Data Backup and Recovery:** Regularly backup your data and store backups in secure off-site locations. Implement reliable backup and recovery mechanisms to ensure data availability in case of accidents, hardware failures, or ransomware attacks. Test restoration procedures periodically to validate the effectiveness of backup systems.

- **Physical Security:** Ensure that physical storage facilities, such as data centers or server rooms, have appropriate security measures in place. Control physical access, monitor environmental conditions, and implement fire suppression systems to protect systems that store sensitive data.

Retention and Destruction Policies

Developing well-defined retention and destruction policies is crucial to manage the lifecycle of data and comply with legal requirements. Here are some considerations for creating effective retention and destruction policies:

- **Retention Period:** Determine the appropriate retention period for different types of data based on legal requirements, business purposes, and industry best practices. Retain data only for as long as necessary and securely dispose of it after the retention period expires.

- **Secure Disposal:** Establish guidelines for the secure disposal of data, including physical documents, electronic records, and backup media. Use secure deletion methods (e.g., overwriting, degaussing, or physical destruction) to prevent data recovery. Document the disposal process to demonstrate compliance.

- **Records Management:** Implement a systematic records management policy to organize and track data throughout its lifecycle. Maintain an inventory of stored data, including its classification, retention period, and archival processes. Regularly review and update records to remove obsolete or expired data.

- **Data Archiving:** Consider the need for data archiving to preserve information that is no longer actively used but may be required for legal, historical, or research purposes. Implement secure and reliable archiving mechanisms to protect archived data from unauthorized access or degradation over time.

Challenges and Considerations

Implementing secure data storage and retention policies may face certain challenges. Consider the following factors:

- **Data Volume and Scalability:** As the volume of data increases, it becomes challenging to store and manage data securely. Consider scalable storage solutions and efficient data management techniques to ensure secure storage and retrieval of large datasets.

- **Third-Party Service Providers:** If you rely on third-party service providers for data storage, ensure that they have appropriate security measures in place. Establish clear contractual obligations and conduct due diligence to verify their compliance with security standards and data protection regulations.

- **Data Loss Prevention:** Implement data loss prevention (DLP) measures to monitor and prevent unauthorized data transmission or exfiltration. Use data loss prevention tools and technologies to detect sensitive information leaving the organization without proper authorization.

Example Scenario

Consider a healthcare organization that stores electronic health records (EHRs). To ensure secure data storage and retention, the organization implements the following measures:

- All EHRs are encrypted both at rest and in transit using strong encryption algorithms. This ensures that even if an attacker gains unauthorized access to the data, it remains unreadable.
- Access to EHRs is restricted to authorized healthcare professionals and staff members with a legitimate need-to-know. Role-based access controls are implemented to enforce data segregation and minimize the risk of unauthorized access.
- The organization conducts regular backups of EHRs and stores them in an off-site location. Backup integrity is verified periodically through restoration testing.
- A systematic records management policy is in place to track the lifecycle of EHRs. Data that is no longer required is securely disposed of using appropriate methods, following legal and regulatory requirements.

By implementing these measures, the healthcare organization ensures the confidentiality, integrity, and availability of the stored EHRs, thereby safeguarding patient privacy and complying with relevant regulations.

Additional Resources

To further explore secure data storage and retention policies, consider the following resources:

- "Data Protection and Privacy: Global Frameworks and Principles" by Peter Yu.
- "HIPAA Privacy and Security: A Healthcare Provider's Guide" by Kevin Beaver.
- "Data Lifecycles: Managing Data for Strategic Advantage" by Roger Reid and Richard Swainson.
- National Institute of Standards and Technology (NIST) Special Publication 800-88: "Guidelines for Media Sanitization."
- Health and Human Services (HHS) Office for Civil Rights (OCR) website for guidance on HIPAA compliance.

Conclusion

Secure data storage and retention policies are vital for safeguarding sensitive information in the health and wellness industry. By understanding data storage requirements, implementing secure storage practices, defining retention and destruction policies, and addressing associated challenges, organizations can ensure the protection of personal data, maintain regulatory compliance, and enhance overall cybersecurity in the digital age.

Data Encryption and Decryption Techniques

In the digital age, where data is constantly being transmitted and stored, it is crucial to protect sensitive information from unauthorized access. One of the most effective ways to achieve this is through data encryption. Data encryption is the process of converting plaintext data into ciphertext, which can only be decoded or decrypted with the correct key. In this section, we will explore different data encryption and decryption techniques commonly used in cybersecurity.

Symmetric Encryption

Symmetric encryption, also known as secret-key encryption, is a type of encryption where the same key is used for both the encryption and decryption processes. This key must be kept secret and securely shared between the sender and the recipient. The most widely used symmetric encryption algorithm is the Advanced Encryption Standard (AES).

AES uses a block cipher, which processes fixed-size blocks of data at a time. The algorithm accepts a key of different lengths and operates on blocks of 128 bits. The data blocks are then transformed through a series of substitution, permutation, and mixing operations. The number of rounds, or iterations, performed depends on the key length (128, 192, or 256 bits).

To illustrate the process, let's consider a scenario where Alice wants to send a confidential message to Bob using symmetric encryption. They both agree on a secret key, and Alice uses this key to encrypt her message. She then sends the encrypted message to Bob, who uses the same key to decrypt and read the original message.

Symmetric encryption is efficient and fast, making it suitable for encrypting large amounts of data. However, the main challenge lies in securely sharing the secret key between the sender and the recipient. If the key is compromised, the confidentiality of the encrypted data is compromised as well.

Asymmetric Encryption

Asymmetric encryption, also known as public-key encryption, overcomes the key sharing challenge of symmetric encryption by using a pair of interconnected keys: a public key and a private key. The public key is used for encryption, while the private key is used for decryption. The two keys are mathematically related, but it is computationally infeasible to derive the private key from the public key.

One of the most widely used asymmetric encryption algorithms is the Rivest-Shamir-Adleman (RSA) algorithm. In RSA, the public and private keys are generated using large prime numbers. The encryption process involves raising the plaintext message to the power of the recipient's public key modulo the product of two large prime numbers. Decryption, on the other hand, involves raising the ciphertext to the power of the recipient's private key modulo the same product of prime numbers.

To illustrate the process, let's consider another scenario where Alice wants to send a confidential message to Bob using asymmetric encryption. Bob generates a key pair (public and private key) and shares his public key with Alice. Alice then uses Bob's public key to encrypt her message and sends it to Bob. Bob can then use his private key to decrypt and read the original message.

Asymmetric encryption provides a secure way to encrypt data without the need to share a secret key. However, it is computationally more expensive than symmetric encryption, making it less suitable for encrypting large amounts of data.

Hybrid Encryption

To harness the benefits of both symmetric and asymmetric encryption, a hybrid encryption approach is often used. In this approach, symmetric encryption is used to encrypt the actual data, while asymmetric encryption is used to securely exchange the symmetric key.

The process begins with the sender and the receiver each having their own key pair. The sender generates a random symmetric key and encrypts the data using this key. The recipient's public key is then used to encrypt the symmetric key, creating a wrapper around the encrypted data. The encrypted symmetric key and the wrapped data are then sent to the recipient. Upon receiving the encrypted data, the recipient uses their private key to decrypt the symmetric key. This symmetric key is then used to decrypt the actual data.

By combining both symmetric and asymmetric encryption, hybrid encryption offers the advantages of strong security provided by asymmetric encryption and the efficiency and speed of symmetric encryption. This approach is commonly used in secure communication protocols like Transport Layer Security (TLS) used for securing internet connections.

Quantum Encryption

As quantum computing continues to advance, traditional encryption methods face the risk of being broken by powerful quantum algorithms. To address this threat, quantum encryption techniques are being developed.

Quantum encryption leverages the principles of quantum mechanics to ensure the secure exchange of encryption keys. One such technique is Quantum Key Distribution (QKD), which utilizes the fundamental properties of quantum mechanics to generate and distribute the encryption key.

QKD relies on the principles of quantum superposition and quantum entanglement. It involves the transmission of quantum states, such as the polarization of photons, through a quantum channel. Any attempt to observe or intercept these quantum states would disrupt their integrity, alerting both the sender and the receiver and rendering the key exchange insecure.

Quantum encryption provides a theoretically secure method for key exchange, as any attempt to eavesdrop on the quantum channel would result in errors detectable by the sender and the receiver. However, implementation challenges and the need for specialized hardware currently limit the widespread adoption of quantum encryption.

Summary

In this section, we have explored different data encryption and decryption techniques. We started with symmetric encryption, which uses the same secret key for both encryption and decryption. We then moved on to asymmetric encryption, which utilizes a pair of interconnected keys: a public key for encryption and a private key for decryption. Hybrid encryption combines the benefits of both symmetric and asymmetric encryption, providing a secure and efficient approach for encrypting data. Lastly, we touched upon quantum encryption, which exploits the principles of quantum mechanics to ensure secure communication.

It is important to note that encryption is just one aspect of data protection. Proper key management, secure key exchange protocols, and implementing encryption within a comprehensive cybersecurity framework are critical for ensuring the confidentiality and integrity of sensitive information.

By understanding data encryption and decryption techniques, individuals and organizations can take proactive measures to safeguard their data, protect privacy, and mitigate the risks associated with cyber threats.

Managing Data Access and Authorization Controls

Data access and authorization controls play a crucial role in ensuring the confidentiality, integrity, and availability of sensitive information in the health and wellness industry. Unauthorized access to patient data can lead to severe privacy breaches and compromise the overall security of healthcare systems. In this section, we will explore various techniques and best practices for managing data access and implementing effective authorization controls.

Principles of Data Access Control

Data access control aims to restrict access to sensitive information to authorized individuals or entities. To achieve this, it is essential to establish a robust access control framework based on the following principles:

1. **Least Privilege Principle:** Users should only be granted the minimum level of privileges necessary to perform their tasks. This principle ensures that users have access only to the data that is essential for their job functions, minimizing the risk of accidental or intentional misuse.

2. **Role-Based Access Control (RBAC):** RBAC is a widely adopted access control model that assigns permissions to users based on their roles and responsibilities within the organization. By categorizing users into roles and assigning access rights accordingly, RBAC simplifies access management and reduces the administrative burden.

3. **Segregation of Duties (SoD):** SoD ensures that no single user has complete control over critical processes or systems. By separating conflicting duties, such as the ability to both create and approve transactions, organizations can prevent fraud, error, and misuse of data.

4. **Need-to-Know Principle:** Users should only be granted access to data that is necessary for their specific job functions. This principle restricts the propagation of sensitive information and reduces the risk of unauthorized data exposure.

Access Control Mechanisms

Implementing effective access control mechanisms is essential to govern data access and prevent unauthorized individuals from viewing, modifying, or deleting sensitive information. Some commonly used access control mechanisms include:

1. **User Authentication:** User authentication is the process of verifying the identity of a user before granting access to the system. It typically involves validating the user's credentials, such as usernames and passwords, using strong authentication methods like two-factor authentication (2FA) or biometric authentication.

2. **Access Control Lists (ACLs):** ACLs are lists that define the access rights of individual users or groups for specific resources. By maintaining a centralized ACL, organizations can enforce fine-grained access control at the resource level, determining who can read, write, or execute specific files, databases, or applications.

3. **Attribute-Based Access Control (ABAC):** ABAC is an access control model that incorporates various attributes, such as user roles, job titles, and environmental conditions, into the decision-making process. ABAC allows for more dynamic and context-aware access control policies based on multiple factors.

4. **Multi-Level Security (MLS):** MLS is a security model that enforces access controls based on data classification levels and user clearances. It ensures that users with appropriate clearances can access classified information while preventing unauthorized disclosure or modification.

5. **Audit Trails:** Audit trails record all access attempts and activities related to sensitive data. By maintaining an audit trail, organizations can review and monitor user actions, detect unauthorized access attempts, and facilitate forensic investigations in case of security incidents.

Best Practices for Authorization Controls

Implementing effective authorization controls is vital to ensure that users only perform authorized actions on data. Here are some best practices to consider when designing and implementing authorization controls:

1. **Regular Access Reviews:** Conduct regular access reviews to ensure that users still require the privileges and access rights they were initially granted.

This practice helps identify and mitigate any unauthorized access or potential security risks resulting from changes in personnel or job functions.

2. **Secure Role Management:** Implement a robust role management process to ensure that roles and permissions are assigned accurately and promptly. Regularly review and update role definitions based on changes in job responsibilities, organizational structure, or regulatory requirements.

3. **Strong Password Policies:** Enforce strong password policies, including password complexity requirements, regular password expiration, and restrictions on password reuse. Consider implementing password management solutions to minimize the risk of password-related security breaches.

4. **Privilege Separation:** Avoid granting unnecessary admin privileges to users. Employ the principle of least privilege and separate administrative accounts from standard user accounts. Limit administrative access to only those individuals who genuinely require it.

5. **Regular Backup and Recovery:** Implement a robust backup and recovery strategy to safeguard data in case of accidental or malicious data loss. Regularly test the recovery process to ensure that critical data can be restored promptly and accurately.

6. **Monitor and Respond to Anomalies:** Implement real-time monitoring and log analysis mechanisms to detect unusual user activity patterns or access attempts. Automated alert systems can help identify and respond to potential security incidents promptly.

Case Study: Implementing Role-Based Access Control (RBAC)

To illustrate the implementation of RBAC in a healthcare setting, let's consider the example of a hospital. The hospital can define roles such as physician, nurse, administrator, and patient. Each role will be associated with specific permissions, dictating what data and functionalities each role can access.

1. Physicians would have access to patients' medical records, be able to order diagnostic tests, and prescribe medications.

2. Nurses would have access to patient vital signs, be able to administer medications, and update patient records.

3. Administrators would have privileges to manage user accounts, configure access control policies, and generate reports.

4. Patients would have limited access to their own medical records, appointment scheduling, and messaging functionality for secure communication with their healthcare providers.

By assigning users to the appropriate roles, the hospital can ensure that each user has the necessary access rights to perform their job functions without compromising data security. Regular access reviews can be conducted to ensure that the roles and permissions assigned to users are still appropriate and necessary.

Conclusion

Managing data access and authorization controls is essential to protect sensitive information in the health and wellness industry. By implementing robust access control mechanisms and following best practices, organizations can minimize the risk of unauthorized access, maintain data confidentiality, and ensure the integrity of healthcare systems. Regular reviews and updates to access permissions, along with effective role management, play a crucial role in maintaining a secure environment for managing data access.

Cloud Computing Security Considerations

Cloud computing has revolutionized the way organizations store, process, and access data. It offers numerous benefits such as scalability, cost-efficiency, and flexibility. However, it also introduces new security challenges that need to be carefully considered. In this section, we will explore the important security considerations for cloud computing in the health and wellness industry.

Data Protection and Privacy

One of the primary concerns when using cloud computing is the protection of sensitive data. Health and wellness organizations deal with highly confidential information, such as medical records and personal health data. Therefore, it is crucial to implement robust security measures to ensure the privacy and integrity of this data.

Encryption: Encryption is a fundamental security measure that ensures data remains secure throughout its lifecycle. When using cloud services, it is essential to encrypt data both at rest and in transit. At-rest encryption involves encrypting data when it is stored in the cloud provider's infrastructure. In contrast, in-transit encryption protects data as it is being transferred between the cloud provider and the organization. Implementing strong encryption algorithms and key management practices is essential to maintain data confidentiality.

Data Segmentation: Cloud environments typically host multiple organizations' data simultaneously. To minimize the risk of unauthorized access, it is crucial to segregate data logically. By segmenting data, organizations can limit access to specific storage buckets, databases, or virtual machines. This ensures that even if one part of the cloud environment is compromised, the attacker cannot easily access sensitive data from other parts.

Access Control: Controlling who can access your data is vital to maintaining security. Cloud service providers offer access control mechanisms that allow organizations to define fine-grained access policies. It is crucial to establish strong authentication mechanisms, such as multi-factor authentication, to ensure that only authorized individuals can access sensitive data.

Vendor Evaluation: When selecting a cloud service provider, thorough evaluation is crucial. The provider should have a robust security infrastructure, including measures like physical security, network monitoring, and incident response capabilities. Additionally, organizations should review the cloud provider's compliance with industry standards and regulations, such as HIPAA in the healthcare industry, to ensure that data protection requirements are met.

Cloud Security Architecture

The security architecture of the cloud environment plays a crucial role in safeguarding data and systems. Organizations must understand and implement proper security controls to mitigate risks effectively.

Network Security: Cloud environments rely heavily on network connectivity. Organizations should establish secure network connections between their on-premises infrastructure and the cloud provider. This can be achieved through technologies such as virtual private networks (VPNs) or dedicated private connections. Implementing firewalls, intrusion detection systems, and regular vulnerability assessments are essential to protect against external attacks.

Identity and Access Management (IAM): IAM plays a critical role in securing cloud environments. It involves managing user identities, their privileges, and their access to cloud resources. Implementing IAM solutions allows organizations to enforce strong access controls, limit privilege escalation, and provide audit trails. Furthermore, IAM can enable organizations to easily revoke access rights when an employee's role changes or they leave the organization, reducing the risk of unauthorized access.

Logging and Monitoring: It is imperative to have a robust logging and monitoring system in place to detect and respond to security incidents promptly. Cloud service providers offer various logging and monitoring services that can be used to track changes, monitor resource usage, and identify potential security threats. By analyzing logs and monitoring system events, organizations can detect anomalous activities, such as unauthorized access attempts or data breaches, and take appropriate actions.

Incident Response: Despite the best preventive measures, security incidents may still occur. It is essential to have an incident response plan in place to minimize the impact of a security breach. The plan should outline the steps to be taken when an incident occurs, including roles and responsibilities, communication protocols, and recovery procedures. Regularly testing the incident response plan ensures that it remains effective and up to date.

Compliance and Legal Considerations

Compliance with industry regulations and legal requirements is crucial for health and wellness organizations. When using cloud computing services, organizations need to ensure that their cloud environment meets these compliance obligations.

Compliance Frameworks: Organizations should be familiar with industry-specific compliance frameworks and regulations, such as HIPAA, GDPR, or PCI DSS. These frameworks outline security controls and best practices that need to be implemented to protect sensitive data. By understanding the compliance obligations, organizations can choose a cloud service provider that aligns with these requirements.

Data Residency: Depending on the jurisdiction, specific regulations may require data to be stored within certain geographical boundaries. Health and wellness organizations need to ensure that their cloud service provider can meet these data residency requirements and maintain compliance.

Data Ownership and Liability: When storing data in the cloud, organizations need to clarify data ownership and liability responsibilities with the cloud service provider. A well-defined contract should outline data ownership, including the rights and responsibilities of both parties. Additionally, organizations should consider the provider's liability in case of a security breach or data loss.

Data Backup and Recovery: Adequate backup and recovery mechanisms are essential in cloud environments. Organizations should have a data backup strategy that ensures their data is regularly backed up and can be restored in the event of a disaster or data loss incident. The cloud service provider should also provide transparent information about their backup and recovery processes.

Training and Employee Awareness

Even with robust security measures and controls in place, human error remains a significant risk. Therefore, it is crucial to provide training and raise employee awareness about cloud security.

Security Training: Organizations should conduct regular security training sessions to educate employees about the importance of cloud security and mitigate the risks associated with it. This training should cover topics such as data protection, phishing awareness, password hygiene, and incident response.

Secure Cloud Usage Guidelines: Establishing clear guidelines for employees regarding the use of cloud services is essential. This ensures that employees understand their roles, responsibilities, and limitations when working with the cloud. Guidelines should cover topics such as data sharing, acceptable cloud providers, and secure configuration settings.

Reporting Security Incidents: Employees should be made aware of the procedures for reporting security incidents or suspicious activities. Prompt reporting allows organizations to respond to incidents quickly and minimize potential damage.

Continuous Monitoring: Organizations should establish procedures for continuous monitoring of cloud environments. This includes monitoring access logs, network traffic, and system activities. Regularly reviewing and analyzing this data can help detect potential security incidents and take appropriate actions.

In summary, cloud computing brings numerous benefits to the health and wellness industry, but it also introduces security considerations that need to be addressed. By implementing strong data protection measures, designing a robust cloud security architecture, ensuring compliance with regulations, and providing regular training and awareness, organizations can effectively mitigate the risks associated with cloud computing and maintain the security and privacy of sensitive data.

Data Breach Response and Incident Management

In today's digital world, data breaches and security incidents have become an unfortunate reality for organizations across various industries, including the health and wellness sector. A data breach occurs when unauthorized individuals gain access to sensitive information, such as personal identifiable information (PII), protected health information (PHI), and financial data. These breaches can have severe consequences, including financial losses, reputational damage, legal liabilities, and compromised patient and consumer trust.

Proactively planning and implementing effective incident response and management strategies is crucial for mitigating the impact of data breaches and security incidents. Incident management refers to the processes and procedures followed when an incident occurs, whereas incident response focuses on the actions taken to address and resolve the incident. In this section, we will explore the key components of data breach response and incident management in the health and wellness industry.

Understanding the Incident Response Lifecycle

The incident response lifecycle provides a systematic approach for managing security incidents effectively. The following are the typical phases in the incident response lifecycle:

1. **Preparation:** Before an incident occurs, organizations should establish an incident response team, define roles and responsibilities, develop an incident response plan, and conduct training and exercises to enhance preparedness. This phase includes activities such as creating an incident response policy, identifying critical assets, and implementing detection mechanisms.

2. **Detection and Analysis:** This phase involves identifying indicators of compromise (IOCs) and analyzing security events to determine if they represent a potential incident. Organizations should have monitoring tools and procedures in place to detect and escalate potential breaches. It is crucial to establish a baseline for normal network and system behavior to enable rapid detection of anomalous activities.

3. **Containment, Eradication, and Recovery:** Once an incident has been confirmed, the focus shifts to containing the incident, eradicating the attackers, and recovering affected systems. This may involve isolating compromised systems, removing malware, patching vulnerabilities, restoring data from backups, or rebuilding systems.

4. **Investigation:** The investigation phase aims to determine the root cause of the incident, identify the scope of the breach, and collect evidence for legal and regulatory purposes. It may involve forensic analysis, log analysis, network traffic analysis, and coordination with relevant law enforcement or external parties.

5. **Remediation and Lessons Learned:** After resolving the incident, organizations should take steps to prevent similar incidents from occurring in the future. This includes implementing security enhancements, updating policies and

procedures, conducting security awareness training, and sharing lessons learned with the incident response team and other stakeholders.

Data Breach Response Strategies

Data breaches require a swift and coordinated response to minimize the impact on individuals and the organization. Here are some key strategies for effectively responding to data breaches in the health and wellness industry:

1. **Activate the Incident Response Team:** As soon as a data breach or security incident is detected, the incident response team should be activated. This team typically includes representatives from IT, cybersecurity, legal, public relations, human resources, and executive management. Their primary role is to coordinate the incident response efforts and ensure that all necessary actions are taken.

2. **Contain the Breach:** It is essential to contain the breach to prevent further unauthorized access and data exfiltration. This may involve isolating affected systems from the network, disabling compromised accounts, or temporarily shutting down affected services. Quick containment measures can help minimize the impact and limit the potential spread of the breach.

3. **Assess the Scope and Impact:** Once the breach is contained, a thorough assessment of the scope and impact of the incident should be conducted. This includes determining the types of data compromised, the number of individuals affected, and the potential consequences of the breach. The assessment helps in making informed decisions about the next steps in the response process.

4. **Notify Affected Individuals:** Organizations are often required by law to notify affected individuals in the event of a data breach. Prompt and transparent communication with affected individuals is crucial to maintaining trust and allowing individuals to take appropriate actions to protect themselves. The notification should include information about the breach, the steps taken to address the situation, and any available resources or support.

5. **Cooperate with Authorities:** Depending on the nature and scope of the breach, organizations may need to involve law enforcement agencies, regulatory bodies, or other relevant authorities. It is important to cooperate fully with these entities and provide any requested information or assistance to aid in the investigation and prosecution of the attackers.

6. **Provide Support and Resources:** Data breaches can be distressing for affected individuals, and organizations should provide support and resources to help them navigate the aftermath. This may include credit monitoring services, identity theft protection, guidance on securing personal information, and assistance with any legal or financial implications.

7. **Learn from the Incident:** Following a data breach, it is crucial to conduct a thorough post-incident analysis to identify areas for improvement. This includes analyzing the root causes of the breach, evaluating the effectiveness of incident response procedures, and updating security controls and policies accordingly. Lessons learned from the incident should be incorporated into future incident response planning and training efforts.

Practical Example: Responding to a Healthcare Data Breach

Let's consider a practical example to illustrate the data breach response and incident management process in the context of the health and wellness industry. Suppose a healthcare organization experiences a data breach involving the theft of patient records containing sensitive medical information.

1. **Preparation:** The organization has a designated incident response team consisting of representatives from IT, cybersecurity, legal, and executive management. They have established an incident response plan that outlines the key steps and responsibilities during a breach. The team regularly conducts training exercises to enhance their preparedness.

2. **Detection and Analysis:** The organization's security monitoring system detects suspicious activities indicating a potential breach. The incident response team is alerted, and an investigation is initiated. The team analyzes log files, network traffic, and system records to determine the scope and nature of the incident.

3. **Containment, Eradication, and Recovery:** Upon confirming the breach, the organization takes immediate action to contain the incident. They isolate the affected systems from the network and temporarily suspend access to the compromised records. The cybersecurity team works to eradicate any malware or unauthorized access points and begins the process of restoring affected systems from backups.

4. **Investigation:** The incident response team collaborates with forensic experts to determine how the breach occurred and the extent of the compromise. They collect evidence, interview staff members, and review system logs to identify the root cause. Law enforcement is engaged to support the investigation.

5. **Remediation and Lessons Learned:** Once the breach is under control, the organization focuses on remediation efforts. They patch vulnerabilities, enhance security controls, and conduct security awareness training for staff members. They also update their incident response plan based on the lessons learned from the breach.

6. **Notifying Affected Individuals and Authorities:** The organization determines the individuals affected by the breach and promptly notifies them, providing information on the incident, potential risks, and available support. They also notify relevant regulatory authorities and cooperate fully with any investigations or inquiries.

7. **Supporting Affected Individuals:** The organization offers affected individuals complimentary credit monitoring services, identity theft protection, and assistance with any legal or financial implications resulting from the breach. They establish a dedicated helpline and website to handle inquiries and provide ongoing support.

By following this incident response and management process, the healthcare organization can effectively address the data breach, minimize the impact on affected individuals, and implement measures to prevent similar incidents in the future.

Conclusion

Data breach response and incident management are critical components of an organization's cybersecurity strategy in the health and wellness industry. Proactively preparing for breaches, having robust incident response plans, and implementing effective response strategies can significantly reduce the risks and consequences associated with data breaches. By promptly detecting, containing, and recovering from breaches, organizations can protect the confidentiality, integrity, and availability of sensitive information, safeguard their reputation, and maintain the trust of patients and consumers. It is equally important to learn from each incident and continuously improve incident response capabilities to stay ahead of evolving cybersecurity threats.

Privacy-Enhanced Technologies for Health and Wellness

In today's digitally connected world, where personal information is constantly at risk of being compromised, it is crucial to implement privacy-enhanced technologies to safeguard the privacy and security of health and wellness data. This section explores various technologies and strategies that can be employed to protect sensitive information and maintain confidentiality in the health and wellness industry.

Secure Data Transmission using Encryption

One of the fundamental methods to enhance privacy is through the use of encryption. Encryption is the process of converting data into a format that can only be read by authorized individuals. By encrypting health and wellness data, even if it were intercepted during transmission, it would be meaningless to any unauthorized parties.

There are several encryption algorithms available, such as Advanced Encryption Standard (AES) and RSA (Rivest-Shamir-Adleman). These algorithms use complex mathematical calculations to scramble and unscramble data. Organizations can employ secure communication protocols like Transport Layer Security (TLS) or Secure Sockets Layer (SSL) to encrypt data during transmission over networks, such as the internet.

Privacy-Preserving Data Mining

In the health and wellness industry, significant amounts of data are collected and analyzed for research and decision-making purposes. However, privacy concerns arise when dealing with sensitive personal information. Privacy-preserving data mining techniques aim to extract useful insights from data without compromising the privacy of individuals.

One approach is differential privacy, which adds controlled noise or randomness to the data before analysis. This ensures that the results of the analysis do not reveal individual-specific information. Another technique is homomorphic encryption, which allows computations to be performed on encrypted data without decrypting it, thus preserving privacy.

De-identification and Anonymization

De-identification and anonymization techniques are commonly used to protect the privacy of individuals in health and wellness data. De-identification involves removing or altering identifying information, such as names, addresses, and social security numbers, from the data to prevent unauthorized identification. Anonymization goes a step further by irreversibly transforming the data so that it cannot be linked back to an individual.

To achieve effective de-identification and anonymization, organizations can employ techniques like data masking, where sensitive information is replaced with realistic but fictional data, or generalization, where specific values are grouped into ranges or categories. This ensures that the data remains useful for analysis while protecting the privacy of individuals.

Privacy-Preserving Authentication

Authentication is crucial to verify the identity of users accessing health and wellness systems. However, traditional authentication mechanisms may require the disclosure of sensitive personal information, posing privacy risks. Privacy-preserving authentication techniques aim to strike a balance between ensuring security and protecting individual privacy.

One such technique is zero-knowledge proof, where a user can prove knowledge of a secret without revealing the secret itself. This allows individuals to authenticate their identity without disclosing specific identifying information. Another approach is the use of biometric authentication, which relies on unique physical or behavioral characteristics. Biometric data, such as fingerprints or iris scans, can be used securely without revealing the actual biometric information.

Consent Management and Privacy Policies

Effective management of user consent and privacy policies is essential to maintain privacy in health and wellness systems. Organizations must ensure that individuals have control over how their personal information is collected, used, and shared. Privacy-enhanced technologies can help facilitate consent management and enforce privacy policies.

Technologies like privacy dashboards and user-centric privacy settings allow individuals to have visibility and control over their personal data. By providing clear and concise information about data collection and usage practices, individuals can make informed decisions about granting or denying consent. Organizations must also establish robust mechanisms to enforce privacy policies, such as data protection protocols and user access controls.

Limitations and Considerations

While privacy-enhanced technologies play a crucial role in protecting personal information in the health and wellness industry, it is important to acknowledge their limitations and considerations. Encryption and anonymization techniques can provide strong protection, but improper implementation or key management can lead to vulnerabilities. Organizations must ensure the proper implementation and ongoing monitoring of these technologies to maintain their effectiveness.

Additionally, it is important to consider the usability and practicality of privacy-enhanced technologies. Balancing privacy and usability can be challenging, as stringent security measures may hinder user experience. Organizations should strive to strike a balance between privacy and usability to avoid creating barriers and resistance to adopting these technologies.

Conclusion

Privacy-enhanced technologies are essential in safeguarding personal information in the health and wellness industry. Encryption, privacy-preserving data mining, de-identification and anonymization, privacy-preserving authentication, and effective consent management are some of the key strategies to enhance privacy and security.

By implementing these technologies and adhering to privacy best practices, organizations can protect sensitive health and wellness data, maintain individual privacy, and build trust with their users. It is crucial for organizations to continuously stay abreast of emerging privacy-enhanced technologies and adapt their strategies to stay ahead of evolving cybersecurity threats.

Cybersecurity in Telehealth and Digital Health Technologies

Telehealth Security and Privacy Considerations

With the increasing reliance on technology in the healthcare industry, telehealth has emerged as a convenient and accessible alternative to traditional in-person medical consultations. Telehealth allows patients to remotely access healthcare services through video conferencing, remote monitoring, and other digital communication channels. While telehealth offers numerous benefits, such as improved access to care and reduced healthcare costs, it also poses unique security and privacy challenges.

Importance of Telehealth Security

Telehealth involves the transmission and storage of sensitive medical information over digital networks. The security and privacy of this information are paramount to avoid unauthorized access, disclosure, or manipulation. Breaches in telehealth security can compromise patient confidentiality, damage trust in telehealth services, and expose healthcare providers to legal and financial repercussions. Therefore, implementing strong security measures is essential to mitigate these risks and protect patient data.

Risk Assessment and Threat Modeling

Before implementing telehealth services, healthcare organizations should conduct a comprehensive risk assessment and threat modeling exercise. This involves identifying potential threats, evaluating their likelihood and impact, and implementing appropriate security measures to address them. Common threats in telehealth include unauthorized access to patient data, interception of communication channels, and malware attacks on telehealth platforms. By understanding these risks and their potential consequences, healthcare organizations can take proactive steps to prevent or mitigate security incidents.

Technical Security Measures

To ensure the security of telehealth services, healthcare organizations should implement a range of technical security measures. These include:

- **Encryption:** All patient data transmitted or stored during telehealth consultations should be encrypted to protect it from unauthorized access. Strong encryption algorithms, such as AES (Advanced Encryption Standard), should be utilized to ensure data confidentiality.

- **Secure Communication Channels:** Telehealth platforms should use secure communication protocols, such as Transport Layer Security (TLS), to ensure the integrity and confidentiality of data shared during consultations. This prevents eavesdropping and data manipulation during transit.

- **Authentication and Access Controls:** Robust authentication mechanisms, such as two-factor authentication (2FA), should be implemented to verify the identity of both healthcare providers and patients during telehealth sessions. Access controls should also be enforced to limit data access to authorized individuals.

- **Secure Storage and Transmission:** Patient data should be securely stored and transmitted in compliance with data protection regulations. Measures such as data encryption, secure cloud storage, and data loss prevention tools should be implemented to safeguard patient information.

- **Regular System Updates and Patch Management:** Telehealth platforms and associated systems should be regularly updated with the latest security patches to address software vulnerabilities. This reduces the risk of exploitation by cybercriminals.

Privacy Considerations

In addition to security measures, telehealth also requires careful attention to privacy considerations to protect the confidentiality of patient information. Key privacy considerations in telehealth include:

- **Informed Consent:** Patients must be informed about the privacy practices of telehealth services and provide consent for the collection, use, and disclosure of their personal health information. This ensures transparency and empowers patients to make informed decisions about their privacy.
- **Data Minimization:** Healthcare providers should only collect and retain the minimum amount of patient data necessary to provide effective telehealth services. Unnecessary collection or retention of patient information increases the risk of privacy breaches.
- **Notice and Right to Access:** Patients should be provided with clear notice about how their personal health information will be used and shared during telehealth consultations. They should also have the right to access their health information, correct inaccuracies, and request its deletion when no longer needed.
- **Data Sharing and Third-Party Agreements:** Healthcare providers should enter into appropriate agreements with telehealth platforms and other third-party service providers to ensure compliance with privacy regulations. These agreements should define how patient data will be handled, shared, and protected.

Compliance with Regulations

Telehealth services must comply with relevant privacy and security regulations, such as the Health Insurance Portability and Accountability Act (HIPAA) in the United States. Compliance involves implementing security safeguards, conducting risk assessments, and adopting policies and procedures to protect patient information. Healthcare organizations should regularly review and update their telehealth practices to align with evolving regulatory requirements.

Training and Awareness

Healthcare providers and staff involved in telehealth should receive comprehensive training on security and privacy best practices. Training should cover topics such as secure communication, data handling procedures, password hygiene, and recognizing social engineering threats. Regular security awareness campaigns can reinforce good security practices and help foster a culture of security within the organization.

Real-World Example: Telehealth Security Incident

To illustrate the importance of telehealth security, consider the case of a telehealth platform that experienced a security breach. The breach exposed the personal and medical information of thousands of patients, resulting in significant reputational and financial damage to the platform and healthcare providers involved. This incident could have been prevented through the implementation of encryption, strong access controls, and regular security updates.

Further Resources

To delve deeper into the topic of telehealth security and privacy, consider exploring the following resources:

- American Telemedicine Association (telemedicine.org): The ATA provides guidelines, resources, and best practices for ensuring the security and privacy of telehealth services.

- Health Insurance Portability and Accountability Act (HIPAA) Security Rule: This U.S. legislation sets standards for the protection of electronic protected health information (ePHI) and provides guidance on implementing security safeguards in telehealth.

- National Institute of Standards and Technology (NIST) Special Publication 800-66, "An Introductory Resource Guide for Implementing the Health Insurance Portability and Accountability Act (HIPAA) Security Rule": This guide provides detailed information on implementing security measures in compliance with HIPAA requirements.

In conclusion, telehealth security and privacy considerations are of utmost importance in the digital healthcare landscape. By implementing robust security measures, addressing privacy concerns, and complying with regulations, healthcare organizations can ensure the confidentiality and integrity of patient data during telehealth interactions.

Securing Electronic Health Records (EHR)

In today's digital age, electronic health records (EHRs) have become an integral part of healthcare systems. EHRs enable healthcare providers to store, manage, and exchange patients' medical information digitally. However, the increased use of EHRs also brings with it new security challenges. Protecting the confidentiality, integrity, and availability of EHRs is crucial to ensure patient privacy and prevent unauthorized access or breaches. In this section, we will explore the various measures and best practices for securing electronic health records.

Importance of EHR Security

Electronic health records contain sensitive and personal information, including medical histories, diagnoses, medications, and test results. Protecting this information is of paramount importance, as unauthorized access or breach could lead to privacy violations, medical identity theft, and even compromised patient care.

Moreover, the Health Insurance Portability and Accountability Act (HIPAA) requires healthcare providers to implement safeguards to protect the privacy and security of patients' health information. Failure to comply with HIPAA regulations can result in severe penalties and damaged reputation for healthcare organizations.

Access Control and Authentication

One of the fundamental steps in securing EHRs is implementing strong access control mechanisms. This involves ensuring that only authorized individuals have the necessary permissions to access EHRs. Healthcare organizations should establish role-based access control (RBAC) and assign appropriate access privileges based on job responsibilities and the principle of least privilege.

Furthermore, implementing robust authentication methods is crucial to verify the identity of individuals accessing EHRs. Healthcare providers should enforce the use of strong passwords or preferably utilize multi-factor authentication (MFA) to add an extra layer of security. MFA can include a combination of something the user knows (password), something the user has (smart card), or something the user is (biometric data).

Encryption of EHRs

Encrypting EHRs is an essential practice to protect patient information from unauthorized access or interception. Encryption involves converting sensitive data into an unreadable format, which can only be decrypted with the correct encryption key. By encrypting EHRs both in transit and at rest, healthcare providers can ensure that even if the data is intercepted or stolen, it remains unintelligible to unauthorized individuals.

There are two main types of encryption: symmetric encryption and asymmetric encryption. Symmetric encryption uses a single key for both encryption and decryption, while asymmetric encryption utilizes a pair of keys (public and private) for encryption and decryption, respectively. Organizations should use industry-standard encryption algorithms and ensure that encryption keys are appropriately managed and protected.

Audit Logging and Monitoring

Implementing logging and monitoring mechanisms is vital for detecting and investigating potential security incidents or unauthorized access to EHRs. Healthcare organizations should maintain detailed audit logs that capture information, such as user activities, access attempts, modifications, and system events related to EHRs.

Regularly reviewing and analyzing audit logs can help identify security breaches, unauthorized access, or insider threats. Real-time monitoring solutions, such as intrusion detection systems (IDS) or security information and event management (SIEM) systems, can provide timely alerts and help in proactive defense against potential threats.

Training and Awareness

Human error is often one of the leading causes of security breaches. To mitigate this risk, healthcare organizations should invest in comprehensive training and awareness programs for all staff members handling EHRs. Training should cover topics such as password security, phishing awareness, social engineering attacks, and adherence to security policies and procedures.

Regularly conducting security awareness campaigns and keeping employees informed about emerging threats and best practices reinforces the importance of EHR security and cultivates a culture of security throughout the organization.

Data Backup and Disaster Recovery

Accidental data loss, system failures, or ransomware attacks can disrupt access to EHRs, leading to compromised patient care. Implementing robust data backup and disaster recovery strategies is critical for mitigating these risks and ensuring the availability and integrity of EHRs.

Healthcare organizations should regularly perform backups of EHRs and store them securely, preferably in an off-site location or in the cloud. Additionally, conducting periodic disaster recovery drills and testing the restoration process can help identify any vulnerabilities in the system and ensure a prompt recovery in the event of a disaster.

Ethical Considerations

Securing EHRs involves not only technical measures but also ethical considerations. Healthcare providers have an ethical obligation to protect patient privacy, ensure the accuracy of medical information, and maintain the confidentiality of sensitive data. This includes having clear policies on information sharing, obtaining informed consent, and respecting patients' rights to control their health information.

Furthermore, healthcare professionals and organizations should adhere to professional ethical standards and guidelines, such as those set forth by medical associations or governing bodies. This ensures that EHR security aligns with professional ethical principles and best practices.

Legal and Regulatory Compliance

Compliance with legal and regulatory requirements is critical for ensuring EHR security. Healthcare organizations must stay abreast of relevant laws, regulations, and standards, such as HIPAA, the General Data Protection Regulation (GDPR), and the Health Information Technology for Economic and Clinical Health (HITECH) Act.

Meeting these compliance requirements involves implementing appropriate administrative, technical, and physical safeguards, conducting regular risk assessments, and addressing any identified vulnerabilities or gaps. Non-compliance can result in severe penalties, legal repercussions, and reputational damage.

Case Study: The Importance of EHR Security

In 2015, Anthem Inc., one of the largest health insurance companies in the United States, experienced a massive data breach that compromised the personal information of nearly 78.8 million individuals. The breach involved unauthorized access to Anthem's EHR database, where names, birthdates, Social Security numbers, and other sensitive data were stored.

The impact of this breach was significant, not only in terms of financial losses for Anthem but also in terms of potential harm to the affected individuals. The breach highlighted the importance of robust EHR security practices, including access controls, encryption, and logging, to prevent unauthorized access and protect patient information.

Resources and Further Reading

1. Health Insurance Portability and Accountability Act (HIPAA): `https://www.hhs.gov/hipaa/` 2. Healthcare Information and Management Systems Society (HIMSS): `https://www.himss.org/` 3. National Institute of Standards and Technology (NIST) - Computer Security Division: `https://www.nist.gov/itl/cs` 4. Office for Civil Rights (OCR) - HIPAA Security Rule: `https://www.hhs.gov/hipaa/for-professionals/security/index.html`

Exercises

1. Discuss the importance of access control in securing electronic health records. Provide examples of authentication methods and access control techniques that can be implemented. 2. Explain the concept of encryption and its role in protecting EHRs. Compare and contrast symmetric and asymmetric encryption algorithms. 3. Describe the significance of auditing and monitoring in EHR security. Discuss the benefits of real-time monitoring systems in detecting security incidents. 4. Develop a training and awareness program outline for healthcare employees to enhance EHR security awareness. Include key topics to cover and methods for evaluating the effectiveness of the program. 5. Assess the ethical considerations involved in EHR security. Discuss the ethical obligations of healthcare professionals and organizations in protecting patient privacy and maintaining confidentiality. 6. Research and discuss a recent healthcare data breach related to EHRs. Analyze the impact of the breach and the security vulnerabilities that led to the incident.

Remember to refer to the additional resources provided for further reading and exploration of the topic.

Secure Communication Platforms for Telehealth

In the rapidly evolving field of telehealth, where healthcare services are delivered remotely through digital communication platforms, ensuring the security and privacy of patient information is of utmost importance. Telehealth communication platforms must provide a secure environment for healthcare professionals and patients to interact, exchange sensitive medical information, and make informed decisions about their health. This section explores the key considerations for selecting and using secure communication platforms in telehealth.

Importance of Secure Communication in Telehealth

Secure communication platforms play a vital role in maintaining patient confidentiality, protecting sensitive medical data, and preventing unauthorized access or misuse of information. By utilizing secure communication platforms, healthcare providers and patients can have peace of mind, knowing that their conversations and shared data are encrypted and secure from potential cyber threats.

End-to-End Encryption

One of the fundamental features of a secure communication platform for telehealth is end-to-end encryption. This encryption technique ensures that data transmitted between the sender and the receiver is only accessible to them and cannot be intercepted or decrypted by unauthorized parties. End-to-end encryption uses cryptographic keys to encode the data at the sender's end and decode it at the receiver's end, ensuring the confidentiality and integrity of the information.

Authentication and Identity Verification

To ensure the privacy and security of telehealth communication, it is crucial to authenticate the identities of both healthcare professionals and patients. Authentication mechanisms like usernames, passwords, and two-factor authentication can be employed to verify the identity of users before granting access to the communication platform. Additionally, digital certificates and public key infrastructure (PKI) can be used to establish trust and validate the authenticity of participants in telehealth sessions.

Secure File Sharing

Telehealth often involves sharing medical records, lab results, and other sensitive documents between healthcare providers and patients. Secure communication platforms should offer secure file-sharing capabilities to enable the transmission of files without compromising their confidentiality. This is achieved through encryption of the files in transit and at rest, ensuring that only authorized individuals can access and view the shared files.

Secure Video Conferencing

Video conferencing has become an integral part of telehealth, allowing remote healthcare consultations and real-time interaction between healthcare professionals and patients. When selecting a secure communication platform, it is essential to ensure that the video conferencing feature incorporates robust security measures. This includes encryption of audio and video streams, secure authentication of participants, and protection against unauthorized access or eavesdropping.

Access Controls and Privacy Settings

To maintain privacy and control over the communication environment, secure telehealth platforms should offer granular access controls and privacy settings. These features allow users to define who can initiate communication and access their information. Additionally, access control policies can be set to restrict certain functionalities or data sharing options based on user roles and permissions. By providing fine-grained access controls, healthcare providers and patients can mitigate the risk of unauthorized access to their sensitive data.

Compliance with Regulatory Standards

Secure communication platforms used in telehealth must adhere to relevant legal and regulatory standards, such as the Health Insurance Portability and Accountability Act (HIPAA) in the United States. Compliance with these standards ensures that the platform implements necessary safeguards to protect patient privacy and maintain the confidentiality, integrity, and availability of sensitive health information. It is essential to choose communication platforms that are certified and compliant with the applicable regulatory requirements in the specific jurisdiction.

Training and Awareness

While selecting and implementing a secure communication platform is crucial, it is equally important to provide comprehensive training and awareness to healthcare professionals and patients. Training programs can educate users on best practices for secure communication, password management, recognizing and reporting security incidents, and maintaining overall cybersecurity hygiene. By fostering a culture of security awareness, telehealth stakeholders can actively contribute to the protection of patient information.

Case Study: Secure Communication Platform XYZ

To illustrate the principles discussed above, let's consider the secure communication platform called XYZ. XYZ provides end-to-end encrypted messaging, file sharing, and video conferencing capabilities specifically designed for telehealth.

XYZ leverages industry-standard encryption algorithms to ensure the confidentiality and integrity of messages and files exchanged between healthcare providers and patients. The platform implements strong authentication mechanisms, including username and password-based login, as well as multi-factor authentication for an added layer of security. It also supports integration with existing identity management systems, such as electronic medical record systems, to simplify user authentication.

In terms of file sharing, XYZ employs encryption both in transit and at rest, ensuring that files are protected from unauthorized access throughout their lifecycle. The platform allows healthcare providers to securely share medical records, lab results, and imaging files with patients, while ensuring that only authorized individuals can access the shared files.

For video conferencing, XYZ uses end-to-end encryption for audio and video streams, keeping patient conversations private and secure. The platform supports secure authentication of participants, preventing unauthorized individuals from joining telehealth sessions. It also offers privacy settings that allow participants to control who can initiate communication and access their video conference sessions.

XYZ is fully compliant with regulatory standards, including HIPAA, and undergoes regular security assessments and audits to ensure the platform's security posture is up to date. The company provides comprehensive training materials and resources to healthcare providers and patients, promoting security awareness and helping users make the most out of the platform's security features.

By leveraging XYZ as a secure communication platform for telehealth, healthcare providers and patients can communicate and share sensitive health information with confidence, knowing that their privacy and security are protected.

Conclusion

Secure communication platforms are essential for maintaining patient confidentiality, protecting sensitive medical data, and preventing unauthorized access in telehealth. End-to-end encryption, authentication mechanisms, secure file sharing, and video conferencing capabilities are essential features to consider when choosing a secure communication platform. Additionally, adherence to regulatory standards, comprehensive training, and promoting security awareness among healthcare professionals and patients are vital components of a robust telehealth communication ecosystem. By prioritizing security and privacy, telehealth stakeholders can ensure a safe and secure environment for remote healthcare delivery.

Cybersecurity in Wearable Devices and Health Apps

In recent years, wearable devices and health apps have gained popularity, allowing individuals to track their health and fitness levels. These devices and apps provide valuable insights into various aspects of our well-being, such as heart rate, sleep patterns, exercise routines, and calorie intake. However, with the increasing dependence on these technologies, it is crucial to address the cybersecurity risks associated with wearable devices and health apps.

Understanding the Risks

Wearable devices and health apps collect and store vast amounts of personal health information. This sensitive data, if compromised, can have severe consequences for individuals, jeopardizing their privacy, security, and overall well-being. Therefore, it is essential to be aware of the potential risks and vulnerabilities in this domain.

One of the primary risks is unauthorized access to personal health data. If a wearable device or health app lacks proper security measures, malicious actors can exploit vulnerabilities to gain access to sensitive information. This can lead to identity theft, financial fraud, or even blackmail.

Another risk is the potential for data manipulation. Hackers can alter the data collected by wearable devices or modify the functionality of health apps, providing inaccurate or misleading information. This can have significant consequences, especially when it comes to medical diagnoses or treatment plans based on faulty data.

Furthermore, wearable devices and health apps often rely on wireless communication protocols to transmit data to other devices or cloud servers. This wireless communication can be intercepted by attackers, compromising the confidentiality and integrity of the data. Additionally, these devices and apps may also face risks such as malware infections and denial-of-service attacks.

Protecting Wearable Devices and Health Apps

To mitigate the cybersecurity risks associated with wearable devices and health apps, several protective measures should be implemented.

First and foremost, developers should prioritize security during the design and development phase. This includes incorporating strong encryption algorithms to protect data at rest and in transit. Additionally, the use of robust authentication mechanisms, such as biometric authentication or two-factor authentication, can help ensure that only authorized users can access the devices or apps.

Regular software updates and patches are crucial to address any known vulnerabilities and protect against emerging threats. Developers should actively monitor security forums and stay up to date with the latest cybersecurity trends to timely address any vulnerabilities or issues.

User education and awareness play a significant role in protecting wearable devices and health apps. Individuals should be aware of the risks and practice good cyber hygiene, such as setting strong passwords, avoiding suspicious links or downloads, and being cautious about sharing personal information.

Furthermore, individuals should carefully review the privacy settings and permissions of wearable devices and health apps. By limiting the data shared with the app or device and restricting unnecessary permissions, individuals can minimize the exposure of their personal information.

For healthcare organizations and providers, it is crucial to implement strict data privacy and access control policies. This includes regular risk assessments, employee training programs, and incident response plans. Implementing appropriate security controls and conducting regular security audits will help mitigate potential vulnerabilities.

Real-world Example: Fitness Tracker Data Breach

In 2018, a popular fitness tracker app suffered a significant data breach, compromising the personal health information of millions of users. The breach occurred due to a vulnerability in the app's user authentication process, allowing hackers to gain unauthorized access to sensitive data.

As a result of the breach, the personal health information of the users, including their exercise routines, heart rate data, and sleep patterns, became exposed to malicious actors. The implications of this breach were far-reaching, as the compromised data could be used for targeted attacks, fraudulent activities, or even blackmail.

This real-world example highlights the importance of robust security measures in wearable devices and health apps. It also underscores the need for continuous monitoring, timely security updates, and user education to prevent such incidents.

Additional Resources

For further exploration of the topic of cybersecurity in wearable devices and health apps, the following resources are recommended:

- **Book:** "Healthcare Cybersecurity: Best Practices for Securing Connected Medical Devices" by Johnathan Tal
- **Article:** "The Security Risks of Wearable Devices" by Mary Johnson
- **Webinar:** "Securing Health Apps: Protecting User Data in a Connected World" by Cybersecurity Professionals Association
- **Guidelines:** "Mobile Health App Security Guidelines" by the National Institute of Standards and Technology (NIST)

These resources provide valuable insights into the challenges of cybersecurity in wearable devices and health apps, along with practical recommendations for addressing the associated risks.

Conclusion

As wearable devices and health apps continue to shape the future of health and wellness, it is crucial to prioritize cybersecurity. By understanding the risks, implementing protective measures, and staying informed about the latest developments in the field, individuals and organizations can ensure the safety and privacy of personal health information. Together, we can create a secure and digitally connected world that enhances our overall well-being.

Internet of Medical Things (IoMT) Security Challenges

The Internet of Medical Things (IoMT) refers to the network of medical devices, wearables, and other healthcare equipment that are connected to the internet, allowing for the collection, exchange, and analysis of health data. While the IoMT offers numerous benefits in terms of healthcare management, patient monitoring, and treatment delivery, it also presents critical security challenges that must be addressed to ensure the confidentiality, integrity, and availability of sensitive medical information.

In this section, we will explore some of the key security challenges associated with the IoMT and discuss strategies and best practices to mitigate these risks. We will delve into the unique vulnerabilities and threats facing the IoMT ecosystem and examine the measures healthcare organizations and individuals can take to protect against potential attacks.

Understanding IoMT Security Risks

The IoMT brings together several interconnected devices and systems, ranging from medical implants and sensors to health tracking wearables and online patient portals. Each of these components presents its own set of security risks, which, if exploited, can have significant consequences for patient safety and privacy.

One of the primary security risks in the IoMT is the potential for unauthorized access to sensitive medical data. With the increasing connectivity of medical devices, hackers could gain access to patients' personal health information, including medical records, test results, and treatment plans. This could result in identity theft, medical fraud, and even jeopardize patient safety if tampered data leads to incorrect diagnoses or treatment interventions.

Another concern is the potential for manipulation or unauthorized control of medical devices. If a device is compromised, an attacker could manipulate its functionality, leading to improper treatment delivery or even life-threatening scenarios. For example, a hacker could tamper with an insulin pump, causing it to deliver excessive amounts of insulin and leading to serious health complications in a diabetic patient.

Additionally, the IoMT ecosystem faces the risk of data breaches. If proper security measures are not in place, hackers may exploit vulnerabilities in the network, device firmware, or communication protocols to gain access to sensitive data. This could result in the exposure of patients' personal information or the loss of valuable medical research data.

Securing the IoMT Ecosystem

To mitigate the security challenges posed by the IoMT, various security measures must be implemented throughout the ecosystem. These measures involve a combination of technical safeguards, policy frameworks, and user awareness.

1. Secure Device Design and Development: Manufacturers play a crucial role in ensuring the security of medical devices. They should follow secure coding practices, perform regular security assessments and penetration testing, and promptly address any identified vulnerabilities. This includes implementing secure authentication mechanisms, encryption protocols, and device firmware updates.

2. **Network Segmentation and Isolation:** To minimize the risk of unauthorized access, healthcare organizations should employ network segmentation, separating sensitive medical devices from other less critical systems. This helps contain potential breaches and limits the attacker's lateral movement within the network.

3. **Access Control and Authentication:** Strong access control mechanisms, such as unique user identification, strong passwords, and multi-factor authentication, should be implemented to restrict unauthorized access to medical devices and the associated data. Additionally, user permissions should be assigned based on the principle of least privilege, ensuring that only authorized personnel can access sensitive data.

4. **Encryption and Data Integrity:** Medical data stored or transmitted within the IoMT ecosystem should be encrypted to protect against unauthorized interception and tampering. Encryption mechanisms, such as secure communication protocols and encryption algorithms, should be employed to ensure the confidentiality and integrity of sensitive data.

5. **Continuous Monitoring and Intrusion Detection:** Healthcare organizations should implement intrusion detection systems and continuously monitor the network for any suspicious activities or anomalies. This allows for the early detection of potential breaches and timely response to mitigate the impact of an attack.

6. **Regular Patching and Updates:** Medical devices and associated software should receive regular updates and patches from manufacturers to address known vulnerabilities. Healthcare organizations should establish procedures for timely deployment of these updates to ensure that devices are protected against the latest threats.

7. **User Education and Awareness:** Healthcare professionals and individuals using IoMT devices should receive comprehensive training on cybersecurity best practices. This includes recognizing potential threats, understanding secure device usage, and adhering to organizational security policies.

8. **Incident Response and Recovery Planning:** Healthcare organizations should develop robust incident response and recovery plans to address potential security incidents promptly. This includes establishing an incident response team,

documenting response procedures, and regularly testing the effectiveness of the plans through simulations and exercises.

Case Study: Securing Wearable Devices

To illustrate the security challenges and solutions in the IoMT ecosystem, let's consider the example of securing wearable devices, such as fitness trackers and smartwatches, which have gained significant popularity in recent years.

Wearable devices collect and transmit personal health data, including heart rate, sleep patterns, and physical activity, making them attractive targets for hackers. To ensure the security of wearable devices, manufacturers should implement strong encryption algorithms to protect data in transit and at rest. Moreover, user authentication mechanisms, such as biometric authentication or PIN codes, should be employed to prevent unauthorized access.

Healthcare organizations can also deploy network monitoring systems to identify abnormal patterns of data transmission and detect potential data breaches. Regular firmware updates should be issued to address any identified vulnerabilities and ensure the security of the devices.

User education and awareness play a critical role in securing wearable devices. Users should be educated about the importance of strong passwords, regular device updates, and avoiding suspicious links or downloads that could compromise their device's security. Encouraging users to be vigilant and report any unusual device behavior can help detect potential security incidents.

Conclusion

The IoMT offers immense potential to revolutionize healthcare delivery and improve patient outcomes. However, the integration of medical devices and systems into the interconnected ecosystem brings forth critical security challenges that must be addressed.

By implementing robust security measures, including secure device design, network segregation, access control, encryption, and user education, healthcare organizations and individuals can mitigate the risks associated with the IoMT. By ensuring the security and privacy of medical data, the IoMT can continue to facilitate advancements in healthcare while safeguarding patient well-being.

Protecting Personal Health Information in Remote Monitoring Systems

Remote monitoring systems have become increasingly popular in the health and wellness industry. These systems allow healthcare providers to collect and monitor patients' health data remotely, providing timely and personalized care. However, with the increased reliance on these systems comes the need to ensure the security and privacy of personal health information (PHI). This section focuses on the strategies and best practices to protect PHI in remote monitoring systems.

Understanding the Importance of Protecting PHI

Personal health information includes sensitive data such as medical records, test results, and health monitoring data. Protecting PHI is crucial to maintain patient privacy, prevent identity theft, and ensure compliance with regulations like the Health Insurance Portability and Accountability Act (HIPAA). Unauthorized access, data breaches, and misuse of PHI can have severe consequences for both patients and healthcare organizations.

Encryption and Data Security

Encryption is a critical component in protecting PHI in remote monitoring systems. It ensures that the data transmitted and stored is secure and unreadable to unauthorized individuals. Implementing strong encryption algorithms and protocols, such as Advanced Encryption Standard (AES) and Transport Layer Security (TLS), can help safeguard sensitive data.

In addition to encryption, other data security measures should be implemented. These include:

- Access controls: Implementing strict access controls ensures that only authorized individuals can access and manipulate PHI. This involves using strong authentication mechanisms like usernames, passwords, and two-factor authentication.

- Data segmentation: Segmenting data ensures that different categories of data are separated, limiting access to only those who need it. For example, separating identifying information from health monitoring data.

- Data minimization: Only collecting and storing the minimum amount of PHI needed for the remote monitoring system's purpose can help reduce the risk of unauthorized access. Unused or expired data should be securely discarded.

- Secure transmission: Remote monitoring systems should use secure communication protocols, such as HTTPS, to transmit data securely over networks. This prevents interception and eavesdropping by unauthorized parties.

Secure Authentication and Authorization

Authentication and authorization are vital in ensuring that only authorized individuals can access PHI in remote monitoring systems. Strong authentication methods, like using unique usernames and complex passwords, should be implemented. Two-factor authentication adds an extra layer of security by requiring additional verification, such as a fingerprint scan or a one-time password.

Authorization mechanisms should be in place to grant access privileges based on roles and responsibilities. Healthcare providers should only have access to the PHI necessary for their specific tasks, and access should be revoked once no longer required.

Continuous Monitoring and Intrusion Detection

Continuous monitoring is crucial for identifying and responding to potential security incidents in remote monitoring systems. Intrusion detection systems can help detect unauthorized access attempts or anomalies in the system's behavior. These systems should be regularly updated and configured to detect known attack patterns and suspicious activities.

In addition to automated monitoring, establishing incident response procedures and protocols is essential. This ensures that any security incidents can be promptly identified, contained, and remediated to minimize potential damage.

Staff Training and Awareness

Human error often poses a significant risk to the security of PHI. It is essential to provide comprehensive training and awareness programs for healthcare staff involved in remote monitoring systems. Training should cover topics such as secure handling of PHI, identifying phishing attempts, and the importance of adhering to security policies and procedures.

Regularly updating staff on emerging security threats and providing refresher training sessions can help maintain a culture of cybersecurity awareness within the organization.

Legal and Regulatory Compliance

Healthcare organizations must comply with legal and regulatory requirements, such as HIPAA, when handling PHI in remote monitoring systems. It is crucial to have a thorough understanding of these regulations and ensure that appropriate measures are in place to meet compliance standards.

Regular audits and assessments can help identify any gaps in compliance and ensure that necessary corrective actions are taken promptly.

Privacy-Enhancing Technologies

Privacy-enhancing technologies (PETs) can provide additional layers of protection for PHI in remote monitoring systems. These technologies aim to preserve privacy by minimizing the amount of sensitive information exposed during data collection and sharing processes. Examples of PETs include anonymization techniques, data masking, and differential privacy algorithms.

By implementing PETs, healthcare organizations can enhance privacy while still deriving meaningful insights from the collected data.

Ethical Considerations

Remote monitoring systems raise ethical considerations regarding patient autonomy, informed consent, and potential unintended consequences. As healthcare providers collect and analyze PHI, it is essential to respect patient preferences and ensure that they have control over their health information.

Ethical guidelines should be established to govern the use of PHI in remote monitoring systems. These guidelines should address issues related to data ownership, data sharing, and the long-term implications of data collection and analysis.

Conclusion

Protecting personal health information in remote monitoring systems is paramount to maintain patient privacy, prevent data breaches, and ensure compliance with regulations. The implementation of robust encryption, secure authentication and authorization mechanisms, continuous monitoring, staff training, and adherence to legal and ethical standards are essential components in safeguarding PHI. By incorporating these strategies, healthcare organizations can enhance the overall security of remote monitoring systems and build trust with patients.

Ethical Considerations in Telehealth and Digital Health Technologies

In the rapidly evolving field of telehealth and digital health technologies, there are important ethical considerations that need to be taken into account. These considerations revolve around privacy, consent, confidentiality, equity, and the overall ethical framework within which telehealth services and digital health technologies operate. In this section, we will explore these ethical considerations and discuss their implications on the delivery of healthcare services.

Privacy and Confidentiality

Privacy and confidentiality are crucial ethical principles in the healthcare context, and they become even more critical in the realm of telehealth and digital health technologies. When patients engage in telehealth consultations or use digital health applications, their personal health information is transmitted and stored electronically. It is essential to ensure that patients' privacy and confidentiality are protected throughout these processes.

Healthcare providers and organizations must implement robust security measures to safeguard patient data from unauthorized access, use, or disclosure. This may include encryption techniques, secure data storage, and strict access controls. Patients should be informed about the security measures in place and have the right to give or withhold their consent for the collection, use, and disclosure of their personal health information.

Furthermore, healthcare professionals must adhere to professional codes of ethics and legal frameworks that govern privacy and confidentiality. They should also educate patients about the potential risks associated with telehealth and digital health technologies and inform them of their rights related to privacy and confidentiality.

Informed Consent

Informed consent is a fundamental ethical principle that ensures patients have the necessary information to make autonomous decisions regarding their healthcare. In the context of telehealth and digital health technologies, obtaining informed consent takes on added complexity.

Healthcare providers must clearly explain the purpose, benefits, and limitations of telehealth consultations or the use of digital health technologies to patients. They should also discuss any potential risks and alternative options. Patients need to understand how their personal health information will be collected, used, and stored, along with the associated privacy and security measures.

Obtaining informed consent may be challenging in certain situations, such as emergencies or when patients have limited technological literacy. In such cases, healthcare providers must make reasonable efforts to ensure that patients have a basic understanding of the telehealth or digital health service. They should also provide ongoing support and assistance to ensure patients can fully participate in their care.

Equitable Access

Ensuring equitable access to telehealth and digital health technologies is a significant ethical consideration. While these technologies have the potential to expand access to healthcare services, they may also exacerbate existing health inequalities.

Barriers such as lack of internet access, limited digital literacy, and language or cultural barriers can prevent certain populations from benefiting from telehealth and digital health technologies. It is crucial to address these inequities and take steps to ensure that vulnerable and marginalized populations have equal access to these services.

Healthcare organizations and policymakers should develop strategies to bridge the digital divide by providing technological resources, training programs, and support for underserved communities. Additionally, healthcare providers should be mindful of cultural and linguistic diversity when using telehealth and digital health technologies. Adapting these technologies to accommodate different needs and preferences can help promote equitable access to healthcare services.

Therapeutic Relationship and Trust

The establishment and maintenance of a strong therapeutic relationship between healthcare providers and patients are essential for effective healthcare delivery. In the context of telehealth and digital health technologies, maintaining this relationship can be challenging due to the lack of physical proximity.

Healthcare providers must make deliberate efforts to build trust and rapport with patients during telehealth consultations or when using digital health technologies. Clear and empathetic communication, active listening, and fostering a non-judgmental environment are crucial in creating a therapeutic relationship.

It is also important to recognize the limitations of telehealth and digital health technologies in facilitating non-verbal cues and physical examinations. Healthcare providers should be transparent with patients about these limitations and coordinate in-person evaluations or referrals when necessary.

Data Ownership and Governance

In the age of telehealth and digital health technologies, the ownership and governance of patient data are increasingly important ethical considerations. Patients should have control over their health data and be informed about how it will be used and shared.

Healthcare organizations and technology companies must ensure that patients' rights to data ownership are respected. This includes providing patients with clear information about data governance practices, opportunities to access and correct their health information, and the ability to determine how and with whom their data is shared.

Additionally, healthcare providers should consider the ethical implications of secondary use of patient data for research, quality improvement, or public health purposes. Striking the right balance between data utilization and privacy protection is vital to maintain public trust in telehealth and digital health technologies.

Ethical Dilemmas and Decision-Making Frameworks

Telehealth and digital health technologies can present healthcare providers with ethical dilemmas and complex decision-making situations. For example, the use of artificial intelligence and machine learning algorithms in diagnostic or treatment processes raises questions about algorithm bias, accountability, and patient autonomy.

Healthcare providers should be equipped with decision-making frameworks that enable them to navigate these ethical dilemmas effectively. Ethical principles such as beneficence, non-maleficence, autonomy, and justice should guide the decision-making process. In cases where there are conflicting ethical obligations, consulting with colleagues, professional bodies, and ethics committees can provide valuable insights.

Patients should also be involved in the decision-making process whenever possible. Shared decision-making models that allow patients to actively participate in their care can help address ethical concerns and promote patient-centered care.

Ethics Committees and Institutional Policies

To ensure adherence to ethical principles and guidelines, healthcare organizations should establish ethics committees and develop institutional policies specific to telehealth and digital health technologies. These committees can provide guidance, oversight, and support for healthcare providers facing ethical dilemmas.

Ethics committees can also contribute to the development of organizational policies and guidelines that address ethical considerations related to telehealth and digital health technologies. These policies should be regularly reviewed and updated to reflect the evolving ethical landscape and changes in regulations or best practices.

Case Study: Ethical Considerations in Remote Monitoring

Remote monitoring technologies, such as wearable devices and sensors, have become increasingly prevalent in healthcare. These technologies allow for continuous monitoring of a patient's vital signs, activity levels, and other health parameters. While they offer the potential for improved patient outcomes and reduced healthcare costs, there are ethical considerations that arise.

One ethical concern is the potential for data breaches and unauthorized access to the patient's health information collected through remote monitoring. Healthcare providers must ensure that robust security measures are in place to protect patient privacy and confidentiality. This includes encryption of data, secure storage, and access controls.

Another ethical consideration is the impact of remote monitoring on the patient's autonomy and sense of privacy. Patients may feel constantly monitored and experience a loss of control over their own bodies and health. Healthcare providers must address these concerns proactively by engaging in open and honest communication about the purpose and benefits of remote monitoring. They should also obtain informed consent and respect patients' decisions regarding the use of remote monitoring technologies.

Furthermore, there may be ethical implications related to the unequal distribution and access to remote monitoring technologies. Some patients may not have the financial means or technological literacy to benefit from these technologies, leading to health disparities. It is crucial to consider these inequities and develop strategies to ensure equal access to remote monitoring for all patients.

In conclusion, ethical considerations must underpin the use of telehealth and digital health technologies to ensure the delivery of safe, effective, and equitable healthcare services. Privacy, informed consent, equitable access, the therapeutic relationship, data ownership, and ethics committees play critical roles in addressing the ethical challenges that arise in telehealth and digital health. Healthcare providers, policymakers, and patients must collaborate to navigate these ethical considerations and promote the responsible use of telehealth and digital health technologies.

Legal and Regulatory Framework for Telehealth Cybersecurity

The rapid growth of telehealth has revolutionized the healthcare industry, allowing patients to access medical services from the comfort of their own homes. However, along with the many benefits, telehealth also presents unique cybersecurity challenges. The sensitive nature of health information and the reliance on technology make it crucial to have a strong legal and regulatory framework in place to ensure the protection of patient data. In this section, we will explore the key laws and regulations that govern telehealth cybersecurity and discuss their implications for healthcare providers and patients.

Health Insurance Portability and Accountability Act (HIPAA)

HIPAA is a federal law enacted in 1996 that sets national standards for the protection of individuals' personal health information (PHI). The Privacy Rule, one of the key components of HIPAA, establishes the requirements for the use and disclosure of PHI by covered entities, including healthcare providers, health plans, and healthcare clearinghouses. The Security Rule, another important aspect of HIPAA, outlines the safeguards that covered entities must implement to protect electronic PHI (ePHI).

In the context of telehealth, HIPAA requires healthcare providers to implement administrative, physical, and technical safeguards to ensure the confidentiality, integrity, and availability of ePHI. This includes measures such as encrypting ePHI, implementing access controls, regularly training employees on HIPAA requirements, and conducting risk assessments to identify potential vulnerabilities.

It is important for healthcare providers offering telehealth services to have a thorough understanding of HIPAA and ensure compliance to protect patient privacy and security.

HITECH Act

The Health Information Technology for Economic and Clinical Health (HITECH) Act, enacted in 2009, reinforces and expands the provisions of HIPAA, especially in relation to electronic health records (EHRs) and technology. The HITECH Act promotes the adoption of EHRs and incentivizes the meaningful use of electronic health information.

From a cybersecurity standpoint, the HITECH Act includes provisions that strengthen the enforcement of HIPAA rules. It empowers the Office for Civil Rights (OCR) to impose significant penalties for non-compliance with HIPAA, including fines for data breaches and violations of privacy and security rules.

Additionally, the HITECH Act introduced the concept of "business associates," entities that work with covered entities and handle ePHI on their behalf. Business associates are also subject to HIPAA regulations and must enter into business associate agreements (BAAs) with covered entities to ensure the protection of ePHI.

Telemedicine Laws and State Regulations

In addition to federal laws like HIPAA and the HITECH Act, telehealth cybersecurity is also governed by a complex web of state laws and regulations. Each state has the authority to regulate telemedicine within its jurisdiction, leading to variations in requirements and standards across different states.

These state laws typically address issues such as licensure, patient consent, prescribing medications remotely, and reimbursement. Some states have specific regulations related to the security and privacy of telehealth services, while others rely on existing laws like HIPAA to govern telemedicine cybersecurity.

Healthcare providers offering telehealth services must be aware of the telemedicine laws and regulations specific to the states in which they operate. This requires staying up-to-date with the evolving landscape of telehealth regulations, as laws and requirements are continually being modified to keep pace with technological advancements and emerging security threats.

Other Relevant Laws and Regulations

Apart from HIPAA, the HITECH Act, and state telemedicine laws, there are other federal laws and regulations that have implications for telehealth cybersecurity:

- **Federal Trade Commission (FTC) Act:** The FTC Act prohibits unfair or deceptive acts or practices in commerce, including healthcare services. The FTC has authority over telehealth providers who engage in deceptive practices related to cybersecurity or fail to adequately protect patient data.
- **Federal Communications Commission (FCC) Regulations:** The FCC plays a role in regulating the telecommunications infrastructure used for telehealth services. They ensure the availability and reliability of broadband networks and promote cybersecurity measures, such as encrypting data transmitted over the network.
- **Drug Enforcement Administration (DEA) Regulations:** For telehealth providers who prescribe controlled substances, compliance with DEA regulations is essential. This includes implementing secure electronic prescribing systems and conducting identity verification and authentication for prescribing practitioners and patients.

Healthcare providers and telehealth platforms must navigate these various laws and regulations to ensure compliance and safeguard patient data.

Implications and Challenges for Telehealth Providers

Complying with the legal and regulatory framework for telehealth cybersecurity presents significant challenges for healthcare providers:

- **Complexity:** The overlapping and constantly evolving laws and regulations can be overwhelming for healthcare providers, especially those operating across multiple states. Staying informed about the latest requirements and understanding how they apply to telehealth practices is essential but time-consuming.
- **Resource Constraints:** Compliance with cybersecurity regulations requires financial and technological resources, which may pose challenges for smaller healthcare providers. Implementing robust security measures, conducting regular risk assessments, and training staff require investments of time and money.

- **Interoperability:** Telehealth providers often rely on multiple technologies and platforms to deliver services. Ensuring interoperability among different systems while maintaining security and privacy can be a complex task. Compatibility issues and vulnerabilities in one system can potentially compromise the entire telehealth ecosystem.

- **Emerging Technologies:** The proliferation of emerging technologies in telehealth, such as remote patient monitoring devices and wearable health trackers, adds another layer of complexity to cybersecurity. Ensuring the security of these devices and protecting the sensitive data they generate is a growing concern.

To overcome these challenges, healthcare providers should prioritize cybersecurity measures, develop comprehensive policies and procedures, and allocate resources to ensure compliance with applicable laws and regulations. Collaboration with legal and cybersecurity professionals can help navigate the complexities of the legal landscape and develop robust cybersecurity programs.

Resources and Best Practices

Given the rapidly evolving nature of telehealth cybersecurity, it is important for healthcare providers to stay informed about the latest laws, regulations, and best practices. Here are some resources to assist healthcare providers in ensuring telehealth cybersecurity compliance:

- HealthIT.gov: The website provides guidance and resources on telehealth, including cybersecurity considerations for healthcare organizations and telehealth providers.

- American Telemedicine Association (ATA): The ATA offers resources and educational materials on telemedicine, including cybersecurity guidelines and best practices.

- National Institute of Standards and Technology (NIST): NIST develops and promotes cybersecurity standards and guidelines applicable to various industries, including healthcare. Their publications provide valuable insights into cybersecurity risk management and mitigation strategies.

Implementing best practices such as conducting regular risk assessments, encrypting data, training employees, and developing an incident response plan can significantly enhance the cybersecurity posture of telehealth providers.

Case Study: Telehealth and the COVID-19 Pandemic

The COVID-19 pandemic has accelerated the adoption of telehealth, with healthcare providers increasingly relying on virtual consultations to ensure continuity of care while minimizing the risk of virus transmission. This sudden surge in telehealth usage has brought unique cybersecurity challenges to the forefront.

During the pandemic, cybercriminals have exploited the increased reliance on telehealth services to launch phishing attacks, ransomware attacks, and other cybersecurity threats. The urgency to deliver care remotely sometimes overrides proper security measures, leading to vulnerabilities in telehealth systems.

To address these challenges, regulatory bodies and industry organizations have released guidance specific to telehealth cybersecurity during the pandemic. These guidelines emphasize the importance of maintaining security and privacy while delivering telehealth services and recommend actions such as encryption, secure authentication, and training for healthcare providers.

The increased focus on telehealth security during the pandemic highlights the critical role of a robust legal and regulatory framework in safeguarding patient data and ensuring the delivery of secure telehealth services.

Exercises

1. Conduct a risk assessment for a telehealth provider, identifying potential vulnerabilities in their system and suggesting appropriate cybersecurity controls to mitigate those risks.

2. Develop a telehealth cybersecurity policy that encompasses the legal and regulatory requirements discussed in this section. Consider the unique challenges of telehealth, such as the use of remote monitoring devices and virtual communication platforms.

3. Research the telemedicine laws and regulations specific to your state and identify any gaps or areas where improvements could be made to enhance telehealth cybersecurity.

4. Interview a healthcare provider who offers telehealth services and discuss the cybersecurity challenges they face in complying with HIPAA, state laws, and other applicable regulations. Share their insights and recommendations for overcoming these challenges.

Conclusion

The legal and regulatory framework for telehealth cybersecurity plays a vital role in protecting patient data and ensuring the integrity and availability of telehealth services. Compliance with laws such as HIPAA and the HITECH Act, along with state telemedicine laws, is essential for healthcare providers offering telehealth services.

The complex and ever-changing nature of telehealth cybersecurity regulations presents challenges for healthcare providers, including the need for resource allocation, navigating interoperability issues, and addressing emerging technologies. However, by prioritizing cybersecurity measures, staying informed about the latest laws and regulations, and implementing best practices, healthcare providers can mitigate risks and secure the future of telehealth.

Secure Communication and Collaboration

Secure Email and Messaging Systems

Encrypting Emails and Attachments

In today's digital age, email has become one of the primary means of communication, both personally and professionally. However, it also poses significant security risks, as emails can easily be intercepted or accessed by unauthorized individuals. To protect sensitive information and ensure the privacy of your emails and attachments, it is essential to encrypt them.

Understanding Email Encryption

Email encryption is a process that scrambles the content of an email and its attachments to make it unreadable to anyone without the decryption key. Encryption ensures that even if an email is intercepted or accessed by unauthorized individuals, the content remains secure and confidential.

There are two primary types of email encryption: symmetric encryption and asymmetric encryption. Symmetric encryption uses a single key to both encrypt and decrypt the email, while asymmetric encryption uses a pair of keys, a public key for encryption and a private key for decryption.

Symmetric Encryption

Symmetric encryption is the simpler form of email encryption. In this method, both the sender and the recipient use the same shared key to encrypt and decrypt the email. The key must be kept secret and securely transmitted to the recipient to ensure the confidentiality of the email.

To encrypt an email using symmetric encryption, you can use various encryption algorithms such as Advanced Encryption Standard (AES) or Triple Data Encryption Standard (3DES). These algorithms apply complex mathematical operations to the email content and attachments, making it virtually impossible for unauthorized individuals to decipher the encrypted data.

Asymmetric Encryption

Asymmetric encryption, also known as public-key encryption, is a more secure but complex method of email encryption. It uses a pair of keys, a public key and a private key, to encrypt and decrypt the email, respectively.

The sender encrypts the email using the recipient's public key, which is freely available to anyone. The encrypted email can only be decrypted using the recipient's private key, which is kept confidential and known only to the recipient. This ensures that only the intended recipient can read the email.

Popular asymmetric encryption algorithms include RSA (Rivest-Shamir-Adleman) and Elliptic Curve Cryptography (ECC). These algorithms offer robust security and are widely used in various encryption applications.

Digital Signatures

In addition to encryption, digital signatures provide an added layer of security to emails. A digital signature verifies the authenticity and integrity of an email, ensuring that it has not been tampered with in transit and comes from the claimed sender.

To create a digital signature, the sender uses their private key to encrypt a hash or a digest of the email's content. The recipient can then use the sender's public key to decrypt the digital signature and compare it with the calculated hash of the received email. If they match, it confirms that the email has not been altered during transmission.

Digital signatures are particularly valuable in preventing spoofing and impersonation attacks. By using digital signatures, recipients can trust the authenticity of the email and be confident that it originated from the claimed sender.

Implementing Email Encryption

To effectively encrypt emails and attachments, you can use various email encryption software and services available in the market. These tools provide user-friendly interfaces and automate the encryption and decryption processes, making it seamless for both the sender and the recipient.

One popular email encryption standard is Pretty Good Privacy (PGP), which is widely used for secure email communication. PGP provides a robust framework for email encryption, digital signatures, and key management. Several email clients and services offer built-in PGP support, allowing you to easily encrypt and sign your emails.

Another widely adopted standard is Secure/Multipurpose Internet Mail Extensions (S/MIME). S/MIME integrates seamlessly with email clients and provides end-to-end encryption and digital signatures. It utilizes X.509 digital certificates to authenticate senders and recipients, ensuring secure communication.

It is important to note that email encryption is only effective when both the sender and the recipient use compatible encryption methods and have the necessary encryption keys. As a sender, it is crucial to verify the recipient's encryption capabilities and securely exchange encryption keys before sending encrypted emails.

Best Practices for Email Encryption

To ensure the security and privacy of your emails and attachments, consider the following best practices for email encryption:

- Use strong encryption algorithms: Choose encryption algorithms with high-security standards, such as AES or RSA, to protect your emails effectively.

- Keep encryption keys secure: Safeguard your encryption keys and never share them with unauthorized individuals. Consider using secure key management solutions to store and manage your keys.

- Regularly update encryption software: Keep your email encryption software up to date to ensure you benefit from the latest security patches and enhancements.

- Verify recipient encryption capabilities: Before sending encrypted emails, verify that the recipient supports email encryption and has the necessary encryption keys.

- Use end-to-end solutions: Consider using comprehensive email encryption solutions that provide end-to-end encryption, digital signatures, and key management functionalities.

- Educate users on email encryption: Train users on the importance of email encryption, how to encrypt emails and attachments, and the significance of securely managing encryption keys.

By adhering to these best practices, you can effectively protect sensitive information, maintain privacy, and securely exchange emails and attachments.

Real-World Example

Let's consider a real-world example to illustrate the importance of email encryption. Emily, a healthcare professional, needs to communicate with her patients via email to provide health-related advice and guidance. Emily understands the importance of protecting patient privacy and ensuring the confidentiality of medical information.

To secure her email communication, Emily decides to use email encryption. She selects an email client that supports PGP encryption and generates a pair of encryption keys—a public key for encryption and a private key for decryption.

Before sending encrypted emails, Emily ensures her patients have compatible email clients and supports PGP encryption. She securely shares her public key with her patients, allowing them to encrypt their emails before sending them to her.

When Emily receives an encrypted email from a patient, she uses her private key to decrypt the email and access its contents securely. Emily can communicate with her patients confidently, knowing that their sensitive medical information remains confidential and protected.

Additional Resources

For further reading on email encryption and its implementation, consider the following resources:

- Schneier, Bruce. *Applied Cryptography: Protocols, Algorithms, and Source Code in C.* John Wiley & Sons, 1995.
- Shelly, Gary B., and Misty E. Vermaat. *Discovering Computers.* Cengage, 2018.
- "Email Encryption." Electronic Frontier Foundation, https://ssd.eff.org/en/module/how-use-pgp-windows.

Remember, email encryption is an essential practice in maintaining the security and privacy of your communications. By incorporating encryption into your email workflows, you can protect sensitive information, prevent unauthorized access, and ensure the confidentiality of your emails and attachments.

Implementing Email Authentication Protocols (SPF, DKIM, DMARC)

In today's digital world, email has become one of the primary means of communication. However, it has also become a prime target for cyber attackers looking to exploit vulnerabilities and gain unauthorized access to sensitive information. To counter these threats, it is essential to implement robust email authentication protocols that can verify the integrity and authenticity of email messages. In this section, we will explore three essential email authentication protocols: SPF, DKIM, and DMARC.

Sender Policy Framework (SPF)

Sender Policy Framework (SPF) is an email authentication protocol that allows the recipient's mail server to verify that the incoming email is sent from an authorized domain. It works by specifying the IP addresses or hostnames authorized to send emails on behalf of a particular domain.

The SPF record is a TXT record published in the domain's DNS settings. It lists all the authorized IP addresses and hostnames, denoted by an SPF mechanism. When an email is received, the recipient's mail server checks the SPF record of the sender's domain to ensure it matches the IP address from which the email originates. If the check fails, the email could be marked as spam or rejected.

SPF provides a simple and effective means of preventing email spoofing and forging, as it verifies the source of the email. It also allows domain owners to set policies on how their emails should be handled when they fail the SPF check.

DomainKeys Identified Mail (DKIM)

DomainKeys Identified Mail (DKIM) is another email authentication protocol that verifies the integrity of the email message and ensures it has not been altered during transit. It uses public-key cryptography to add a digital signature to the email header.

Here's how DKIM works:

1. The sending mail server generates a unique private-public key pair for the domain. 2. The email message header is hashed using a specific algorithm, such as SHA-256 or SHA-1. 3. The generated hash is then encrypted using the private key, creating the digital signature. 4. The digital signature is added to the DKIM-Signature header field in the email. 5. The recipient's mail server retrieves the public key from the domain's DNS records. 6. The mail server verifies the email's integrity by decrypting the digital signature using the public key and comparing it to the hashed email header.

If the signature is valid and matches the hashed header, the email is considered authentic and unaltered. DKIM provides end-to-end authentication, ensuring that even if the email passes through intermediate servers, its integrity is maintained.

Domain-based Message Authentication, Reporting, and Conformance (DMARC)

Domain-based Message Authentication, Reporting, and Conformance (DMARC) is an email authentication protocol that combines the benefits of SPF and DKIM, providing a comprehensive approach to email authentication.

DMARC allows domain owners to set policies on how their emails should be handled if they fail the SPF or DKIM checks. These policies include monitoring, quarantining, or rejecting emails that do not meet the specified authentication criteria.

Here's how DMARC works:

1. The domain owner publishes a DMARC record in their DNS settings, specifying the desired policies and email addresses for receiving DMARC reports. 2. When an email is received, the recipient's mail server checks the SPF and DKIM authentication results. 3. If the email passes both the SPF and DKIM checks, it is delivered to the recipient's inbox. 4. If the email fails either the SPF or DKIM check, the recipient's mail server checks the DMARC policy for further instructions. 5. Based on the DMARC policy, the email may be marked as spam, quarantined, or rejected.

DMARC also provides valuable reporting capabilities by generating reports detailing the authentication results of inbound emails. These reports help domain owners identify and mitigate email authentication issues, strengthen their email security, and monitor for potential abuse.

Best Practices and Considerations

Implementing SPF, DKIM, and DMARC protocols requires careful planning and consideration. Here are some best practices to ensure a successful implementation:

1. Regularly monitor DMARC reports and analyze the authentication results to identify any potential issues. 2. Gradually implement DMARC by starting with a "monitoring only" policy before moving to a "quarantine" or "reject" policy. 3. Test the impact of implementing the protocols on your email deliverability and ensure it doesn't inadvertently affect legitimate email flows. 4. Use a reliable DNS provider to ensure the proper publication of SPF, DKIM, and DMARC records.

5. Keep SPF, DKIM, and DMARC records up to date by reviewing and updating them periodically or when changes occur in your email infrastructure.

By implementing SPF, DKIM, and DMARC, organizations can significantly reduce the risk of email-based attacks and ensure the integrity, authenticity, and proper handling of email messages. These protocols provide a robust defense against email spoofing, phishing attempts, and other malicious activities, enhancing the overall security of your email communication.

Conclusion

In this section, we explored the importance of implementing email authentication protocols, specifically SPF, DKIM, and DMARC. These protocols play a crucial role in verifying the authenticity of emails and ensuring their integrity during transit. By adopting these protocols, organizations can significantly enhance their email security posture and protect their users and sensitive information from cyber threats. Remember to regularly monitor and update your email authentication records to maintain the effectiveness of these protocols.

Secure Instant Messaging and Collaboration Tools

In today's digitally connected world, instant messaging and collaboration tools have become an essential part of communication for individuals and organizations alike. Whether it is for personal use or professional purposes, these tools allow us to connect and collaborate in real-time, regardless of our physical locations. However, with the convenience of instant communication comes the risk of security vulnerabilities and breaches.

Instant messaging and collaboration tools can be susceptible to various security threats, including unauthorized access, data breaches, and malware attacks. Therefore, it is crucial to implement security measures to protect sensitive information and ensure secure communication. In this section, we will explore the key considerations and best practices for using secure instant messaging and collaboration tools.

Understanding the Risks

Before discussing the security measures, let's first understand the risks associated with insecure instant messaging and collaboration tools. Some common risks include:

- **Unauthorized Access:** Without proper security measures, anyone can potentially access your conversations and data.
- **Data Breaches:** Insecure messaging platforms can be vulnerable to data breaches, where sensitive information can be leaked or stolen.
- **Malware Attacks:** Instant messaging platforms can be used to spread malware through malicious links or file attachments.
- **Phishing Attacks:** Attackers may impersonate trusted individuals or organizations to trick users into revealing sensitive information or clicking on malicious links.

Now that we understand the risks, let's explore the best practices for ensuring secure instant messaging and collaboration.

End-to-End Encryption

One of the most critical security measures for instant messaging and collaboration tools is end-to-end encryption. With end-to-end encryption, the communication between users is encrypted from the sender's device to the recipient's device, ensuring that only the intended recipients can access the message content.

End-to-end encryption prevents unauthorized access and minimizes the risk of data breaches. Even if the communication is intercepted, the encrypted content will be meaningless to the attackers without the decryption keys.

Popular instant messaging platforms like Signal, WhatsApp, and Telegram offer end-to-end encryption by default. It is essential to choose platforms that prioritize user privacy and provide strong encryption mechanisms.

Multi-Factor Authentication

To strengthen the security of your instant messaging and collaboration accounts, it is advisable to enable multi-factor authentication (MFA). MFA adds an extra layer of security by requiring users to provide additional verification factors, typically beyond just a password.

Common MFA methods include:

- **One-Time Passwords (OTP):** Users receive a unique code on their registered mobile device, which they need to enter along with their password.
- **Biometric Verification:** Users authenticate using their fingerprint, face recognition, or other biometric identifiers.

- **Hardware Tokens:** Users use physical devices, such as security keys or smart cards, to authenticate their identities.

By enabling MFA, even if an attacker manages to obtain your password, they would still need the additional verification factor to gain access to your account.

Secure File Transfer

In collaborative environments, the ability to share files quickly and securely is crucial. When using instant messaging and collaboration tools, it is important to consider the security of file transfers to protect sensitive information.

Ideally, choose platforms that offer secure file transfer capabilities, ensuring that files are encrypted during transit. Additionally, utilizing file encryption tools or compressing files with passwords before sharing can provide an extra layer of security.

It is also essential to exercise caution when receiving files from unknown senders, as they may contain malware or other malicious content. Always scan files with reliable antivirus software before opening them.

Regular Updates

Keeping your instant messaging and collaboration tools up to date is crucial for maintaining security. Software updates often include security patches and bug fixes that address vulnerabilities discovered in previous versions.

Regularly check for updates and ensure that your instant messaging and collaboration tools are running the latest versions. Additionally, enable automatic updates whenever possible to stay protected from emerging security threats.

Safe Usage Practices

In addition to technical security measures, adopting safe usage practices is equally important when using instant messaging and collaboration tools. Here are some best practices to follow:

- **Verify Contacts:** Before sharing sensitive information or engaging in confidential conversations, verify the identity of the individuals you are communicating with. This helps prevent falling victim to impersonation attacks.

- **Be Cautious with Links and Attachments:** Avoid clicking on suspicious links or downloading file attachments from unknown or untrusted sources. Exercise caution even when the message comes from a known contact, as their account may have been compromised.
- **Avoid Sharing Sensitive Information:** Refrain from sharing confidential or sensitive information, such as passwords or financial details, over instant messaging platforms. Consider using more secure communication methods, such as encrypted emails or secure file sharing platforms, for such sensitive information.
- **Use Public Wi-Fi with Caution:** When using instant messaging and collaboration tools on public Wi-Fi networks, be cautious about potential risks. Public Wi-Fi networks can be easily compromised, so avoid transmitting sensitive information unless you are connected through a secure VPN.
- **Regularly Audit and Remove Unused Accounts:** Periodically review your instant messaging and collaboration accounts and remove any unused or unnecessary accounts. By reducing the number of active accounts, you can minimize the risk of potential security breaches.

Following these safe usage practices helps protect your data and maintain a secure communication environment.

Case Study: The Importance of Secure Instant Messaging in Healthcare

Consider a real-world scenario in the healthcare industry. Healthcare professionals often need to communicate sensitive patient information securely and efficiently. Instant messaging platforms provide a convenient way to collaborate and discuss patient cases with colleagues without the need for face-to-face meetings.

However, without proper security measures, the unauthorized access or exposure of patient information can have severe consequences, ranging from privacy breaches to compromised treatments. Therefore, healthcare organizations must prioritize secure instant messaging solutions and ensure compliance with healthcare privacy regulations, such as the Health Insurance Portability and Accountability Act (HIPAA) in the United States.

By implementing end-to-end encryption, enabling multi-factor authentication, and following safe usage practices, healthcare professionals can maintain the confidentiality and integrity of patient-related communications, minimizing the risk of data breaches and privacy violations.

Conclusion

Secure instant messaging and collaboration tools play a vital role in our digitally connected world. By implementing robust security measures, such as end-to-end encryption, multi-factor authentication, and safe usage practices, individuals and organizations can protect sensitive information, maintain privacy, and ensure secure communication.

Remember, the responsibility to maintain security lies with both the users and the service providers. Stay informed about the latest security practices and choose platforms that prioritize user privacy and data protection. By doing so, we can foster a safer digital environment for instant messaging and collaboration in various sectors, including healthcare, business, and personal communication. Safe communication and collaboration lead to enhanced productivity, improved decision-making, and, most importantly, the protection of sensitive information.

Securing Voice and Video Communication Platforms

Securing voice and video communication platforms is essential in the digital age, especially in the health and wellness industry where sensitive information is often transmitted. This section focuses on the best practices and techniques for ensuring the confidentiality, integrity, and availability of voice and video communication platforms.

Threats to Voice and Video Communication

Voice and video communication systems are susceptible to various threats, including:

- **Eavesdropping:** Unauthorized parties may intercept and listen to conversations, potentially compromising sensitive information.

- **Man-in-the-Middle Attacks:** Attackers can intercept and manipulate the communication between two parties without their knowledge, leading to unauthorized access or data leakage.

- **Denial of Service (DoS) Attacks:** Attackers can flood the communication system with a high volume of requests, rendering it unable to handle legitimate traffic.

- **Call and Video Spoofing:** Attackers can manipulate caller IDs or video feeds to deceive recipients and gain unauthorized access.

To mitigate these threats, several measures can be implemented to secure voice and video communication platforms.

Encryption

Encryption is crucial for ensuring the confidentiality of voice and video communication. It involves the use of cryptographic algorithms to encode communication in such a way that only authorized parties can decrypt and understand it.

End-to-End Encryption is a robust encryption technique that ensures only the intended recipients can access the communication. It encrypts the data at the source and decrypts it at the destination, making it virtually impossible for attackers to eavesdrop or intercept the communication.

Secure Real-Time Transport Protocol (SRTP) is a widely used encryption protocol for securing voice and video communication. It encrypts the media streams between communication endpoints, preventing unauthorized access and tampering.

Transport Layer Security (TLS) can also be employed to secure signaling and control communication between endpoints. It provides authentication and encryption of control messages, protecting against man-in-the-middle attacks.

Authentication and Access Control

Authentication ensures that only authorized users can access voice and video communication platforms. It verifies the identities of the participants and prevents unauthorized access.

Secure Signaling Protocols like Session Initiation Protocol (SIP) can be used for user authentication and registration. SIP allows participants to exchange encryption keys and authenticate each other before establishing a communication session.

Strong User Authentication methods, such as passwords and biometric authentication, should be implemented to ensure that only authenticated individuals can access the communication platform.

Access Control mechanisms should be in place to restrict access to voice and video communication platforms. Only authorized users should have the necessary privileges to initiate or join communication sessions.

Firewalls and Intrusion Detection Systems

Firewalls and intrusion detection systems play a vital role in securing voice and video communication platforms.

Firewalls establish a barrier between the internal network and external networks, monitoring and controlling incoming and outgoing traffic. They can be configured to allow specific protocols and ports required for voice and video communication, while blocking unauthorized access attempts.

Intrusion Detection Systems (IDS) monitor network traffic for suspicious activities or patterns that could indicate a potential attack. They can detect and alert administrators about unauthorized access attempts, DoS attacks, or other malicious activities.

Regular Updates and Patch Management

Keeping voice and video communication platforms updated with the latest security patches is crucial for safeguarding against known vulnerabilities.

Regular Updates should be installed for the operating systems, applications, and firmware used in the communication infrastructure. These updates often include security fixes and enhancements that address known vulnerabilities.

Patch Management processes should be in place to ensure timely deployment of security patches. This includes testing patches in a controlled environment and scheduling their deployment to minimize disruption to communication services.

Employee Training and Awareness

Training employees on the importance of secure voice and video communication is essential in maintaining a secure environment.

Security Awareness Training should cover topics such as recognizing and reporting suspicious activities, avoiding phishing attempts, and adhering to secure communication practices.

Encryption and Authentication Best Practices should be emphasized, educating employees on how to properly use encryption tools, authenticate participants, and identify potential security risks.

Secure Communication Policies and Procedures should be established and clearly communicated to employees. This includes guidelines on choosing strong passwords, securely sharing access credentials, and reporting any security incidents promptly.

Monitoring and Auditing

Effective monitoring and auditing of voice and video communication platforms help detect and respond to security incidents in a timely manner.

Network Traffic Monitoring involves continuously monitoring network traffic for suspicious activities, such as abnormal traffic patterns or unauthorized access attempts. Advanced analytical techniques can be employed to identify potential security threats.

Audit Logs should be enabled for voice and video communication platforms. These logs capture details of communication sessions, allowing administrators to investigate any suspicious activities, perform forensic analysis, and ensure compliance with security policies.

Regular Security Audits should be conducted to evaluate the effectiveness of security controls and identify any vulnerabilities. External security experts can be engaged to perform penetration testing and assess the overall security posture of the communication infrastructure.

Example Scenario: Securing a Healthcare Teleconferencing Platform

Consider a teleconferencing platform used by healthcare professionals to discuss patient cases. It is essential to secure this platform to protect patient privacy and ensure confidential communication.

1. **Encryption:** Implement end-to-end encryption using SRTP to secure the voice and video streams between participants. Ensure the encryption keys are securely managed.
2. **Authentication and Access Control:** Require participants to authenticate themselves using strong, unique passwords. Implement access controls to restrict unauthorized access to the teleconferencing platform.
3. **Firewall and IDS:** Configure the firewall to allow only necessary incoming and outgoing traffic for the teleconferencing platform. Employ an IDS to monitor for any suspicious activities or potential attacks.
4. **Regular Updates and Patch Management:** Keep the teleconferencing platform up to date with the latest security patches to address any known vulnerabilities. Establish a patch management process to ensure timely deployment of patches.
5. **Employee Training and Awareness:** Provide training to healthcare professionals on secure teleconferencing practices, including encryption usage, authentication, and recognizing potential security risks.

6. **Monitoring and Auditing:** Monitor network traffic for any anomalies and enable audit logs to capture details of teleconferencing sessions. Perform regular security audits to identify vulnerabilities and ensure compliance with security policies.

By implementing these security measures, healthcare professionals can securely communicate and collaborate using the teleconferencing platform, protecting patient confidentiality and ensuring compliance with privacy regulations.

Additional Resources

For further information and resources on securing voice and video communication platforms, refer to the following:

- "Secure Communication Systems: Design, Analysis, and Implementation" by Abubakar Sadiq Hussaini.
- "Voice and Video Conferencing Fundamentals" by Scott Firestone, Thiya Ramalingam, and Steve Fry.
- National Institute of Standards and Technology (NIST) publications on securing communication systems (e.g., NIST SP 800-57 Part 1 and Part 2).

Remember, securing voice and video communication platforms is an ongoing process that requires continuous monitoring, updates, and user awareness. By implementing the best practices outlined in this section, organizations can minimize the risks associated with voice and video communication and protect sensitive information in the health and wellness industry.

Best Practices for Secure File Sharing and Document Collaboration

File sharing and document collaboration have become essential in today's digital world. However, it is crucial to ensure the security and confidentiality of shared files and documents, especially in the health and wellness industry. In this section, we will discuss best practices for secure file sharing and document collaboration to protect sensitive information from unauthorized access.

Implement Strong Access Controls

One of the fundamental steps in secure file sharing and document collaboration is to implement strong access controls. This means that only authorized individuals should have access to the shared files and documents. Here are some best practices to consider:

- Use role-based access controls (RBAC) to assign permissions based on job roles and responsibilities. This ensures that individuals only have access to the files and documents necessary for their work.
- Regularly review and update access privileges to reflect changes in job roles or responsibilities of individuals within the organization. This prevents unauthorized access to sensitive information.
- Implement two-factor authentication (2FA) or multi-factor authentication (MFA) to add an extra layer of security. This requires users to provide additional verification, such as a fingerprint or a one-time password, when accessing shared files and documents.

Encrypt Shared Files and Documents

Encryption is an effective way to protect shared files and documents from unauthorized access. By encrypting the data, even if it gets intercepted or accessed by unauthorized parties, it will be in an unreadable format. Here's how you can ensure encryption for shared files and documents:

- Use end-to-end encryption when transferring files, which means the data is encrypted on the sender's device and decrypted only on the recipient's device. This ensures that the data remains encrypted throughout the entire transmission process.
- Utilize strong encryption algorithms, such as AES-256 (Advanced Encryption Standard with a key length of 256 bits), to protect the confidentiality of shared files and documents.
- Implement encryption at rest, which means that the files and documents are encrypted when stored on servers or cloud platforms. This ensures that even if the storage is compromised, the data remains encrypted and inaccessible to unauthorized individuals.

Choose Secure File Sharing and Collaboration Platforms

When selecting a file sharing and collaboration platform, it is crucial to choose a secure and trustworthy solution. Consider the following best practices:

- Select platforms that have robust security features, such as data encryption, access controls, and audit logs. Review their security certifications and industry compliance to ensure they meet the necessary standards for protecting sensitive information.

- Look for platforms that offer granular access controls, allowing you to define permissions at the user, folder, or file level. This ensures that only authorized individuals can view, edit, or share specific files and documents.

- Consider platforms that provide features like access expiration, remote wipe, or watermarking to further enhance the security of shared files and documents.

Train Users on Secure Practices

Even with strong security measures in place, human error can still lead to security breaches. It is essential to provide training and education to users on secure file sharing and document collaboration practices. Here are some key points to cover in user training:

- Emphasize the importance of password security and encourage the use of strong and unique passwords for accessing file sharing and collaboration platforms.

- Educate users on the risks of phishing attacks and social engineering techniques used to trick individuals into disclosing sensitive information. Provide examples and tips on how to identify and report suspicious emails or messages.

- Instruct users on the proper use of file sharing and collaboration platforms, including how to set appropriate access controls, encrypt files, and share documents securely.

- Raise awareness about potential risks of using personal devices or unsecured networks for file sharing and collaboration. Encourage users to use company-approved devices and secure networks whenever possible.

Regularly Update and Patch Systems

To maintain the security of file sharing and document collaboration systems, it is crucial to keep them updated with the latest security patches and software updates.

Regular updates ensure that any vulnerabilities or bugs are fixed, reducing the risk of unauthorized access. Consider the following best practices:

- Enable automatic updates for file sharing and collaboration software to ensure that the latest security patches are applied promptly.
- Regularly monitor and review security advisories from the vendors of file sharing and collaboration platforms to stay informed about any new vulnerabilities or security updates.
- Develop a patch management process that includes testing updates in a controlled environment before deploying them to the production environment. This helps minimize any potential disruptions caused by updates.

Monitor and Audit File Sharing Activities

Monitoring and auditing file sharing activities can help detect and prevent unauthorized access or data breaches. Here are some best practices for effective monitoring and auditing:

- Implement logging and monitoring mechanisms that track file access, modifications, and sharing activities. This helps identify any suspicious or unauthorized activities.
- Regularly review access logs and monitor for any unusual patterns or behaviors that may indicate a security breach.
- Conduct periodic security audits to assess the effectiveness of security controls and identify any potential vulnerabilities or weaknesses in the file sharing and collaboration systems.

Example Scenario: Secure File Sharing in a Healthcare Organization

Imagine a healthcare organization that needs to securely share patient records with authorized healthcare professionals. They have implemented the following best practices for secure file sharing and document collaboration:

- Access controls: The organization ensures that only authorized healthcare professionals, such as doctors and nurses, have access to patient records. They use RBAC to assign appropriate permissions based on job roles.

- Encryption: All patient records are encrypted using strong encryption algorithms when in transit and at rest. This ensures that the records remain secure even if intercepted or accessed without authorization.
- Secure file sharing platform: The organization opts for a secure file sharing platform that provides end-to-end encryption, granular access controls, and necessary security certifications and compliance.
- User training: Healthcare professionals undergo regular training on secure file sharing practices, including password security, identifying phishing attacks, and using the file sharing platform securely.
- Regular updates and patches: The organization keeps the file sharing platform up to date by enabling automatic updates and regularly reviewing security advisories from the vendor.
- Monitoring and auditing: The organization implements logging and monitoring mechanisms to track file access and sharing activities. They conduct regular security audits to ensure the effectiveness of security controls.

By following these best practices, the healthcare organization can ensure the secure sharing of patient records, protecting sensitive information and maintaining the confidentiality of patient data.

Resources and Further Reading

For more information on secure file sharing and document collaboration, the following resources may be helpful:

1. National Institute of Standards and Technology (NIST) Special Publication 800-171: "Protecting Controlled Unclassified Information in Nonfederal Systems and Organizations"
2. Health Insurance Portability and Accountability Act (HIPAA) Security Rule
3. European Union General Data Protection Regulation (EU GDPR)
4. Cloud Security Alliance (CSA) guidance on file sharing and collaboration security

5. OWASP Secure File Upload Cheat Sheet: `https://cheatsheetseries.owasp.org/cheatsheets/File_Upload_Cheat_Sheet.html`

Remember, secure file sharing and document collaboration are critical components of cybersecurity in the health and wellness industry. By implementing these best practices, you can minimize the risks of unauthorized access, data breaches, and protect sensitive information.

Secure Collaboration Tools for Health and Wellness Professionals

In today's digitally connected world, collaboration among health and wellness professionals is crucial for providing optimal care and ensuring the overall wellbeing of individuals. However, with the increasing prevalence of cyber threats and attacks, it is essential to use secure collaboration tools to protect sensitive information and maintain the confidentiality of patient data. This section will explore the various secure collaboration tools available to health and wellness professionals, highlighting their features, benefits, and best practices for implementation.

Secure Messaging Systems

One of the most commonly used collaboration tools in the healthcare industry is secure messaging systems. These platforms offer encrypted messaging capabilities, ensuring that communication between healthcare professionals remains confidential and secure. Additionally, secure messaging systems often come with features such as message recall, message expiration, and secure file sharing, further enhancing collaboration.

For example, the HIPAA-compliant secure messaging app MedSecureChat allows healthcare professionals to securely communicate and share patient information. It uses end-to-end encryption and requires user authentication to ensure that only authorized individuals can access the messages. Furthermore, this app incorporates features like read receipts and message recall, enabling efficient and secure communication.

When using secure messaging systems, it is important to adhere to best practices. First, healthcare professionals should ensure that they are using a system that complies with relevant privacy regulations, such as HIPAA in the United States. Additionally, strong access controls, such as two-factor authentication, should be implemented to prevent unauthorized access. Users should also be cautious when sharing sensitive information and verify the recipient's identity to avoid accidental data breaches.

Collaboration and Document Sharing Platforms

Collaboration and document sharing platforms are valuable tools for health and wellness professionals who need to work together on projects, share documents, and collaborate remotely. These platforms offer features such as real-time document editing, version control, and secure file sharing, allowing healthcare professionals to collaborate effectively while maintaining data security.

One prominent example is Microsoft Teams, an all-in-one collaboration platform that integrates chat, video meetings, file storage, and application integration. Teams provides a secure environment for collaboration, with encrypted communication channels and robust data protection measures. Additionally, it allows for seamless integration with other Microsoft Office applications, making it a convenient choice for healthcare professionals accustomed to using these tools.

When using collaboration and document sharing platforms, it is crucial to follow security best practices. Users should always review and understand the privacy and security settings of the platform they are using. It is important to restrict access to shared documents and ensure that only authorized individuals can view or edit sensitive information. Regularly updating and patching these platforms is also vital to address any security vulnerabilities.

Virtual Meeting and Video Conferencing Platforms

In the age of telehealth and remote work, virtual meeting and video conferencing platforms have become indispensable for health and wellness professionals. These tools allow individuals to conduct secure and private video conferences, enabling remote consultations, team meetings, and collaborations.

Zoom is a widely recognized video conferencing platform that provides end-to-end encryption for secure video calls. It offers extensive controls to prevent unauthorized access and also allows participants to join meetings via a unique meeting ID or password. Additionally, Zoom provides features like virtual backgrounds and screen sharing, enhancing the overall user experience.

To ensure secure virtual meetings and video conferences, healthcare professionals should consider implementing the following measures. First, they should select platforms that offer robust encryption and privacy features. It is important to protect meeting links and passwords, only sharing them with authorized participants. Healthcare professionals should also be aware of the potential for "Zoom bombing" or other similar security threats and take steps to mitigate the risks. This can include using waiting rooms, enabling meeting registration, and locking meetings once all participants have joined.

Best Practices for Secure Collaboration

While using secure collaboration tools is essential, it is equally important to follow best practices to maintain data security and privacy. Here are some general guidelines that health and wellness professionals should consider:

- Regularly update collaboration tools and applications to ensure they are equipped with the latest security patches and features.

- Use strong, unique passwords for all collaboration accounts and enable two-factor authentication whenever possible.

- Train all staff members on the proper and secure use of collaboration tools, emphasizing the importance of data protection and privacy.

- Establish policies and procedures for sharing and storing sensitive data, including guidelines on secure file sharing and data retention.

- Regularly review access permissions to collaboration platforms, ensuring that only authorized individuals have access to sensitive information.

- Monitor collaboration platforms for any suspicious activities or unauthorized access and promptly respond to any identified security incidents.

By following these best practices, health and wellness professionals can ensure that their collaboration efforts are secure, protecting patient data and upholding confidentiality.

Case Study: Secure Collaboration in a Telehealth Setting

Consider the scenario of a group of healthcare professionals working in a telehealth setting. They need to securely collaborate on patient care plans, share medical records, and communicate effectively. Here's how they can leverage secure collaboration tools:

1. **Secure Messaging Systems:** The healthcare professionals can use a secure messaging app, like MedSecureChat, to exchange patient information securely, ask questions, and discuss treatment plans. They can leverage features like message recall in case of accidental data sharing.

2. **Collaboration and Document Sharing Platforms:** The team can utilize collaboration platforms, such as Microsoft Teams, to jointly review and edit documents, access patient records, and update care plans in real-time. They can ensure that each document has the appropriate access controls, limiting visibility to authorized personnel only.

3. **Virtual Meeting and Video Conferencing Platforms:** Telehealth sessions and team meetings can be conducted using secure video conferencing tools like Zoom. The professionals can ensure that meetings are password-protected, use waiting rooms to verify participant identities, and lock meetings once everyone has joined.

By incorporating these secure collaboration tools into their telehealth workflow, the healthcare professionals can maintain the privacy and security of patient information while effectively collaborating on patient care.

Conclusion

Secure collaboration tools play a vital role in maintaining the privacy and security of patient information in the health and wellness industry. By utilizing secure messaging systems, collaboration and document sharing platforms, and virtual meeting and video conferencing platforms, healthcare professionals can effectively collaborate while ensuring the confidentiality of sensitive data. It is crucial to follow best practices, regularly update and patch these tools, and train all staff members on secure collaboration techniques. Through the use of secure collaboration tools and proper security measures, health and wellness professionals can enhance their teamwork, ultimately benefiting the overall wellbeing of their patients.

Protecting Sensitive Information During Communication and Collaboration

In today's digital age, effective communication and collaboration are vital for the success of any organization in the health and wellness industry. However, it is equally important to ensure that sensitive information remains protected during these processes. This section will discuss various strategies and best practices for safeguarding sensitive information during communication and collaboration, helping you maintain the confidentiality and integrity of your data.

Understanding the Importance of Protecting Sensitive Information

Sensitive information in the health and wellness industry includes personal health records, financial data, proprietary research, and intellectual property. Breaches of such information can have severe consequences, including identity theft, reputational damage, and regulatory non-compliance. Therefore, it is crucial to understand the significance of protecting sensitive information.

One way to classify sensitive information is by its level of sensitivity. This can be done by assessing the potential impact of unauthorized disclosure, alteration, or destruction of the information. Additionally, it is important to identify the legal and regulatory requirements specific to your organization regarding the protection of sensitive information.

Implementing Encryption for Secure Communication

Encryption is a powerful tool for protecting sensitive information during communication and collaboration. By encrypting data, you ensure that only authorized individuals can access and understand it. This is achieved by converting the original information into an unreadable format using cryptographic algorithms.

End-to-end encryption is particularly relevant when sharing sensitive information between individuals or organizations. In this method, the information remains encrypted from the sender to the recipient, minimizing the risk of interception and exposure to unauthorized parties.

There are several encryption methods available, including symmetric encryption and asymmetric encryption. Symmetric encryption uses a single key for both encryption and decryption, while asymmetric encryption involves a pair of keys: a public key for encryption and a private key for decryption. Implementing strong encryption algorithms and key management practices will enhance the security of your sensitive information.

Secure Document and File Sharing Practices

Document and file sharing are common activities in the health and wellness industry, especially when collaborating with other professionals or sharing information with patients. To protect sensitive information during these activities, it is necessary to follow secure document and file sharing practices.

First, ensure that the platforms or tools you use for sharing documents and files are secure and offer the necessary encryption and access controls. Avoid using insecure file transfer methods, such as unencrypted email attachments or file-sharing services with lax security measures.

Second, consider implementing access controls to restrict who can view, edit, or download shared documents and files. This can involve using password protection, granting specific permissions to individuals, or employing digital rights management (DRM) solutions.

Third, regularly review and audit shared documents and files to identify any unauthorized access or suspicious activities. By monitoring who accesses and modifies sensitive information, you can detect and respond to any potential security breaches in a timely manner.

Role-based Access Control and User Authentication

Protecting sensitive information during communication and collaboration requires implementing proper user authentication and role-based access control (RBAC) measures. RBAC restricts access to sensitive information based on users' roles and responsibilities within the organization.

Implementing RBAC ensures that only authorized individuals have access to sensitive information, based on the principle of least privilege. Different roles within the organization may have different levels of access, and access permissions should be regularly reviewed and updated as needed.

User authentication mechanisms, such as passwords, multi-factor authentication (MFA), and biometric authentication, further enhance the security of sensitive information. Strong and unique passwords, coupled with additional authentication factors such as fingerprint or facial recognition, provide an additional layer of security in the event that passwords are compromised.

Regularly educating users about the importance of strong passwords, avoiding password reuse, and being vigilant against phishing attacks can significantly reduce the risk of unauthorized access to sensitive information.

Training and Awareness for Secure Communication and Collaboration

One of the most effective ways to protect sensitive information during communication and collaboration is by fostering a culture of security awareness within your organization. This involves providing regular training and education to employees on secure communication and collaboration practices.

Training sessions should cover topics such as best practices for encryption, secure document sharing, RBAC, user authentication, and identifying and reporting potential security threats. Real-world examples and case studies can help illustrate the consequences of mishandling sensitive information and emphasize the importance of following security protocols.

Furthermore, it is essential to create a feedback mechanism, encouraging employees to report any security concerns or suspicious activities regarding communication and collaboration. This allows for prompt investigation and response, minimizing the potential impact of security incidents.

Summary

Protecting sensitive information during communication and collaboration requires a comprehensive approach that incorporates encryption, secure document sharing practices, RBAC, user authentication, and ongoing training and awareness. By implementing these strategies, you can ensure the confidentiality, integrity, and availability of sensitive information in the health and wellness industry.

Remember, protecting sensitive information is not a one-time effort but an ongoing process. Regularly review and update your security measures to adapt to emerging threats and maintain a proactive stance against potential cybersecurity risks. By doing so, you contribute to a safer and more secure digital environment for everyone involved in health and wellness.

Employee Training and Awareness for Secure Communication and Collaboration

Employee training and awareness play a crucial role in ensuring secure communication and collaboration within an organization. By providing employees with the necessary knowledge and skills, organizations can significantly reduce the risk of security breaches and protect sensitive information from falling into the wrong hands. In this section, we will explore the importance of employee training and awareness for secure communication and collaboration, as well as some key strategies and best practices to implement.

Understanding the Importance of Employee Training and Awareness

Employees are often the weakest link in the cybersecurity chain. They may unknowingly engage in behaviors that put the organization at risk, such as clicking on phishing emails, using weak passwords, or sharing sensitive information with unauthorized individuals. Therefore, it is crucial to provide employees with the necessary training and raise their awareness about the importance of secure communication and collaboration.

Training employees on secure communication and collaboration practices not only helps protect sensitive data but also enhances the overall security posture of the organization. When employees understand the risks and consequences of their actions, they are more likely to adopt secure behaviors, report potential security incidents, and actively contribute to maintaining a secure working environment.

Key Training Strategies for Secure Communication and Collaboration

When developing a training program for secure communication and collaboration, it is important to consider the specific needs and requirements of the organization. Here are some key strategies and best practices to implement:

1. **Tailor training to different job roles:** Different job roles may have varying levels of exposure to cybersecurity risks. Tailoring the training content to address the specific needs and responsibilities of each role ensures that employees receive the most relevant and effective training.

2. **Use real-world examples and case studies:** Simulating real-world scenarios and providing examples of recent security breaches can help employees understand the potential consequences of their actions and make them more vigilant. Case studies can also provide practical insights into how secure communication and collaboration practices can mitigate risks.

3. **Interactive and engaging training methods:** Traditional classroom-style training may not be as effective in capturing employees' attention and promoting learning. Consider incorporating interactive elements, such as quizzes, games, simulations, and hands-on exercises, to actively engage employees and make the training more enjoyable.

4. **Regular training sessions and refreshers:** Cybersecurity threats and best practices are constantly evolving. Ongoing training sessions and periodic refreshers help ensure that employees stay up to date with the latest security trends and are aware of any new risks or vulnerabilities.

5. **Promote a culture of security awareness:** Security awareness should not be limited to formal training sessions. Encourage employees to report suspicious activities, provide incentives for good security practices, and create an open environment where employees feel comfortable discussing security concerns.

6. **Provide resources and support:** Make sure employees have easy access to resources such as user manuals, guidelines, and frequently asked questions related to secure communication and collaboration tools. Establish a support system where employees can seek assistance or clarification on security-related matters.

Best Practices for Secure Communication and Collaboration

In addition to training, organizations should implement best practices for secure communication and collaboration. These practices should be reinforced through regular reminders, policy enforcement, and technical controls. Here are some key best practices to consider:

- **Use strong authentication mechanisms:** Implement multi-factor authentication (MFA) to add an extra layer of security when accessing sensitive information or collaborating with others.

- **Encrypt sensitive data:** Utilize encryption technologies to protect sensitive information during transmission and storage. This ensures that even if data is intercepted, it remains unreadable and unusable to unauthorized individuals.

- **Be cautious of email communications:** Train employees to be vigilant when handling emails, especially those containing attachments or links. Encourage them to verify the authenticity of emails and avoid clicking on suspicious links or downloading attachments from unknown sources.

- **Secure file sharing:** Use secure file sharing platforms or encryption techniques when sharing sensitive documents externally. Ensure that access controls are in place to restrict unauthorized access.

- **Collaborate securely:** When collaborating with external parties, implement secure collaboration tools and establish guidelines for sharing information. Clearly define roles and permissions to control access to sensitive data.

- **Secure video conferencing:** When conducting video conferences, ensure the use of secure platforms that utilize encryption and authentication mechanisms. Share meeting links and passwords securely only with authorized participants.

- **Regularly update software and systems:** Keep all communication and collaboration tools up to date with the latest security patches and updates.

Outdated software may contain vulnerabilities that can be exploited by attackers.

- **Report and respond to security incidents:** Train employees on the proper procedures for reporting security incidents. Establish clear lines of communication and response processes to mitigate the impact of potential breaches.

The Role of Employees in Maintaining Security

Employees play a critical role in maintaining the security of an organization's communication and collaboration systems. By following secure practices and being vigilant, employees can significantly reduce the risk of security breaches. Here are a few key responsibilities employees should be aware of:

- **Password hygiene:** Employees should create strong, unique passwords and avoid sharing them with others. Passwords should be changed regularly and not reused across multiple accounts.

- **Phishing awareness:** Employees should be able to recognize phishing attempts and suspicious communications. They should refrain from clicking on unknown links or providing sensitive information in response to suspicious requests.

- **Privacy and confidentiality:** Employees should understand the importance of protecting sensitive information and abide by privacy and confidentiality policies. Sharing sensitive information with unauthorized individuals or discussing confidential matters in insecure environments should be strictly avoided.

- **Awareness of security policies:** Employees should familiarize themselves with the organization's security policies and guidelines for communication and collaboration. They should follow these policies and report any violations or potential risks to the appropriate channels.

- **Reporting incidents:** Employees should report any suspicious activities, security incidents, or potential breaches to the designated IT or security personnel. This allows for timely response and mitigation of the incident.

Conclusion

Employee training and awareness are essential for maintaining secure communication and collaboration within organizations. By providing employees with the necessary knowledge and skills and promoting a culture of security awareness, organizations can significantly reduce the risk of security breaches and protect sensitive information. Implementing best practices and encouraging employees to take an active role in maintaining security will create a more resilient and secure working environment. Remember, cybersecurity is a shared responsibility, and every employee plays a crucial role in protecting sensitive data and maintaining a secure organization.

Monitoring and Auditing Communication and Collaboration Platforms

Effective monitoring and auditing of communication and collaboration platforms is crucial for maintaining the security and privacy of sensitive information in the health and wellness industry. These platforms, such as email systems, instant messaging tools, and file sharing platforms, are used extensively for communication among healthcare professionals and patients. However, they can also become entry points for cyber attacks and data breaches if not properly monitored and audited.

Understanding the Importance of Monitoring and Auditing

Monitoring and auditing communication and collaboration platforms provide several benefits. It allows organizations to detect and respond to security incidents in a timely manner, ensuring that any unauthorized access or suspicious activities are identified and addressed promptly. Additionally, monitoring and auditing help organizations demonstrate compliance with relevant cybersecurity laws, regulations, and industry standards.

By monitoring and auditing these platforms, healthcare organizations can identify potential vulnerabilities and weaknesses in their systems, networks, and processes. This enables them to proactively implement appropriate controls and measures to prevent security incidents and maintain the integrity, confidentiality, and availability of their communication and collaboration platforms.

Types of Monitoring and Auditing

There are various methods and techniques for monitoring and auditing communication and collaboration platforms. Some common approaches include:

1. **Log Monitoring:** Monitoring logs generated by communication and collaboration platforms can provide valuable insights into security events and activities, such as login attempts, file transfers, and message exchanges. By analyzing these logs, organizations can identify any abnormal or suspicious behaviors and take appropriate actions.

2. **Network Traffic Analysis:** Analyzing network traffic within the organization can help detect any unusual patterns or anomalies that may indicate a security incident. Network traffic analysis tools can capture and analyze data packets to identify potential threats or unauthorized access attempts.

3. **User Activity Monitoring:** Monitoring user activity on communication and collaboration platforms can help identify any unauthorized or inappropriate actions. This can include monitoring file access, message content, and user behavior patterns. User activity monitoring can be performed through centralized logging, endpoint monitoring, or user behavior analytics (UBA) tools.

4. **Data Loss Prevention (DLP):** Implementing DLP solutions can help prevent the unauthorized transfer or leakage of sensitive data through communication and collaboration platforms. DLP tools can identify and classify sensitive information, enforce data handling policies, and prevent data exfiltration.

5. **Penetration Testing and Vulnerability Assessments:** Periodic penetration testing and vulnerability assessments can identify potential weaknesses and vulnerabilities in communication and collaboration platforms. By simulating real-world cyber attacks, organizations can evaluate the effectiveness of their security controls and identify areas for improvement.

6. **Audit Trails and Records:** Maintaining audit trails and records of activities on communication and collaboration platforms is essential for accountability and compliance purposes. These records can provide a documented history of user actions, system changes, and security incidents, facilitating incident investigations and ensuring regulatory compliance.

Best Practices for Monitoring and Auditing

To ensure effective monitoring and auditing of communication and collaboration platforms, healthcare organizations should consider following these best practices:

- **Establish Clear Logging and Monitoring Policies:** Define and implement clear policies and procedures for logging and monitoring activities on communication and collaboration platforms. This includes specifying what should be logged, how long logs should be retained, and who has access to the logs.

- **Automate Monitoring and Alerting:** Utilize automated monitoring and alerting systems to promptly detect and respond to security events. These systems can generate alerts or notifications when predefined thresholds or suspicious activities are detected, enabling immediate investigation and remediation.

- **Regularly Review and Analyze Logs:** Routinely review and analyze logs generated by communication and collaboration platforms to identify any abnormal or suspicious activities. Implement log aggregation and analysis tools to simplify this process and enable centralized monitoring.

- **Implement User Behavior Analytics (UBA):** User behavior analytics tools can help identify anomalous user behavior on communication and collaboration platforms. By establishing baseline user activity patterns, UBA tools can detect and alert on any deviations from normal behavior, such as unauthorized access attempts or data exfiltration.

- **Encrypt Logs and Audit Trails:** Ensure that logs and audit trails are encrypted to protect the integrity and confidentiality of the recorded information. This prevents unauthorized access or tampering of logs, ensuring their reliability and usefulness during incident investigations and audits.

- **Regularly Update and Patch Monitoring Tools:** Keep monitoring tools up to date with the latest security patches and updates. This helps address any known vulnerabilities in the monitoring systems themselves and ensures their effectiveness in detecting and responding to security incidents.

- **Perform Regular Penetration Testing:** Conduct periodic penetration testing exercises to assess the effectiveness of security controls on communication and collaboration platforms. This helps identify any potential weaknesses or vulnerabilities that could be exploited by attackers.

- **Educate Employees on Monitoring and Auditing Policies:** Provide training and awareness programs to educate employees on the importance of monitoring and auditing communication and collaboration platforms. This includes educating employees on recognizing suspicious activities, reporting security incidents, and adhering to established monitoring and auditing policies.

- **Document and Retain Audit Trail Records:** Maintain detailed records of audit trail activities and retain them for the required period as per legal, regulatory, and industry requirements. These records should be securely stored and easily accessible for incident investigations and compliance audits.

Case Study: Detecting and Responding to Insider Threats

An employee working in a healthcare organization accessed confidential patient records without valid authorization using the organization's internal messaging platform. The organization had implemented monitoring and auditing mechanisms to detect such incidents.

The monitoring system flagged the employee's activities as suspicious, as it identified multiple attempts to access patient records outside the employee's normal job responsibilities. An alert was automatically generated and sent to the organization's security team.

Upon receiving the alert, the security team quickly initiated an investigation. They analyzed the employee's access logs, communication history, and other correlated data to gather evidence. The audit trail also provided insights into the employee's interactions with other staff members and potential collaborators.

Based on their findings, the security team confronted the employee and terminated their access to sensitive systems immediately. The organization took appropriate action, including notifying the affected patients and initiating legal proceedings against the employee.

This case study demonstrates the importance of proactive monitoring and auditing. By having effective monitoring and auditing mechanisms in place, the organization was able to detect and respond to the insider threat incident promptly, minimizing the potential impact on patient privacy and preventing further unauthorized access.

Secure Social Media Usage

Risks of Personal Data Exposure on Social Media

In today's digital age, social media has become an integral part of our lives. We use platforms like Facebook, Twitter, and Instagram to connect with friends, share our thoughts, and express ourselves. However, it is important to be aware of the risks associated with sharing personal information on social media.

1. Privacy Settings and Account Protection: Before delving into the risks, it is crucial to understand the importance of properly configuring privacy settings on social media platforms. Adjusting these settings allows you to control who can see your posts, photos, and personal information. It is essential to review and update these settings regularly to ensure that your data remains private.

2. Personal Data Exposure: One of the major risks of sharing personal information on social media is the potential exposure of sensitive data. By posting personal details such as your full name, address, phone number, or date of birth, you are providing a treasure trove of information to potential hackers and cybercriminals. This data can be used for identity theft, phishing attacks, or other fraudulent activities.

3. Social Engineering Attacks: Another risk associated with personal data exposure on social media is the increased susceptibility to social engineering attacks. Cybercriminals can gather information from your social media profiles to create targeted phishing emails or manipulate you into revealing sensitive information. For example, they might impersonate a friend or acquaintance and ask for personal details, banking information, or passwords.

4. Reputation and Image Damage: Sharing personal information, photos, or opinions on social media can have long-lasting consequences. Employers, educational institutions, or potential future partners often search social media profiles for information about individuals. Revealing too much information or posting inappropriate content can damage your reputation and affect future opportunities.

5. Location Tracking: Many social media platforms allow you to check-in at different locations or share your current whereabouts. While this feature may seem innocent, it can also pose risks to your privacy and personal safety. Sharing your location publicly can make you a target for physical threats or burglaries, especially if your home address is easily accessible.

6. Third-Party Data Collection: Social media platforms often collect and share user data with third-party advertisers and marketers. This can lead to targeted advertising, personalized content, and potential data breaches. It is important to

review the privacy policies of social media platforms and understand what data is being collected and how it is being used.

7. Oversharing and Overexposure: It is essential to exercise caution when sharing personal information or intimate details on social media. Oversharing can not only jeopardize your privacy and personal safety but also leave you vulnerable to online stalking, harassment, or cyberbullying. It is important to think twice before sharing personal experiences, financial information, or private conversations.

To protect your personal information on social media, consider the following tips:

1. Review and update privacy settings regularly to ensure your personal data is only visible to trusted connections. 2. Be mindful of the information you share online and avoid revealing sensitive details such as your full address or contact information. 3. Use strong and unique passwords for your social media accounts, and enable two-factor authentication for an extra layer of security. 4. Be cautious of friend requests or messages from unknown individuals, as they may be attempting to gather personal information or engage in social engineering attacks. 5. Regularly monitor your social media profiles for any suspicious or unauthorized activity. 6. Avoid posting location updates or check-ins that may compromise your personal safety. 7. Educate yourself about the privacy policies and data collection practices of social media platforms to make informed decisions about sharing personal information.

By understanding the risks associated with personal data exposure on social media and implementing these protective measures, you can ensure a safer and more secure online presence. Remember, your personal information is valuable, and it is always better to be cautious and proactive in safeguarding it. Stay informed, stay vigilant, and enjoy the benefits of social media without compromising your privacy.

Secure Privacy Settings and Account Protection

In this section, we will explore the importance of securing privacy settings and protecting user accounts in the context of health and wellness. Given the increasing reliance on digital platforms and the potential risks of data breaches, it is crucial to take proactive measures to safeguard sensitive personal information. We will discuss various techniques and best practices that can be employed to enhance the security of privacy settings and protect user accounts.

Understanding the Importance of Privacy Settings

Privacy settings are a critical aspect of managing the accessibility of personal information shared on various online platforms. They allow users to control who can access their data and what can be seen or shared. In the context of health and wellness, protecting the privacy of personal health information is of utmost importance. Therefore, understanding and appropriately configuring privacy settings is essential to maintain confidentiality and prevent unauthorized access.

By utilizing privacy settings effectively, users can limit the visibility of their profiles, posts, and personal information to only trusted individuals or networks. This ensures that sensitive health-related data remains confidential and prevents potential misuse.

Configuring Privacy Settings on Social Media

One area where strong privacy settings are crucial is social media platforms. These platforms often provide granular control over who can view and interact with user profiles and posts. Some important considerations when configuring privacy settings on social media include:

- **Profile Visibility:** Review and configure the visibility of your profile, including profile pictures, personal information, and contact details. Limit the accessibility to friends or trusted connections only.

- **Post Visibility:** Choose the audience for each post, ensuring that health-related posts or sensitive information are shared with a select group of individuals or restricted to private settings.

- **Tagging and Mentions:** Manage the settings related to tagging and mentions. It is advisable to review and approve tags before they appear on your profile to maintain control over the content associated with your account.

- **Third-Party Apps:** Monitor and manage the permissions and access granted to third-party applications integrated with social media accounts. Remove any unnecessary or suspicious applications that could potentially compromise your privacy.

Regularly reviewing and updating privacy settings on social media platforms can provide an added layer of protection for personal information, ensuring that only intended recipients have access to it.

Securing Account Credentials

While privacy settings play a vital role in protecting personal information, it is equally important to secure the user accounts themselves. Weak or compromised account credentials can lead to unauthorized access and potential data breaches. Here are some best practices to safeguard account credentials:

- **Strong and Unique Passwords:** Use strong, complex passwords that are not easily guessable. Avoid using common words or personal information. It is advisable to use a combination of uppercase and lowercase letters, numbers, and special characters. Furthermore, each account should have a unique password to prevent a single breach from compromising multiple accounts.
- **Multi-Factor Authentication (MFA):** Enable multi-factor authentication whenever possible. This adds an additional layer of security by requiring a second form of verification, such as a code sent to a mobile device, along with the account password.
- **Avoiding Phishing Attempts:** Be cautious of phishing attempts, where attackers masquerade as legitimate entities to trick users into revealing their account credentials. Practice vigilance when clicking on links or downloading attachments from unsolicited emails or suspicious websites.
- **Regularly Update Credentials:** As a precautionary measure, periodically update passwords and security questions associated with user accounts. This reduces the risk of unauthorized access, particularly if a data breach has occurred on a third-party platform that the user interacts with.

Implementing these practices for securing account credentials significantly enhances the overall security of user accounts and reduces the likelihood of unauthorized access.

Ongoing Account Monitoring

In addition to configuring privacy settings and securing account credentials, it is crucial to monitor user accounts regularly. This proactive approach allows for the detection and response to any suspicious activities or potential security breaches. Some recommendations for ongoing account monitoring are:

- **Account Activity Notifications:** Enable account activity notifications, which alert users of any unusual login attempts or changes to account settings. These notifications help users identify potential security breaches promptly.

- **Regularly Review Account Activity:** Periodically review account activity logs to check for any unauthorized access or suspicious activities. Look for any unfamiliar devices, locations, or login timestamps.
- **Suspicious Content Reporting:** Be proactive in reporting any suspicious content, contacts, or messages to the platform administrators. This helps in the identification and mitigation of potential security risks.
- **Stay Informed of Security Threats:** Stay updated on the latest security threats and vulnerabilities. By being aware of emerging risks, users can take appropriate preventive measures to protect their accounts.

By regularly monitoring user accounts, individuals can quickly respond to potential security incidents and take necessary action to protect their personal information.

Educating Users on Privacy and Account Security

Educating users about the importance of privacy and account security is paramount in enhancing overall cybersecurity. Promoting awareness and providing guidance on best practices empowers individuals to actively protect their personal information. Some effective educational strategies include:

- **User Awareness Campaigns:** Conduct user awareness campaigns to highlight the importance of privacy and account security. Use real-world examples and case studies to demonstrate potential risks and their implications.
- **Online Training Resources:** Provide online training resources, such as videos, tutorials, and interactive modules, that educate users on configuring privacy settings, securing account credentials, and identifying potential threats.
- **Security Guidelines and Policies:** Develop and share comprehensive security guidelines and policies that outline the expectations and requirements for protecting personal information. Make these resources easily accessible to users.
- **Regular Training and Refreshers:** Offer regular training sessions and refresher courses to ensure that individuals are up-to-date with the latest privacy and security practices. Continual education is vital in addressing evolving cyber threats.

Through user education initiatives, individuals can develop a strong understanding of privacy and account security, making them proactive participants in their own cybersecurity.

Case Study: Protecting Personal Information on a Health and Wellness Platform

Consider the case of a health and wellness platform that allows users to track their exercise routines, calorie intake, and monitor their overall well-being. To protect personal information on this platform, the following privacy settings and account protection measures can be implemented:

- Privacy Settings:
  - Configure the profile visibility to only trusted connections or a selected group of individuals within the platform.
  - Ensure that the health-related data recorded on the platform is not shared with the public and is accessible only to the user or specified individuals.
  - Limit the visibility of personal achievements or goals to maintain privacy.
- Account Protection:
  - Enforce the use of strong and unique passwords for user accounts on the platform.
  - Encourage users to enable multi-factor authentication to enhance account security.
  - Monitor account activity logs regularly to identify any unauthorized access or suspicious activities.
  - Provide clear instructions and guidance on reporting any privacy concerns or security incidents.

By implementing these measures, the health and wellness platform can ensure that users' personal information remains secure and their privacy is respected.

Conclusion

In summary, securing privacy settings and protecting user accounts are essential for safeguarding personal information in the digital landscape of health and wellness. Configuring privacy settings appropriately on various platforms, securing account credentials, ongoing account monitoring, and user education are key practices to enhance privacy and security. By following these best practices, individuals can maintain control over their personal information, mitigate potential risks, and enjoy a safer online experience in the health and wellness domain.

Recognizing and Avoiding Social Engineering Attacks on Social Media

In the digital age, social media platforms have become an integral part of our daily lives, allowing us to connect with friends, family, and colleagues, and share our thoughts, experiences, and personal information. However, the widespread use of social media has also made it an attractive target for cybercriminals who employ various techniques to deceive and manipulate users for their malicious purposes. This section will explore social engineering attacks on social media platforms, how to recognize and avoid them, and steps you can take to protect yourself.

Understanding Social Engineering Attacks

Social engineering attacks leverage psychological manipulation and deception to exploit the trust and naivety of individuals in order to obtain sensitive information, gain unauthorized access to systems, or carry out fraudulent activities. On social media platforms, these attacks can take various forms, such as:

- **Phishing:** Cybercriminals create fraudulent messages or posts that appear to be from a trustworthy source, such as a friend, family member, or a reputable company. These messages often contain malicious links or attachments that, when clicked, can lead to the compromise of your account or the installation of malware on your device.

- **Spoofing:** Attackers impersonate legitimate individuals or organizations by creating fake accounts or profiles. They may use the names, logos, and other identifying information of well-known brands or public figures to deceive users into sharing confidential information or clicking on malicious links.

- **Baiting:** Cybercriminals dangle enticing offers, such as free giveaways, exclusive discounts, or sensational news, to lure users into clicking on their posts or links. These offers are designed to exploit users' curiosity or desire to obtain something for free, leading them to unknowingly disclose private information or unwittingly install malware.

- **Quid pro quo:** In this type of attack, attackers offer something in return for sensitive information. For example, they may promise to provide access to exclusive content or special privileges if users reveal their account credentials or other personal details.

- **Pretexting:** Cybercriminals create elaborate fictional scenarios to gain users' trust and extract sensitive information. They may impersonate a friend, colleague, or customer service representative and engage in extensive conversations to convince users of their legitimacy before requesting personal information.

It's important to recognize and be wary of these tactics to protect yourself and your personal information on social media.

Recognizing Social Engineering Attacks

Being able to identify social engineering attacks on social media platforms is the first step in protecting yourself. Here are some common signs that may indicate a possible attack:

- **Unsolicited messages or posts:** If you receive a private message, comment, or post from someone you don't know or weren't expecting, exercise caution. Cybercriminals often target individuals who are more likely to trust messages from unfamiliar sources.

- **Unrealistic offers or requests:** Be skeptical of offers or requests that seem too good to be true. For instance, if someone is promising you a large sum of money or an unbelievable deal, it's likely a scam. Similarly, be cautious if someone requests sensitive information, such as your social security number or credit card details, especially if they're not a trusted entity.

- **Grammatical and spelling errors:** Many social engineering attacks originate from non-native English speakers or poorly constructed automated systems, resulting in obvious grammatical and spelling mistakes in their messages or posts. Pay attention to such errors, as they can be a red flag.

- **Urgency or fear-inducing language:** Attackers often create a sense of urgency or fear to manipulate their victims. If a message or post tries to pressure you into taking immediate action or threatens negative consequences for not complying, it's likely a social engineering ploy.

- **Unusual or suspicious links:** Hover over any links shared with you on social media before clicking on them to see the actual URL. If the link appears unrelated to the message or post or directs you to a suspicious website, refrain from clicking on it, as it could be a phishing attempt.

It's crucial to remain skeptical and vigilant while using social media platforms to protect yourself from social engineering attacks.

Protecting Yourself from Social Engineering Attacks

To minimize the risk of falling victim to social engineering attacks on social media, here are some proactive steps you can take:

- **Think before you click:** Before clicking on any links or opening attachments, consider the source and the context of the message. If something seems suspicious or doesn't feel right, it's best to err on the side of caution and avoid clicking on it.

- **Verify the sender's identity:** If you receive a message or post that seems suspicious, independently verify the identity of the sender before responding or taking any further action. Reach out to the person or organization through a different channel, such as a verified website or official contact information, to confirm the legitimacy of the communication.

- **Keep personal information private:** Be cautious about sharing personal details, such as your full name, address, phone number, or financial information, on social media platforms. Limit the amount of publicly available information about yourself to minimize the risk of identity theft or targeted scams.

- **Enable privacy settings:** Configure your social media account settings to enhance your privacy. Restrict access to your profile information, posts, and photos to only those you trust. Regularly review and update your privacy settings as new features and options become available.

- **Educate yourself and stay informed:** Stay up-to-date on the latest social engineering techniques and attack trends. Familiarize yourself with the common signs of social engineering attacks and learn how to recognize and avoid them. By staying informed, you can better protect yourself and help others in your network stay safe too.

- **Use security software and keep it updated:** Install reputable security software on your devices, such as antivirus and anti-malware programs, and keep them up to date. These software solutions can help detect and prevent known threats, providing an additional layer of protection against social engineering attacks.

By following these proactive measures, you can significantly reduce your vulnerability to social engineering attacks on social media platforms.

Real-World Example

Consider the following real-world example to illustrate the dangers of social engineering attacks on social media:

Sarah, an avid social media user, receives a direct message on her favorite social networking platform from a person claiming to be a representative of a popular online shopping website. The message informs her that she has won a gift card worth $500 and provides a link to claim the prize. Excited about the offer, Sarah clicks on the link without thinking twice and is redirected to a website that asks for her personal information, including her credit card details.

In this scenario, Sarah fell victim to a social engineering attack known as a phishing scam. The fraudulent message exploited her desire for a free gift and the false sense of trust associated with the representative's claim. By clicking on the link and providing her personal information, Sarah unknowingly compromised her financial security.

This example emphasizes the importance of being cautious and skeptical while engaging with messages and posts on social media, even if they appear to be from reputable sources.

Conclusion

Social engineering attacks on social media platforms continue to pose a significant threat to users' personal information and online security. By understanding the different forms of attacks and how to recognize and avoid them, you can better protect yourself from falling victim to these schemes. Taking proactive measures such as thinking before clicking, verifying senders' identities, limiting the sharing of personal information, and staying informed about the latest attack trends can go a long way in safeguarding your online presence and overall digital wellbeing. Stay vigilant and skeptical while using social media platforms, and remember that prevention is key in the battle against social engineering attacks.

Securing Social Media Profiles for Health and Wellness Professionals

In today's digitally connected world, social media has become an integral part of our personal and professional lives. For health and wellness professionals, social media platforms offer a unique opportunity to engage with patients or clients, share valuable information, and promote their services. However, it is essential to recognize the potential risks and ensure the security of social media profiles to protect sensitive information and maintain professional integrity. In this section, we will explore the best practices for securing social media profiles while maximizing their benefits.

Understanding the Risks

Social media platforms are not immune to cybersecurity threats, and health and wellness professionals must be aware of the potential risks associated with these platforms. Some common risks include:

- **Privacy breaches:** Social media platforms often have privacy settings that users can configure. However, misconfigurations or vulnerabilities in these settings can expose personal information to unauthorized individuals.
- **Phishing attacks:** Cybercriminals may attempt to trick users into revealing their sensitive information, such as login credentials, through deceptive messages or links shared on social media.
- **Reputation damage:** Inappropriate or controversial content posted on social media profiles can harm the professional reputation of health and wellness professionals.
- **Data leaks:** Social media platforms may experience data breaches that result in the exposure of users' personal information.
- **Social engineering attacks:** Attackers may impersonate health and wellness professionals or their clients to gain access to sensitive information or deceive others.

Understanding these risks is crucial for devising an effective strategy to secure social media profiles.

Implementing Best Practices

To enhance the security of social media profiles, health and wellness professionals should follow these best practices:

1. **Enable Strong Authentication:** Utilize strong and unique passwords for social media accounts. Enable two-factor authentication (2FA) whenever possible

to add an extra layer of security. This could involve receiving a verification code via SMS or using an authenticator app.

2. **Configure Privacy Settings:** Review and configure the privacy settings for social media profiles. Limit the visibility of personal information to trusted connections only. Regularly audit and update privacy settings as platforms may introduce new options or change default settings.

3. **Be Mindful of User-Generated Content:** Exercise caution when interacting with user-generated content on social media. Avoid clicking suspicious links or downloading files from untrusted sources as they may contain malware or lead to phishing attempts.

4. **Regularly Update Software:** Keep social media applications and associated devices up to date with the latest security patches and software updates. This helps protect against known vulnerabilities that attackers may exploit.

5. **Practice Safe Posting and Sharing:** Be mindful of the content posted on social media profiles. Avoid sharing sensitive information such as personal contact details, patient information, or work-related confidential information. Think twice before sharing photos or tagging locations that could compromise privacy or security.

6. **Educate and Train Employees:** If health and wellness professionals manage social media accounts for their organization, it is essential to educate staff on the risks and best practices of social media usage. Provide training on how to identify and respond to potential threats, such as suspicious messages or phishing attempts.

7. **Regularly Monitor and Audit Profiles:** Regularly monitor social media profiles and review account activities. Enable notifications for account logins or suspicious activities. Conduct periodic audits to ensure that the profiles align with the desired security and privacy settings.

8. **Secure Mobile Devices:** As social media usage extends to mobile devices, ensure the security of smartphones and tablets used for accessing social media accounts. Implement device encryption, enable screen locks, and use trusted and up-to-date mobile security applications.

9. **Stay Informed:** Keep up-to-date with the latest trends and security practices in social media. Follow reputable sources and industry experts for insights and guidance on securing social media profiles.

Case Study: Securing a Twitter Profile

Consider the case of Dr. Sarah, a renowned nutritionist with a significant social media presence. Dr. Sarah actively uses Twitter to share valuable insights, interact with followers, and promote her services. However, she is concerned about the security of her Twitter profile. Let's explore the steps she can take to enhance the security of her account.

1. **Strengthen Password and Enable 2FA:** Dr. Sarah should immediately update her Twitter password with a strong, unique combination of characters. Additionally, she should enable two-factor authentication to add an extra layer of security.

2. **Configure Privacy Settings:** Dr. Sarah should review her Twitter privacy settings and limit the visibility of her tweets and profile information to trusted followers only. She should also consider enabling the option to review and approve follower requests.

3. **Be Cautious of Direct Messages:** Dr. Sarah should exercise caution when receiving direct messages from unknown or suspicious accounts. She should avoid clicking on links or providing personal information unless she can verify the sender's identity.

4. **Regularly Monitor Account Activity:** Dr. Sarah should regularly monitor her Twitter account for any unauthorized activities, such as unusual login attempts or suspicious tweets. Enabling login notifications can help her stay vigilant.

5. **Educate Staff on Social Media Best Practices:** If Dr. Sarah has a team managing her social media accounts, she should ensure they receive proper training on social media best practices. This will help prevent accidental exposure of sensitive information or falling victim to social engineering attacks.

By implementing these recommended practices, Dr. Sarah can significantly improve the security of her Twitter profile while effectively utilizing the platform to engage with her audience.

Additional Resources

Securing social media profiles is an ongoing process, and health and wellness professionals should stay informed about the latest best practices and emerging threats. Here are some additional resources that can provide valuable insights:

- **Healthcare Information and Management Systems Society (HIMSS) Social Media Privacy Toolkit:** Provides guidance and resources on securing social media profiles in the healthcare industry.

- **Federal Trade Commission (FTC) Social Media: A Guide for Individuals and Businesses:** Offers tips and best practices for securing social media accounts and protecting sensitive information.

- **Cybersecurity and Infrastructure Security Agency (CISA) Social Media Security Tips:** Provides practical recommendations for securing social media profiles and reducing the risk of cyber threats.

Using these resources, health and wellness professionals can stay up to date with the latest security practices, further enhance their skills, and ensure the highest level of protection for their social media profiles.

Conclusion

Securing social media profiles is essential for health and wellness professionals to protect sensitive information, maintain professional integrity, and reduce the risk of cybersecurity threats. By understanding the risks, implementing best practices, and staying informed about the latest security trends, professionals can maximize the benefits of social media platforms while minimizing the potential risks. Remember, securing social media profiles is an ongoing effort that requires continuous monitoring, adaptation, and proper education for both professionals and their staff. Stay vigilant, stay informed, and enjoy the benefits of social media in a secure and responsible manner.

Educating Employees on Responsible Social Media Usage

In today's digitally connected world, social media has become an integral part of our personal and professional lives. However, the use of social media in the workplace also presents significant cybersecurity risks. To mitigate these risks, it is crucial to educate employees on responsible social media usage. This section will discuss the importance of such education and provide guidance on how to effectively educate employees on responsible social media practices.

Understanding the Risks

The first step in educating employees about responsible social media usage is to provide a comprehensive understanding of the risks associated with using social media in the workplace. These risks include:

- **Data Breaches:** Inadvertent disclosure of sensitive information through social media platforms can lead to data breaches and compromise the organization's security.

- **Phishing Attacks:** Social media platforms are often used as a medium for phishing attacks, where malicious actors trick employees into revealing sensitive information or downloading malware.

- **Reputation Damage:** Inappropriate or unprofessional behavior on social media can damage the reputation of both employees and the organization.

- **Intellectual Property Theft:** Sharing confidential or proprietary information on social media can result in intellectual property theft and financial losses.

- **Compliance Violations:** Violating industry regulations or internal policies through social media usage can lead to legal and financial consequences for the organization.

By understanding these risks, employees can grasp the importance of responsible social media usage and the potential impact on cybersecurity and overall organizational well-being.

Establishing Social Media Usage Policies

To guide employees in their social media activities, organizations should establish clear and comprehensive social media usage policies. These policies should outline acceptable and unacceptable behaviors, as well as provide guidance on privacy settings, sharing of company information, and engagement with external parties.

The policies should also highlight the importance of maintaining a professional image and the potential consequences of non-compliance. It is essential to make these policies easily accessible and regularly communicate any updates to ensure employees stay informed.

Training Programs

Developing effective training programs is critical to educate employees on responsible social media usage. These programs should be tailored to the specific needs of the organization and its workforce. Here are some key components to consider when designing such programs:

- **Interactive Workshops:** Conducting interactive workshops where employees can learn about the risks, best practices, and case studies related to social media usage enables hands-on learning and engagement.

- **Role-Playing Exercises:** Engaging employees in role-playing exercises can simulate real-life social media scenarios, allowing them to practice appropriate responses and decision-making.
- **Scenarios and Examples:** Providing employees with scenarios and examples of both responsible and irresponsible social media usage can help them understand the practical implications of their actions.
- **Guest Speakers and Experts:** Inviting industry experts and guest speakers with expertise in cybersecurity and social media can provide valuable insights and perspectives, enhancing the training experience.
- **Continuous Learning:** Social media landscape and cybersecurity threats evolve rapidly. It is crucial to encourage continuous learning by providing access to resources, webinars, and updated training materials.

Monitoring and Reporting Mechanisms

To ensure adherence to social media usage policies, organizations should implement monitoring and reporting mechanisms. These mechanisms can help detect and mitigate potential risks and incidents. Some essential considerations include:

- **Social Media Monitoring Tools:** Utilize dedicated tools to monitor social media platforms for mentions of the organization, its employees, or any sensitive information. This can enable proactive detection of security threats and potential reputational risks.
- **Anonymously Reporting Incidents:** Establish a confidential and anonymous reporting channel for employees to report any social media-related incidents or concerns without fear of retaliation.
- **Regular Auditing:** Conduct routine audits of employees' social media activities to ensure compliance with the organization's policies. These audits can identify areas for improvement and provide valuable feedback to enhance training programs.

Encouraging Responsible Social Media Usage

In addition to strict policies and training, organizations should foster a culture of responsible social media usage. This can be achieved through various strategies:

- **Lead by Example:** Organizational leaders should demonstrate responsible social media behavior to set the tone for employees.
- **Positive Reinforcement:** Recognize and reward employees who consistently adhere to responsible social media practices and contribute to a secure online environment.
- **Open Communication Channels:** Encourage open communication between employees and management regarding any social media concerns or incidents. This helps create a supportive and proactive cybersecurity culture.
- **Regular Refreshers:** Conduct periodic refresher courses or awareness campaigns to reinforce responsible social media practices and remind employees of the potential risks.

Case Study: Social Media Mishap

To illustrate the consequences of irresponsible social media usage, let's consider a case study involving a healthcare organization, Secure Health Solutions (SHS). An employee of SHS, unaware of the organization's social media usage policies, shares a photo containing sensitive patient information on their personal social media account. The photo gets reposted, ultimately leading to a data breach and damaging SHS's reputation. This incident serves as a reminder of the importance of educating employees on responsible social media practices to prevent such mishaps.

Conclusion

Educating employees on responsible social media usage is crucial to safeguarding personal information and maintaining cybersecurity in the workplace. By providing comprehensive training programs, establishing clear policies, and fostering a culture of responsible social media usage, organizations can mitigate risks and promote a secure online environment. Remember, responsible social media usage is not only essential for cybersecurity but also for safeguarding the overall well-being of individuals and organizations.

Monitoring and Managing Social Media Presence

In today's digital age, social media has become an integral part of our personal and professional lives. However, with the increasing use of social media platforms, the risk of cyber threats and privacy breaches has also grown. It is crucial for health and wellness professionals to monitor and manage their social media presence to ensure the safety and security of their personal information as well as their patients' data.

Understanding the Risks of Social Media

Social media platforms offer numerous benefits, such as enhancing communication, expanding professional networks, and promoting health and wellness services. However, it is essential to be aware of the risks associated with social media usage. Some common risks include:

- Privacy breaches: Social media platforms may inadvertently expose personal information, which can be used by cybercriminals for identity theft or other malicious activities.
- Reputation damage: Inappropriate or unprofessional content on social media can harm the reputation and credibility of health and wellness professionals.
- Social engineering attacks: Cyber attackers may exploit the information shared on social media platforms to manipulate or deceive individuals into disclosing sensitive information or engaging in harmful activities.
- Malware and phishing attacks: Social media platforms can serve as a vector for spreading malware or initiating phishing attacks, leading to compromised accounts and stolen data.

By understanding these risks, health and wellness professionals can take appropriate measures to safeguard their social media presence and mitigate potential threats.

Establishing a Social Media Monitoring Strategy

To effectively monitor and manage their social media presence, health and wellness professionals should develop a comprehensive strategy. This strategy should include the following steps:

1. Identify social media platforms: Determine which social media platforms are most relevant to your profession and target audience. Focus your efforts on these platforms to maximize engagement and reach.
2. Set up monitoring tools: Utilize social media monitoring tools to track mentions, comments, and messages related to your professional accounts.

These tools provide real-time notifications, allowing you to respond promptly and address any concerns.

3. Define monitoring objectives: Clearly outline what you aim to achieve through social media monitoring. Whether it is increasing brand awareness, monitoring patient feedback, or counteracting misinformation, having clear objectives will guide your monitoring efforts.

4. Establish monitoring frequency: Decide how frequently you will perform social media monitoring. Regular monitoring is crucial to detect and respond to potential threats promptly. Consider dedicating specific time slots or utilizing automated monitoring tools to streamline the process.

5. Determine response protocols: Establish guidelines for addressing different types of social media interactions. Define response timeframes, tone of communication, and escalation procedures for handling both positive and negative interactions.

By establishing a comprehensive monitoring strategy, health and wellness professionals can gain control over their social media presence and effectively mitigate risks.

Best Practices for Social Media Management

In addition to monitoring, effective management of social media presence is vital to maintain professionalism and protect sensitive information. Here are some best practices for managing social media accounts:

- Secure account settings: Utilize strong and unique passwords for each social media platform. Enable two-factor authentication whenever possible to provide an extra layer of security.

- Regularly review privacy settings: Familiarize yourself with the privacy settings of each platform and adjust them to control the visibility of your personal and professional information. Limit the sharing of personal details to trusted connections only.

- Think before posting: Before sharing content on social media, consider the potential impact on your personal and professional reputation. Avoid posting sensitive or confidential information and be mindful of the language and tone used in your posts.

- Avoid engaging with malicious accounts: Be cautious when interacting with unknown or suspicious accounts. Avoid clicking on suspicious links, and report or block accounts that exhibit malicious behavior.

- Educate employees and colleagues: Provide training and guidelines to your employees or colleagues regarding responsible social media usage. Ensure they understand the risks associated with social media and the importance of maintaining professionalism online.

- Conduct regular audits: Periodically review the content shared on your social media accounts to ensure compliance with professional standards. Remove or update any outdated or inappropriate content.

By following these best practices, health and wellness professionals can effectively manage their social media presence and minimize the risk of privacy breaches and reputation damage.

Real-World Example: Managing Social Media Presence in a Healthcare Practice

Dr. Taylor, a renowned psychiatrist, wants to ensure the secure management of her social media presence while maintaining a professional image. She takes the following steps to monitor and manage her social media accounts effectively:

- Dr. Taylor identifies the most relevant social media platforms for her practice, including Facebook, Twitter, and LinkedIn.

- She sets up social media monitoring tools that notify her whenever her name or practice is mentioned on these platforms.

- Dr. Taylor defines her monitoring objectives, which include addressing patient queries, sharing mental health tips, and countering misinformation related to psychiatry.

- She dedicates 20 minutes each morning to review and respond to social media interactions. For automated monitoring, she uses tools that provide daily summaries of her social media activity.

- Dr. Taylor establishes response protocols, ensuring that patient queries are answered within 24 hours and negative interactions are handled promptly and professionally.

- She secures her social media accounts with strong passwords and enables two-factor authentication whenever possible.
- Dr. Taylor regularly reviews her privacy settings, ensuring that her personal information is only visible to trusted connections.
- Before posting content, she considers its potential impact and ensures that it aligns with professional ethics and standards.

By implementing these practices, Dr. Taylor effectively monitors and manages her social media presence, ensuring the security of her personal information and maintaining a reputable online image.

Conclusion

Monitoring and managing social media presence is essential for health and wellness professionals to protect their personal information, maintain professionalism, and safeguard patient data. By understanding the risks, establishing a monitoring strategy, following best practices, and utilizing proper tools, professionals can confidently engage with social media platforms while minimizing the potential impact of cyber threats. With a proactive approach to social media management, health and wellness professionals can thrive in the digital world and enhance their overall wellbeing and professional success.

Crisis Communication and Social Media

In today's digitally connected world, social media has become a powerful tool for communication and information sharing. However, during times of crisis, it can also pose significant challenges for organizations in terms of managing their reputation and handling public relations. In this section, we will explore the importance of crisis communication in the context of social media and discuss strategies for effectively managing crises in the health and wellness industry.

Understanding Crisis Communication

Crisis communication refers to the process of conveying information and managing public perception during a crisis situation. It involves the strategic dissemination of accurate and timely information to minimize negative consequences, maintain trust, and protect the reputation of the organization.

Social media has revolutionized the way crises unfold and are communicated. It allows for rapid dissemination of information and provides individuals with a platform to share their opinions and experiences. As a result, organizations must carefully navigate social media during times of crisis to ensure they control the narrative and address concerns effectively.

Planning for Crisis Communication

Effective crisis communication begins with thorough planning and preparation. Organizations should develop a crisis communication plan that outlines the necessary steps to be taken in the event of a crisis. This plan should include:

- Identification of potential crises: Identify the types of crises that could occur in the health and wellness industry, such as data breaches, product recalls, or allegations of malpractice.
- Designation of spokespersons: Identify individuals within the organization who are responsible for communicating with the media, stakeholders, and the public during a crisis.
- Preparing key messages: Develop key messages that address the crisis and convey important information to stakeholders.
- Monitoring social media: Implement a system to monitor social media platforms for mentions of the organization, key personnel, and any crisis-related keywords.
- Establish protocols for responding: Define the procedures for responding to social media posts, including who should respond, what should be said, and the appropriate tone and language to use.

By proactively planning and establishing protocols, organizations can respond quickly and effectively to crisis situations.

Social Media Crisis Response Strategies

When a crisis occurs and is amplified through social media, organizations need to act swiftly and appropriately to manage the situation. Here are some key strategies for crisis communication on social media:

- Monitor social media platforms: Regularly monitor social media platforms to identify any potential crisis situations and address them promptly.

- Respond promptly: Acknowledge the crisis and respond to inquiries, concerns, and complaints in a timely manner. Promptly addressing and empathizing with stakeholders' concerns can help mitigate the negative impact of the crisis.

- Be transparent and honest: Provide accurate and transparent information to stakeholders. Avoid speculation or sharing unverified information that could further escalate the crisis.

- Apologize when necessary: If the organization is at fault, apologize sincerely and take responsibility for the situation. Offering an apology can help rebuild trust and demonstrate a commitment to resolving the issue.

- Engage with influencers: Identify influential individuals or organizations within the health and wellness industry and engage with them to help disseminate accurate information and counter misinformation.

- Provide regular updates: Keep stakeholders informed with regular updates on the progress and steps being taken to address the crisis. This helps to maintain credibility and demonstrates proactive management of the situation.

- Use visual content: Incorporate visual content, such as infographics or videos, to communicate complex information in an easily understandable format.

- Monitor sentiment and feedback: Continuously monitor the sentiment and feedback from stakeholders on social media. This feedback can help gauge public perception and identify areas where additional communication or actions are necessary.

By adopting these strategies, organizations can effectively manage crises on social media and maintain their reputation and credibility.

Case Study: Crisis Communication in the Health and Wellness Industry

To illustrate the importance of crisis communication in the health and wellness industry, let's consider a hypothetical case study:

Imagine a health and wellness company that manufactures dietary supplements. The company receives reports of adverse reactions from some customers who consumed one of their products. Word spreads quickly on social media, with users sharing their negative experiences and expressing concerns about product safety.

In this scenario, the company should immediately activate its crisis communication plan and implement the following strategies:

- Monitor social media platforms for mentions of the company and the product in question.
- Respond promptly to each mention, acknowledging the customers' concerns and assuring them that the company is investigating the issue.
- Provide regular updates on the progress of the investigation and any actions being taken to address the problem.
- Engage with influencers in the health and wellness industry to share accurate information about the company's response to the issue.
- Offer refunds or replacements to affected customers as a goodwill gesture and to demonstrate the company's commitment to customer satisfaction.
- Conduct an internal investigation to identify the cause of the adverse reactions and take necessary steps to prevent similar incidents in the future.

Through these strategies, the company can effectively manage the crisis, address customers' concerns, and work towards rebuilding trust in its brand.

Conclusion

Crisis communication is essential in the digital age, especially when social media can amplify the impact of a crisis. Organizations in the health and wellness industry must be prepared to respond swiftly and effectively to crisis situations on social media platforms. By planning ahead, adopting appropriate strategies, and engaging with stakeholders transparently, organizations can protect their reputation and maintain public trust even during challenging times.

Secure Remote Access and Virtual Meetings

VPNs for Secure Remote Access to Work Systems

In today's digitally connected world, many health and wellness professionals rely on remote access to work systems for various tasks such as accessing electronic health records, collaborating with colleagues, and conducting telehealth consultations. However, the security of these remote connections is of utmost importance to ensure the privacy and confidentiality of sensitive personal and patient information. This is where Virtual Private Networks (VPNs) come into play.

Understanding VPNs

A VPN is a secure and encrypted connection that allows users to access a private network, such as a work system, over the internet. It creates a virtual tunnel between the user's device and the work system, ensuring that all data transmitted between them is encrypted and protected from unauthorized access.

VPNs provide several key benefits for remote access to work systems:

- **Data Encryption:** VPNs use encryption algorithms to convert data into unreadable ciphertext, preventing unauthorized individuals from intercepting and understanding the transmitted data.
- **Secure Authentication:** VPNs employ various authentication methods, such as digital certificates or username/password combinations, to verify the identity of the user before granting access to the work system.
- **Anonymity and Privacy:** By routing internet traffic through a remote server, VPNs mask the user's IP address and location, enhancing privacy and protecting against online tracking.
- **Bypassing Geographical Restrictions:** VPNs can be used to bypass geographical restrictions imposed by content providers, allowing health and wellness professionals to access work systems from anywhere in the world.

Types of VPNs

There are several types of VPNs available, each with its own strengths and weaknesses. The choice of VPN type depends on the specific requirements and constraints of the health and wellness organization.

1. **Remote Access VPNs:** Also known as client-to-site VPNs, these VPNs allow individual users to remotely connect to a private network. Users install VPN client software on their devices and establish a secure connection to the work system. Remote Access VPNs are commonly used by health and wellness professionals who work from home or travel frequently.
2. **Site-to-Site VPNs:** Also known as network-to-network VPNs, these VPNs establish a secure connection between different physical locations of

an organization. They are typically used by large health and wellness organizations with multiple offices or facilities that need to connect and share resources securely.

3. **Cloud VPNs:** As more health and wellness organizations adopt cloud computing technologies, cloud-based VPNs have gained popularity. These VPNs provide secure connectivity between on-premises networks and cloud infrastructure, allowing seamless integration of cloud services into the organization's network.

4. **Mobile VPNs:** With the increasing use of mobile devices in the health and wellness industry, mobile VPNs have become essential. These VPNs are specifically designed for smartphones and tablets, providing secure access to work systems while on the go. Mobile VPNs often have additional features to optimize performance and battery life on mobile devices.

Implementing VPNs for Secure Remote Access

To ensure the effective implementation of VPNs for secure remote access to work systems, health and wellness organizations need to consider the following aspects:

1. **VPN Solution Evaluation:** It is crucial to carefully evaluate different VPN solutions based on the organization's requirements, security features, ease of use, scalability, and compatibility with existing infrastructure. Consulting with cybersecurity professionals and conducting pilot testing can help in selecting the most suitable VPN solution.

2. **Strong Encryption and Authentication:** The selected VPN solution should use strong encryption algorithms, such as AES (Advanced Encryption Standard), and support robust authentication methods, such as digital certificates or two-factor authentication. This ensures that the data transmitted through the VPN tunnel is adequately protected, and only authorized users can gain access.

3. **VPN Gateway Configuration:** Proper configuration of the VPN gateway is crucial to ensure its security and reliability. This includes setting up firewall rules, enabling logging and monitoring features, optimizing network performance, and implementing intrusion detection and prevention systems to detect and mitigate potential attacks.

4. **User Education and Awareness:** Health and wellness professionals must be educated on the importance of using VPNs for secure remote access and provided with clear instructions on how to set up and use the VPN client software. Regular training sessions and awareness programs can help reinforce best practices and ensure that users understand how to protect their remote connections effectively.

5. **Continuous Monitoring and Maintenance:** VPNs require regular monitoring and maintenance to ensure their ongoing security. This includes monitoring VPN logs for any unusual activities, promptly applying software updates and patches, and conducting periodic security assessments and audits to identify and address any vulnerabilities.

Real-World Example

Consider the case of a healthcare organization that offers telehealth services to patients. The organization has a team of remote healthcare professionals who need secure access to patient records and communication tools. To provide secure remote access, the organization decides to implement a Remote Access VPN solution.

They evaluate different VPN vendors based on their security features, compatibility with existing systems, ease of use, and cost. After careful consideration, they choose a VPN solution that uses AES-256 encryption and supports two-factor authentication for enhanced security. The VPN solution also integrates seamlessly with their existing electronic health record system.

The organization sets up a VPN gateway at their data center and configures firewall rules to allow VPN traffic. They provide clear instructions to the remote healthcare professionals on how to install the VPN client software on their devices and authenticate using their unique credentials.

To ensure continuous security, the organization regularly monitors VPN logs, applies software updates to the VPN gateway, and conducts periodic security assessments. They also provide ongoing training and awareness sessions to the healthcare professionals, emphasizing best practices for secure remote access.

Through the implemented VPN solution, the remote healthcare professionals can securely connect to the organization's network, access patient records, collaborate with colleagues, and provide telehealth services to patients while maintaining the highest standards of privacy and confidentiality.

Conclusion

VPNs play a crucial role in ensuring secure remote access to work systems in the health and wellness industry. By implementing the appropriate VPN solution and following best practices, health and wellness professionals can protect sensitive information, maintain privacy, and enhance the overall security of their remote connections. It is essential for organizations to closely evaluate VPN solutions, educate users, and continuously monitor and maintain the VPN infrastructure to effectively mitigate cybersecurity risks and safeguard the wellbeing of both individuals and organizations.

Exercises

1. Explain the concept of a VPN and its significance in securing remote access to work systems.

2. Compare and contrast the different types of VPNs, highlighting their use cases and benefits in the health and wellness industry.

3. Discuss the factors that health and wellness organizations should consider when implementing VPNs for secure remote access to work systems.

4. Research and identify a real-world case study where the use of VPNs resulted in the protection of sensitive personal or patient information. Present your findings and discuss the key lessons learned from the case study.

5. Imagine you are a cybersecurity consultant for a health and wellness organization. Design a training program for healthcare professionals on the effective use of VPNs for secure remote access. Outline the key topics to be covered and the training methods to be employed.

Additional Resources

- Bejtlich, R. (2016). The Practice of Network Security Monitoring: Understanding Incident Detection and Response. No Starch Press.

- Cheswick, W. R., & Bellovin, S. M. (2003). Firewalls and Internet Security: Repelling the Wily Hacker. Addison-Wesley Professional.

- Gasior, D. (2016). Understanding Virtual Private Networks. Artech House.

- Harkins, D., & Roberts, P. (2017). Network Security Architectures. Cisco Press.

- Velte, A. T., Velte, T. J., & Elsenpeter, R. C. (2012). Virtual Private Networks: Technologies and Solutions. McGraw-Hill Education.

- National Institute of Standards and Technology (NIST). (2020). NIST Special Publication 800-113: Guide to SSL VPNs. Retrieved from https://doi.org/10.6028/NIST.SP.800-113

Trick: To remember the acronym "VPN," think of it as a "Virtual Privacy Network" that protects your remote connections.

Caveat: While VPNs provide secure remote access, it is essential to remember that they are just one part of an organization's overall cybersecurity strategy. Organizations should implement additional security measures, such as strong access controls and regular security awareness training, to ensure comprehensive cybersecurity protection.

Secure Remote Desktop Access and Virtual Private Servers

In today's digital age, the ability to access resources remotely is crucial for many organizations, including those in the health and wellness industry. Secure remote desktop access and virtual private servers (VPS) play a significant role in facilitating this remote access while maintaining a high level of security. In this section, we will explore the importance of securing remote desktop access and VPS, discuss best practices for implementation, and highlight key considerations for safeguarding sensitive information.

The Importance of Secure Remote Desktop Access

Remote desktop access allows users to connect to a computer or server in a different location. This capability is particularly valuable for health and wellness professionals who often need to access patient records and critical systems from outside the office or clinic. However, without proper security measures in place, remote desktop access can expose sensitive information to potential threats.

One of the primary risks associated with remote desktop access is the potential for unauthorized access. If an attacker gains access to an organization's remote desktop, they can potentially exploit vulnerabilities, steal sensitive data, or even launch further attacks on the internal network. To mitigate these risks, it is crucial to implement robust security measures.

Securing Remote Desktop Access

To ensure the security of remote desktop access, organizations should follow best practices for implementation and maintenance. Here are some key considerations:

1. Use Strong Authentication Mechanisms: Implementing strong authentication mechanisms is essential to protect remote desktop access. Require users to utilize complex passwords or consider using multi-factor authentication (MFA), such as biometrics or hardware tokens, to add an additional layer of security.

2. Limit Access and Privileges: Only grant remote desktop access privileges to authorized individuals who need it for their job functions. Restrict access based on the principle of least privilege, ensuring that users have only the necessary permissions to perform their tasks. Regularly review and update access privileges to align with the principle of least privilege.

3. Implement Network Segmentation: To enhance security, create a separate network segment specifically for remote desktop access. This can help isolate potential threats and reduce the exposure of critical systems to external attackers.

4. Enable Strong Encryption: Encrypting remote desktop communication can prevent eavesdropping and unauthorized access to transmitted data. Always use secure encryption protocols, such as Transport Layer Security (TLS), to protect the confidentiality and integrity of remote desktop sessions.

5. Regularly Update and Patch Systems: Keeping remote desktop systems up to date with the latest security patches is crucial. Regularly check for updates and apply necessary patches to mitigate vulnerabilities that may be exploited by attackers.

6. Monitor and Log Activities: Implement logging and monitoring mechanisms to track remote desktop access and detect any suspicious activities. Analyzing log data can help identify potential security incidents and enable prompt response and recovery.

Virtual Private Servers (VPS)

A virtual private server (VPS) is a virtual machine that provides users with a dedicated and isolated environment within a shared physical server. VPSs are commonly used for hosting websites, applications, and other services because of their flexibility and cost-effectiveness. When it comes to security, VPSs offer several advantages over traditional shared hosting environments.

1. Enhanced Isolation: Unlike shared hosting, where multiple websites or applications reside on the same server, VPSs provide a higher level of isolation. Each VPS operates independently, with its own dedicated resources, file system, and operating system. This isolation minimizes the risk of one compromised website or application affecting others.

2. **Control and Customization:** With a VPS, users have greater control and customization options compared to shared hosting. They can install security software, configure firewalls, and implement tailored security measures to meet their specific requirements.

3. **Scalability and Performance:** VPSs offer scalability, allowing users to adjust resources based on their needs. This flexibility ensures optimal performance and enables organizations to grow their infrastructure seamlessly while meeting security requirements.

4. **Data Backup and Disaster Recovery:** VPS providers often offer backup and disaster recovery solutions, ensuring data resilience and availability. Users can schedule regular backups and restore data in the event of data loss or system failures.

5. **Regular System Updates:** VPS providers typically handle system updates, including security patches and software upgrades. Regular updates help safeguard the underlying infrastructure and reduce the risk of vulnerabilities.

Best Practices for VPS Security

To ensure the security of VPS environments, organizations should consider the following best practices:

1. **Choose a Reputable VPS Provider:** Select a reliable VPS provider with a strong track record in security and customer support. Research the provider's reputation, security practices, and data protection measures before making a decision.

2. **Enable Firewall Protection:** Activate a firewall on your VPS to monitor and control incoming and outgoing network traffic. Configure firewall rules to allow only necessary connections and services.

3. **Regularly Update and Patch the VPS:** Keep your VPS up to date by promptly applying security patches and updates. Regularly check for updates and ensure that the operating system, software, and applications are patched to the latest versions.

4. **Implement Access Controls:** Follow the principle of least privilege and carefully manage user access on the VPS. Use strong passwords or implement MFA for enhanced authentication. Regularly review and update user privileges to minimize security risks.

5. **Backup Data Regularly:** Establish a regular backup routine to ensure data integrity and availability. Store backups securely, preferably offsite or in a separate location to protect against potential data loss or system failures.

6. **Monitor VPS Activities:** Implement monitoring and logging mechanisms to track VPS activities and detect any signs of unauthorized access or suspicious behavior. Regularly review log files to identify potential security incidents and take appropriate actions.

Real-World Example - Remote Desktop Vulnerability

In 2019, a critical vulnerability was discovered in Microsoft's Remote Desktop Protocol (RDP). The vulnerability, named BlueKeep, allowed attackers to remotely execute code and potentially spread malware across vulnerable systems without user interaction. This vulnerability affected older versions of the Windows operating system, making it a significant risk for organizations relying on remote desktop access.

The BlueKeep vulnerability highlighted the importance of promptly applying security patches and updates. To mitigate the risk, Microsoft released security updates for affected versions of Windows, urging users to update their systems immediately. Organizations that failed to patch their systems in a timely manner faced an increased risk of exploitation and potential compromise of sensitive information.

This real-world example emphasizes the need for strong security practices and regular updates to safeguard remote desktop access and protect against emerging vulnerabilities.

Conclusion

Secure remote desktop access and virtual private servers are central to maintaining productivity and accessing critical resources in today's digitally connected world. By implementing best practices, such as strong authentication mechanisms, network segmentation, encryption, regular updates, and robust access controls, organizations can mitigate the risks associated with remote access and ensure the security of sensitive information.

In the next section, we will explore secure communication and collaboration tools, focusing on ensuring the confidentiality and integrity of communication channels within the health and wellness industry.

Securing Virtual Meetings and Video Conferencing Platforms

In today's digitally connected world, virtual meetings and video conferencing have become an essential part of communication for individuals and businesses alike. With the rise of remote work and telecommuting, it is important to ensure the security and privacy of virtual meetings to protect sensitive information from unauthorized access and potential breaches. This section will explore the various measures and best practices that can be implemented to secure virtual meetings and video conferencing platforms.

Understanding the Risks

Virtual meetings and video conferencing platforms are susceptible to various security risks that can compromise the confidentiality, integrity, and availability of the communication. Some of the common risks include:

- Unauthorized access: Hackers or malicious actors gaining unauthorized access to the meeting and eavesdropping on sensitive conversations.

- Data interception: Interception of data transmitted during the meeting, including audio, video, and files shared.

- Denial of service (DoS) attacks: Malicious attempts to overload the virtual meeting infrastructure, rendering it unusable for legitimate participants.

- Malware and phishing attacks: Distribution of malware or attempts to trick participants into revealing sensitive information through phishing attacks.

- Lack of encryption: Inadequate encryption of the communication, leaving it vulnerable to interception and unauthorized access.

- Weak authentication: Weak or inadequate authentication mechanisms that can be exploited by attackers to gain unauthorized access.

Best Practices for Securing Virtual Meetings

To secure virtual meetings and video conferencing platforms, it is essential to follow the best practices outlined below:

1. **Choose a secure and reputable platform:** Select a virtual meeting platform that prioritizes security and has a proven track record of implementing robust security measures. Popular platforms such as Zoom, Microsoft Teams, and Cisco Webex offer significant security features and regular updates to address vulnerabilities.

2. **Use strong meeting passwords:** Implement strong passwords for each meeting and share them securely with participants. Avoid using easily guessable passwords and encourage participants to choose strong passwords as well.

3. **Enable waiting rooms or participant access controls:** Utilize waiting rooms or participant access controls to ensure that only authorized individuals can join the meeting. This helps prevent unauthorized participants from entering the meeting and accessing sensitive information.

4. **Encrypt communications:** Enable end-to-end encryption for all audio, video, and data transmitted during the meeting. Encryption ensures that the communication is secure and cannot be intercepted by unauthorized parties.

5. **Update software and applications:** Regularly update the virtual meeting software and applications to the latest versions. Updates often include security patches that address vulnerabilities and protect against potential threats.

6. **Beware of phishing attempts:** Educate participants about the risks of phishing attacks and advise them to be cautious while clicking on any links or downloading files during the meeting. Encourage them to verify the authenticity of any shared content before accessing or downloading.

7. **Limit screen sharing privileges:** Restrict screen sharing capabilities to authorized participants only. This prevents any unauthorized sharing of inappropriate or sensitive content during the meeting.

8. **Disable file transfer:** Control file transfer capabilities within the platform to prevent the sharing of potentially malicious files. Only enable file transfer when necessary and ensure that files are scanned for malware before being shared.

9. **Monitor participant activity:** Assign a host or moderator who can monitor participant activity during the meeting. This helps identify any suspicious behavior or unauthorized participants and take appropriate actions to mitigate potential risks.

10. **Record meetings securely:** If recording the meeting is necessary, ensure that the recorded content is stored securely and only accessible to authorized individuals. Delete the recordings when they are no longer needed to reduce the risk of unauthorized access.

Example Scenario: Securing a Virtual Board Meeting

Consider a scenario where a healthcare organization is conducting a virtual board meeting to discuss sensitive financial information and strategic plans. To ensure the security of the meeting, the following steps can be taken:

1. The organization selects a reputable virtual meeting platform known for its security features and strong encryption mechanisms.

2. A unique and strong password is set for the meeting and shared securely with the board members. The password should be a combination of alphanumeric characters and symbols.

3. The waiting room feature is enabled, allowing the host to admit participants only after verifying their identities. This prevents unauthorized access to the meeting.

4. All communications during the meeting, including audio, video, and data, are encrypted using end-to-end encryption to maintain confidentiality.

5. The host regularly updates the virtual meeting software to ensure that the latest security patches are applied and any vulnerabilities are addressed.

6. Participants are educated about the risks of phishing attempts and advised to exercise caution when clicking on links or downloading files shared during the meeting.

7. Screen sharing capabilities are restricted to authorized participants only, preventing any unwanted or sensitive content from being shared inappropriately.

8. File transfer is disabled during the meeting unless specifically required. Files shared are scanned for malware before being shared with the participants.

9. The host actively monitors participant activity during the meeting for any suspicious behavior or unauthorized access. Immediate action is taken to address any identified risks.

10. If the meeting needs to be recorded for documentation purposes, the host ensures that the recording is securely stored and accessible only to authorized individuals. The recording is deleted once it is no longer needed.

By following these best practices, the healthcare organization can significantly reduce the risk of unauthorized access or data breaches during the virtual board meeting.

Additional Resources

For more information and resources on securing virtual meetings and video conferencing platforms, refer to the following:

- National Institute of Standards and Technology (NIST) Special Publication 800-44: "Guidelines on Securing Public Web Servers"
- The Internet Engineering Task Force (IETF) RFC 3552: "Guidelines for Writing RFC Text on Security Considerations"
- Center for Internet Security (CIS) Controls and Benchmarks for Secure Configuration of Virtual Meeting Platforms
- Official documentation and support materials provided by the virtual meeting platform used by the organization
- Certified cybersecurity professionals specializing in secure communication and collaboration platforms

Remember, securing virtual meetings and video conferencing platforms is a continuous effort. Stay updated with the latest security practices and regularly review and improve the security measures you have in place to protect your sensitive information during virtual meetings.

Two-Factor Authentication for Remote Access

In today's interconnected world, remote access has become an integral part of our lives, allowing us to work from anywhere and stay connected with our colleagues, clients, or even healthcare providers. However, with the increasing number of cyber threats, it is essential to implement strong security measures to protect sensitive information during remote access. One such effective security measure is two-factor authentication (2FA).

Understanding Two-Factor Authentication

Two-factor authentication adds an additional layer of security to the traditional username and password login process. It requires users to provide two different types of authentication factors to verify their identity. These factors usually fall into one of the following categories:

1. **Knowledge factor:** Something the user knows, such as a password or a PIN.

2. **Possession factor:** Something the user possesses, such as a mobile device or a security token.

3. **Biometric factor:** Something unique to the user's physical characteristics, such as a fingerprint or facial recognition.

By combining two factors, it significantly reduces the risk of unauthorized access, even if one factor is compromised.

Implementing Two-Factor Authentication

To enable two-factor authentication for remote access, organizations should follow these best practices:

1. **Select a reliable authentication method:** There are various 2FA methods available, such as SMS codes, mobile apps, hardware tokens, or biometrics. Choose a method that suits the needs of your organization and provides a high level of security.

2. **Integrate with your remote access solution:** Ensure that your remote access solution supports two-factor authentication. Most modern remote access tools and virtual private network (VPN) software support 2FA integration.

3. **Enforce 2FA for all users:** Make two-factor authentication mandatory for all employees and users who require remote access to sensitive systems or data. This ensures consistent and comprehensive security across the organization.

4. **Educate users about 2FA:** Provide clear instructions and training to users on how to set up and use two-factor authentication. Emphasize the importance of protecting their authentication factors and the benefits of 2FA in preventing unauthorized access.

5. **Regularly review and update authentication methods:** Stay informed about the latest 2FA technologies and regularly review their effectiveness. Consider implementing adaptive authentication methods that evaluate risk factors and adjust security requirements accordingly.

Real-World Example: Two-Factor Authentication in Healthcare

Let's consider a real-world scenario in the healthcare industry. Dr. Sarah needs to access patient records remotely, which contain sensitive and confidential information. The healthcare facility has implemented two-factor authentication to secure remote access for all healthcare providers.

Dr. Sarah logs into the remote access portal using her username and password (knowledge factor). Once authenticated, she receives a one-time passcode on her mobile phone (possession factor) via a text message. She enters the passcode along with her username and password to complete the authentication process.

In this example, by combining the knowledge factor (username and password) and possession factor (mobile phone for receiving the passcode), the healthcare facility ensures that only authorized healthcare providers can access patient records remotely.

Caveats and Considerations

While two-factor authentication provides enhanced security, it is important to consider the following caveats:

- **User experience:** Depending on the implementation method, 2FA can introduce additional steps for users during the login process. Organizations should strive to balance security with user convenience to ensure adoption and compliance.

- **Backup and recovery options:** Organizations must have contingency plans in place if the user's primary authentication factor (such as a mobile phone) is lost, stolen, or unavailable. Alternative backup methods or recovery processes should be established.

- **Integration challenges:** Integrating two-factor authentication with existing systems and applications may require technical expertise. It is important to evaluate compatibility and seek support from vendors or experts if needed.

Conclusion

Two-factor authentication provides an effective way to strengthen remote access security. By incorporating an additional authentication factor, organizations can significantly reduce the risk of unauthorized access to sensitive information. It is crucial for organizations to understand the benefits and best practices of implementing two-factor authentication to ensure the security and privacy of their remote access systems and data.

Managing Third-Party Access and Vendor Security

In today's interconnected world, organizations often rely on third-party vendors and service providers to meet their business needs. However, with the increasing number of cyber threats, it is essential to manage the access of these external parties and ensure the security of their systems and data. This section will explore the importance of managing third-party access and provide practical guidance on vendor security.

The Importance of Managing Third-Party Access

Third-party vendors play a crucial role in the operations of many organizations, including those in the health and wellness industry. These vendors may provide services such as cloud computing, data storage, software development, or IT support. While outsourcing certain tasks can bring cost savings and expertise, it also introduces additional risks.

One of the major risks associated with third-party access is the potential for unauthorized access to sensitive information. If a vendor's system is compromised, it could lead to a breach of the organization's data. Additionally, a vendor's security practices may not align with the organization's cybersecurity standards, making them a weak link in the overall security posture.

By managing third-party access effectively, organizations can mitigate these risks and ensure the confidentiality, integrity, and availability of their systems and data. This involves implementing appropriate security controls, monitoring vendor activities, and establishing clear contractual obligations.

Vendor Security Assessment

Before granting access to a third-party vendor, it is crucial to assess their security posture and ensure they meet the necessary security requirements. The following steps can help organizations conduct a thorough vendor security assessment:

1. **Identify critical vendors:** Begin by identifying the vendors who have access to sensitive systems or handle confidential information. This could include cloud service providers, software development firms, or data storage providers.

2. **Review vendor security practices:** Request the vendor's security policies, procedures, and other relevant documentation. This will provide insights into their approach to cybersecurity. Look for evidence of strong access controls, encryption, regular security audits, and incident response plans.

3. **Perform on-site assessments:** Conduct on-site visits, if feasible, to assess the physical security measures in place. This could include reviewing the vendor's data center or office facility to ensure they have appropriate safeguards in place.

4. **Assess vendor's compliance:** Determine whether the vendor complies with relevant security standards and regulations. This could include ISO 27001, HIPAA, or GDPR. Request evidence of certifications or audits conducted by third-party assessors.

5. **Review incident response capabilities:** Evaluate the vendor's incident response capabilities and assess their ability to detect, respond, and recover from cybersecurity incidents. Request documented incident response plans and review their effectiveness.

6. **Evaluate subcontractor relationships:** Understand whether the vendor engages subcontractors and assess their security posture as well. Ensure that the subcontractor's security measures align with the organization's requirements.

Based on the vendor security assessment, organizations can make an informed decision about granting third-party access and manage vendor relationships more effectively.

Establishing Secure Vendor Agreements

Once a vendor has been assessed and deemed suitable for access, it is crucial to establish a secure vendor agreement that outlines the expectations and responsibilities of both parties. A comprehensive vendor agreement should include the following components:

1. **Security requirements:** Clearly define the security requirements that the vendor must meet. This may include specific security controls, encryption standards, incident notification procedures, and access management practices. Ensure that the agreement aligns with the organization's cybersecurity policies and regulatory requirements.

2. **Data handling and protection:** Specify how the vendor should handle and protect the organization's data. Include provisions for data encryption, data retention, backup and recovery, and data breach notification. Clearly define ownership and responsibility for data throughout the vendor's engagement.

3. **Audit and monitoring rights:** Establish the organization's rights to audit and monitor the vendor's security practices and systems. This may involve periodic security assessments, vulnerability scans, or penetration tests. Clearly state the frequency, scope, and reporting requirements for these assessments.

4. **Incident response and notification:** Define the vendor's responsibilities in the event of a cybersecurity incident. This should include their obligation to notify the organization promptly, cooperate in the investigation, and take appropriate remedial actions. Specify the timeline and reporting requirements for incident response.

5. **Termination and transition:** Outline the process for terminating the vendor's access and transitioning to a different vendor if necessary. Include provisions for data transfer, data sanitization, and return or destruction of confidential information.

6. **Indemnification and liability:** Clarify the allocation of liability between the organization and the vendor in case of security breaches or other cybersecurity incidents. Determine the extent to which the vendor will indemnify the organization for any losses arising from their actions or omissions.

By establishing a robust vendor agreement, organizations can set clear expectations for security and ensure that vendors understand their responsibilities in safeguarding sensitive information.

Ongoing Vendor Management

Managing third-party access is not a one-time activity. Organizations must engage in ongoing vendor management to ensure the continued security of their systems and data. The following practices can help ensure effective vendor management:

- **Regular vendor audits:** Conduct regular security audits to assess the vendor's compliance with the agreed-upon security requirements. This could include both technical assessments and policy reviews.
- **Security incident reporting and response:** Establish mechanisms for the vendor to promptly report any security incidents or breaches. Define the incident response procedures that both parties should follow in the event of a cybersecurity incident.
- **Continuous monitoring:** Implement continuous monitoring tools and techniques to track the vendor's compliance with security controls. This could involve network monitoring, log analysis, or vulnerability scanning.
- **Periodic contract review:** Regularly review and update the vendor agreement to reflect changes in the organization's security requirements or regulatory landscape. Ensure that the agreement remains relevant and enforceable.
- **Employee education and awareness:** Provide training and awareness programs for employees who interact with third-party vendors. This will help them understand the importance of vendor security and their role in maintaining it.
- **Vendor risk ranking:** Develop a risk ranking system to prioritize vendor assessments and allocate resources accordingly. Focus more attention on vendors with higher access privileges or those handling more sensitive information.

By incorporating these practices into their vendor management program, organizations can proactively address security risks associated with third-party access.

Case Study: Vendor Security Breach and Lessons Learned

To highlight the importance of managing third-party access and vendor security, let's consider a real-world case study.

In 2017, Equifax, one of the largest credit reporting agencies in the United States, suffered a massive data breach that exposed the personal information of over 147 million individuals. The breach was a result of a vulnerability in a web application built by a third-party vendor.

Equifax's failure to properly manage the vendor's access and monitor their security practices resulted in significant reputational and financial damage. In the aftermath of the breach, Equifax faced numerous lawsuits, regulatory investigations, and a loss of customer trust.

From this case study, we can learn several key lessons:

- Conduct regular security assessments of third-party vendors and review their security practices to identify vulnerabilities and weaknesses.
- Clearly define security requirements in vendor agreements and ensure they align with the organization's security policies and regulatory obligations.
- Establish robust incident response procedures that encompass vendor responsibilities in the event of a cybersecurity incident.
- Implement continuous monitoring and auditing programs to track vendor compliance with security controls and address any emerging risks promptly.
- Provide ongoing employee education and awareness programs to emphasize the importance of vendor security and foster a culture of cybersecurity.

By applying these lessons, organizations can reduce the risk of vendor-related data breaches and maintain a more secure environment.

Conclusion

Managing third-party access and ensuring vendor security is of paramount importance in today's interconnected world. By conducting thorough vendor security assessments, establishing secure contracts, and implementing robust vendor management practices, organizations can minimize the potential risks associated with third-party access. Ongoing monitoring, employee education, and incident response planning are critical components of effective vendor security management. By adopting these practices, organizations can strengthen their overall cybersecurity posture and safeguard their valuable systems and data.

Secure Access Control Policies and Procedures

Access control is a fundamental aspect of cybersecurity that focuses on managing and regulating access to digital resources and sensitive information. In the context of health and wellness, secure access control policies and procedures ensure that only authorized individuals can access and interact with critical data and systems. This section will explore the principles and best practices involved in developing effective access control policies and procedures to safeguard sensitive information in the health and wellness industry.

Access Control Fundamentals

Before diving into the specifics of creating access control policies and procedures, it is important to understand the fundamental principles that underpin access control mechanisms. These principles include:

1. **Least Privilege:** The principle of least privilege states that individuals should only be granted the minimum level of access necessary to perform their job functions. By adhering to this principle, organizations can limit the potential damage that can occur if an account is compromised or misused.

2. **Need-to-Know:** Similar to the principle of least privilege, the need-to-know principle ensures that individuals are only granted access to information and resources that are necessary for their specific roles or responsibilities. This principle helps minimize the risk of unauthorized disclosure or misuse of sensitive data.

3. **Separation of Duties:** Separation of duties requires dividing tasks and privileges among multiple individuals to prevent a single person from having full control over critical operations. This principle helps mitigate the risk of insider threats and unauthorized activities.

4. **Authentication:** Authentication is the process of verifying the identity of a user, device, or system before granting access to resources. Common authentication methods include passwords, biometrics, smart cards, and two-factor authentication (2FA). Strong authentication mechanisms are essential for ensuring the integrity of access control.

5. **Authorization:** Authorization determines the actions and operations that an authenticated user or entity is allowed to perform on a system or data. It involves defining and managing access rights and permissions based on roles,

groups, or attributes. Implementing robust authorization mechanisms is crucial for enforcing access control policies.

By incorporating these fundamental principles into access control policies, organizations can effectively manage security risks associated with unauthorized access.

Developing Access Control Policies and Procedures

Developing access control policies and procedures requires a systematic approach that aligns with the organization's overall security objectives. The following steps outline the key considerations for creating effective access control frameworks:

1. **Identify Critical Assets and Resources:** Start by identifying the critical assets and resources that need protection. This may include databases, electronic health records (EHRs), financial systems, and intellectual property. Understanding the value and importance of these assets will help in prioritizing access control measures.

2. **Define User Roles and Access Levels:** Determine the roles and responsibilities within the organization and define the access levels associated with each role. This can be done by categorizing users into different groups based on their job functions and granting appropriate access privileges according to the principle of least privilege.

3. **Establish Access Control Policies:** Develop policies that outline access control requirements, including authentication mechanisms, password complexity rules, session management, and user account management. These policies should be clear, concise, and easily understandable to ensure compliance by all users.

4. **Implement Access Control Technologies:** Deploy access control technologies that align with the organization's security requirements. This may include user authentication systems, access control lists (ACLs), role-based access control (RBAC), and attribute-based access control (ABAC). It is important to regularly update and patch these technologies to address any vulnerabilities.

5. **Enforce Data Privacy and Confidentiality:** Access control should not only focus on restricting access to sensitive data but also incorporate measures to preserve data privacy and confidentiality. Encryption, anonymization, and

pseudonymization techniques can be employed to protect data both at rest and in transit.

6. **Regularly Audit and Monitor Access:** Implement a logging and auditing system to monitor user access activities and detect any suspicious or anomalous behavior. Regularly review access logs, perform user access reviews, and conduct internal and external security audits to ensure compliance and identify any security gaps.

By following these steps, organizations can establish robust and effective access control policies and procedures that align with industry best practices.

Challenges and Considerations

Implementing secure access control policies and procedures in the health and wellness industry comes with its own set of challenges and considerations. Some of these include:

- **Balancing Security and Usability:** Striking the right balance between security and user convenience is crucial. Access control mechanisms should be strong enough to prevent unauthorized access but not overly complex to impede legitimate users from performing their tasks efficiently.

- **User Training and Awareness:** Users play a significant role in maintaining the effectiveness of access control. Organizations should provide regular training and awareness programs to educate users about the importance of access control, password hygiene, and the risks associated with sharing credentials.

- **Third-Party Access:** Organizations often collaborate with third-party vendors and external partners who require access to certain systems or data. Establishing secure access controls for third-party entities is essential to prevent unauthorized access or data breaches through these external connections.

- **Compliance with Regulations:** The health and wellness industry is subject to various regulations and standards, such as HIPAA (Health Insurance Portability and Accountability Act) and GDPR (General Data Protection Regulation). Access control policies and procedures must comply with these regulations to protect patient privacy and avoid legal consequences.

Addressing these challenges requires a comprehensive approach that includes ongoing monitoring, regular risk assessments, and continuous improvement of access control frameworks.

Case Study: Access Control in a Healthcare Organization

To better understand the practical implementation of access control policies and procedures, let's consider a case study of a healthcare organization.

ABC Healthcare is a large hospital that handles a vast amount of sensitive patient data. To ensure secure access to this data, ABC Healthcare has implemented several access control measures.

First, they have categorized their employees into roles based on job functions, such as doctors, nurses, administrative staff, and IT professionals. Each role is assigned specific access privileges based on the principle of least privilege. For example, doctors have access to patient records, while administrative staff have limited access to financial and administrative systems.

To enforce strong authentication, ABC Healthcare has implemented two-factor authentication (2FA) for all employees. This requires users to provide a unique password and a one-time verification code generated by a mobile app or a physical token.

Furthermore, ABC Healthcare has implemented a granular access control system that restricts access to specific patient records based on the need-to-know principle. Only authorized users with a legitimate reason to access certain records can do so.

Regular audits and monitoring of access logs are conducted to identify any unauthorized access attempts or anomalies. Incident response procedures are in place to address any security incidents promptly.

In this case study, the access control policies and procedures implemented by ABC Healthcare demonstrate a comprehensive approach to protecting sensitive patient data while ensuring efficient and secure access for authorized personnel.

Conclusion

Secure access control policies and procedures are crucial for protecting sensitive information and systems in the health and wellness industry. By adhering to the fundamental principles of access control, organizations can effectively manage and regulate access to critical resources. Developing robust access control frameworks requires careful planning, implementation of appropriate technologies, and ongoing monitoring and improvement. By addressing the challenges and considerations specific to the industry, organizations can establish a strong security posture that safeguards sensitive data and promotes trust among stakeholders.

Employee Training on Secure Remote Access

Remote access to work systems has become increasingly common in today's digital world. With the rise of telecommuting and virtual teams, employees often need to access sensitive company resources from outside the office. However, this convenience also brings security risks that need to be addressed through proper employee training. In this section, we will explore the importance of secure remote access and provide guidelines for effective employee training.

Understanding the Risks of Remote Access

Remote access allows employees to connect to their work systems and access company data and applications from outside the physical office environment. While this brings flexibility and productivity benefits, it also exposes the organization to various cybersecurity risks. Some of the key risks associated with remote access include:

- **Unauthorized access:** If remote access is not properly secured, attackers may be able to gain unauthorized access to sensitive company resources.
- **Data breaches:** Remote access introduces the risk of data breaches, as sensitive data may be transmitted and stored on less secure devices and networks.
- **Malware and ransomware:** Remote access increases the chances of employees unknowingly downloading malware or falling victim to ransomware attacks.
- **Loss or theft of devices:** Remote access often involves using personal devices, which increases the risk of loss or theft and potential exposure of sensitive information.

Given these risks, it is crucial to educate employees about the best practices for secure remote access.

Developing a Comprehensive Training Program

A comprehensive training program on secure remote access should cover the following key areas:

1. **Introduction to remote access security:** Start by explaining the importance of secure remote access and how it impacts the overall cybersecurity posture of the organization. Emphasize the potential risks and consequences of insecure practices.

2. **Policies and procedures:** Provide employees with a clear understanding of the organization's policies and procedures related to remote access. Explain the acceptable use of company resources, password management guidelines, and data protection requirements.

3. **Securing personal devices:** Educate employees on the steps they should take to secure their personal devices when accessing work systems remotely. This includes enabling device encryption, installing security updates, and using strong passwords.

4. **Network security:** Teach employees about the importance of using secure networks when connecting remotely. Emphasize the risks of using public Wi-Fi networks and encourage the use of virtual private networks (VPNs) for secure connections.

5. **Authentication methods:** Train employees on the different methods of authentication used for remote access, such as passwords, biometric authentication, and two-factor authentication. Explain the benefits and limitations of each method and how to use them appropriately.

6. **Phishing awareness:** Educate employees about the risks of phishing attacks and how to identify and report suspicious emails or messages. Emphasize the importance of never sharing login credentials or sensitive information in response to unsolicited requests.

7. **Safe file handling:** Provide guidelines on how to handle files securely when accessing them remotely. Teach employees about file encryption, secure file transfer methods, and the importance of scanning files for malware before opening them.

8. **Incident reporting:** Instruct employees on the proper procedures for reporting security incidents or suspicious activities related to remote access. Establish clear channels of communication and ensure employees feel comfortable reporting any potential issues.

Interactive and Engaging Training Methods

To ensure the effectiveness of the training program, it is essential to make the training interactive and engaging. Here are some strategies to consider:

- **Case studies and real-world examples:** Incorporate real-world examples and case studies of remote access security breaches to illustrate the potential consequences of insecure practices. This helps employees understand the relevance and importance of the training content.

- **Simulated phishing exercises:** Conduct simulated phishing exercises to test employees' ability to identify and respond to phishing attacks. Provide immediate feedback on their performance and offer additional training if necessary.

- **Interactive e-learning modules:** Develop interactive e-learning modules that allow employees to learn at their own pace and engage with the content through quizzes, interactive scenarios, and simulations.

- **Hands-on workshops:** Organize hands-on workshops where employees can practice secure remote access techniques using virtual lab environments. Provide step-by-step instructions and encourage employees to ask questions and seek clarification.

Ongoing Reinforcement and Evaluation

Employee training on secure remote access should not be a one-time event. To ensure long-term effectiveness, consider the following strategies:

- **Regular refreshers:** Conduct periodic refreshers on secure remote access to reinforce the training content and keep employees up to date with the latest threats and best practices.

- **Internal communication and reminders:** Regularly communicate with employees through internal newsletters, emails, or intranet announcements to remind them of the importance of secure remote access and any updates to policies or procedures.

- **Evaluation and metrics:** Establish metrics to evaluate the effectiveness of the training program. Monitor remote access-related security incidents, user feedback, and employee compliance with policies to identify areas for improvement.

- **Continuous improvement:** Continuously review and update the training program based on feedback and emerging threats. Incorporate new technologies, tools, and techniques to ensure employees are equipped with the most relevant knowledge and skills.

By implementing a comprehensive training program that emphasizes secure remote access, organizations can significantly reduce the risk of security incidents and better protect their sensitive data and resources.

Conclusion

Employee training on secure remote access is crucial for maintaining a strong cybersecurity posture in today's remote work environment. By educating employees about the risks associated with remote access and providing practical guidelines for secure practices, organizations can significantly mitigate the potential security threats. Remember to continuously reinforce the training content, evaluate the effectiveness of the program, and adapt to ever-evolving cybersecurity landscape to stay ahead of emerging threats.

Collaboration and Security in Cloud Computing

Understanding Cloud Computing Models and Security Risks

Cloud computing has revolutionized the way businesses and organizations manage their data and applications. It provides convenient, on-demand access to a shared pool of computing resources, such as servers, storage, and applications, over the internet. However, along with its many benefits, cloud computing also introduces new security risks and challenges. In this section, we will explore the different cloud computing models, their respective security risks, and best practices for ensuring the security of cloud-based systems.

Cloud Computing Models

There are three main cloud computing models: Infrastructure as a Service (IaaS), Platform as a Service (PaaS), and Software as a Service (SaaS). Each model offers a different level of control and responsibility to the cloud service provider and the customer.

Infrastructure as a Service (IaaS) IaaS is the most customizable and flexible cloud computing model. It provides virtualized infrastructure resources such as virtual machines, storage, and networks. With IaaS, customers are responsible for managing their applications, data, runtime, and middleware, while the cloud service provider takes care of the underlying infrastructure. Examples of IaaS providers include Amazon Web Services (AWS) EC2, Microsoft Azure, and Google Cloud Compute Engine.

Platform as a Service (PaaS) PaaS provides a platform for developers to build, deploy, manage, and scale applications without having to worry about infrastructure. Customers can focus on coding and developing their applications, while the PaaS provider handles the underlying servers, storage, and networking. This model offers a higher level of abstraction compared to IaaS. Examples of PaaS providers include Heroku, Google App Engine, and Red Hat OpenShift.

Software as a Service (SaaS) SaaS is the most user-friendly cloud computing model. It delivers software applications over the internet, accessible through a web browser, without the need for installation or maintenance. The cloud service provider hosts the application and takes care of all infrastructure and maintenance tasks. Users only need to access the application and use it for their specific needs. Popular examples of SaaS applications include Salesforce, Microsoft Office 365, and Dropbox.

Security Risks in Cloud Computing

While cloud computing offers numerous benefits, it is not without its security risks. Here are some of the common security risks associated with cloud computing:

Data Breaches One of the primary concerns in cloud computing is the risk of unauthorized access to sensitive data. Data breaches can occur due to weak access controls, misconfiguration of cloud resources, or vulnerabilities in the cloud provider's infrastructure. Attackers may target valuable data stored in the cloud, such as customer records, intellectual property, or financial information.

Insecure APIs Application Programming Interfaces (APIs) enable communication and interaction between different software systems and services. Insecure APIs in cloud environments can be a potential entry point for attackers. If APIs are not properly secured, attackers can exploit vulnerabilities to gain unauthorized access, manipulate data, or launch attacks on cloud-based applications.

Insider Threats Insider threats are security risks posed by authorized individuals within an organization. In the context of cloud computing, insider threats can include malicious or negligent actions by employees, contractors, or third-party service providers with access to the cloud infrastructure. These individuals may intentionally or unintentionally disclose sensitive information or compromise the security of the cloud environment.

Data Loss and Availability Cloud service providers typically ensure data redundancy and availability within their infrastructure. However, technical failures, natural disasters, or other unforeseen events can cause data loss or service disruptions. Organizations must have contingency plans and backup strategies in place to mitigate the risk of data loss and ensure business continuity.

Lack of Control and Visibility When an organization decides to migrate to the cloud, it relinquishes some control and visibility over its data and infrastructure. This lack of control can make it challenging to monitor and assess security controls, detect vulnerabilities or misconfigurations, and respond to security incidents effectively. Organizations must carefully consider the security measures and transparency offered by cloud service providers to address this risk.

Best Practices for Securing Cloud Computing

To mitigate the security risks associated with cloud computing, organizations should implement the following best practices:

Data Encryption Implement strong encryption mechanisms to protect data both at rest and in transit. Encryption ensures that even if data is intercepted or stolen, it remains unreadable by unauthorized individuals. Organizations should leverage encryption techniques such as symmetric and asymmetric encryption, secure key management, and transport layer security protocols.

Access Control and Identity Management Enforce robust access controls and strong authentication mechanisms to prevent unauthorized access to cloud resources. Implement user identity and access management solutions, including role-based access controls, multi-factor authentication, and privileged access management. Regularly review and update access permissions to align with the principle of least privilege.

Security Monitoring and Incident Response Implement centralized security monitoring and real-time threat detection mechanisms in cloud environments. Monitor and analyze logs, events, and network traffic to identify security incidents or anomalies. Develop an incident response plan that outlines the actions to be taken in the event of a security breach and regularly test and update this plan.

Vendor Due Diligence Before selecting a cloud service provider, conduct a thorough assessment of their security measures, certifications, and compliance with relevant regulations. Evaluate their incident response capabilities, data protection practices, and commitment to security. Ensure that the cloud service provider maintains transparency and provides appropriate security controls to meet your organization's requirements.

Data Backup and Recovery Implement regular data backup procedures to ensure the availability and integrity of critical data. Store backups in separate locations or with a different cloud service provider to protect against data loss due to technical failures or disasters. Test the restoration process periodically to ensure its effectiveness.

Employee Education and Awareness Educate employees about the security risks and best practices associated with cloud computing. Provide training on how to identify and report phishing attacks, secure password management, and safe cloud usage. Foster a culture of security awareness and encourage employees to adhere to security policies and procedures.

In conclusion, cloud computing offers significant advantages in terms of scalability, cost-efficiency, and accessibility. However, organizations must be aware of the security risks and implement appropriate measures to protect their data and applications in the cloud. Understanding the different cloud computing models and their associated security risks is crucial for ensuring the confidentiality, integrity, and availability of cloud-based systems. By following best practices and staying up to date with emerging threats, organizations can leverage the benefits of cloud computing while maintaining a strong security posture.

Best Practices for Secure Cloud Storage and File Sharing

In today's interconnected world, cloud storage and file sharing have become essential tools for individuals and organizations alike. However, the convenience of these services also presents risks to the security and privacy of sensitive data. In this section, we will discuss the best practices for ensuring secure cloud storage and file sharing, mitigating the potential risks, and protecting your valuable information.

Understanding the Risks

Before we delve into the best practices, it is important to understand the potential risks associated with cloud storage and file sharing. These risks include:

- Unauthorized access: Hackers can exploit vulnerabilities in cloud storage services or gain unauthorized access to your account, compromising the confidentiality and integrity of your data.

- Data breaches: Cloud storage services may experience security breaches, leading to the exposure of sensitive or confidential information.

- Malware infection: Malicious software can infect files stored in the cloud, allowing cybercriminals to gain control over your system or steal your data.

- Insider threats: Your data may be at risk from individuals within your organization who have access to your cloud storage account.

- Data loss: Cloud storage providers can suffer from technical failures or hardware malfunctions, resulting in the permanent loss of your data.

To mitigate these risks and ensure the security of your cloud storage and file sharing, follow these best practices:

Choose a Trusted Cloud Storage Provider

The first step to secure cloud storage and file sharing is selecting a reputable and trustworthy cloud storage provider. Look for providers that prioritize security and have a strong track record of protecting user data. Consider factors such as encryption, access controls, data backup procedures, and compliance with relevant regulations.

Implement Strong Authentication

Authentication plays a crucial role in securing your cloud storage and file sharing. Implement robust authentication measures such as multi-factor authentication (MFA) to ensure that only authorized individuals can access your account. MFA combines two or more verification factors, such as passwords, biometrics, or one-time authentication codes, providing an extra layer of security.

Encrypt Your Data

Encryption is an essential practice for protecting the confidentiality of your data. Ensure that your cloud storage provider offers end-to-end encryption, which ensures that your data is encrypted both at rest and in transit. End-to-end encryption guarantees that only you and authorized recipients can access and decrypt the data, even if it is intercepted by unauthorized parties.

Manage Access Controls

To prevent unauthorized access, it is crucial to manage access controls effectively. Limit access privileges to only those individuals who require access to specific files or folders. Regularly review and revoke access for former employees or individuals no longer requiring access. This helps reduce the risk of insider threats and unauthorized data access.

Regularly Update and Patch

Keep your cloud storage infrastructure and associated software up to date with the latest security patches. Cloud storage providers often release updates to address vulnerabilities and improve security. Regularly applying these updates ensures that your cloud storage remains protected against known security vulnerabilities.

Backup Your Data

Data loss can occur due to multiple factors, including hardware failures or accidental deletions. Regularly backup your data to a separate cloud storage account or an offline storage device. This ensures that even if your primary cloud storage is compromised or experiences a failure, you can restore your data from the backup.

Monitor and Audit Activity

Monitoring and auditing activity within your cloud storage account helps you identify any unauthorized access attempts or suspicious behavior. Enable logging and notifications for critical events such as failed login attempts or unusual file activities. Regularly review these logs and investigate any anomalies promptly.

Educate Users

User awareness and training are crucial in maintaining the security of cloud storage and file sharing. Educate users about best practices, such as strong password management, caution when sharing files externally, and identifying phishing attempts. Regularly reinforce security awareness to ensure users remain vigilant and proactive in protecting sensitive data.

Conduct Regular Security Assessments

Regularly assess the security of your cloud storage and file sharing practices. This may include penetration testing, vulnerability scanning, and risk assessments to identify any weaknesses or areas for improvement. Address any vulnerabilities or deficiencies promptly to mitigate potential risks.

Cloud Storage and File Sharing Best Practices Checklist

To summarize, here is a checklist of best practices for secure cloud storage and file sharing:

- Choose a trusted cloud storage provider
- Implement strong authentication measures like multi-factor authentication
- Encrypt your data with end-to-end encryption
- Manage access controls and regularly review access privileges
- Keep your cloud storage infrastructure and software up to date
- Regularly backup your data
- Monitor and audit activity within your cloud storage account
- Educate users about security best practices

- Conduct regular security assessments

By following these best practices, you can ensure that your cloud storage and file sharing activities are secure and protect your valuable data from unauthorized access, breaches, and other potential risks.

Conclusion

Secure cloud storage and file sharing are essential for safeguarding sensitive and valuable data. By implementing these best practices, you can enhance the security and integrity of your data in the cloud. Remember, the responsibility to protect your information rests with you, so stay vigilant, keep up with latest security practices, and continuously assess and improve the security measures you have in place.

Cloud Security Controls and Compliance Considerations

In today's digital world, cloud computing has become an integral part of the health and wellness industry. It provides numerous benefits such as scalability, cost-efficiency, and flexibility. However, with the adoption of cloud services comes the need for robust security controls to protect sensitive health and wellness data. This section will explore the various security controls and compliance considerations that organizations should take into account when utilizing cloud computing in the healthcare sector.

Security Controls in Cloud Computing

When it comes to cloud security, organizations must implement a layered approach to protect their data. Let's discuss some key security controls that are critical in a cloud computing environment:

1. **Authentication and Access Controls:** Strong authentication mechanisms, such as multi-factor authentication (MFA), should be implemented to ensure that only authorized individuals can access cloud resources. Access controls, such as role-based access control (RBAC), should be established to limit user privileges and enforce the principle of least privilege.

2. **Data Encryption:** Encrypting data at rest and in transit is essential to maintain its confidentiality. Organizations should use industry-standard encryption algorithms to protect sensitive data when it resides in the cloud or is transferred between cloud service providers (CSPs) and users.

3. **Network Security:** Robust network security controls, including firewalls, intrusion detection and prevention systems (IDPS), and virtual private networks (VPNs), should be implemented to safeguard the cloud infrastructure from malicious activities and unauthorized access.

4. **Vulnerability Management:** Regular vulnerability assessments and penetration testing should be performed to identify and address potential weaknesses in the cloud environment. Prompt patching of software and firmware vulnerabilities is also crucial to prevent exploitation by attackers.

These are just a few examples of the security controls that organizations need to consider when leveraging cloud computing services in the health and wellness industry. It is important to note that security controls should be tailored to the specific requirements and risk appetite of each organization.

Compliance Considerations in Cloud Computing

In the healthcare sector, compliance with regulatory requirements and industry standards is of utmost importance. When using cloud services, organizations must ensure that they comply with the relevant regulations and standards. Let's discuss some key compliance considerations in cloud computing:

1. **HIPAA Compliance:** The Health Insurance Portability and Accountability Act (HIPAA) sets the standards for protecting sensitive health information. Cloud service providers must offer HIPAA-compliant services and sign business associate agreements (BAAs) with covered entities. Organizations should assess the cloud provider's security measures and data protection capabilities to ensure compliance with HIPAA regulations.

2. **GDPR Compliance:** If an organization operates in the European Union or handles personal data of EU residents, it must comply with the General Data Protection Regulation (GDPR). Cloud service providers should have appropriate data protection mechanisms in place and adhere to GDPR requirements, including data subject rights, data breach notification, and lawful basis for data processing.

3. **ISO 27001 Certification:** The International Organization for Standardization (ISO) 27001 certification demonstrates that an organization has implemented an Information Security Management System (ISMS) and follows best practices for information security.

Choosing a cloud service provider with ISO 27001 certification can provide assurance that the provider has robust security controls in place.

4. **Data Sovereignty:** Organizations must consider the location of their data in the cloud to ensure compliance with data sovereignty laws. Some countries have restrictions on moving certain types of data across borders. It is important to understand where cloud data centers are located, as well as the data privacy laws and regulations of those jurisdictions.

By addressing these compliance considerations, organizations can ensure that they are meeting the necessary regulatory requirements when utilizing cloud computing services.

Case Study: Cloud Security Controls and Compliance in Healthcare

Let's consider a real-world example to illustrate the importance of cloud security controls and compliance in the healthcare industry.

Case Study: XYZ Healthcare System

XYZ Healthcare System is a large healthcare organization that utilizes cloud services for storing and processing patient data. To ensure the security and privacy of patient information, XYZ Healthcare System has implemented a range of security controls and compliance measures:

1. **Authentication and Access Controls:** XYZ Healthcare System enforces strong password policies and implements multi-factor authentication for accessing cloud resources. User privileges are carefully managed using role-based access controls to minimize the risk of unauthorized access.

2. **Data Encryption:** XYZ Healthcare System encrypts patient data both at rest and in transit. Data stored in the cloud is encrypted using industry-standard encryption algorithms, and secure communication protocols are used when transferring data to and from the cloud.

3. **Network Security:** To protect against network-based threats, XYZ Healthcare System employs firewalls and IDPS to monitor and block malicious activities. Remote access to cloud resources is secured using VPNs, and network traffic is segmented to isolate sensitive data and workloads.

4. **Vulnerability Management:** Regular vulnerability assessments and penetration testing are conducted to identify and mitigate vulnerabilities in

the cloud environment. XYZ Healthcare System maintains a proactive approach to patching software and firmware vulnerabilities to minimize the risk of exploitation.

5. **HIPAA Compliance:** As a healthcare organization, XYZ Healthcare System ensures that its cloud service provider signs a business associate agreement (BAA) and offers HIPAA-compliant services. The provider implements robust physical, technical, and administrative safeguards to protect patient data.

6. **ISO 27001 Certification:** XYZ Healthcare System chooses a cloud service provider that has achieved ISO 27001 certification. This certification gives assurance that the provider follows internationally recognized information security best practices.

By implementing these security controls and considering compliance requirements, XYZ Healthcare System minimizes the risk of data breaches and ensures the security and privacy of patient information in the cloud.

Conclusion

Cloud computing offers significant advantages to the health and wellness industry but requires careful consideration of security controls and compliance requirements. Organizations must deploy robust security controls to protect sensitive data, such as strong authentication mechanisms, data encryption, network security, and vulnerability management. Additionally, compliance considerations, including HIPAA, GDPR, ISO 27001, and data sovereignty, must be addressed to ensure adherence to relevant regulations and industry standards. By implementing these security controls and compliance measures, organizations can confidently leverage cloud computing while safeguarding their data in the digital age.

In the next section, we will explore secure communication and collaboration tools that are essential for maintaining privacy and security in the health and wellness industry.

Securing Data in Cloud-Based Collaboration Tools

In today's digital age, cloud-based collaboration tools have become an essential part of the health and wellness industry. These tools enable seamless communication, file sharing, and collaboration among healthcare professionals, researchers, and patients. However, the increasing reliance on cloud-based solutions also comes with cybersecurity risks that need to be addressed to ensure the security and privacy of sensitive data. In this section, we will explore the best practices and strategies for securing data in cloud-based collaboration tools.

Understanding the Security Challenges

Cloud-based collaboration tools offer numerous advantages, such as enhanced accessibility, scalability, and cost-effectiveness. However, they also introduce unique security challenges that must be addressed. Some of the key security challenges in this context include:

- **Data Breaches:** Cloud storage and collaboration platforms can be attractive targets for hackers due to the potential wealth of sensitive information they hold.

- **Data Loss:** The risk of accidental data loss or deletion is ever-present in cloud-based environments. Technical errors or human mistakes can lead to permanent loss of data if not properly mitigated.

- **Unauthorized Access:** Cloud-based collaboration tools may be accessed by multiple users and require robust access controls to prevent unauthorized individuals from gaining access to sensitive information.

- **Insider Threats:** Malicious or unintentional actions by authorized users pose a significant risk to the security of data stored in cloud-based collaboration tools. Proper measures must be implemented to detect and mitigate insider threats.

- **Compliance and Legal Requirements:** Health and wellness organizations are subject to various regulatory requirements and legal obligations, such as HIPAA (Health Insurance Portability and Accountability Act). Ensuring compliance with these regulations while using cloud-based collaboration tools is critical.

Best Practices for Securing Data

To mitigate the security risks associated with cloud-based collaboration tools, organizations should implement a comprehensive set of security best practices. These practices include:

1. **Strong Authentication and Access Controls:** Implementing strong authentication measures, such as multi-factor authentication (MFA) and role-based access controls (RBAC), ensures that only authorized individuals can access the data. User access and permissions should be regularly reviewed and updated based on job roles and responsibilities.

2. **Data Encryption:** Encrypting data at rest and in transit is essential to protect sensitive information from unauthorized access. Encryption should be implemented using robust encryption algorithms, and keys should be securely managed.

3. **Regular Data Backups:** Regularly backing up data stored in cloud collaboration tools is crucial for data recovery in the event of accidental deletion, data corruption, or other data loss incidents. Backups should be stored in a separate secure location, preferably offline.

4. **Continuous Monitoring and Intrusion Detection:** Deploying intrusion detection systems (IDS) and continuously monitoring the cloud infrastructure can help detect and prevent unauthorized access or suspicious activities. This includes monitoring access logs, network traffic, and system logs.

5. **Data Classification and Access Policies:** Classify data based on sensitivity and implement access policies accordingly. Only authorized users should have access to sensitive or confidential information, and data should be shared strictly on a need-to-know basis.

6. **Vendor Security Evaluation:** Before adopting a cloud-based collaboration tool, thoroughly assess the security measures implemented by the vendor. This includes evaluating the vendor's security certifications, compliance with industry standards, and their data protection practices.

7. **Employee Training and Awareness:** Properly train employees on cybersecurity best practices, including safe data handling, password hygiene, and recognizing phishing attacks. Regular awareness programs and training sessions should be conducted to keep employees informed about the latest threats and mitigation measures.

8. **Contractual Agreements:** Ensure that the contractual agreements with cloud service providers explicitly state the security and privacy requirements, including data protection, encryption, and compliance with applicable regulations. Regular audits may be required to verify compliance.

9. **Data Retention and Disposal Policies:** Implement data retention and disposal policies that dictate how long data should be stored and how it should be securely disposed of at the end of its lifecycle. This reduces the risk of unauthorized access to outdated or unnecessary data.

Real-World Example: Securing Patient Data in a Cloud-Based Collaboration Tool

Let's consider a real-world example to illustrate the importance of securing patient data in a cloud-based collaboration tool.

ABC Healthcare is a multi-specialty clinic that utilizes a cloud-based collaboration tool to facilitate communication and information sharing among its healthcare providers. The clinic follows strict data privacy regulations, including HIPAA compliance, and contains confidential patient records.

To secure patient data in the cloud-based collaboration tool, ABC Healthcare implements the following measures:

- **Multi-Factor Authentication (MFA):** All healthcare providers are required to enable MFA when accessing the cloud collaboration tool. This ensures that even if a password is compromised, an additional layer of authentication is needed for access.

- **Data Encryption:** Patient data is encrypted both at rest and in transit using strong encryption algorithms. Encryption keys are stored separately from the data and are regularly rotated to enhance security.

- **Access Controls and Data Classification:** ABC Healthcare implements role-based access controls to restrict access to patient data based on job roles and responsibilities. Additionally, patient data is classified based on sensitivity, and only authorized users with a need-to-know are granted access.

- **Regular Data Backups:** The clinic performs regular backups of patient data stored in the cloud collaboration tool. Backups are encrypted and stored in a separate secured location to ensure data recoverability in case of any data loss incidents.

- **Employee Training and Awareness:** ABC Healthcare conducts regular training sessions for its healthcare providers on data privacy and cybersecurity best practices. This includes topics such as password hygiene, recognizing phishing attempts, and proper handling of patient data.

By implementing these security measures, ABC Healthcare significantly reduces the risk of unauthorized access, data breaches, and other security incidents related to patient data stored in the cloud collaboration tool.

Conclusion

Securing data in cloud-based collaboration tools is paramount in the health and wellness industry. By understanding the security challenges, implementing best practices, and staying compliant with industry regulations, organizations can minimize the risk of data breaches, unauthorized access, and data loss incidents. Additionally, regular employee training and awareness programs play a crucial role in maintaining a strong cybersecurity posture. By following these principles and implementing robust security measures, health and wellness professionals can leverage cloud-based collaboration tools while ensuring the confidentiality, integrity, and availability of sensitive data.

Managing Cloud Service Providers and Contracts

Cloud computing has revolutionized the way organizations store and process data by allowing them to leverage the power of remote servers and resources. However, when it comes to cybersecurity, relying on cloud service providers (CSPs) introduces additional challenges and risks. In this section, we will explore best practices for managing CSPs and contracts to ensure the security and integrity of your data.

Understanding the Role of Cloud Service Providers

Cloud service providers play a crucial role in the storage, management, and processing of data for organizations. They offer a variety of services, ranging from infrastructure-as-a-service (IaaS) to software-as-a-service (SaaS). The responsibilities of CSPs can vary depending on the type of service being offered.

When selecting a CSP, it is essential to assess their security capabilities and practices. Look for CSPs that have implemented robust security controls, including physical and logical access controls, data encryption, and regular security audits. Additionally, consider their track record in terms of data breaches and their incident response capabilities.

Contractual Considerations

Once you have selected a CSP, it is crucial to establish a clear and comprehensive contract that outlines the rights, responsibilities, and expectations of both parties.

The contract should include the following key considerations:

1. **Service Level Agreements (SLAs):** SLAs define the performance metrics and availability guarantees provided by the CSP. This includes uptime guarantees, response times for support requests, and data recovery timeframes in case of an outage or disaster. Ensure that the SLAs align with your organization's needs and that there are appropriate financial penalties for breaches.

2. **Data Ownership and Control:** Clarify the ownership rights and control over the data stored in the cloud. It is important to retain ownership of your data and have the ability to move or delete it as needed. Understand the CSP's data retention policies and ensure they comply with your organization's regulations and requirements.

3. **Data Security and Privacy:** Establish clear expectations regarding data security and privacy measures. The contract should specify the encryption methods employed, access controls, and the CSP's compliance with relevant regulations, such as the Health Insurance Portability and Accountability Act (HIPAA) or the General Data Protection Regulation (GDPR).

4. **Data Breach and Incident Response:** Define the procedures and responsibilities in case of a data breach or security incident. This includes notification and reporting requirements, as well as the remediation steps the CSP will take to mitigate the impact of the breach. Make sure the contract includes provisions for regular security assessments and penetration testing.

5. **Vendor Lock-In and Exit Strategy:** Plan for the possibility of changing CSPs or bringing the data back in-house. The contract should specify the data migration process, including the format in which the data will be provided, and any associated costs. Avoid vendor lock-in by using open standards and ensuring data portability.

Performing Due Diligence

Before entering into a contract with a CSP, it is important to conduct a thorough due diligence process. This process involves evaluating the CSP's security posture, compliance with regulations, financial stability, and reputation in the industry. Consider the following steps:

1. Conduct a comprehensive security assessment: Evaluate the CSP's security controls, incident response capabilities, and adherence to relevant standards and regulations. This can be done by reviewing independent security audits, requesting documentation, and performing on-site visits.

2. Review past incidents and breaches: Research the CSP's history of incidents and breaches. Analyze their incident response plans and determine if they align with your organization's requirements.

3. Assess compliance with regulations: Ensure that the CSP complies with any industry-specific regulations that apply to your organization. For example, if you deal with protected health information (PHI), ensure that the CSP complies with HIPAA.

4. Evaluate financial stability: A CSP's financial stability is crucial to ensure the longevity of the service and their ability to invest in security measures. Request financial statements or conduct background research to assess their financial standing.

5. Seek references and customer feedback: Reach out to other organizations that have used the CSP's services and gather feedback on their performance, reliability, and responsiveness to security concerns.

Continuous Monitoring and Oversight

Once the contract with the CSP is in place, it is essential to continuously monitor their performance and ensure ongoing compliance with security requirements. Consider the following measures:

1. Regular audits and assessments: Conduct periodic audits and assessments to evaluate the CSP's compliance with security standards and contractual obligations. This can include vulnerability assessments, penetration testing, and security control reviews.

2. Incident monitoring and reporting: Monitor for any security incidents or breaches and ensure that the CSP promptly reports and addresses them. Establish clear communication channels for incident reporting and response.

3. Contract review and updates: Periodically review the contract with the CSP to ensure that it remains up to date with changing security requirements and industry standards. This can include revisiting SLAs, data protection provisions, or any other contractual clauses.

4. Stay informed about industry trends: Stay updated on emerging threats, vulnerabilities, and best practices in cloud security. Attend conferences, participate in industry forums, and engage with cybersecurity professionals to ensure that your organization remains at the forefront of cloud security.

Example: Evaluating a Cloud Service Provider

Let's consider an example to illustrate the process of evaluating a CSP. XYZ Healthcare, a large hospital network, is considering moving its patient data to a cloud environment. They have shortlisted two CSPs and need to assess their suitability.

XYZ Healthcare conducts a security assessment of both CSPs, reviewing their security controls, data protection measures, and compliance with healthcare regulations. They request documentation on incident response plans, perform on-site visits to evaluate physical security, and review the CSPs' performance in recent independent security audits.

Additionally, XYZ Healthcare contacts other healthcare organizations that have used the CSPs' services to gather feedback on their experiences. They learn about any past incidents, the CSPs' responsiveness, and the level of trust among their customers.

Based on their due diligence, XYZ Healthcare selects a CSP that demonstrates a strong security posture, compliance with healthcare regulations, and positive customer feedback. They negotiate a comprehensive contract that includes clearly defined responsibilities, security controls, incident response procedures, and strong SLAs.

After migrating the data to the cloud, XYZ Healthcare continuously monitors the CSP's performance, conducts periodic security audits, and stays informed about emerging cloud security trends. This proactive approach ensures the security and privacy of their patients' data in the cloud.

Resources and Further Reading

- Cloud Security Alliance (CSA): `https://cloudsecurityalliance.org/`

- National Institute of Standards and Technology (NIST) Special Publication 800-145: *The NIST Definition of Cloud Computing*: `https://nvlpubs.nist.gov/nistpubs/Legacy/SP/nistspecialpublication800-145.pdf`

- European Union Agency for Cybersecurity (ENISA) Cloud Security Guidelines: `https://www.enisa.europa.eu/topics/csrm/cloud-and-big-data-security/cloud-security`
- Health Insurance Portability and Accountability Act (HIPAA): `https://www.hhs.gov/hipaa/index.html`
- General Data Protection Regulation (GDPR): `https://gdpr-info.eu/`

In conclusion, managing cloud service providers and contracts requires careful consideration of security, privacy, and compliance aspects. By selecting the right CSP and establishing a comprehensive contract, organizations can leverage the benefits of cloud computing while safeguarding their data and ensuring the integrity of their operations. Regular monitoring and ongoing oversight are essential to maintain a secure cloud environment.

Monitoring and Auditing Cloud Computing Services

In the realm of cybersecurity, monitoring and auditing are essential components of maintaining the security and integrity of cloud computing services. As organizations increasingly adopt cloud solutions for storing and processing sensitive data, it becomes crucial to implement effective monitoring and auditing practices to ensure the privacy, confidentiality, and availability of information.

The Importance of Monitoring and Auditing

Monitoring refers to the continuous observation and analysis of activities within a cloud computing environment to identify potential security threats, breaches, or irregularities. It involves collecting and analyzing data from various sources, such as network logs, system logs, and application logs, to detect abnormalities or suspicious activities that may indicate a security incident. On the other hand, auditing focuses on evaluating the effectiveness of security controls, policies, and procedures to ensure compliance with regulatory requirements and industry best practices.

There are several key reasons why monitoring and auditing cloud computing services is crucial:

- **Threat detection and prevention:** By monitoring and auditing cloud environments, organizations can proactively identify and respond to security incidents, such as unauthorized access attempts, malware infections, or data breaches. This enables the implementation of timely countermeasures to mitigate risks and prevent potential damages.

- **Compliance adherence:** Many industries, including healthcare and finance, have strict regulatory requirements regarding the protection of sensitive data. By monitoring and auditing cloud services, organizations can ensure compliance with these regulations, such as HIPAA (Health Insurance Portability and Accountability Act) or GDPR (General Data Protection Regulation).

- **Performance optimization:** Monitoring and auditing can also help identify performance bottlenecks or inefficiencies within a cloud environment. By analyzing system logs and performance metrics, organizations can optimize resource allocation, identify capacity issues, and improve overall system performance.

- **Incident response and forensic investigations:** In the event of a security incident or data breach, the ability to monitor and audit cloud services becomes crucial for conducting thorough incident response activities and forensic investigations. Detailed logs and audit trails facilitate the identification of the attack vectors, the scope of compromise, and the extent of the damage, aiding in the recovery and remediation process.

Components of Cloud Computing Monitoring and Auditing

Effective monitoring and auditing of cloud computing services require the implementation of various components and techniques. Let's explore some essential elements:

- **Log Management:** Centralized log management is critical for capturing, aggregating, and analyzing logs generated by different components of the cloud infrastructure. It involves collecting logs from virtual machines, network devices, databases, and other relevant sources. Log management solutions, such as ELK Stack (Elasticsearch, Logstash, Kibana) or Splunk, provide the ability to search, correlate, and visualize log data for effective monitoring and auditing.

- **Intrusion Detection and Prevention Systems (IDPS):** IDPS solutions play a crucial role in monitoring cloud environments for potential security breaches. These systems analyze network traffic, system logs, and application behavior to detect and prevent malicious activities. IDPS can generate alerts or trigger automated responses to mitigate unauthorized access attempts, suspicious network traffic, or other security incidents.

- **Vulnerability Scanning:** Regular vulnerability assessments are essential for identifying weaknesses or misconfigurations within cloud infrastructure. Vulnerability scanning tools, such as Nessus or OpenVAS, can automatically identify known vulnerabilities in operating systems, applications, and network devices. By monitoring and auditing the results of vulnerability scans, organizations can promptly address identified vulnerabilities and maintain a secure cloud environment.

- **User and Entity Behavior Analytics (UEBA):** UEBA solutions utilize machine learning algorithms and behavioral analysis techniques to detect anomalous or malicious activities based on user behavior. By monitoring users' actions in cloud environments, UEBA tools can identify deviations from normal behavior, such as unusual login patterns, excessive data access, or data exfiltration attempts. This helps organizations spot potential insider threats or compromised accounts.

- **Configuration and Change Management:** Monitoring and auditing cloud computing services also involve tracking and managing changes to the cloud infrastructure configuration over time. Through configuration management tools, organizations can ensure that all changes adhere to security policies, minimize the attack surface, and prevent unauthorized modifications to critical components. Additionally, change management processes help maintain an accurate inventory of assets and configurations.

- **Automated Compliance Auditing:** Cloud environments may need to comply with various regulatory frameworks, industry standards, or internal security policies. Automated compliance auditing solutions can continuously evaluate the configuration of cloud resources, assess adherence to security controls, and generate compliance reports. Through regular audits, organizations can identify and rectify non-compliant settings, ensuring the cloud infrastructure meets required security standards.

Challenges and Considerations

While monitoring and auditing of cloud computing services offer numerous benefits, several challenges and considerations should be addressed to ensure their effectiveness:

- **Data Volume and Retention:** Cloud environments generate vast amounts of data, including logs, metrics, and events. Organizations must develop strategies for efficiently handling, storing, and retaining this data for monitoring and auditing purposes. Cloud-native services, such as Amazon CloudWatch or Azure Monitor, can assist in managing and analyzing large-scale data sets.

- **Costs and Resource Utilization:** Implementing comprehensive monitoring and auditing solutions can incur additional costs, particularly when using cloud-managed services or third-party tools. Organizations should carefully evaluate the trade-offs between cost and the level of visibility required for their specific cloud environment. Proper resource utilization planning is also crucial to avoid performance degradation or overprovisioning.

- **Privacy and Compliance:** Monitoring and auditing activities may involve capturing and analyzing sensitive data, including user information or personally identifiable information (PII). Organizations must ensure compliance with privacy regulations and implement appropriate anonymization or encryption techniques to protect sensitive data during monitoring and auditing processes.

- **Integration and Interoperability:** Cloud environments often consist of diverse components and services from different vendors. Effective monitoring and auditing require seamless integration and interoperability between these components, enabling the aggregation and correlation of data from multiple sources. Open standards and APIs (Application Programming Interfaces) can facilitate the integration of monitoring and auditing tools into cloud infrastructure.

- **Incident Response and Remediation:** Monitoring and auditing are only effective if organizations have well-defined incident response plans in place. Prompt response to identified security incidents and timely remediation of vulnerabilities or misconfigurations are crucial to maintaining a secure cloud environment. Integration with incident response and ticketing systems streamlines the coordination and resolution of security events.

Best Practices and Recommendations

To establish effective monitoring and auditing practices in cloud computing services, organizations should consider the following best practices:

- Define clear monitoring and auditing objectives based on the organization's security requirements and compliance obligations.
- Develop a comprehensive monitoring and auditing strategy that covers all relevant components, including network infrastructure, virtual machines, applications, and data storage.
- Regularly review and update logging configurations to capture relevant events and activities. Define log retention policies to comply with legal, regulatory, or internal requirements.
- Implement real-time alerts and notifications to promptly identify and respond to security incidents or anomalies.
- Establish baseline behavior patterns for users, applications, and network traffic to facilitate the detection of abnormal activities.
- Integrate monitoring and auditing tools with incident response processes to ensure a streamlined response to security incidents.
- Continuously evaluate and improve the effectiveness of monitoring and auditing practices through assessments and audits.
- Stay up-to-date with emerging threats, new monitoring techniques, and compliance regulations to adapt monitoring and auditing practices accordingly.

Conclusion

Monitoring and auditing cloud computing services play a significant role in maintaining a secure and compliant environment. By implementing effective monitoring and auditing practices, organizations can detect, mitigate, and prevent security incidents, ensure regulatory compliance, optimize system performance, and enhance overall cybersecurity posture. It is essential to understand the unique challenges associated with monitoring and auditing in the cloud and follow best practices to derive maximum benefit from these practices. By doing so, organizations can establish and maintain a robust and secure cloud computing environment.

Cloud-Based Disaster Recovery and Business Continuity Planning

Cloud-based disaster recovery and business continuity planning are critical components of a robust cybersecurity strategy for health and wellness organizations. In today's digital age, where cyber threats and data breaches are on the rise, organizations must have measures in place to ensure the resilience of their systems and the continuity of their operations. In this section, we will explore the importance of cloud-based solutions for disaster recovery and business continuity planning, and provide practical guidelines for implementation.

Understanding Disaster Recovery and Business Continuity

Disaster recovery refers to the process of restoring IT infrastructure and critical systems after a disruptive event, such as a cyber attack, natural disaster, or equipment failure. On the other hand, business continuity involves maintaining uninterrupted operations during such events and ensuring the availability of essential services to customers or patients.

Traditionally, organizations relied on physical infrastructure and on-premises backup solutions for disaster recovery and business continuity. However, with the advent of cloud computing, organizations now have access to scalable and cost-effective solutions that offer increased flexibility, responsiveness, and reliability.

Advantages of Cloud-Based Disaster Recovery

Cloud-based disaster recovery offers several advantages over traditional approaches:

- **Reduced Costs:** Cloud-based solutions eliminate the need for expensive hardware and infrastructure, as well as the associated maintenance and management costs. With a pay-as-you-go model, organizations can scale their disaster recovery capabilities based on their specific needs, resulting in significant cost savings.

- **Flexibility and Scalability:** Cloud providers offer a wide range of options for disaster recovery, allowing organizations to tailor their solutions to their unique requirements. With the ability to easily scale resources up or down, organizations can quickly adapt to changing demands and optimize their disaster recovery capabilities as needed.

- **Enhanced Reliability:** Cloud providers typically operate multiple data centers in geographically dispersed locations, ensuring redundancy and minimizing the risk of data loss. This distributed infrastructure reduces the impact of localized disasters and enhances the overall reliability of the disaster recovery solution.

- **Faster Recovery Time:** Cloud-based disaster recovery solutions often provide faster recovery times compared to traditional methods. With preconfigured templates and automated processes, organizations can quickly restore critical systems and resume operations, minimizing downtime and the associated financial losses.

Implementing Cloud-Based Disaster Recovery

To effectively implement cloud-based disaster recovery and business continuity planning, organizations should follow these guidelines:

1. **Identify Critical Systems and Data:** Conduct a thorough assessment of your organization's IT infrastructure to identify the critical systems, applications, and data that are essential for business operations. This will help prioritize the allocation of resources and ensure that the most critical assets are protected.

2. **Define Recovery Point Objectives (RPO) and Recovery Time Objectives (RTO):** RPO refers to the maximum acceptable amount of data loss in the event of a disaster, while RTO specifies the target time for recovering and restoring systems. It is crucial to define realistic RPO and RTO objectives, taking into consideration the cost implications and the impact on business operations.

3. **Choose a Cloud Service Provider:** Select a reputable cloud service provider that meets your organization's specific security and compliance requirements. Consider factors such as data center locations, data encryption capabilities, and the provider's track record in delivering reliable disaster recovery solutions.

4. **Backup and Replication Strategy:** Determine the appropriate backup and replication strategy based on your RPO and RTO objectives. Cloud providers offer various options, including continuous data replication, periodic data backup, and hybrid approaches. Consider factors such as data sensitivity, network bandwidth, and cost when designing your strategy.

5. **Testing and Validation:** Regularly test your disaster recovery plan to ensure its effectiveness and reliability. Conduct simulated disaster scenarios and

evaluate the recovery process, documenting any lessons learned and making necessary adjustments. It is crucial to involve key stakeholders and regularly review and update the plan as your organization's needs evolve.

6. **Compliance and Security Considerations:** Ensure that your cloud-based disaster recovery solution complies with relevant industry regulations, such as HIPAA for healthcare organizations. Implement appropriate security measures, such as data encryption, access controls, and monitoring, to protect sensitive information and mitigate the risk of unauthorized access or data breaches.

Real-World Example: Cloud-Based Disaster Recovery in a Healthcare Organization

Imagine a large healthcare organization that relies heavily on digital systems to deliver critical patient care services. In the event of a natural disaster, such as a hurricane, the organization's on-premises servers and infrastructure may become inaccessible or damaged, leading to significant disruptions in patient care.

To mitigate this risk, the organization decides to implement a cloud-based disaster recovery solution. They identify their critical systems, including electronic health records (EHR) and communication platforms, and define their RPO and RTO objectives.

The organization selects a reputable cloud service provider that specializes in healthcare IT solutions. They design a backup and replication strategy that includes periodic data backup to the cloud, continuous replication of critical systems, and regular testing of the disaster recovery plan.

During a simulated disaster scenario, the organization's IT team initiates the disaster recovery process. The cloud-based solution quickly restores the EHR system and communication platforms, allowing healthcare professionals to access patient information and communicate with each other. The organization's operations continue with minimal disruptions, ensuring the delivery of uninterrupted patient care services.

Resources and Further Reading

For more information on cloud-based disaster recovery and business continuity planning, consider the following resources:

- "Disaster Recovery Planning: Preparing for the Unthinkable" by Jon William Toigo.

- "Cloud Computing: Concepts, Technology & Architecture" by Thomas M. Erl et al.
- "NIST Special Publication 800-34 Rev. 1: Contingency Planning Guide for Federal Information Systems" by the National Institute of Standards and Technology.
- AWS Disaster Recovery whitepaper: `https://aws.amazon.com/whitepapers/disaster-recovery/`
- Microsoft Azure Site Recovery documentation: `https://docs.microsoft.com/en-us/azure/site-recovery/`

Conclusion

Cloud-based disaster recovery and business continuity planning provide organizations with a scalable, cost-effective, and reliable solution to protect their critical systems and ensure uninterrupted operations. By following best practices and leveraging the advantages of cloud computing, health and wellness organizations can enhance their cybersecurity posture and effectively mitigate the risks posed by cyber threats and disruptive events. It is essential to regularly review, test, and update the disaster recovery plan to adapt to the evolving threat landscape and organizational requirements.

Employee Training on Secure Cloud Collaboration

Employee training is a crucial aspect of ensuring the security of cloud collaboration in a health and wellness organization. With the increasing use of cloud computing services in the industry, it is essential to educate employees about the potential risks and best practices associated with secure cloud collaboration. This section focuses on the key elements of employee training, including the importance of training, topics to cover, training methods, and evaluation of training effectiveness.

Importance of Employee Training

Employee training plays a vital role in mitigating the risks associated with cloud collaboration. It helps employees understand the significance of secure practices, promotes awareness of potential threats, and empowers them to make informed decisions while collaborating on cloud platforms. By investing in comprehensive training programs, organizations can foster a culture of security and create a workforce equipped with the knowledge and skills needed to protect sensitive data in the cloud.

Topics to Cover

When designing employee training programs on secure cloud collaboration, it is essential to cover specific topics that are relevant to the organization's cloud environment. Some key topics to consider include:

1. Introduction to cloud collaboration: Provide an overview of cloud computing concepts, benefits, and risks, with a focus on collaboration tools and platforms used within the organization.

2. Cloud security fundamentals: Educate employees about the fundamental principles of cloud security, including data privacy, access controls, encryption, and secure authentication methods.

3. Cloud collaboration best practices: Highlight the recommended practices for secure cloud collaboration, such as using strong passwords, enabling two-factor authentication, being cautious of sharing sensitive information, and regularly updating software and applications.

4. Understanding cloud service provider (CSP) security: Familiarize employees with the security measures and protocols implemented by the organization's chosen cloud service provider. Explain the importance of reviewing and understanding the CSP's security and privacy policies.

5. Data classification and handling: Teach employees how to classify, handle, and share data appropriately in the cloud, based on its sensitivity and regulatory requirements. Emphasize the need to follow data protection guidelines and secure file sharing practices.

6. Recognizing and reporting anomalies: Train employees to identify suspicious activities, such as unauthorized access attempts, unusual data transfers, or unusual system behavior. Instruct them on how to report these incidents to the appropriate IT or cybersecurity team.

7. Incident response and recovery: Provide guidelines on the steps to follow in the event of a security incident or data breach. Educate employees on their roles and responsibilities during incident response efforts and the importance of timely reporting.

8. Regular security awareness updates: Highlight the need for ongoing security awareness training to keep employees up to date with emerging threats and evolving best practices in secure cloud collaboration.

Training Methods

Employers have several options when it comes to delivering employee training on secure cloud collaboration. Some effective training methods include:

1. Classroom-based training: Organize face-to-face training sessions led by an instructor who specializes in cloud security. This approach allows for interactive discussions, real-time feedback, and personalized guidance.

2. Online training modules: Develop interactive e-learning modules that employees can access at their convenience. Include quizzes and assessments to reinforce learning and measure knowledge retention.

3. Webinars and virtual workshops: Conduct live webinars or virtual workshops, where employees can participate remotely. These sessions can incorporate demonstrations, case studies, and Q&A sessions.

4. Training materials and resources: Create a repository of training materials, such as instructional videos, infographics, and written guidelines. Make these resources easily accessible to employees for self-paced learning and reference.

5. Simulation exercises: Use simulation exercises to simulate real-world scenarios and test employee response to security incidents. This practical approach helps employees apply their knowledge and develop incident response capabilities.

Evaluation of Training Effectiveness

To ensure the effectiveness of employee training programs on secure cloud collaboration, organizations should implement evaluation strategies. Some methods to assess training effectiveness include:

1. Knowledge assessments: Conduct pre-training and post-training assessments to measure the increase in employee knowledge and awareness of secure cloud collaboration practices.

2. Training feedback surveys: Distribute surveys to gather feedback from employees about the training content, delivery, and relevance. Use this feedback to improve future training programs.

3. Performance monitoring: Regularly monitor employees' adherence to secure cloud collaboration practices and assess their ability to apply the knowledge gained from training.

4. Incident response exercises: Periodically conduct simulated incident response exercises to assess employees' ability to respond effectively to security incidents in a cloud collaboration environment.

5. Continuous improvement: Continuously review and update training programs to address emerging threats, evolving technologies, and changes in the organization's cloud collaboration tools and platforms.

By regularly evaluating the effectiveness of employee training, organizations can identify areas for improvement and make necessary adjustments to the training content and delivery methods.

Conclusion

Employee training on secure cloud collaboration is critical for safeguarding sensitive data and promoting a culture of security within health and wellness organizations. By covering essential topics, using varied training methods, and evaluating training effectiveness, organizations can empower employees to collaborate securely in the cloud and contribute to the overall cybersecurity posture of the organization.

Remember, ongoing education and training are essential due to the ever-evolving cybersecurity landscape. Encourage employees to stay informed about the latest trends, emerging threats, and best practices in secure cloud collaboration. Through continuous learning, organizations can stay ahead of potential risks and ensure the safe and effective use of cloud technologies in the health and wellness industry.

Recommended Resources: - "Cloud Security and Privacy: An Enterprise Perspective on Risks and Compliance" by Tim Mather, Subra Kumaraswamy, and Shahed Latif - "Cloud Computing Security: Foundations and Challenges" by John R. Vacca - "The Cloud Security Ecosystem: Technical, Legal, Business, and Management Issues" by Ryan Ko, Kim-Kwang Raymond Choo, and Dianxiang Xu

Exercises: 1. Research and compare different cloud collaboration platforms' security features. Create a document outlining the strengths and weaknesses of each platform, and recommend the most secure platform for your organization. 2. Develop a simulated incident response exercise for employees, focusing on responding to a security incident in a cloud collaboration environment. Create a step-by-step guide and evaluate employees' response to the simulated incident. 3. Design an infographic highlighting the essential best practices for secure cloud collaboration. Use visually engaging elements to capture employees' attention and promote the adoption of secure practices. 4. Conduct a survey to gather feedback from employees on their understanding and awareness of secure cloud collaboration practices. Use the survey results to identify areas of improvement and develop targeted training initiatives.

Cybersecurity in Healthcare Facilities

Securing Physical Access to Health and Wellness Facilities

Access Control Systems and Physical Security Measures

Access control systems and physical security measures are essential components of a comprehensive cybersecurity strategy for health and wellness facilities. These measures ensure that only authorized individuals can gain physical access to sensitive areas, such as data centers, server rooms, or restricted areas within a facility. In this section, we will explore the principles of access control, various access control technologies, and best practices for implementing physical security measures.

Principles of Access Control

Access control is the process of managing and controlling the flow of individuals, vehicles, or materials into and within a facility or specific areas within the facility. The goal is to ensure that only authorized personnel or entities can access certain areas, while also preventing unauthorized access or breaches.

There are three fundamental principles of access control:

1. Identification: This involves establishing the identity of an individual or entity. It typically involves the use of identification credentials, such as ID cards, badges, or biometric identifiers like fingerprints or facial recognition.

2. Authentication: Once the identity is established, the system verifies the authenticity of the identification credentials. This is typically done by

comparing the presented credentials with stored data in a database or using biometric authentication techniques.

3. Authorization: After successful authentication, the system determines whether the authenticated individual or entity has the necessary privileges and permissions to access a particular area or resource. This is typically managed through access control policies and permissions.

Access Control Technologies

To implement effective access control systems, health and wellness facilities can utilize various technologies that help enforce the principles mentioned earlier. Here are some commonly used access control technologies:

- ID Cards and Badges: ID cards and badges are physical credentials issued to authorized personnel. These credentials typically include information about the individual, such as their name, photograph, and department. They can be easily displayed and used to grant access to specific areas through card readers or badge readers.

- Biometric Identification: Biometric identification involves using unique physical or behavioral characteristics of individuals to establish their identity. Common biometric identifiers include fingerprints, palm prints, facial recognition, and iris scans. Biometric systems provide a high level of security as they are difficult to forge or replicate.

- Key Cards and Key Fobs: Key cards and key fobs are electronic devices that allow authorized individuals to gain access to specific areas. These devices can be programmed with access rights and can be easily deactivated or reprogrammed if lost or stolen.

- Proximity Readers: Proximity readers are used in combination with access cards or fobs. These readers can detect the presence of the card or fob when it is brought within a certain distance. They eliminate the need for physical contact with the reader and provide a quick and convenient way to grant access.

- Access Control Panels and Software: Access control panels are the central control units that manage and enforce access control policies. They are responsible for granting or denying access based on authentication and authorization. Access control software provides a user-friendly interface to manage and configure access control policies, monitor access logs, and generate reports.

- Video Surveillance Systems: Video surveillance systems, including Closed Circuit Television (CCTV) cameras, provide a visual record of activities within and around the facility. They can be integrated with access control systems to capture video footage of individuals accessing secured areas, enhancing the security and accountability of access control.

Best Practices for Physical Security Measures

In addition to implementing access control systems, health and wellness facilities should adhere to best practices for physical security measures to further enhance the overall security posture. Here are some key best practices to consider:

1. Perimeter Security: Secure the perimeter of the facility with physical barriers, such as fences, gates, or bollards, to prevent unauthorized access. Implement technologies like video surveillance and motion sensors to detect any suspicious activities.

2. Visitor Management: Implement a robust visitor management system to ensure that only authorized visitors gain access to the facility. This can include procedures for visitor registration, issuing visitor badges, and escorting visitors to their designated areas.

3. Security Awareness Training: Provide regular security awareness training to employees, contractors, and visitors to educate them about the importance of physical security and the role they play in maintaining a secure environment. Train them on how to identify and report suspicious activities.

4. Incident Response Plan: Develop and regularly test an incident response plan that includes procedures for responding to physical security incidents, such as facility breaches or unauthorized access attempts. This plan should outline roles, responsibilities, and communication protocols during incidents.

5. Security Guards: Employ trained security personnel who are responsible for monitoring and enforcing physical security measures. Security guards can provide a physical presence and respond to security incidents promptly.

6. Access Control Audits: Conduct regular audits and reviews of access control systems to ensure their effectiveness. This includes reviewing access logs,

maintaining an up-to-date list of authorized personnel, and deactivating or revoking access for employees who no longer require it.

7. Physical Asset Management: Implement asset tracking and inventory management systems to keep track of equipment and assets within the facility. This helps prevent theft or unauthorized removal of sensitive equipment.

Example: Implementing Access Control in a Healthcare Facility

Let's consider the example of a healthcare facility that wants to improve its access control systems and physical security measures. The facility decides to implement a combination of access control technologies and best practices to enhance security.

First, the facility upgrades its access control system by implementing key card readers at all entry points. Authorized employees are issued proximity key cards that grant them access to designated areas based on their job roles and responsibilities. The access control software is used to manage card assignments, access rights, and generate access logs.

In addition, the facility installs video surveillance cameras in critical areas, such as server rooms and medication storage areas. The cameras are connected to a central monitoring system, and access to the footage is restricted to authorized security personnel.

The facility also develops and implements a comprehensive visitor management system. Visitors are required to register at the front desk, provide identification, and receive a visitor badge. Escorts are assigned to visitors to ensure they are accompanied and directed to the appropriate areas.

To enforce physical security measures, security guards are deployed to monitor access points, patrol the facility, and respond to any security incidents. Regular security awareness training is provided to employees, emphasizing the importance of maintaining a secure environment and reporting any suspicious activities.

Finally, the facility conducts periodic access control audits to identify any vulnerabilities or discrepancies in the system. The audits help ensure that access privileges are regularly reviewed, and access credentials are timely revoked when an employee leaves the organization.

By implementing these access control technologies and physical security measures, the healthcare facility significantly enhances its overall security posture. It reduces the risk of unauthorized access, theft, or tampering with sensitive information or equipment.

Conclusion

Access control systems and physical security measures play a vital role in protecting health and wellness facilities from unauthorized access and breaches. By implementing a combination of access control technologies and best practices, organizations can create a secure environment that safeguards sensitive information, assets, and the overall wellbeing of individuals within the facility. Regular audits, security awareness training, and incident response planning are essential components of these efforts. Ensuring a robust access control system and physical security measures is instrumental in mitigating cybersecurity risks and maintaining a safe and secure healthcare environment.

Securing Medical Equipment and Internet-of-Things (IoT) Devices

In the era of digital connectivity, the use of Internet-of-Things (IoT) devices in the health and wellness industry has grown exponentially. From smart wearable devices to connected medical equipment, these IoT devices offer numerous advantages in terms of patient monitoring, data collection, and healthcare delivery. However, with the increasing reliance on IoT devices comes the need to address the security challenges associated with them.

Understanding the Security Risks

Medical equipment and IoT devices are vulnerable to various security risks that can compromise patient safety and privacy. These risks include:

- **Unauthorized Access:** IoT devices connected to the healthcare network can become potential entry points for attackers. If not properly secured, unauthorized individuals can access these devices and tamper with their settings or extract sensitive data.

- **Data Breaches:** IoT devices collect and transmit patient data, making them a valuable target for cybercriminals. A data breach can expose personal health information, leading to significant privacy violations and potential identity theft.

- **Malware Attacks:** IoT devices can be infected with malware, such as viruses or ransomware, which can disrupt their functionality or allow attackers to gain control over them. Malware attacks can compromise the integrity of medical equipment and pose a threat to patient safety.

- **Lack of Patching and Updates:** Many IoT devices in the healthcare industry have limited capabilities to receive software updates and security patches. This leaves them vulnerable to known vulnerabilities that attackers can exploit.

Addressing these security risks is crucial to ensure the safe and reliable operation of medical equipment and protect the privacy of patient data.

Establishing Robust Security Measures

To secure medical equipment and IoT devices, healthcare organizations should implement a comprehensive set of security measures. These measures can include:

- **Risk Assessment:** Conducting a risk assessment helps identify vulnerabilities and potential threats associated with medical equipment and IoT devices. It provides a foundation for creating an effective security strategy tailored to the organization's specific needs.

- **Access Controls:** Implementing strong access controls is essential to prevent unauthorized access to medical equipment and IoT devices. This can include user authentication mechanisms such as passwords, biometrics, or smart cards. Additionally, access privileges should be granted on a need-to-know basis to limit the number of individuals who can interact with the devices.

- **Secure Configuration:** Ensuring that medical equipment and IoT devices are configured securely is vital. This includes changing default passwords, disabling unnecessary services, and enabling encryption where possible. Regular firmware updates should also be applied to address known vulnerabilities and exploit patches.

- **Network Segmentation:** Separating IoT devices from the main healthcare network through network segmentation helps contain potential attacks. By isolating IoT devices, the impact of a security breach can be limited, reducing the risk to critical systems and patient data.

- **Encryption:** Implementing strong encryption protocols for data at rest and in transit is crucial. This ensures that sensitive information transmitted between medical equipment and IoT devices remains confidential and cannot be intercepted by unauthorized individuals.

- **Monitoring and Logging:** Continuous monitoring and logging of IoT devices enable the timely detection of security incidents. Suspicious activities or unusual behavior should trigger alerts to allow immediate investigation and response.

- **Vendor Management:** Working closely with IoT device vendors is essential. Organizations should collaborate with vendors to ensure that security is a priority in the design, development, and maintenance of medical equipment and IoT devices.

Case Study: Pacemaker Security

As an example of the security challenges in securing medical equipment, let's consider the case of pacemakers. Pacemakers are implantable medical devices that help regulate a person's heartbeat. With the advancement of IoT, modern pacemakers are equipped with wireless communication capabilities, allowing healthcare providers to monitor the device remotely.

However, the wireless connectivity of pacemakers introduces security risks. An attacker could potentially intercept the communication between the pacemaker and the monitoring system or gain unauthorized access to reprogram the pacemaker, which can have life-threatening consequences.

To mitigate these risks, pacemaker manufacturers have implemented various security measures. These include:

- **Encryption:** Pacemakers use encryption algorithms to secure communication between the device and the monitoring system, ensuring that the data exchanged remains private and tamper-proof.

- **Authentication:** Strong authentication mechanisms, such as unique cryptographic keys, are used to verify the identity of the pacemaker and the monitoring system. This prevents unauthorized devices from connecting or communicating with the pacemaker.

- **Firmware Updates:** Manufacturers regularly release firmware updates that address security vulnerabilities and enhance the pacemaker's security features. Healthcare providers must ensure that pacemakers are up to date with the latest firmware to mitigate risk.

- **Physical Security:** Physical security measures, such as tamper-evident seals, are employed to protect the pacemaker from unauthorized access. These measures make it difficult for attackers to physically tamper with the device without leaving visible evidence.

While these security measures are essential, it is important to note that no system is entirely foolproof. As threats continue to evolve, manufacturers, healthcare providers, and regulatory bodies must remain vigilant and proactive in addressing emerging security challenges.

Conclusion

Securing medical equipment and IoT devices is crucial to protect patient safety and privacy. Healthcare organizations should implement robust security measures, such as access controls, secure configurations, encryption, and network segmentation. Collaboration with vendors, ongoing monitoring, and regular security updates are also vital to address emerging threats. By prioritizing security in the design and operation of medical equipment and IoT devices, the health and wellness industry can ensure a safer and more secure digital future.

Securing Physical Storage and Record Keeping Areas

Physical storage and record keeping areas play a crucial role in maintaining the privacy and security of sensitive information in the health and wellness industry. These areas often contain valuable documents, medical records, and other physical assets that need to be protected from unauthorized access, theft, or physical damage. In this section, we will discuss various strategies and best practices for securing physical storage and record keeping areas.

Importance of Physical Security

Physical security is a fundamental aspect of overall cybersecurity. While technological measures such as encryption and firewalls are essential, physical security ensures that unauthorized individuals cannot physically access sensitive information. It acts as the first line of defense against theft, tampering, and unauthorized disclosure of physical documents and assets.

Access Control Systems

Implementing access control systems is crucial for securing physical storage and record keeping areas. Access control systems restrict entry to authorized personnel only, ensuring that sensitive information is accessible only to those who need it. There are several components that contribute to an effective access control system:

- **Physical Barriers:** Install physical barriers such as locked doors, gates, and fences to prevent unauthorized access. Equip these barriers with tamper-proof locks and alarms that can detect any unauthorized attempts to gain entry.

- **Identification and Authentication:** Use identification and authentication mechanisms such as badges, key cards, or biometric systems (fingerprint or iris scanners) to verify the identity of individuals seeking access.

- **Visitor Management:** Implement a robust visitor management system that requires visitors to sign in and out, provide identification, and be escorted by authorized personnel while in sensitive areas.

Surveillance Systems

Surveillance systems play a vital role in enhancing the physical security of storage and record keeping areas. When strategically placed, surveillance cameras can act as a deterrent for potential intruders and provide crucial evidence in the event of any security incidents. Here are some key considerations for deploying surveillance systems:

- **Camera Placement:** Identify critical areas within storage and record keeping areas, such as entrance points, file storage areas, and document processing areas, where surveillance cameras should be installed. Ensure that there are no blind spots and that cameras cover the entire space effectively.

- **Monitoring and Recording:** Configure the surveillance system to continuously monitor and record activities within the storage and record keeping areas. Regularly review and analyze the footage to detect any suspicious activities or security breaches.

- **Data Protection:** Protect the surveillance camera footage by storing it in a secure location separate from the storage and record keeping areas. Implement appropriate levels of access controls to ensure that only authorized personnel can access the footage.

Sensitive Document Storage

Proper storage of sensitive documents is essential to prevent unauthorized access, loss, or damage. Here are some best practices for securing sensitive document storage:

- **Lockable Cabinets and Safes:** Use lockable cabinets or safes to store physical documents. Ensure that the cabinets or safes are made of durable materials and have tamper-proof locks.
- **Access Controls:** Limit access to sensitive document storage areas to authorized personnel only. Keep a record of individuals who access these areas and regularly review the logs for any anomalies.
- **Organizational Policies and Procedures:** Develop and enforce clear policies and procedures for handling and storing sensitive documents. Train employees on the importance of document security and ensure that they adhere to the established guidelines.
- **Labeling and Classification:** Clearly label and classify sensitive documents to ensure that they are appropriately handled and stored. Use color-coded labels or tags to easily identify different document types and their associated security requirements.

Record Retention and Destruction Policies

Proper record retention and destruction policies are essential to ensure that sensitive information is not retained longer than necessary and is securely disposed of when no longer needed. Here are some considerations for establishing record retention and destruction policies:

- **Legal and Regulatory Requirements:** Familiarize yourself with the legal and regulatory requirements for record retention and destruction specific to the health and wellness industry. Ensure that your policies align with these requirements and are regularly updated to reflect any changes.
- **Secure Destruction Methods:** Implement secure destruction methods, such as shredding or incineration, for physical documents that have reached the end of their retention periods. Use certified third-party vendors for maximum security and compliance.

- **Documentation and Auditing:** Maintain proper documentation of the entire record retention and destruction process, including the identification of documents, retention periods, destruction dates, and methods used. Regularly audit these processes to ensure compliance.

Employee Training and Awareness

Educating employees about the importance of physical security and providing training on security protocols is crucial for maintaining a secure environment. Here are some key points to consider:

- **Security Awareness Programs:** Develop and conduct regular security awareness programs that educate employees about the significance of physical security measures, the potential risks, and the expected behavior in sensitive areas.

- **Role-Based Training:** Tailor training programs to address the specific roles and responsibilities of different employees. Provide targeted training for individuals who handle sensitive documents or have access to storage areas.

- **Reporting and Incident Response:** Train employees to recognize and report any suspicious activities or security incidents involving physical storage and record keeping areas. Establish clear protocols for reporting incidents and responding to security breaches.

Caveats and Challenges

While implementing physical security measures, it is important to be aware of certain caveats and challenges:

- **Physical Environment:** Consider environmental factors such as temperature, humidity, and fire hazards that can impact the security of physical storage areas. Implement appropriate measures to mitigate these risks, such as fire suppression systems or environmental monitoring systems.

- **Maintenance and Regular Inspections:** Regularly inspect and maintain physical security measures to ensure their effectiveness. Repair or replace any damaged locks, barriers, or surveillance equipment promptly.

- **Employee Compliance:** Even with robust physical security measures in place, employees play a critical role in maintaining security. It is essential to cultivate a culture of security awareness and ensure that employees understand and follow the established security protocols.

Conclusion

Securing physical storage and record keeping areas is vital for protecting sensitive information in the health and wellness industry. By implementing access control systems, surveillance systems, and proper document storage and retention practices, organizations can significantly enhance the physical security of their sensitive assets. However, it is crucial to remember that physical security measures should work in conjunction with other cybersecurity strategies to provide comprehensive protection against both physical and digital threats.

Employee Training on Facility Security Policies

Employee training on facility security policies is crucial to ensure the overall cybersecurity of health and wellness facilities. It helps to create a culture of security awareness and promotes responsible behavior among employees. This section will discuss the importance of employee training, key components of facility security policies, and best practices for effective training programs.

Importance of Employee Training

Employees play a vital role in maintaining the security of health and wellness facilities. They are often the first line of defense against potential security threats. Without proper training, employees may not be aware of the risks and vulnerabilities that exist within the facility or the potential consequences of their actions.

Effective training programs help employees understand their responsibilities in safeguarding sensitive information and assets. They educate employees on the importance of following security policies and procedures, as well as the potential impact of security breaches on patients, staff, and the overall reputation of the facility.

By investing in employee training, health and wellness facilities can:

- Enhance the cybersecurity posture of the organization
- Promote a security-conscious culture among employees
- Mitigate the risk of human error leading to security incidents

- Improve incident detection and response capabilities
- Comply with industry regulations and standards
- Protect patient confidentiality and trust

Overall, employee training is a critical component of a comprehensive cybersecurity strategy for health and wellness facilities.

Key Components of Facility Security Policies

Before developing training programs, it is essential to establish robust facility security policies that outline the expectations and requirements for employees. These policies should cover various areas of facility security, including:

1. **Physical Access Control:** Policies should define the rules for accessing the facility, including badge requirements, visitor registration processes, and restricted areas. It should also cover how to handle lost or stolen badges and the importance of reporting suspicious activities or individuals.

2. **Asset Protection:** Policies should highlight the importance of protecting physical assets, such as medical equipment, computers, and other valuable resources. This includes guidelines for securing personal belongings, reporting theft or damage, and proper disposal of sensitive information.

3. **Data Security:** Policies should address the protection of electronic and physical data within the facility. This includes guidelines for secure data storage, handling, and disposal. It should also cover the importance of strong passwords, data encryption, and regular data backups.

4. **Incident Reporting and Response:** Policies should establish clear procedures for reporting and responding to security incidents. This includes guidelines for reporting suspicious emails, lost devices, or potential breaches. It should also define the roles and responsibilities of employees during an incident and the escalation process.

5. **Internet and Email Usage:** Policies should outline acceptable use policies for internet and email communications. This includes guidelines for safe browsing habits, downloading attachments, and avoiding phishing scams. It should also emphasize the need to report any suspicious or unauthorized activities.

These policy components serve as a foundation for employee training programs on facility security.

Best Practices for Employee Training

To ensure the effectiveness of employee training on facility security policies, the following best practices should be followed:

1. **Tailor Training to Job Roles:** Different job roles within the facility may have varying security responsibilities. Training programs should be tailored to address the specific needs and requirements of each role. For example, administrative staff may receive training on data handling and incident reporting, while IT staff may require training on network security and vulnerability management.

2. **Engage Employees with Real-World Examples:** Make training engaging and relatable by incorporating real-world examples of security incidents and their impact. This helps employees understand the consequences of their actions and reinforces the importance of following security policies.

3. **Provide Hands-On Exercises:** Include hands-on exercises and simulations to allow employees to apply their knowledge and skills in realistic scenarios. This helps to reinforce learning and prepares employees to respond effectively to security incidents.

4. **Regularly Update and Reinforce Training:** Cybersecurity threats evolve over time, so it is crucial to provide regular updates and refresher training sessions to keep employees informed about new risks and mitigation strategies. Reinforcement can be achieved through periodic security awareness campaigns, quizzes, and reminders.

5. **Measure Training Effectiveness:** Develop metrics and assessments to measure the effectiveness of training programs. This could include quizzes or simulated phishing campaigns to evaluate employees' knowledge and behavior regarding security practices. Use the results to identify areas for improvement and modify training programs accordingly.

6. **Promote a Culture of Security:** Foster a culture of security awareness by recognizing and rewarding employees who demonstrate good security practices. Encourage open communication channels for reporting potential security incidents or concerns without fear of retribution.

By following these best practices, health and wellness facilities can ensure that employee training on facility security policies is effective and contributes to a strong cybersecurity posture.

Example Scenario

To illustrate the importance of employee training on facility security policies, consider the following scenario:

Dr. Smith is a healthcare professional working at a busy wellness facility. One day, he receives an email from an unknown sender claiming to provide important patient information. The email includes a suspicious link, but Dr. Smith, who has not received proper training on email security, clicks on the link without verifying its authenticity.

Unfortunately, the link leads to a malicious website that installs malware on Dr. Smith's computer. The malware allows attackers to gain unauthorized access to the facility's network, compromising patient data and causing significant financial and reputational damage to the facility.

This scenario highlights the risks associated with a lack of employee training on facility security policies. With proper training, Dr. Smith could have recognized the email as a phishing attempt and reported it to the appropriate personnel, thus preventing the security breach.

Resources for Employee Training

Several resources are available to assist health and wellness facilities in developing and delivering effective employee training programs on facility security policies. These include:

- **Industry Associations and Organizations:** Industry associations often provide cybersecurity resources and training materials tailored to the health and wellness industry. Examples include the Healthcare Information and Management Systems Society (HIMSS) and the American Health Information Management Association (AHIMA).

- **Government Agencies:** Government agencies such as the Department of Health and Human Services (HHS) offer cybersecurity guidelines and training resources specific to the healthcare sector. These resources can help facilities comply with regulatory requirements and best practices.

- **Vendor-Specific Training:** Many cybersecurity vendors offer training programs designed for healthcare professionals and employees. These programs provide industry-specific knowledge and practical guidance on protecting sensitive information and assets.

- **Online Training Platforms:** Numerous online platforms offer cybersecurity training courses that are suitable for health and wellness facilities. These courses cover various aspects of cybersecurity and can be customized to meet the specific needs of the organization.

- **Internal IT and Security Teams:** Internal IT and security teams can develop and deliver training programs based on the facility's specific security policies and requirements. They can leverage their expertise to provide targeted training to employees.

Health and wellness facilities should explore these resources and adapt them to meet their unique training needs.

Conclusion

Employee training on facility security policies is critical for maintaining robust cybersecurity in health and wellness facilities. By investing in training programs, organizations can foster a culture of security awareness, promote responsible behavior among employees, and mitigate the risk of security incidents. It is essential to develop comprehensive facility security policies, tailor training programs to job roles, engage employees with real-world examples, provide hands-on exercises, and regularly update and measure training effectiveness. By following these best practices, health and wellness facilities can enhance their cybersecurity posture and protect the sensitive information and assets they hold.

Surveillance Systems and Security Cameras

Video Surveillance Systems and Data Protection

Video surveillance systems play a crucial role in enhancing the security of healthcare facilities by monitoring entrances, parking lots, critical areas, and other sensitive locations. However, it's essential to ensure that the data collected by these systems is adequately protected to maintain privacy and prevent unauthorized access or misuse. This section will discuss the principles of video surveillance systems and various measures to safeguard the collected data.

Principles of Video Surveillance Systems

Video surveillance systems consist of cameras, video recorders, monitors, and storage devices. These systems capture, record, and store video footage to provide a visual record of activities in and around healthcare facilities. The principles underlying video surveillance systems include:

- **Camera placement:** Proper placement of cameras is crucial to ensure effective coverage of critical areas while respecting privacy regulations. Care must be taken to avoid capturing sensitive information such as patient medical records or private conversations.
- **Monitoring and recording:** Surveillance cameras should continuously monitor the designated areas and record high-resolution video footage. This footage can be used for investigation purposes or as evidence in case of security incidents.
- **Retention period:** The recorded video footage should be retained for a specific period according to legal and regulatory requirements. This ensures that the data is available for review if needed while preventing unnecessary storage of outdated footage.
- **Access control and authentication:** Only authorized personnel should have access to the video surveillance system and recorded data. Strong authentication mechanisms, such as two-factor authentication, should be implemented to prevent unauthorized access.
- **Data encryption:** To ensure the confidentiality of the recorded video footage, it should be encrypted during storage and transmission. Encryption algorithms, such as AES (Advanced Encryption Standard), can be used to protect the data from unauthorized viewing.

Safeguarding Video Surveillance Data

Securing the data collected by video surveillance systems is essential to protect patient privacy, maintain compliance with regulations, and prevent data breaches. Here are some measures to safeguard video surveillance data:

- **Access controls:** Implement strict access controls to limit who can access the video surveillance system and recorded data. Access should be granted based on job roles and responsibilities, and strong passwords or biometric authentication should be used to authenticate users.

- **Encryption:** Apply encryption techniques to safeguard the confidentiality of the recorded video footage. Encryption should be utilized during storage and transmission to protect against unauthorized access, even if the data is intercepted.

- **Physical security:** Ensure that the physical infrastructure hosting the video surveillance system is adequately secured. This includes securing the server rooms, surveillance control centers, and storage areas to prevent unauthorized access or theft of equipment.

- **Network security:** Protect the video surveillance system from network-based attacks by implementing firewalls, intrusion detection and prevention systems, and regular security updates. Encryption should also be applied to network communication to secure video data in transit.

- **Regular maintenance and updates:** Keep the video surveillance system up to date with the latest firmware, patches, and security upgrades. Regularly check for vulnerabilities and address them promptly to prevent exploitation.

- **Data backup and disaster recovery:** Backup the recorded video footage and implement a disaster recovery plan to ensure data availability in case of system failure or physical damage. Regularly test the backup and recovery processes to verify their effectiveness.

- **Monitoring and auditing:** Continuously monitor the video surveillance system for any irregularities or suspicious activities. Implement auditing mechanisms to track system access, video data modifications, and changes to system configurations.

- **Privacy policies and training:** Develop and enforce privacy policies specific to video surveillance systems. Regularly train employees on privacy regulations, the proper handling of video data, and the consequences of unauthorized access or misuse.

Real-World Example: Integrated Security Solutions

One real-world example of safeguarding video surveillance data is the implementation of integrated security solutions. These solutions combine video surveillance with other security systems, such as access control and alarm systems, to enhance the overall security posture of healthcare facilities.

By integrating video surveillance with access control systems, authorized personnel can be granted access to specific areas based on their roles, and the video footage can be synchronized with access events. This integration allows for more effective monitoring and investigation of security incidents.

Additionally, the integration of video surveillance with alarm systems enables real-time monitoring of critical areas. If an alarm is triggered, such as an unauthorized entry or an equipment tampering alert, the video surveillance system can immediately provide live video feeds to security personnel, allowing for a quick response to the situation.

Such integrated security solutions not only enhance the protection of video surveillance data but also provide a more comprehensive approach to healthcare facility security.

Resources and Further Reading

To learn more about video surveillance systems and data protection in healthcare facilities, consider the following resources:

- "Video Surveillance Policy and Procedure" by the International Association for Healthcare Security and Safety (IAHSS).
- "Guidelines for Privacy, Security, and Safety in Health Video Surveillance" by the Healthcare Security and Safety Foundation (HSSF).
- "HIPAA Compliance and Surveillance Video: Legal Pitfalls for Health Care Providers" by the Security Industry Association (SIA).
- "Video Surveillance Best Practices: Data Privacy and Cybersecurity" by the National Center for Spectator Sports Safety and Security (NCS4).

These resources provide comprehensive guidance on the implementation and management of video surveillance systems while maintaining compliance with privacy regulations and ensuring data protection.

Conclusion

Video surveillance systems are vital tools for maintaining the security of healthcare facilities. However, it is equally important to protect the data generated by these systems to safeguard patient privacy and prevent unauthorized access. By implementing proper access controls, encryption, physical and network security measures, regular maintenance, and training, healthcare facilities can ensure the confidentiality and integrity of their video surveillance data. Integrated security solutions further enhance the effectiveness of video surveillance by combining it with other security systems. By following best practices and staying up to date with the latest technologies and regulations, healthcare facilities can establish robust and secure video surveillance systems.

Privacy Considerations in Video Monitoring

Video monitoring has become a common practice in various settings, including healthcare facilities, to enhance security and ensure the safety of patients, employees, and visitors. However, it is important to consider privacy implications when implementing video monitoring systems. This section will explore the key privacy considerations involved in video monitoring and provide guidelines for healthcare facilities to protect individuals' privacy while maintaining a secure environment.

Legal and Ethical Framework

When deploying video monitoring systems, healthcare facilities need to adhere to legal and ethical guidelines to safeguard individuals' privacy rights. These guidelines may vary depending on the country or region, but they typically include the following elements:

- **Notice:** Individuals should be informed about the presence of video monitoring through clear signage and prominent display of privacy policies. This allows them to make an informed decision about being in the monitored area.
- **Consent:** In some regions, capturing and storing video footage may require obtaining consent from individuals who are being monitored. Consent may be obtained through explicit agreements or implied consent, depending on local laws.
- **Purpose limitation:** Video monitoring should only be used for the intended purpose, such as enhancing security or investigating specific incidents. Any use of the footage beyond the stated purpose should be prohibited.
- **Retention and deletion:** Healthcare facilities should establish clear policies regarding the retention period for video footage. Retaining footage for longer than necessary increases the risk of unauthorized access and potential misuse. Once the retention period is over, the footage must be promptly deleted.

- **Access control:** Access to video footage should be restricted to authorized personnel who have a legitimate need to view it. Healthcare facilities should implement access control measures, such as secure login credentials and role-based access management, to ensure that only authorized individuals can access the footage.

Compliance with legal and ethical guidelines not only protects individuals' privacy but also helps healthcare facilities maintain trust with their patients, employees, and the public.

Minimizing Intrusion and Protecting Sensitive Areas

To minimize the intrusion on individuals' privacy, healthcare facilities should carefully consider the placement and coverage of surveillance cameras. Cameras should be positioned to focus only on necessary areas, such as entrances, exits, and high-security zones, while avoiding capturing private or sensitive spaces like restrooms, patient rooms, or counseling rooms.

In areas where video monitoring is necessary, healthcare facilities can adopt privacy-enhancing techniques. One approach is to use privacy filters or masks that blur or obscure certain parts of the video feed in real-time. For example, a privacy mask can be applied to block out sensitive areas within a camera's field of view. This ensures that even if unauthorized individuals gain access to the footage, they cannot discern private information or identities.

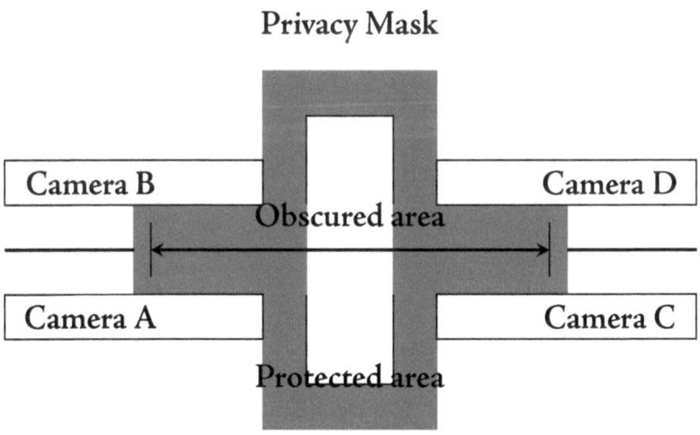

Figure 0.1: Example of privacy masks applied to cameras in a healthcare facility.

Figure 0.1 illustrates an example where privacy masks are applied to cameras in a healthcare facility. The obscured area represents the regions where sensitive information or private activities occur, while the protected area is where the camera can capture activities deemed necessary for security purposes.

Data Security and Access Controls

In addition to protecting individuals' privacy through legal and ethical measures, healthcare facilities must also secure the video footage to prevent unauthorized access and potential misuse. Here are some key data security measures for video monitoring systems:

- **Encryption:** Video footage should be encrypted both during transmission and storage to safeguard its confidentiality and integrity. Healthcare facilities should employ strong encryption algorithms and ensure that encryption keys are properly managed.
- **Secure storage:** Video footage should be stored in a secure location with restricted access. The storage systems should have sufficient capacity to retain footage for the designated retention period. Regular backups should be performed to prevent data loss in case of system failures or physical damage.
- **Access controls:** Access to video footage should be limited to authorized individuals only. Strong authentication mechanisms, such as multi-factor authentication, should be implemented to ensure that only authorized personnel can access the footage. Role-based access control should also be applied to restrict access based on job responsibilities and the principle of least privilege.

By implementing robust data security measures, healthcare facilities can protect the privacy of individuals captured in the video footage while ensuring the integrity and confidentiality of the data.

Transparency and Accountability

Maintaining transparency and accountability is crucial in video monitoring to build trust with individuals and comply with legal requirements. Healthcare facilities should establish clear policies regarding video monitoring and make them easily accessible to patients, employees, and the public. These policies should outline the purpose of video monitoring, the types of activities captured, retention periods, and any third-party involvement in managing the video footage.

Regular audits and monitoring should be conducted to ensure compliance with the established policies and regulations. Security incidents or breaches involving the video monitoring system should be promptly investigated, and appropriate actions should be taken to address any vulnerabilities or weaknesses.

Case Study: Privacy Protection in a Hospital Video Monitoring System

Consider a case where a hospital is implementing a video monitoring system to enhance security and ensure a safe environment for patients and staff. The hospital aims to strike a balance between security needs and individuals' privacy. They take the following steps to protect privacy in their video monitoring system:

- The hospital places cameras strategically in public areas, such as entrances, waiting areas, and parking lots, avoiding locations where individuals expect privacy, such as patient rooms or restrooms.

- Clear signs are posted at the entrances and in the monitored areas, informing individuals about the use of video monitoring for security purposes.

- Privacy masks are applied to cameras, blurring or obscuring sensitive areas within the camera's field of view. This ensures that the cameras only capture activities necessary for security while protecting privacy in areas where sensitive information might be exposed.

- Access to the video footage is restricted to authorized personnel through a secure login system. Each personnel's access privileges are based on their roles and responsibilities within the hospital.

- The hospital encrypts the video footage during transmission and storage to maintain its confidentiality. Strong encryption algorithms are used, and encryption keys are securely managed.

- Regular audits are conducted to ensure compliance with privacy policies and legal regulations. Any incidents or breaches are thoroughly investigated, and corrective measures are taken to prevent future occurrences.

By implementing these measures, the hospital can effectively protect individuals' privacy while maintaining a secure environment through video monitoring.

Conclusion

Video monitoring can be a valuable tool for enhancing security in healthcare facilities. However, it is essential to consider privacy considerations and ensure compliance with legal and ethical guidelines. By following the principles outlined in this section, healthcare facilities can strike the right balance between security and privacy, building trust and maintaining a secure environment for patients, employees, and visitors.

Monitoring and Auditing Surveillance Systems

Monitoring and auditing surveillance systems are essential components of maintaining the security and integrity of healthcare facilities. These systems play a crucial role in deterring and detecting unauthorized access, theft, or other security breaches. In this section, we will explore the importance of monitoring and auditing surveillance systems, best practices for performing these tasks, and the tools and techniques used in the process.

Importance of Monitoring and Auditing

Surveillance systems are deployed in healthcare facilities to monitor and record activities within and around the premises. They provide visual evidence in case of security incidents and serve as a deterrent against criminal activities. However, simply installing surveillance cameras is not sufficient; regular monitoring and auditing are crucial to ensure the effectiveness of these systems.

Monitoring involves actively observing live feeds from surveillance cameras in real-time. It allows security personnel to identify and respond to suspicious activities promptly. Auditing, on the other hand, involves reviewing recorded video footage to investigate past incidents or verify compliance with security protocols. Both monitoring and auditing help identify security gaps, validate system functionality, and ensure that the surveillance systems are being used appropriately.

Best Practices for Monitoring

Effective monitoring of surveillance systems requires the establishment of well-defined procedures and the use of appropriate tools. Here are some best practices for monitoring:

- **Establish monitoring schedules:** Define specific timeframes for active monitoring based on the operational needs and risk levels of the healthcare facility. High-risk areas such as access control points, medication storage areas, and critical infrastructure should receive more frequent monitoring.

- **Designate competent personnel:** Assign trained security personnel to actively monitor surveillance feeds. These individuals should have a clear understanding of the system's capabilities and be capable of recognizing suspicious activities.

- **Maintain situational awareness:** Monitor screens or video walls in a well-organized control room that provides a comprehensive view of all monitored areas. Ensure that the monitors are positioned ergonomically for maximum visibility.

- **Implement incident response protocols:** Establish communication channels and protocols for notifying appropriate personnel in case of suspicious or criminal activities. This includes establishing links with security teams, law enforcement, and other relevant stakeholders.

- **Regular training and awareness:** Provide ongoing training sessions for security personnel to enhance their skills in monitoring and recognizing potential threats. This training should cover common security vulnerabilities and techniques used by criminals to avoid detection.

- **Leverage analytics and automation:** Utilize video analytics software to automate the monitoring process. These tools can detect specific events or behaviors of interest, such as unauthorized access or loitering, and generate alerts for further investigation.

Best Practices for Auditing

Auditing surveillance systems involves reviewing recorded video footage to ensure compliance, investigate incidents, or gather evidence. Here are some best practices for auditing:

- **Establish auditing procedures:** Define standardized procedures for conducting audits, including the frequency of audits, areas to be audited, and criteria for evaluating the compliance and effectiveness of surveillance systems.

- **Retain video footage:** Implement a robust system for storing and archiving video footage, considering the retention requirements mandated by applicable laws and regulations. Ensure that the storage infrastructure is secure, reliable, and scalable to accommodate long-term storage needs.

- **Perform regular audits:** Conduct routine audits of the recorded video footage to identify any anomalies, security breaches, or system malfunctions. These audits should focus on critical areas and events that pose a higher risk to the healthcare facility.

- **Document audit findings:** Maintain detailed documentation of audit findings, including the nature of incidents, actions taken, and recommendations for system improvements. This documentation can serve as evidence during investigations or legal proceedings.

- **Collaborate with stakeholders:** Work closely with internal and external stakeholders, including law enforcement agencies and security consultants, to conduct thorough and impartial audits. This collaboration can provide expert insights and validate the effectiveness of the surveillance system.

- **Update policies and procedures:** Continuously evaluate and update auditing policies and procedures to align with emerging technologies, regulatory changes, and industry best practices. Regularly review and update the standard operating procedures (SOPs) for video auditing to ensure their relevance and effectiveness.

Tools and Techniques

Monitoring and auditing surveillance systems can be facilitated by various tools and techniques. Some key ones are:

- **Video management software (VMS):** VMS platforms provide centralized control and management of surveillance cameras. They allow security personnel to view live video feeds, search recorded footage, and configure system settings. VMS platforms often include advanced features such as video analytics and integration with access control systems.

- **Video analytics:** Video analytics software uses advanced algorithms to analyze video feeds in real-time. It can automatically detect and alert security personnel about specific events or behaviors, such as unauthorized access, loitering, or object removal. Video analytics can significantly reduce the manual effort required for monitoring large-scale surveillance systems.

- **Intelligent video surveillance:** Intelligent video surveillance systems combine video analytics with sophisticated algorithms to provide advanced capabilities such as facial recognition, license plate recognition, and object tracking. These systems enhance security by automatically identifying and tracking individuals or objects of interest.

- **Audit trail and system logs:** Surveillance systems should generate audit trails and system logs that record events such as system configuration changes, user accesses, and video export activities. These audit trails provide an essential source of information during investigations and audits, ensuring the integrity and accountability of the system.

- **Physical access controls:** Physical access controls should be implemented to secure the areas where surveillance system infrastructure is located. This includes using secure cabinets or rooms, limiting access to authorized personnel only, and implementing electronic locks or biometric access control systems.

Challenges and Considerations

Monitoring and auditing surveillance systems in healthcare facilities come with several challenges and considerations:

- **Privacy concerns:** It is crucial to strike a balance between security needs and patient privacy rights. Ensure compliance with applicable laws and regulations governing the capture and storage of video recordings, including obtaining informed consent when required.

- **Data protection:** Video footage contains sensitive information, and care must be taken to protect it from unauthorized access, tampering, or loss. Encryption, secure storage, and strict access control measures should be in place to safeguard the integrity and confidentiality of video data.

- **System scalability:** Healthcare facilities may experience changes in their infrastructure, expansions, or renovations. Surveillance systems must be designed with scalability in mind to accommodate future growth and ensure that monitoring and auditing capabilities can adapt to changing requirements.

- **System reliability and maintenance:** Regular maintenance and testing of surveillance systems are essential to ensure their continued functionality.

Procedures should be in place to promptly address hardware or software failures, camera malfunctions, and connectivity issues.

- **Training and awareness:** Proper training for security personnel on monitoring and auditing procedures is vital for maximizing the effectiveness of surveillance systems. Ongoing awareness campaigns can also help educate employees and visitors about the presence of surveillance cameras and their role in enhancing safety and security.

Conclusion

Monitoring and auditing surveillance systems are critical components of the overall security strategy in healthcare facilities. By actively monitoring live video feeds and reviewing recorded footage, security personnel can identify potential security threats, investigate incidents, and deter criminal activities. Implementing best practices for monitoring and auditing, leveraging appropriate tools and techniques, and staying mindful of privacy concerns and system maintenance are key to ensuring a safe and secure environment in healthcare facilities.

Network Security in Healthcare Facilities

Secure Wi-Fi Networks and Guest Access

In today's digitally connected world, Wi-Fi networks have become essential for both personal and professional use. However, with the increased reliance on Wi-Fi, there is also an increased risk of security breaches and unauthorized access. In this section, we will explore the importance of securing Wi-Fi networks and the best practices for guest access.

Importance of Secure Wi-Fi Networks

Wi-Fi networks are susceptible to various security threats, such as unauthorized access, eavesdropping, and man-in-the-middle attacks. Securing Wi-Fi networks is crucial to protect sensitive data, including personal information, medical records, and financial transactions. By implementing robust security measures, health and wellness organizations can ensure the confidentiality, integrity, and availability of their network resources.

Wi-Fi Security Protocols

To secure Wi-Fi networks, one of the fundamental steps is to implement strong Wi-Fi security protocols. The most commonly used protocols include:

- **WPA2 (Wi-Fi Protected Access II):** WPA2 is currently the most secure protocol for Wi-Fi networks. It provides robust encryption and authentication mechanisms to prevent unauthorized access and eavesdropping. WPA2 supports two encryption modes: Personal and Enterprise.

- **WPA3 (Wi-Fi Protected Access III):** WPA3 is the latest Wi-Fi security protocol, offering enhanced security features compared to WPA2. It provides stronger encryption, protection against brute-force attacks, and improved authentication protocols.

- **802.1X/EAP (Extensible Authentication Protocol):** This protocol is commonly used in enterprise Wi-Fi networks. It enables centralized authentication and accounting, using a separate authentication server, such as a RADIUS (Remote Authentication Dial-In User Service) server. 802.1X/EAP provides mutual authentication, ensuring that both the client and the access point verify each other's identity.

Best Practices for Wi-Fi Network Security

Implementing the following best practices can significantly enhance the security of Wi-Fi networks:

1. **Change Default SSID and Password:** By default, Wi-Fi access points come with pre-configured network names (SSID) and passwords. It is crucial to change these defaults to prevent unauthorized access. Choose unique, strong passwords that include a combination of upper and lowercase letters, numbers, and special characters. Regularly update passwords to maintain security.

2. **Enable Network Encryption:** To secure wireless communications, enable encryption protocols such as WPA2 or WPA3. Encryption ensures that data transmitted over the network is indecipherable to unauthorized users. Avoid using outdated encryption protocols, such as WEP (Wired Equivalent Privacy), as they are vulnerable to security breaches.

3. **Segment Wi-Fi Networks:** Segmenting the Wi-Fi network can help isolate different categories of users or devices. For example, separate guest Wi-Fi networks from internal networks to restrict unauthorized access to sensitive information. Use virtual LANs (VLANs) to create logical network segments.
4. **Implement Network Access Control:** Implement network access control mechanisms to authenticate and authorize devices before allowing them to connect to the Wi-Fi network. This can be achieved using 802.1X/EAP, which requires users to provide credentials for access.
5. **Enable Firewalls:** Enable firewalls on Wi-Fi access points and routers to filter incoming and outgoing network traffic. Firewalls can help block malicious traffic and protect the network from unauthorized access attempts.
6. **Disable Remote Management:** Disable the remote management feature on Wi-Fi access points to prevent unauthorized access to device settings. If remote management is required, restrict access to trusted IP addresses and use secure protocols, such as SSH (Secure Shell) or HTTPS (Hypertext Transfer Protocol Secure).
7. **Regularly Update Firmware:** Keep Wi-Fi access points, routers, and other network devices up to date with the latest firmware. Manufacturers often release firmware updates to address security vulnerabilities and improve the overall performance and stability of the devices. Regularly check for firmware updates and apply them promptly.

Guest Wi-Fi Access

In health and wellness facilities, providing guest Wi-Fi access is essential for patient satisfaction and convenience. However, guest networks pose a security risk if not properly secured. Here are some best practices for implementing secure guest Wi-Fi access:

1. **Segment Guest Network:** Segment the guest network from the internal network to prevent guest users from accessing sensitive information or other devices on the network. This can be done by using separate VLANs or network subnets.
2. **Set Time and Bandwidth Limits:** Limit the duration of guest Wi-Fi access and allocate a specific bandwidth to ensure fair usage and prevent abuse. This helps maintain network performance and prevents unauthorized users from remaining connected for extended periods.

3. **Implement Captive Portal:** Use a captive portal to authenticate guest users before granting them access to the network. This can involve a simple username and password authentication or even integrating with social media accounts for a seamless login experience.

4. **Isolate Guest Devices:** Implement client isolation on the guest network to prevent guest devices from communicating with each other. This adds an extra layer of security and prevents attacks between guest devices.

5. **Provide a Terms of Service Agreement:** Display a terms of service agreement that guest users must accept before gaining access to the guest network. This agreement should include an acceptable use policy and clearly state the consequences of violating the policy.

By following these best practices, health and wellness organizations can ensure secure Wi-Fi networks for both internal users and guest access, reducing the risk of unauthorized access and maintaining the privacy and integrity of sensitive data.

Summary

Securing Wi-Fi networks and implementing best practices for guest access are critical in maintaining the confidentiality, integrity, and availability of health and wellness data. By using strong Wi-Fi security protocols, segmenting networks, enabling network access control, and following recommended security measures, organizations can mitigate security risks and provide a safe browsing experience for users. Regularly updating firmware and continuously monitoring network security are also essential to protect against emerging threats. Remember, a well-secured Wi-Fi network contributes to overall cybersecurity and enhances the wellbeing of both individuals and organizations in the health and wellness industry.

Network Segmentation and VLANs

In today's interconnected world, where many devices are connected to the same network, the security of the network becomes a critical concern. Network segmentation and VLANs (Virtual Local Area Networks) are essential tools for enhancing network security and managing network traffic effectively. This section will explore the concepts and benefits of network segmentation and VLANs, as well as provide guidance on their implementation in the context of cybersecurity for health and wellness.

Understanding Network Segmentation

Network segmentation is the process of dividing a larger network into smaller, isolated segments, known as subnets, to improve security, performance, and manageability. Each subnet operates as its own mini-network, with its own set of devices and resources, and is separated from other subnets using routers, firewalls, or switches.

The primary objective of network segmentation is to reduce the attack surface, preventing unauthorized access and lateral movement across the network in the event of a security breach. By dividing the network into smaller segments, an attacker's ability to move laterally and gain access to critical assets is limited. Even if one subnet is compromised, the attacker will still face barriers to accessing other subnets, thereby minimizing the impact and scope of a breach.

Additionally, network segmentation helps to improve network performance by reducing network congestion. By separating devices into different segments based on their functions or locations, network traffic can be managed more efficiently. This leads to improved data transfer speeds and decreased latency, resulting in a better overall user experience.

Virtual Local Area Networks (VLANs)

A VLAN, short for Virtual Local Area Network, is a logical network that allows devices to communicate with each other as if they were in the same physical network, regardless of their physical location. VLANs are created by grouping devices based on specific criteria, such as department, function, or security requirements, rather than their physical proximity.

The main advantage of VLANs is that they provide logical isolation within a physical network infrastructure. By grouping devices into VLANs, traffic can be isolated and contained within specific segments, preventing unauthorized access from devices outside the VLAN. This isolation enhances security by minimizing the potential attack surface and limiting the lateral movement of attackers.

VLANs also offer flexibility and scalability in network management. Administrators can easily reconfigure VLAN assignments as organizational needs change without physically relocating devices or rewiring the network infrastructure. This flexibility allows for efficient management of network resources, minimizing time and effort required to adapt to evolving business needs.

Implementing Network Segmentation and VLANs

To implement network segmentation using VLANs, several steps need to be followed:

1. **Identify segmentation criteria:** Determine the criteria for segmenting the network, such as department, function, or security requirements. This will depend on the specific needs and structure of the health and wellness organization.

2. **Design the VLAN architecture:** Create a VLAN plan that defines the number and purpose of each VLAN, including which devices and resources will be grouped together.

3. **Configure VLANs on network devices:** Configure VLANs on the network switches or routers by assigning specific ports to each VLAN. This ensures that devices within each VLAN can communicate with each other while restricting communication with devices in other VLANs.

4. **Implement VLAN access controls:** Define and enforce access control policies to regulate traffic between VLANs. This can be achieved through the use of firewall rules, access control lists, or network segmentation devices.

5. **Monitor and maintain VLANs:** Regularly monitor the VLANs to ensure proper functioning, detect any anomalies or potential security breaches, and apply necessary updates or patches to maintain the security and performance of the network.

Benefits and Considerations

Implementing network segmentation through VLANs offers several benefits, particularly in the context of cybersecurity for health and wellness:

- **Improved security:** Network segmentation reduces the attack surface, limiting the impact of a security breach and preventing unauthorized access to critical assets. VLANs provide logical isolation, further enhancing security by restricting communication between devices in different VLANs.

- **Enhanced performance:** By segregating network traffic into different VLANs, network congestion is minimized, resulting in improved data transfer speeds and reduced latency. This ensures optimal performance for critical health and wellness applications and services.

- **Flexibility and scalability:** VLANs offer the flexibility to reconfigure network resources as organizational needs change, without the need for physical reconfiguration. This allows for efficient resource management and easy adaptation to evolving business requirements.

- **Simplified network management:** Network segmentation through VLANs simplifies the management of network resources, as devices and resources can be easily assigned to specific VLANs. This streamlines administration tasks and improves the overall efficiency of the network infrastructure.

While network segmentation through VLANs provides significant benefits, it is important to consider some caveats:

- **Complexity:** Implementing VLANs requires careful planning and configuration, and it can be complex, particularly in larger environments. Proper design and documentation are crucial to ensure a secure and efficient VLAN implementation.

- **Security risks:** It is essential to implement proper access controls and regularly monitor VLANs to prevent unauthorized access and data breaches. Misconfigurations or weaknesses in VLAN configurations can potentially expose sensitive information, so thorough testing and ongoing management are necessary.

- **Network performance impact:** Improper configuration or excessive segmentation can lead to unnecessary network complexity and degrade overall network performance. It is essential to strike a balance between security and performance requirements when designing and implementing VLANs.

Example Application: Securing IoT Devices with VLANs

In the context of health and wellness, the Internet of Things (IoT) devices, such as smart medical devices and wearables, play an increasingly significant role. These devices often connect to the network wirelessly and may introduce potential security vulnerabilities if not properly secured.

One practical application of VLANs in the health and wellness industry is securing IoT devices. By creating a dedicated VLAN for IoT devices, these devices can be isolated from other critical network segments, such as patient data storage or administrative systems. This isolation limits the attack surface and prevents potential security breaches from spreading to other parts of the network.

For example, a health facility can create a VLAN specifically for smart medical devices, such as connected infusion pumps, patient monitors, or implantable devices. These devices can be assigned to the IoT VLAN, which is separate from other network segments. By implementing proper access controls, only authorized devices and services can communicate with the IoT VLAN, reducing the risk of unauthorized access or tampering with critical medical devices.

In this scenario, network administrators can implement additional security measures, such as network traffic monitoring and anomaly detection systems, to detect any suspicious behavior on the IoT VLAN. Regular monitoring of the traffic within the VLAN can help identify potential security breaches or unauthorized access attempts.

By securing IoT devices with VLANs, health and wellness organizations can protect critical medical devices from cyber threats, ensuring both patient safety and the integrity of healthcare services.

Additional Resources

For further exploration of network segmentation and VLANs, the following resources are recommended:

- R. Bejtlich, C. Mandia, and K. Liston. *Network Security Monitoring: Best Practices for Identifying and Mitigating Threats in Your Network.* O'Reilly Media, 2014.
- C. Lynch. *Network Security Through Data Analysis: From Data to Action.* O'Reilly Media, 2014.
- C. Little, R. Charles, and J. Aitken. *Network Security: A Beginner's Guide.* McGraw-Hill, 2016.
- Standards for VLANs: IEEE 802.1Q (VLAN Tagging) and IEEE 802.1ah (Provider Backbone Bridges).

Conclusion

Network segmentation using VLANs is an essential component of a comprehensive cybersecurity strategy for health and wellness organizations. It provides improved security, network performance, and flexibility while enabling effective management of network resources. By understanding the principles and best practices of network segmentation and VLANs, health and wellness professionals can enhance the security and integrity of their network infrastructure, safeguarding sensitive patient data and ensuring the reliable delivery of healthcare services.

Wireless Intrusion Prevention Systems (WIPS)

In the digital age, wireless networks play a crucial role in our daily lives, enabling us to connect to the internet and communicate wirelessly. However, with this convenience comes the risk of unauthorized access and attacks on wireless networks. Wireless Intrusion Prevention Systems (WIPS) are designed to mitigate these risks by monitoring and securing wireless networks against potential threats. In this section, we will explore the fundamentals of WIPS, their benefits, and their implementation in healthcare facilities.

Understanding Wireless Network Security

Wireless networks transmit data over the airwaves, making them vulnerable to interception and unauthorized access. Attackers can exploit vulnerabilities in wireless networks to gain unauthorized access to sensitive information or disrupt network operations. To ensure the security of wireless networks, it's essential to implement robust security measures, and this is where WIPS comes into play.

What is a Wireless Intrusion Prevention System (WIPS)?

A Wireless Intrusion Prevention System (WIPS) is a network security solution designed to detect and prevent unauthorized access to wireless networks. Unlike traditional intrusion detection systems, which focus on wired networks, WIPS is specifically geared towards securing wireless networks. It utilizes a combination of techniques, including monitoring, detection, and prevention, to safeguard wireless networks and the devices connected to them.

Benefits of WIPS in Healthcare Facilities

Healthcare facilities handle sensitive patient data and have a high volume of wireless devices, making them attractive targets for cyber attacks. Implementing WIPS in healthcare facilities offers several benefits:

- **Threat Detection:** WIPS continuously monitors wireless network traffic, detecting any unauthorized or suspicious activities. It can identify rogue access points, unauthorized devices, and potential attacks, allowing for immediate response and mitigation.

- **Attack Prevention:** WIPS employs various countermeasures to prevent attacks on wireless networks. It can enforce policies and access controls, block unauthorized devices, and disrupt malicious activities, ensuring the integrity and security of the network.
- **Compliance and Regulatory Requirements:** Healthcare facilities are subject to various compliance and regulatory requirements, such as HIPAA (Health Insurance Portability and Accountability Act). WIPS helps fulfill these requirements by providing network security monitoring, intrusion prevention, and incident response capabilities.
- **Improved Network Performance:** By actively monitoring and managing wireless network traffic, WIPS can optimize network performance. It identifies and mitigates bandwidth-hogging activities, interference issues, and network misconfigurations, ensuring a stable and reliable wireless network for healthcare operations.

Detecting and Mitigating Wireless Network Threats

WIPS employs a range of techniques to detect and mitigate wireless network threats. Some key techniques include:

- **Wireless Packet Inspection:** WIPS inspects wireless packets to identify rogue access points, unauthorized devices, and suspicious network activities. It analyzes packet headers and payloads to detect anomalies, unauthorized protocols, and known attack signatures.
- **Radio Frequency (RF) Spectrum Analysis:** By performing RF spectrum analysis, WIPS can identify sources of interference, unauthorized access points, and unusual RF patterns. It helps detect wireless attacks, such as jamming or denial of service attacks, and ensures that wireless networks operate within designated frequency bands.
- **Device Fingerprinting:** WIPS uses device fingerprinting techniques to identify and classify wireless devices connected to the network. It maintains a database of known devices and compares the characteristics of connected devices to detect unauthorized or unknown devices.
- **Wireless Intrusion Detection:** WIPS continuously monitors wireless network traffic for suspicious activities and known attack signatures. It can detect various types of attacks, including unauthorized access attempts, man-in-the-middle attacks, and network reconnaissance.

- **Intrusion Prevention and Response:** Upon detection of an intrusion or suspicious activity, WIPS can take immediate action to mitigate the threat. It can block unauthorized devices, terminate malicious connections, and dynamically adjust network access control policies to prevent further intrusions.

Implementation Considerations

When implementing WIPS in healthcare facilities, several considerations should be taken into account:

- **Coverage and Placement:** WIPS sensors or access points should be strategically placed to ensure comprehensive coverage of the wireless network. They should be positioned in critical areas, such as waiting rooms, patient treatment areas, and administrative areas, to provide effective monitoring and protection.

- **Integration with Existing Network Infrastructure:** WIPS should seamlessly integrate with the existing network infrastructure of healthcare facilities. It should be compatible with wireless access points, network switches, and other network components to ensure smooth operation and management.

- **Scalability and Performance:** Healthcare facilities often have large and complex wireless networks. WIPS solutions should be scalable to accommodate the growing number of devices and network traffic. They should also have minimal impact on network performance to prevent interruptions in critical healthcare operations.

- **Configuration and Management:** WIPS solutions should provide user-friendly interfaces for configuration and management. They should offer centralized management capabilities, allowing administrators to monitor and manage the wireless network security from a single console.

- **Ongoing Monitoring and Maintenance:** Continuous monitoring and maintenance are crucial for the effective operation of WIPS. Regular monitoring of alerts, logs, and reports generated by WIPS helps identify vulnerabilities and potential security issues. It enables proactive response and timely updates to security policies and configurations.

Conclusion

Wireless Intrusion Prevention Systems (WIPS) are vital components in ensuring the security and integrity of wireless networks in healthcare facilities. By detecting and preventing unauthorized access, WIPS helps protect sensitive patient data, comply with regulatory requirements, and maintain the overall security posture of healthcare operations. Implementing WIPS requires careful consideration of coverage, integration, scalability, configuration, and ongoing maintenance. With the ever-evolving cybersecurity landscape, WIPS serves as an essential defense against wireless network threats, contributing to a safer and more secure healthcare environment.

Securing Remote Access for Healthcare Staff

Remote access plays a crucial role in the healthcare industry, allowing healthcare staff to access critical systems and patient records from outside the healthcare facility. However, it also poses significant security risks if not properly secured. In this section, we will explore best practices and strategies to ensure secure remote access for healthcare staff.

Understanding the Risks

Before diving into the strategies, it's essential to understand the risks associated with remote access in healthcare. Unauthorized access to patient records, tampering with data, and potential loss or theft of sensitive information are some of the primary concerns. Additionally, compromised remote access can lead to breaches of healthcare networks and systems.

Implementing VPNs for Secure Remote Access

One of the most effective ways to secure remote access in healthcare is by implementing Virtual Private Networks (VPNs). VPNs create a secure encrypted connection between the remote user and the healthcare network, ensuring that data transmitted is protected from interception and tampering.

To implement VPNs effectively, the following steps should be taken:

1. **Use Strong Encryption:** Ensure that your VPN solution uses strong encryption protocols such as IPSec or SSL/TLS to protect data during transmission.

2. **Enforce Two-Factor Authentication (2FA):** Require healthcare staff to use two-factor authentication when connecting through VPNs. This adds an extra layer of security by requiring both a password and a second form of verification, such as a code sent to a mobile device.

3. **Limit Access Privileges:** Grant remote access only to staff members who genuinely require it for their job functions. Implement role-based access controls to ensure that access privileges are appropriate and limited to the necessary systems and data.

4. **Regularly Update VPN Software:** Keep the VPN software and firmware up to date to ensure that any vulnerabilities are patched promptly.

Securing Remote Desktop Access and Virtual Private Servers

In healthcare, remote desktop access allows healthcare staff to access and control their work computers remotely. However, it is crucial to secure remote desktop access to prevent unauthorized access and potential breaches.

The following steps should be taken to secure remote desktop access:

1. **Use Strong Authentication:** Require strong passwords and enforce 2FA for remote desktop access. Implement account lockout policies to prevent brute-force attacks on login credentials.

2. **Limit Network Exposure:** Use firewalls to restrict remote desktop access to only trusted IP addresses or virtual private networks (VPNs). This ensures that access is limited to authorized individuals and reduces the risk of unauthorized access.

3. **Regularly Monitor and Log Remote Desktop Sessions:** Implement logging mechanisms to monitor remote desktop sessions and detect any suspicious activities. Regularly review the logs to identify and respond to any potential security incidents.

4. **Update Remote Access Software:** Keep the remote access software, such as Remote Desktop Protocol (RDP), up to date with the latest security patches to address any known vulnerabilities.

When it comes to virtual private servers (VPS), which are often used to host healthcare applications and services, securing remote access is equally crucial. The following measures should be implemented:

1. **Disable Default Accounts and Unused Services:** Disable any default accounts on the VPS and remove any unnecessary or unused services. This reduces the potential attack surface and minimizes the risk of unauthorized access.
2. **Strong Authentication and Access Controls:** Enforce strong passwords and limit remote access to authorized individuals. Implement access controls to restrict access to authorized IP addresses or VPNs.
3. **Regular Patching and Updates:** Keep the VPS operating system and software up to date with the latest security patches. This ensures that any known vulnerabilities are addressed promptly.
4. **Implement Intrusion Detection Systems (IDS) and Intrusion Prevention Systems (IPS):** Use IDS and IPS to detect and prevent unauthorized access attempts and suspicious activities on the VPS. Configure these systems to generate alerts or take proactive actions to mitigate potential threats.

Managing Third-Party Access and Vendor Security

In healthcare settings, it is common for third-party vendors, such as software providers or IT service providers, to require remote access to healthcare systems. However, managing and securing such access is vital to prevent unauthorized entry or malicious actions.

Consider the following practices for managing third-party access and vendor security:

1. **Vendor Due Diligence:** Before granting remote access privileges, conduct thorough due diligence on the third-party vendor. Ensure they have appropriate security measures in place and comply with relevant regulations and standards.
2. **Secure Remote Access Agreement:** Establish a formal agreement that outlines the responsibilities of both parties regarding remote access. Clearly define the scope of access, security requirements, and expectations for protecting sensitive information.
3. **Access Controls and Monitoring:** Implement access controls to restrict vendor access to only the necessary systems and data. Monitor and log vendor activities to detect any potential security incidents.

4. **Regular Audits and Assessments:** Conduct regular audits and assessments of vendor security practices to ensure compliance. This can include vulnerability assessments, penetration testing, and periodic reviews of vendor policies and procedures.

5. **Terminate Access for Inactive Vendors:** When a vendor's services are no longer required, promptly revoke their remote access privileges to mitigate the risk of unauthorized access.

Secure Access Control Policies and Procedures

In addition to implementing specific security measures, healthcare organizations should establish strong access control policies and procedures to govern remote access. These policies and procedures should include the following:

1. **Authentication and Authorization:** Clearly define the authentication methods, including passwords and 2FA, for remote access. Specify the authorization levels and the process for granting and revoking access privileges.

2. **User Account Management:** Establish guidelines for user account creation, management, and termination. This should include password complexity requirements, account lockout policies, and removal of accounts for terminated employees or contractors.

3. **Audit Logs and Monitoring:** Define the logging requirements for remote access activities, including which activities should be logged and for how long. Implement a system for reviewing and analyzing audit logs to detect any suspicious activities.

4. **Incident Response:** Develop an incident response plan that covers remote access security incidents. Clearly outline the steps to be taken in the event of a breach or unauthorized access, including containment, investigation, and communication procedures.

5. **Training and Awareness:** Provide regular training and awareness programs for healthcare staff regarding remote access security. This should cover best practices, potential risks, and how to identify and report security incidents.

Summary

Securing remote access for healthcare staff is crucial to safeguard patient data and protect healthcare systems. By implementing secure VPNs, securing remote desktop access and virtual private servers, managing third-party access, and establishing robust access control policies, healthcare organizations can mitigate the risks associated with remote access. It is imperative to regularly update and review security measures to adapt to evolving threats and ensure ongoing protection. By employing these strategies, healthcare institutions can maintain the confidentiality, integrity, and availability of systems and patient information.

Resources

Here are some additional resources for further reading on securing remote access in healthcare:

- NIST Special Publication 800-46: Guide to Enterprise Telework, Remote Access, and Bring Your Own Device (BYOD) Security: Provides detailed guidelines on securing remote access for organizations.
- HITRUST CSF: A comprehensive framework that includes remote access security controls specific to the healthcare industry.
- OWASP Secure Coding Practices: Offers best practices for secure coding, which can be applied to remote access solutions in healthcare.

Incident Response and Network Security Monitoring

Incident response and network security monitoring are crucial components of an effective cybersecurity strategy in healthcare facilities. In this section, we will explore the importance of incident response and network security monitoring, as well as the key steps involved in handling security incidents and ensuring the continuous monitoring of network systems.

The Importance of Incident Response

Incident response is a systematic approach to addressing and managing security incidents in a timely and efficient manner. It allows organizations to detect, respond to, and recover from cybersecurity breaches effectively. In the healthcare industry, where sensitive patient information is at risk, incident response plays a vital role in preventing data breaches, minimizing the impact of incidents, and maintaining the trust of patients.

Network Security Monitoring

Network security monitoring involves the continuous monitoring of network systems, including network traffic, devices, and infrastructure, to identify and respond to security threats. It helps organizations to detect and mitigate potential security incidents, identify vulnerabilities, and ensure the integrity and availability of network resources.

Key Steps in Incident Response

Effective incident response follows a systematic approach that includes the following key steps:

1. Preparation: This step involves establishing an incident response plan, defining roles and responsibilities, and identifying the necessary tools and resources to effectively respond to security incidents. It also includes conducting regular training and simulations to ensure the readiness of the incident response team.

2. Detection and Analysis: Detecting security incidents early is crucial to minimize their impact. Incident detection involves implementing security monitoring tools, such as Intrusion Detection Systems (IDS) and Security Information and Event Management (SIEM) systems, to identify potential threats and anomalies in network traffic. Once an incident is detected, it needs to be analyzed to understand the nature and extent of the breach.

3. Containment and Eradication: This step involves isolating the affected systems and network segments to prevent further spread of the incident. It may include temporarily disconnecting compromised systems from the network, disabling user accounts, or removing malicious files. The goal is to eradicate the incident and restore the normal functioning of the affected systems.

4. Recovery: After containing and eradicating the incident, organizations must restore affected systems and data from backups, if available. This step may also involve patching vulnerabilities, strengthening security controls, and implementing additional preventive measures to prevent similar incidents in the future.

5. Post-Incident Analysis: Conducting a thorough post-incident analysis is vital to understand the root causes of the incident, evaluate the effectiveness of the incident response process, and identify areas for improvement. This analysis helps organizations refine their incident response plans and implement preventive measures to mitigate future risks.

Security Monitoring in Healthcare Facilities

Continuous network security monitoring is critical in healthcare facilities to ensure the early detection and response to security incidents. Here are some key aspects of network security monitoring in healthcare:

1. SIEM Systems: Security Information and Event Management (SIEM) systems enable healthcare organizations to collect, analyze, and correlate security event logs from various network devices, servers, and applications. This centralized monitoring and analysis provide real-time insights into potential security threats and help organizations respond promptly.

2. Intrusion Detection Systems (IDS): IDS tools monitor network traffic and detect patterns or anomalies that indicate potential intrusions or malicious activities. IDS can be network-based or host-based, providing an additional layer of security to identify and mitigate security risks.

3. Log Monitoring: Monitoring system and application logs allows healthcare facilities to track user activities, identify suspicious behavior, and detect unauthorized access attempts. Log monitoring provides valuable information for incident response and forensic investigations.

4. Threat Intelligence: Keeping up-to-date with the latest threats and vulnerabilities is essential in network security monitoring. Healthcare facilities can subscribe to threat intelligence feeds and collaborate with industry peers to stay informed about emerging threats and preventive measures.

5. Incident Response Automation: Implementing automation tools and playbooks can aid in incident response and reduce response time. Automated incident response workflows enable rapid containment and remediation of security incidents.

Challenges and Best Practices

Implementing effective incident response and network security monitoring in healthcare facilities comes with its own set of challenges. These challenges include the complexity of IT infrastructure, limited resources, and the evolving nature of cyber threats. To address these challenges, the following best practices can be followed:

1. Collaboration and Communication: Incident response is a team effort that requires clear communication and collaboration among IT teams, security personnel, and stakeholders. Establishing effective lines of communication and coordinated decision-making processes is crucial during security incidents.

2. Regular Training and Awareness: Healthcare organizations should provide ongoing cybersecurity training to their staff, focusing on incident response procedures, recognizing potential threats, and reporting incidents promptly. It is essential to raise awareness about the importance of incident response and network security monitoring at all levels of the organization.

3. Incident Response Partnerships: Forming partnerships with external incident response teams, law enforcement agencies, and cybersecurity vendors can provide healthcare facilities with additional expertise and resources during security incidents. These partnerships enhance incident response capabilities and aid in a more effective response to threats.

4. Continuous Improvement: Cybersecurity is an ever-changing landscape, and healthcare organizations must continually evaluate and improve their incident response and network security monitoring capabilities. Regularly reviewing incident response plans, conducting drills and exercises, and staying updated with the latest security practices and technologies are critical for staying ahead of emerging threats.

Case Study: Incident Response and Network Security Monitoring in a Healthcare Facility

Let's consider a case study to understand how incident response and network security monitoring are implemented in a healthcare facility.

Scenario: Hospital X has implemented a comprehensive incident response and network security monitoring program. They have a dedicated incident response team consisting of IT professionals, security analysts, and legal representatives. The team is responsible for handling security incidents and maintaining the security posture of the organization.

Incident Detection: The SIEM system deployed by Hospital X constantly monitors network traffic, system logs, and user activities. One day, the SIEM system generates an alert indicating a potential unauthorized access attempt to a critical patient database. The incident response team immediately starts investigating the alert.

Containment and Eradication: After initial investigation, the incident response team verifies the intrusion attempt and isolates the affected systems from the network. They initiate the incident response process as per the predefined protocols. The team conducts a thorough analysis to determine the extent of the breach and removes the unauthorized access from the affected systems.

Post-Incident Analysis: Once the incident is contained and eradicated, the incident response team conducts a post-incident analysis. They review logs, system configurations, and other relevant data to understand how the breach occurred and identify any vulnerabilities that were exploited. Based on the analysis, the team recommends security enhancements and updates the incident response plan accordingly.

Continuous Monitoring and Prevention: Hospital X continues to monitor network traffic, system logs, and user activities to detect and prevent future security incidents. They regularly update their security controls, conduct security awareness training for employees, and collaborate with external incident response teams to stay ahead of emerging threats.

Key Takeaways

Incident response and network security monitoring are critical components of a robust cybersecurity strategy in healthcare facilities. Key takeaways from this section include:

1. Incident response enables organizations to detect, respond to, and recover from security incidents promptly. 2. Network security monitoring provides continuous visibility into network systems to identify and mitigate security threats. 3. Key steps involved in incident response include preparation, detection and analysis, containment and eradication, recovery, and post-incident analysis. 4. Security monitoring in healthcare facilities involves using SIEM systems, IDS tools, log monitoring, and leveraging threat intelligence. 5. Collaboration, regular training, incident response partnerships, and continuous improvement are essential for effective incident response and network security monitoring. 6. Real-world case studies help illustrate the practical implementation and benefits of incident response and network security monitoring in healthcare facilities.

By implementing robust incident response and network security monitoring practices, healthcare facilities can minimize the impact of security incidents, safeguard patient data, and ensure the overall security and resilience of their IT infrastructure.

Employee Training on Network Security Awareness

Employee training on network security awareness is an essential component in any organization's cybersecurity strategy. It equips employees with the knowledge and skills to identify and respond to network security threats, thereby minimizing the risk of successful cyber attacks. In this section, we will explore the key aspects of employee training on network security awareness, including the importance of training, the scope of the training program, training methods, and evaluating the effectiveness of the training.

Importance of Network Security Awareness Training

Employees are often the first line of defense against cyber attacks. By training them on network security awareness, organizations can empower employees to recognize potential security threats, adhere to security best practices, and report suspicious activities promptly. Here are some key reasons why network security awareness training is crucial:

- **Prevention of Social Engineering Attacks:** Social engineering attacks, such as phishing and pretexting, rely on tricking employees into revealing sensitive information or granting unauthorized access. By educating employees on these attack vectors, they can learn how to identify and avoid falling victim to such attacks.

- **Protection of Confidential Information:** Employees handle sensitive and confidential data on a daily basis. Network security awareness training can help them understand the importance of protecting this information and the potential consequences of data breaches, thereby promoting a culture of data security.

- **Mitigation of Human Error Risks:** Many cybersecurity incidents occur due to human errors, such as weak passwords, unsecure Wi-Fi usage, or accidental sharing of sensitive information. Training employees on proper security practices can significantly reduce the risks associated with these errors.

- **Compliance with Regulations:** Organizations operating in the health and wellness industry need to comply with various data privacy and security regulations, such as the Health Insurance Portability and Accountability Act (HIPAA) and the General Data Protection Regulation (GDPR). Network security awareness training helps employees understand their obligations and responsibilities in relation to these regulations.

Scope of Network Security Awareness Training

The scope of network security awareness training should cover a wide range of topics to ensure comprehensive coverage of potential security threats. Here are some important areas that should be included in the training program:

- **Phishing Awareness:** Employees should be trained to identify phishing emails and messages, understand the techniques used by attackers, and avoid clicking on suspicious links or downloading malicious attachments.
- **Password Security:** Training should emphasize the importance of using strong passwords, avoiding password reuse, and regularly updating passwords. Employees should also be educated on the risks of sharing passwords and the benefits of using password management tools.
- **Secure Wi-Fi Usage:** Employees should be aware of the risks associated with unsecured Wi-Fi networks, such as man-in-the-middle attacks. Training should cover the importance of connecting to trusted networks and the use of virtual private networks (VPNs) for secure remote access.
- **Physical Security:** Topics such as securing workstations, locking screens when leaving the desk, and preventing unauthorized physical access to sensitive areas should be included to ensure holistic security awareness.
- **Safe Use of Removable Media:** Employees should be trained on the risks of using external storage devices and the potential introduction of malware. Best practices for scanning removable media and securely transferring data should also be covered.
- **Mobile Device Security:** The use of mobile devices, such as smartphones and tablets, introduces additional security risks. Training should address topics like device encryption, secure app installation, and the importance of installing updates promptly.

Training Methods

When it comes to training methods, organizations have a range of options to choose from. A combination of different methods can be effective in maximizing the impact of network security awareness training. Here are some common training methods:

- **In-Person Training Sessions:** In-person training sessions allow for direct interaction with employees and facilitate better engagement. Trainers can customize the content based on the organization's specific needs and address questions and concerns in real-time.
- **Online Training Modules:** Online training modules offer the flexibility of self-paced learning. They can include interactive elements like quizzes and

simulations to reinforce learning. Online training can be accessed from anywhere, making it convenient for employees in remote locations.

- **Video Tutorials:** Short video tutorials can be an effective way to deliver key messages in an engaging manner. They can be used as standalone training resources or as supplementary material to reinforce topics covered in other training methods.

- **Simulated Phishing Exercises:** Simulated phishing exercises allow employees to experience simulated phishing attacks in a controlled environment. These exercises can help employees recognize phishing attempts and reinforce the training they have received.

- **Role-Playing Activities:** Role-playing activities can be used to simulate real-life scenarios, such as responding to a security incident or handling a suspicious phone call. This approach helps employees apply their knowledge and skills in a practical context.

It is important to tailor the training methods to the organization's culture, available resources, and the specific needs of the employees. A combination of different methods can help cater to different learning styles and ensure maximum retention of knowledge.

Evaluating Training Effectiveness

To measure the effectiveness of network security awareness training, organizations can implement various evaluation methods. These methods provide insights into the learning outcomes, identify areas for improvement, and help organizations refine their training programs. Here are some evaluation methods to consider:

- **Knowledge Assessments:** Pre and post-training assessments can be used to evaluate employees' knowledge and understanding of network security concepts. By comparing the results, organizations can gauge the effectiveness of the training in improving employees' knowledge.

- **Simulated Phishing Tests:** Regularly conducting simulated phishing tests can help assess employees' ability to identify and report phishing attempts. The results can provide valuable insights into the effectiveness of the training in mitigating social engineering risks.

- **Feedback Surveys:** Anonymous feedback surveys allow employees to provide their opinions and suggestions regarding the training program. This feedback can reveal areas of improvement and help organizations tailor future training sessions to better meet employees' needs.
- **Observation and Reporting:** Encouraging employees to actively report any suspicious activities or potential security incidents can serve as an indicator of improved network security awareness. Regular reporting and incident data analysis can highlight progress and areas for further training.

It is essential to continuously monitor and evaluate the effectiveness of the training program. This ensures that it remains up to date with the evolving threat landscape and provides employees with the knowledge and skills needed to address emerging cybersecurity challenges.

Training Tips and Best Practices

Here are some additional tips and best practices to enhance the effectiveness of network security awareness training:

- **Regular Training Updates:** Cybersecurity threats are constantly evolving, and new attack techniques emerge regularly. It is crucial to update the training materials periodically to address emerging threats and incorporate the latest best practices.
- **Management Support:** Obtaining support from top management is vital to foster a culture of security awareness. When employees see that the management is committed to cybersecurity, they are more likely to prioritize security practices.
- **Gamification:** Introducing gamification elements, such as leaderboards and rewards, can increase employee engagement and motivation to participate in the training. This approach makes the training experience more enjoyable and memorable.
- **Continued Reinforcement:** Reinforcing training materials through regular reminders, newsletters, and posters can help employees retain key information and reinforce security best practices in their day-to-day work.
- **Tailored Training for Different Roles:** Consider customizing training materials to match the specific roles and responsibilities of employees. This

ensures that the training is relevant and applicable to their job functions and enhances their understanding of security risks.

- **Collaboration and Sharing:** Encourage employees to share their knowledge and experiences with their colleagues. This not only promotes a collaborative and supportive environment but also reinforces good network security practices.

Conclusion

Employee training on network security awareness plays a critical role in protecting organizations from cybersecurity threats. By providing employees with the necessary knowledge and skills, organizations can create a workforce that is vigilant, security-conscious, and capable of defending against network security risks. Through effective training methods, comprehensive coverage of relevant topics, and continuous evaluation, organizations can establish a strong security culture that is adaptable to the evolving threat landscape.

For further resources and training materials, organizations can consult reputable cybersecurity organizations, industry-specific training programs, and online resources that provide up-to-date information on network security awareness. By investing in employee training, organizations can significantly enhance their overall cybersecurity posture and safeguard their valuable assets.

Incident Response and Disaster Recovery in Healthcare

Establishing an Incident Response Plan

In today's digitally connected world, where cyber threats are becoming more sophisticated and prevalent, it is essential for health and wellness organizations to establish an effective incident response plan. An incident response plan outlines the steps and procedures to be followed in the event of a cybersecurity incident, such as a data breach or a system compromise. This section will discuss the key elements involved in establishing an incident response plan and provide practical guidance on its implementation.

Understanding the Importance of an Incident Response Plan

An incident response plan is a proactive measure that helps organizations effectively respond to and manage cybersecurity incidents, minimizing their impact and ensuring a swift recovery. By having a well-defined incident response plan in place, health and wellness organizations can:

- Reduce the time it takes to identify and respond to incidents, minimizing the damage caused.
- Minimize the disruption to business operations and ensure continuity of services.
- Maintain trust and confidence among customers, patients, and stakeholders.
- Protect sensitive data and prevent its unauthorized disclosure or misuse.
- Comply with legal and regulatory requirements related to cybersecurity incident reporting.

Key Components of an Incident Response Plan

An effective incident response plan typically consists of the following key components:

1. **Preparation:** This phase involves conducting a risk assessment to identify potential vulnerabilities and threats, documenting the organization's critical assets and systems, and defining the roles and responsibilities of the incident response team. It also includes establishing communication channels and establishing relationships with external stakeholders, such as law enforcement agencies and cybersecurity experts.

2. **Detection and Analysis:** In this phase, the focus is on detecting and analyzing cybersecurity incidents. This involves implementing monitoring and detection tools, such as intrusion detection systems and security information and event management (SIEM) systems. The incident response team should be trained on how to recognize and classify different types of incidents and perform a thorough analysis to determine the scope and impact of the incident.

3. **Containment and Eradication:** This phase involves taking immediate actions to contain the incident and prevent further damage. This may

include isolating affected systems from the network, shutting down compromised accounts, or blocking malicious IP addresses. Once containment measures are in place, the incident response team should work on eradicating the root cause of the incident and removing any malware or unauthorized access points.

4. **Recovery:** The focus of this phase is on restoring affected systems and services to normal operations. This may involve restoring data from backups, rebuilding compromised systems, or applying security patches. The incident response team should also perform a post-incident review to identify lessons learned and make improvements to prevent similar incidents in the future.

5. **Post-Incident Activities:** After the incident has been resolved and operations have returned to normal, it is important to conduct post-incident activities. This includes documenting the incident, analyzing the incident response process, and updating the incident response plan based on lessons learned. It is also crucial to communicate with stakeholders about the incident and any actions taken to mitigate its impact.

Implementing the Incident Response Plan

Implementing an incident response plan requires a coordinated effort involving multiple stakeholders and ongoing training and testing. Here are some key steps to consider:

- **Engage Stakeholders:** Involve key stakeholders, such as senior management, IT departments, legal counsel, and public relations, in the development and implementation of the incident response plan. Their input and support are crucial for the success of the plan.

- **Assign Roles and Responsibilities:** Clearly define the roles and responsibilities of the incident response team members. This includes designating a team leader, incident handlers, communications coordinators, and liaisons with external entities.

- **Develop Communication Procedures:** Establish communication procedures that outline how internal and external communication will be managed during a cybersecurity incident. This includes identifying primary and alternate communication channels, establishing contact lists, and defining the protocols for reporting and escalating incidents.

- **Define Incident Severity Levels:** Establish a clear framework for classifying and prioritizing incidents based on their severity and impact. This will help the incident response team allocate resources and respond appropriately to each incident.

- **Train and Test the Plan:** Conduct regular training sessions with the incident response team to ensure they are familiar with their roles and responsibilities. Additionally, perform periodic tabletop exercises and simulations to test the effectiveness of the plan and identify areas for improvement.

- **Review and Update the Plan:** It is essential to review and update the incident response plan regularly to reflect changes in the organization's IT infrastructure, emerging threats, and best practices. This ensures that the plan remains effective and relevant over time.

Common Challenges and Best Practices

Establishing an incident response plan can present certain challenges. Here are some common challenges and best practices for addressing them:

- **Lack of Awareness and Understanding:** Many organizations underestimate the importance of an incident response plan or have a limited understanding of its components. Educating stakeholders about the benefits and necessity of the plan is crucial for obtaining their support.

- **Limited Resources and Expertise:** Small health and wellness organizations may face resource constraints and may not have dedicated cybersecurity teams. In such cases, seeking external assistance, such as partnering with managed security service providers or industry groups, can help augment their capabilities.

- **Inadequate Testing and Maintenance:** Failure to regularly test and update the incident response plan can render it ineffective. Conducting regular exercises and reviewing the plan ensures that it remains robust and aligned with the organization's evolving needs.

- **Lack of Integration with Business Continuity Planning:** Incident response plans should be closely integrated with business continuity and disaster recovery plans to ensure a coordinated and comprehensive approach to managing and recovering from cybersecurity incidents.

Real-World Example

A healthcare organization recently experienced a data breach where patient personal information was accessed by unauthorized individuals. The incident response team immediately activated the incident response plan, following the predefined procedures.

First, they contained the breach by isolating the affected systems from the network and shutting down compromised accounts. They then conducted a thorough investigation to determine the scope and impact of the breach. Simultaneously, they engaged external cybersecurity experts to assist with the analysis and containment efforts.

After eradicating the root cause of the breach and restoring affected systems, the incident response team implemented additional security measures to prevent future incidents. They also communicated with affected patients, providing guidance on steps to protect their identities and offering support services.

Following the incident, the organization conducted a detailed post-incident review to identify areas for improvement. They updated the incident response plan based on the lessons learned and provided additional training to the incident response team. The incident response plan was regularly tested through tabletop exercises and simulations to ensure its effectiveness.

Additional Resources

For further information on establishing an incident response plan and building a resilient cybersecurity strategy for health and wellness organizations, refer to the following resources:

- National Institute of Standards and Technology (NIST) Computer Security Incident Handling Guide
- International Organization for Standardization (ISO) 27035:2016 Information Security Incident Management
- Health Information Sharing and Analysis Center (H-ISAC) Incident Response Playbook

Remember, having an incident response plan is not only about being prepared for cyber threats, but it also demonstrates a commitment to safeguarding the privacy and security of health and wellness information. By implementing an effective incident response plan, organizations can effectively mitigate the impact of cybersecurity incidents, recover quickly, and instill confidence in their stakeholders.

Backup and Recovery Strategies for Healthcare Data

In the fast-paced and interconnected world of healthcare, the importance of backup and recovery strategies for healthcare data cannot be overstated. Healthcare facilities generate and rely on enormous volumes of sensitive data, including electronic health records, medical images, lab results, and patient information. Any loss or corruption of this data can have severe consequences, including compromised patient care and regulatory non-compliance. Therefore, it is imperative for healthcare organizations to implement robust backup and recovery strategies to safeguard their data and ensure its availability in the event of any unforeseen incidents.

Understanding the Need for Backup and Recovery

Before delving into the specifics of backup and recovery strategies, it is essential to understand why they are necessary. Healthcare data is subject to various risks, such as hardware failures, software glitches, cyber attacks, natural disasters, and human errors. These risks can result in data loss, data corruption, or system downtime, all of which can significantly impact patient care, operational continuity, and regulatory compliance. Backup and recovery strategies provide a safety net, allowing organizations to restore their systems and recover their data quickly and efficiently in the face of these risks.

Key Components of Backup and Recovery Strategies

A comprehensive backup and recovery strategy for healthcare data should include the following key components:

1. **Data Inventory and Classification:** Begin by conducting a thorough inventory and classification of all healthcare data in your organization. Categorize the data based on its criticality, sensitivity, and regulatory requirements. This step helps prioritize backup and recovery efforts, ensuring that critical data is protected appropriately.

2. **Data Backup Frequency and Retention:** Determine the appropriate backup frequency based on the rate of data change and the criticality of the data. Critical data may require more frequent backups, while less critical data can

be backed up less frequently. Additionally, establish retention policies to define how long backups should be kept to meet compliance and operational requirements.

3. **Backup Methods:** Choose suitable backup methods based on your organization's infrastructure, data volume, and recovery time objectives. Common backup methods include full backups, incremental backups, and differential backups. Full backups capture the entire dataset, incremental backups only record changes since the last backup, and differential backups record changes since the last full backup.

4. **Off-Site Storage and Geographic Redundancy:** Storing backup copies off-site is critical to protect against physical disasters, such as fires or floods, that can destroy both primary data and on-site backups. Geographic redundancy ensures that backup copies are stored in multiple locations, further enhancing data protection.

5. **Encryption and Data Integrity:** Apply encryption mechanisms to protect sensitive healthcare data during transmission and storage. Encryption ensures that even if backup tapes or devices are compromised, the data remains inaccessible to unauthorized individuals. Additionally, implement mechanisms, such as checksums, to ensure data integrity during backup and recovery processes.

6. **Testing and Validation:** Regularly test and validate the backup and recovery processes to ensure their effectiveness. Conduct simulated recovery exercises to identify and address any gaps or issues that could hinder successful data restoration. Testing also helps assess the recovery time objective (RTO) and recovery point objective (RPO) for different systems and datasets.

7. **Documentation and Standard Operating Procedures:** Document the backup and recovery procedures, including step-by-step instructions, configurations, and contact information for key personnel. This documentation serves as a reference during crises and should be easily accessible to the IT team or any designated personnel responsible for data recovery.

Challenges and Considerations

Implementing backup and recovery strategies for healthcare data can be complex due to the unique challenges and considerations in the healthcare industry. Some of these challenges include:

- **Data Volume and Scalability:** Healthcare organizations deal with vast amounts of data, which requires scalable backup and recovery solutions that can handle the increasing volume of data over time.
- **Regulatory Requirements:** Healthcare data is subject to strict regulations, such as the Health Insurance Portability and Accountability Act (HIPAA) in the United States. Backup and recovery strategies must comply with these regulations to avoid penalties and ensure patient privacy and security.
- **Interoperability and Compatibility:** Healthcare facilities use a variety of systems and applications, each with its own data formats and protocols. Backup and recovery solutions must be compatible with these systems to ensure seamless data restoration.
- **Human Factors:** Human errors, such as accidental deletions or misconfigurations, can lead to data loss. Educating employees about proper backup and recovery procedures and enforcing user access controls are essential to minimize these risks.
- **Continuous Monitoring and Auditing:** Regularly monitor and audit the backup and recovery processes to identify any discrepancies, failures, or potential vulnerabilities. This proactive approach ensures that any issues are addressed promptly and prevents data loss or corruption.

Case Study: Backup and Recovery in a Hospital Setting

Consider a scenario where a hospital wants to establish a reliable backup and recovery system for its electronic health records (EHR) database. The hospital's IT team can follow the steps outlined below:

1. Perform a thorough inventory of the EHR data, identifying critical patient information, lab results, diagnostic images, and other relevant data.
2. Categorize the data based on its sensitivity and regulatory requirements. Prioritize the backup and recovery efforts accordingly.
3. Implement a backup solution that includes incremental backups on a daily basis, combined with weekly full backups. Store the backups securely on-site and regularly transfer copies to an off-site location to ensure geographic redundancy.

4. Apply encryption to both the transmission and storage of backup data. Use strong encryption algorithms to protect patient privacy and prevent unauthorized access to the backups.

5. Regularly test the backup and recovery processes by performing simulated recovery exercises. This helps identify any weaknesses or bottlenecks and allows for adjustments to be made to the backup strategy if necessary.

6. Document the backup and recovery procedures, including step-by-step instructions, configurations, and contact information for responsible personnel. This documentation should be easily accessible to authorized individuals and updated as needed.

By implementing this backup and recovery strategy, the hospital can ensure that its EHR data is protected, complying with regulatory requirements, and that patient care remains uninterrupted even in the face of unforeseen incidents.

Summary

Backup and recovery strategies for healthcare data are critical in ensuring the availability, integrity, and confidentiality of patient information. By conducting a thorough data inventory, implementing appropriate backup methods, storing backups off-site, and regularly testing the recovery processes, healthcare organizations can mitigate the risks associated with data loss, corruption, and system downtime. Furthermore, considering the unique challenges and regulations in the healthcare industry, a tailored and well-documented backup and recovery strategy is essential for maintaining operational continuity and providing high-quality patient care.

Continuity of Operations Planning (COOP)

Continuity of Operations Planning (COOP) is a critical aspect of cybersecurity in healthcare facilities. It involves developing and implementing strategies to ensure the uninterrupted delivery of essential services and to minimize the impact of any disruption or disaster.

COOP is essential in the healthcare industry because any disruption in operations can have severe consequences for patient care and safety. Whether it's a natural disaster, a cyber attack, or a pandemic, healthcare facilities need to be prepared to continue their operations and maintain their critical functions.

Identifying Essential Functions

The first step in developing a COOP is to identify the essential functions of the healthcare facility. These are the functions that must continue even in the face of a disruption or disaster. Examples of essential functions include patient care, emergency response, medical supplies management, laboratory services, and communication systems.

In order to identify these essential functions, healthcare facilities should conduct a Business Impact Analysis (BIA). This analysis assesses the potential impacts of disruptions on different areas of the facility and helps prioritize which functions are critical and must be maintained.

Developing a COOP Plan

Once the essential functions have been identified, the next step is to develop a COOP plan. This plan outlines the strategies and procedures that will be implemented to ensure the continuity of operations during a disruption.

The COOP plan should include:

- Clear roles and responsibilities: Clearly define the roles and responsibilities of key personnel during a disruption. This ensures that everyone knows what they need to do and who is accountable for each task.

- Communication plan: Establish a communication plan to ensure that information is shared effectively during a disruption. This includes both internal communication among staff and external communication with patients, vendors, and other stakeholders.

- Alternate facilities and resources: Identify alternate facilities and resources that can be used in case the primary facility becomes unavailable. This may include backup locations, equipment, and supplies.

- Data backup and recovery: Implement a robust data backup and recovery system to ensure that critical patient information and records are protected and can be accessed during a disruption.

- Training and awareness: Conduct regular training and awareness programs to ensure that staff is familiar with the COOP plan and their roles in executing it. This includes training on emergency response procedures, communication protocols, and the use of alternate systems and resources.

- Testing and exercising: Regularly test and exercise the COOP plan to identify any gaps or areas for improvement. This may involve conducting drills, tabletop exercises, or full-scale simulations to evaluate the effectiveness of the plan and identify areas that need to be addressed.

Challenges and Considerations

Developing and implementing a COOP plan in a healthcare facility comes with its own set of challenges and considerations. Some of the key challenges and considerations include:

- Resource constraints: Healthcare facilities often have limited resources, both financial and human. Developing and implementing a comprehensive COOP plan requires a significant investment of resources, which may be a challenge for some facilities.

- Compliance requirements: Healthcare facilities must comply with various regulations and standards related to data privacy and security. The COOP plan should take these requirements into account and ensure that patient information is protected during a disruption.

- Coordination with external entities: During a disruption, healthcare facilities may need to coordinate with external entities, such as government agencies, emergency services, and other healthcare providers. The COOP plan should include provisions for this coordination to ensure a seamless response.

- Evolving threats: The cybersecurity landscape is constantly evolving, with new threats emerging all the time. The COOP plan should be flexible and adaptable, able to address both existing and emerging threats to the healthcare facility's operations.

Case Study: Hurricane Preparedness

To illustrate the importance of COOP planning, let's consider a case study of a healthcare facility located in a hurricane-prone area. The facility, which provides critical care services, has developed a comprehensive COOP plan to ensure the continuity of operations during a hurricane.

The COOP plan includes the following strategies and procedures:

- Evacuation plan: The facility has identified alternate locations where patients can be safely evacuated in case the primary facility is at risk. The plan includes transportation arrangements and communication protocols to ensure a smooth evacuation process.

- Backup power: The facility has installed backup power generators to ensure that essential functions can continue even in the event of a power outage. The COOP plan includes procedures for testing and maintaining these generators to ensure their reliability.
- Data backup and recovery: The facility has implemented a secure off-site data backup system to ensure that patient information is protected and can be accessed during a hurricane. The COOP plan includes procedures for regular backups and testing of the data recovery process.
- Communication plan: The facility has established multiple channels of communication, including backup phone systems, satellite phones, and secure messaging platforms. The COOP plan includes protocols for communication with staff, patients, and external stakeholders during a hurricane.
- Training and awareness: The facility conducts regular training and awareness programs to ensure that staff is familiar with the COOP plan and emergency response procedures. This includes training on hurricane preparedness, patient evacuation, and the use of emergency equipment and supplies.

Through their COOP plan, the healthcare facility is able to effectively respond to hurricanes and ensure the continuity of critical care services, minimizing the impact on patient care and safety.

Conclusion

Continuity of Operations Planning (COOP) is a vital component of cybersecurity in healthcare facilities. By identifying essential functions, developing a comprehensive COOP plan, and addressing challenges and considerations, healthcare facilities can ensure the uninterrupted delivery of critical services during disruptions and disasters.

Effective COOP planning requires resource allocation, compliance with regulations, coordination with external entities, and adaptability to evolving threats. Through case studies like hurricane preparedness, healthcare facilities can learn from real-world examples and develop strategies to mitigate risks and maintain operational continuity during challenging times.

By prioritizing COOP and incorporating it into their overall cybersecurity framework, healthcare facilities can protect patient care, strengthen their resilience, and contribute to a safer and more secure cyber world in the health and wellness industry.

Conducting Security Assessments and Penetration Testing

Security assessments and penetration testing are essential components of a comprehensive cybersecurity strategy for health and wellness organizations. These processes help identify vulnerabilities and weaknesses in the network, systems, and applications, allowing proactive measures to be taken to strengthen security defenses. In this section, we will explore the principles, methodologies, and best practices for conducting security assessments and penetration testing.

Understanding the Objectives of Security Assessments and Penetration Testing

The primary objective of a security assessment is to evaluate the effectiveness of an organization's security controls and identify potential vulnerabilities. A comprehensive security assessment includes various techniques such as vulnerability scanning, network mapping, configuration reviews, and policy analysis. The assessment focuses on identifying weaknesses in areas such as network infrastructure, operating systems, applications, and data security.

Penetration testing, on the other hand, goes beyond identifying vulnerabilities and aims to exploit them to gain unauthorized access or cause specific impact on the systems. The objective of penetration testing is to simulate real-world attacks and assess the organization's ability to detect and respond to such attacks. By identifying vulnerabilities and demonstrating their exploitation, penetration testing helps organizations understand their potential exposure and prioritize remediation efforts.

Principles of Security Assessments

To ensure the effectiveness of security assessments, it is crucial to follow certain principles. These principles guide the assessment process and help organizations obtain accurate and reliable results:

1. **Scope Definition:** Clearly define the scope of the assessment, including the systems, applications, and networks to be assessed. This helps focus the assessment efforts and ensures that all critical components are included.

2. **Risk Assessment:** Conduct a risk assessment to identify the most critical assets and prioritize them for assessment. This ensures that limited resources are allocated to areas with the highest potential impact.

3. **Methodology Selection:** Select the appropriate methodology based on the objectives of the assessment. Common methodologies include black-box testing, white-box testing, and gray-box testing. Each methodology has its advantages and limitations, and the selection should be based on the organization's specific needs.

4. **Data Gathering & Analysis:** Gather relevant data about the systems, applications, and networks being assessed. This includes network diagrams, system configurations, application documentation, and security policies. Analyze the collected data to identify potential vulnerabilities and weaknesses.

5. **Testing Execution:** Execute the testing activities according to the defined methodology. This may include vulnerability scanning, penetration attempts, social engineering exercises, and application testing. Ensure that testing is conducted in a controlled and safe environment to minimize any impact on the production systems.

6. **Reporting & Remediation:** Document and report the findings of the assessment, including identified vulnerabilities, their potential impact, and recommended remediation actions. The report should provide clear and actionable recommendations to mitigate the identified risks.

Key Steps in a Penetration Testing Process

A successful penetration testing process consists of several key steps that ensure a comprehensive evaluation of an organization's security posture. These steps include:

1. **Planning Phase:** Define the objectives, scope, and rules of engagement for the penetration testing exercise. Establish clear communication channels with the organization's stakeholders and obtain the necessary permissions for the assessment.

2. **Information Gathering:** Collect as much information as possible about the target environment. This includes network mapping, system identification, application fingerprinting, and enumeration of services running on the network.

3. **Vulnerability Analysis:** Identify and exploit vulnerabilities within the target environment. This involves conducting vulnerability assessments, scanning for known vulnerabilities, and analyzing the potential impact of identified weaknesses.

4. **Exploitation:** Attempt to exploit identified vulnerabilities to gain unauthorized access or obtain sensitive information. This step helps assess the effectiveness of the organization's security controls and their ability to detect and respond to attacks.

5. **Post-Exploitation:** Once access has been gained, assess the extent of compromise and attempt to escalate privileges, explore further vulnerabilities, or pivot to other systems. This simulates the actions performed by real-world attackers.

6. **Reporting & Recommendations:** Document the findings of the penetration testing exercise and present them in a clear and concise report. Include details of the vulnerabilities exploited, the impact of successful attacks, and provide recommendations for remediation.

7. **Remediation & Verification:** Work with the organization to implement measures to address the identified vulnerabilities and weaknesses. Conduct a follow-up assessment to verify that the remediation efforts have been effective.

Best Practices for Security Assessments and Penetration Testing

To ensure the effectiveness and integrity of security assessments and penetration testing, it is essential to follow industry best practices. Some of these best practices include:

1. **Engage Qualified Professionals:** Hire experienced and certified professionals with expertise in security assessments and penetration testing. They should possess in-depth knowledge of various testing techniques, methodologies, and tools.

2. **Maintain Confidentiality:** Ensure strict confidentiality throughout the assessment process. This includes signing non-disclosure agreements, limiting access to assessment results, and handling any sensitive data obtained during the testing.

3. **Adhere to Legal and Ethical Standards:** Comply with all legal and ethical standards during the assessment. Obtain proper authorization from the organization being assessed, and ensure that all testing activities adhere to applicable legislation and regulations.

4. **Use Updated Tools and Techniques:** Utilize the latest tools and techniques for security assessments and penetration testing. Regularly update and patch the testing tools to ensure they can identify the latest vulnerabilities and attack vectors.

5. **Consider Business Impact:** Take into account the potential impact on business operations during the assessment process. Coordinate with the organization to schedule testing activities during non-critical periods to minimize disruptions.

6. **Document Everything:** Maintain detailed documentation of all assessment activities, including the methodologies used, test results, and recommendations. This documentation serves as a valuable reference for future assessments and helps track the progress of remediation efforts.

Real-World Example: Penetration Testing for a Telehealth Platform

Consider the case of a telehealth platform that allows patients to connect with healthcare providers remotely. To ensure the security of sensitive patient information and maintain the trust of users, the platform undergoes regular penetration testing.

The penetration testing team starts by defining the scope of the assessment, including all components of the platform, such as the web application, mobile application, backend systems, and infrastructure. They perform thorough information gathering, identifying the different technologies, protocols, and potential vulnerabilities associated with each component.

Using a combination of automated scanning tools and manual techniques, the team identifies vulnerabilities such as weak authentication, insecure APIs, and potential data leakage points. They attempt to exploit these vulnerabilities, validating their impact by gaining unauthorized access to sensitive patient data.

Once successful exploits are identified, the team documents their findings and recommends remediation actions to the organization. These recommendations may include strengthening access controls, implementing secure coding practices, and conducting regular security awareness training for employees.

The organization implements the recommended remediation actions and conducts a follow-up assessment to verify the effectiveness of the implemented measures. By regularly conducting penetration testing, the telehealth platform ensures that it remains resilient against emerging cyber threats and maintains a high level of security for its users.

Additional Resources

For further exploration of security assessments and penetration testing, the following resources are recommended:

- Bejtlich, R. (2018). *The Practice of Network Security Monitoring: Understanding Incident Detection and Response.* No Starch Press.
- Engebretson, P. (2016). *The Basics of Hacking and Penetration Testing: Ethical Hacking and Penetration Testing Made Easy.* Syngress.
- NIST Special Publication 800-115. (2017). *Technical Guide to Information Security Testing and Assessment.* National Institute of Standards and Technology.

These resources provide comprehensive insights into the principles, techniques, and methodologies of security assessments and penetration testing, enabling organizations in the health and wellness industry to enhance their cybersecurity defenses.

Employee Training on Incident Response and Disaster Recovery

Employee training plays a crucial role in the overall cybersecurity strategy of health and wellness facilities. This is especially true when it comes to incident response and disaster recovery, as effective training can significantly mitigate the impact of cyber threats and ensure a swift and coordinated response. In this section, we will explore the key elements of employee training on incident response and disaster recovery, including the importance of training, essential skills and knowledge, and best practices for creating an effective training program.

The Importance of Employee Training

Incident response and disaster recovery are complex processes that require skilled and knowledgeable personnel to handle them effectively. Training employees on these critical aspects of cybersecurity ensures that they understand their roles and responsibilities during an incident and can respond appropriately. By providing employees with the necessary knowledge and skills, organizations can enhance their incident response capabilities and minimize the potential damage caused by cyber attacks.

Furthermore, employee training fosters a culture of security awareness and preparedness within the organization. When employees are well-trained and understand the importance of incident response and disaster recovery, they become proactive in identifying potential threats and taking preventive measures. This proactive approach can significantly reduce the likelihood of successful cyber attacks and improve the overall security posture of the organization.

Essential Skills and Knowledge

To effectively respond to incidents and manage the recovery process, employees need to possess certain skills and knowledge. Here are some essential areas that should be covered in employee training on incident response and disaster recovery:

1. Incident Identification and Reporting: Employees should be trained to recognize and report potential security incidents promptly. This includes understanding the indicators of compromise, suspicious behaviors, and abnormal system activities.

2. Incident Response Procedures: Employees should be familiar with the organization's incident response plan, including the steps to be followed and the roles and responsibilities of each team member. This training should cover incident triage, containment, eradication, and recovery.

3. Communication and Coordination: Effective communication is critical during an incident. Employees should be trained on how to report incidents to the appropriate teams and stakeholders in a timely and accurate manner. They should also be educated on how to coordinate with other team members and external entities, such as law enforcement or incident response vendors.

4. Technical Skills: Depending on their roles, employees may need technical skills related to incident response and recovery. This could include knowledge of network protocols, system administration, malware analysis, forensic analysis, and vulnerability management.

5. Business Continuity and Disaster Recovery: Employees should understand the organization's business continuity and disaster recovery plans. This includes knowing the backup and recovery processes, offsite data storage arrangements, and the steps to restore critical systems and services.

Best Practices for Training Programs

When developing employee training programs for incident response and disaster recovery, organizations should consider the following best practices:

1. Tailor the Training: Recognize that different roles within the organization may require different levels of training. Develop training programs that are tailored to specific job functions to ensure that employees receive the necessary skills and knowledge relevant to their roles.

2. Use Real-World Scenarios: Make the training engaging and practical by using real-world scenarios and case studies. This helps employees understand the potential impact of cyber threats on the organization and reinforces the importance of incident response and recovery.

3. Hands-on Exercises: Provide hands-on exercises and simulations to allow employees to apply their training in a controlled environment. This practical experience helps them become more confident and competent in incident response and disaster recovery.

4. Regular Training Updates: Cyber threats and attack techniques evolve rapidly. To keep employees up to date with the latest trends, it is important to provide regular training updates and refresher courses. This ensures that their skills and knowledge remain relevant and effective.

5. Continuous Evaluation and Improvement: Regularly evaluate the effectiveness of the training program by collecting feedback from employees and conducting assessments. Use this feedback to identify areas for improvement and refine the training program accordingly.

Example Scenario: Ransomware Attack Response Training

As an example, let's consider a training scenario focused on responding to a ransomware attack, which is a common and significant threat to health and wellness organizations:

1. Introduction: Provide an overview of ransomware attacks, their impact on the organization, and why it is crucial for employees to understand how to respond to such incidents.

2. Recognizing Indicators: Train employees to identify early indicators of a ransomware attack, such as suspicious emails, unexpected file encryption, or system slowdowns.

3. Reporting Procedures: Explain how employees should report a potential ransomware incident, including who to contact and the information that needs to be provided.

4. Incident Response Plan: Familiarize employees with the organization's incident response plan for ransomware attacks. This includes the steps to contain the attack, disconnect infected systems, and isolate the network.

5. Communication and Coordination: Teach employees how to communicate the incident to the incident response team, IT personnel, and management. Emphasize the importance of clear and timely communication.

6. Recovery Process: Provide an overview of the recovery process, including the restoration of backups, system scanning for remnants of the ransomware, and ensuring system integrity before reconnecting to the network.

7. Prevention Techniques: Educate employees on best practices for preventing ransomware attacks, such as being cautious with email attachments, regularly updating software and operating systems, and avoiding suspicious websites.

8. Testing and Simulations: Conduct hands-on exercises, such as simulated ransomware attacks, to allow employees to practice their response skills. Provide feedback and guidance during these exercises.

9. Evaluation and Refinement: Gather feedback from employees after the training session and use it to evaluate and refine the training program for future sessions.

Additional Resources

To support employee training on incident response and disaster recovery, organizations can make use of the following resources:

1. Online Training Courses: Many cybersecurity organizations offer online courses specifically tailored to incident response and disaster recovery. These courses often include practical exercises and assessments.

2. Industry Guidelines and Frameworks: Organizations can refer to industry best practices and frameworks, such as NIST Special Publication 800-61 or ISO 27035, which provide detailed guidance on incident response and recovery.

3. Internal Experts and Consultants: Tap into the knowledge and expertise of internal cybersecurity professionals or engage external consultants who specialize in incident response and disaster recovery training.

4. Incident Post-Mortems: Share the lessons learned from past incidents within the organization. These post-mortems help employees understand the real-world impact of cyber attacks and highlight the importance of incident response and recovery.

Conclusion

Employee training is a vital component of an effective incident response and disaster recovery strategy. By providing employees with the necessary skills and knowledge, organizations can enhance their incident response capabilities, foster a culture of security awareness, and strengthen their overall cybersecurity posture. Through tailored training programs, organizations can empower employees to respond effectively and mitigate the impact of cyber threats on the organization.

Cybersecurity Training and Awareness

Importance of Cybersecurity Training for Health and Wellness Professionals

Creating a Culture of Security Awareness

In today's digitally connected world, where personal information is constantly at risk, it is crucial to create a culture of security awareness in the health and wellness industry. Establishing this culture helps to educate and empower individuals to protect themselves and their organizations from cybersecurity threats. In this section, we will explore the importance of creating a culture of security awareness, discuss key strategies for achieving this goal, and provide resources to support your efforts.

The Importance of Security Awareness

Security awareness is not just the responsibility of IT professionals; it requires the active involvement of every individual within an organization. By fostering a culture of security awareness, health and wellness professionals can better understand the potential risks and take proactive measures to mitigate them. This awareness helps to protect sensitive patient information, maintain the integrity of health records, and safeguard the overall well-being of both individuals and organizations.

Key Strategies for Creating a Culture of Security Awareness

1. Leadership and Commitment: Establishing a culture of security awareness starts with leadership commitment. Executives and managers must prioritize cybersecurity and communicate its importance to all staff members. By setting the

example, leaders can inspire employees to take responsibility for security practices in their everyday work.

2. Training and Education: Conduct regular cybersecurity training sessions to educate employees on current threats, best practices, and organizational policies. Provide information on common attack vectors, such as phishing and social engineering, and teach employees how to identify and respond to these threats. Training should be tailored to the specific roles and responsibilities of health and wellness professionals, emphasizing the unique risks they face.

3. Communication and Reinforcement: Regularly communicate security policies and updates to all staff members. Use newsletters, email updates, and other internal communication channels to reinforce the importance of cybersecurity and provide reminders of best practices. Encourage open communication and create a culture where employees feel comfortable reporting potential security incidents or concerns.

4. Employee Engagement: Engage employees in security initiatives by involving them in discussions, decision-making processes, and policy development. Encourage them to share their ideas and suggestions for improving security practices. By involving employees in these efforts, they will feel more invested and accountable for maintaining a secure environment.

5. Rewards and Recognition: Recognize and reward employees who actively participate in maintaining a secure workplace. This can include acknowledging their contributions during team meetings, offering incentives for reporting security incidents, or implementing a formal recognition program. Celebrate successes and milestones in creating a culture of security awareness to reinforce positive behaviors.

6. Continuous Improvement: Cybersecurity threats and technologies are constantly evolving, so it is essential to continuously update and improve security awareness initiatives. Conduct regular assessments to identify areas for improvement, gather employee feedback, and adjust training programs accordingly. Stay up-to-date with the latest industry trends, best practices, and regulations to ensure that security awareness efforts remain relevant and effective.

Resources for Creating a Culture of Security Awareness

To support your efforts in creating a culture of security awareness, various resources are available. Here are a few examples:

1. Online Training Programs: Many organizations offer comprehensive cybersecurity training courses, specifically tailored to the health and wellness

industry. These programs cover topics such as data protection, email security, social engineering awareness, and incident response.

2. Security Awareness Campaigns: Take advantage of cybersecurity awareness campaigns like National Cybersecurity Awareness Month, which occurs every October. These campaigns provide resources, posters, and educational materials that can be distributed to employees.

3. Industry Associations and Networks: Join industry associations and networks focused on cybersecurity in healthcare. These organizations often provide access to resources, webinars, and networking opportunities to enhance security awareness initiatives.

4. Government Websites and Regulatory Bodies: Government websites and regulatory bodies, such as the Department of Health and Human Services, provide guidance and resources on cybersecurity in the healthcare sector. These resources include best practices, frameworks, and compliance guidelines.

5. Security Awareness Tools: Consider implementing security awareness tools that provide simulated phishing attacks, awareness training modules, and progress tracking. These tools help measure the effectiveness of training efforts and identify areas for improvement.

Remember, creating a culture of security awareness is an ongoing process that requires commitment, education, communication, engagement, and continuous improvement. By implementing these strategies and utilizing available resources, health and wellness professionals can contribute to a safer and more secure digital environment for themselves and their organizations.

Conclusion

Creating a culture of security awareness is vital for the health and wellness industry to protect sensitive data and maintain trust with patients. By prioritizing cybersecurity, providing ongoing training, fostering open communication, engaging employees, and leveraging available resources, organizations can build a strong defense against cyber threats. Remember, cybersecurity is everyone's responsibility, and it is through collective efforts that we can create a safer digital landscape for health and wellness. Stay vigilant, stay informed, and together, we can make a difference.

Tailoring Training Programs to Health and Wellness Industry Needs

In order to effectively address the unique cybersecurity challenges in the health and wellness industry, it is crucial to tailor training programs specifically to the needs of professionals in this field. This section will explore the key considerations and strategies for developing training programs that align with the industry's demands.

Understanding the Health and Wellness Industry

To effectively tailor training programs, it is essential to have a deep understanding of the health and wellness industry. This industry encompasses a wide range of organizations and professionals, including healthcare providers, wellness centers, fitness facilities, and more. Each of these entities has distinct roles, responsibilities, and cybersecurity risks.

Training programs should take into account the specific types of data and information handled in the health and wellness industry. This includes personal identifiable information (PII), electronic health records (EHRs), financial information, and sensitive research data. The potential impact of a cybersecurity breach in this sector can be severe, ranging from compromised patient privacy to physical harm.

Identifying Industry-Specific Threats

Once the nuances of the health and wellness industry are understood, it is critical to identify the industry-specific threats and vulnerabilities. By analyzing the common attack vectors and threat landscape, training programs can focus on addressing the most prevalent risks.

Some industry-specific threats in the health and wellness sector include:

- Healthcare ransomware attacks: Malicious actors target healthcare organizations to encrypt critical data and demand ransom, causing significant disruptions to patient care.

- Medical device vulnerabilities: With the proliferation of Internet of Things (IoT) devices in the healthcare industry, ensuring the security of these devices and protecting them from unauthorized access is vital.

- Insider threats: Healthcare professionals, contractors, and employees with privileged access can potentially misuse their credentials or inadvertently expose sensitive data.

- Telehealth vulnerabilities: As telehealth services become more prevalent, securing the communication platforms and protecting patient data during virtual consultations is of utmost importance.

By identifying these industry-specific threats, training programs can be customized to address the unique challenges faced by health and wellness professionals.

Cybersecurity Best Practices in Health and Wellness

Training programs tailored to the health and wellness industry should encompass a wide range of cybersecurity best practices. These best practices should be focused on the specific needs and workflows of professionals in this sector.

Some key areas of focus for training programs include:

- Strong authentication and access controls: Emphasize the importance of using strong and unique passwords, implementing multi-factor authentication, and regularly reviewing access privileges to prevent unauthorized access.

- Data privacy and protection: Educate health and wellness professionals on data protection regulations, such as the Health Insurance Portability and Accountability Act (HIPAA) and the General Data Protection Regulation (GDPR). Train them on the appropriate handling and safeguarding of sensitive data, including encryption techniques and secure storage practices.

- Social engineering awareness: Teach healthcare professionals how to recognize and respond to social engineering attacks, such as phishing emails, phone scams, and impersonation attempts. Provide real-world examples to illustrate the potential impact of falling victim to these tactics.

- Incident response and reporting: Provide comprehensive training on incident response protocols and reporting procedures. Health and wellness professionals should be equipped to detect, contain, and mitigate cyber incidents in a timely and effective manner.

- Ongoing education and awareness: Promote a culture of cybersecurity awareness by encouraging continuous education and training. Highlight the importance of staying updated on the latest cyber threats, emerging technologies, and best practices through regular workshops, webinars, and industry conferences.

Engaging and Interactive Training Approaches

To ensure the effectiveness of training programs, it is important to adopt engaging and interactive approaches. Traditional lecture-style training may not be as impactful as hands-on exercises, simulations, and real-world scenarios.

Some suggested training activities include:

- Simulated phishing campaigns: Conduct periodic simulated phishing campaigns to test employees' awareness and responsiveness to phishing attacks. Provide immediate feedback and additional training based on individual performance.

- Tabletop exercises: Organize tabletop exercises to simulate cyber incidents and engage health and wellness professionals in active problem-solving. This allows participants to practice their incident response skills in a controlled environment.

- Case studies and group discussions: Present real-world case studies to illustrate the impact of cyber threats in the health and wellness industry. Encourage participants to discuss and analyze the best course of action in each scenario, fostering critical thinking and collaboration.

- Hands-on technical training: Provide hands-on training sessions to familiarize health and wellness professionals with common cybersecurity tools and techniques. This can include training on secure file sharing, encryption software, and secure communication platforms.

- Gamified learning: Develop interactive learning platforms or games that promote cybersecurity knowledge and skills. This can enhance engagement and make the learning experience more enjoyable for participants.

Resources and Continued Support

Training programs should not end with a one-time session. It is crucial to provide ongoing support and resources to reinforce the knowledge and skills acquired during training.

Some resources and support mechanisms to consider include:

- Reference materials: Provide participants with comprehensive training materials, such as handbooks, guides, and cheat sheets. These resources can serve as references for cybersecurity best practices and procedures.

- Online learning platforms: Establish online platforms or learning management systems to host training modules, webinars, and interactive quizzes. This allows participants to access materials and resources at their convenience.

- Helpdesk and support channels: Implement a dedicated helpdesk or support channels to address participants' questions, concerns, and ongoing training needs. This ensures that professionals in the health and wellness industry have access to the support they need to continually enhance their cybersecurity practices.

- Continuing education opportunities: Encourage health and wellness professionals to pursue continuing education opportunities in cybersecurity, such as certifications or specialized courses. Highlight the value of staying updated on the evolving landscape of cybersecurity threats and countermeasures.

Conclusion

Tailoring training programs to the specific needs of the health and wellness industry is crucial for building a resilient cybersecurity culture. By understanding the industry, identifying industry-specific threats, leveraging best practices, adopting engaging training approaches, and providing ongoing support, professionals in the health and wellness sector can develop the necessary knowledge and skills to protect against cyber threats effectively. Through continuous education and awareness, the industry can stay ahead of emerging threats and contribute to a safer and more secure cyber world for health and wellness.

Ongoing Education and Continuing Professional Development

In the ever-evolving field of cybersecurity, ongoing education and continuing professional development are crucial for health and wellness professionals to stay ahead of the latest threats and best practices. This section explores the importance of ongoing education, highlights the main challenges in this area, and provides practical strategies for fostering a culture of lifelong learning.

The Importance of Ongoing Education

Cybersecurity is a rapidly evolving field, with new threats and vulnerabilities emerging on a regular basis. Ongoing education is essential for health and wellness professionals to keep pace with these changes and ensure they have the knowledge and skills necessary to protect themselves and their organizations.

Continuous learning in cybersecurity allows professionals to stay up-to-date with the latest technologies, industry standards, and regulatory requirements. It helps them understand emerging attack vectors and defense mechanisms, enabling them to make informed decisions and implement effective security measures.

Moreover, ongoing education fosters a culture of security awareness within healthcare organizations. It empowers employees to take an active role in safeguarding sensitive data and encourages them to adopt proactive security practices in their day-to-day activities. This not only enhances the overall cybersecurity posture of the organization but also helps protect the privacy and well-being of patients.

Challenges in Ongoing Education

While ongoing education is critical, there are several challenges that health and wellness professionals may face in this area. These challenges include:

- Limited time: Health and wellness professionals often have demanding schedules, leaving them with limited time for additional training and education.

- Lack of resources: Access to quality cybersecurity training programs and resources can be limited, especially for non-technical professionals who require tailored education.

- Technological advancements: The rapid pace of technological advancements poses a challenge, as professionals must constantly update their knowledge and skills to keep pace with new technologies and their associated security risks.

- Changing threat landscape: Cyber threats are constantly evolving, making it necessary for professionals to stay abreast of emerging trends and attack techniques.

Addressing these challenges requires proactive measures and a commitment to continuous learning.

Strategies for Ongoing Education

To foster ongoing education and continuing professional development in the field of cybersecurity, consider the following strategies:

1. Create a culture of learning: Encourage and support a culture of learning within your organization. Emphasize the importance of ongoing education, promote self-directed learning, and provide resources and opportunities for professional development.

2. Allocate dedicated time: Recognize the importance of ongoing education by allocating dedicated time for learning activities. This can include attending training sessions, participating in webinars, or engaging in self-paced online courses.

3. Stay updated with industry publications: Subscribe to industry publications and newsletters to stay informed about the latest cybersecurity trends, technologies, and best practices. These publications often provide valuable insights and practical tips that can enhance your knowledge base.

4. Engage in professional networks: Join professional networks, forums, and communities focused on cybersecurity in the health and wellness industry. Engaging with peers, sharing experiences, and participating in discussions can broaden your knowledge and expose you to new ideas and perspectives.

5. Pursue certifications: Consider obtaining relevant cybersecurity certifications to enhance your professional credentials. Certifications provide a structured learning path and demonstrate your commitment to ongoing education to employers and clients.

6. Attend conferences and workshops: Participate in cybersecurity conferences, workshops, and seminars to expand your network, learn from industry experts, and gain exposure to the latest technologies and methodologies.

7. Establish mentoring relationships: Seek out mentors who can guide you in your professional development journey. Mentors can provide valuable insights, share their experiences, and offer guidance on navigating the cybersecurity landscape.

8. Take part in hands-on exercises: Engage in hands-on exercises and practical simulations to reinforce your knowledge and skills. These exercises allow you

to apply theoretical concepts in real-world scenarios, preparing you for the challenges you may encounter in your professional practice.

9. Share knowledge within your organization: Actively share your knowledge and experiences with colleagues within your organization. This can be done through informal knowledge sharing sessions, lunch-and-learn sessions, or formal training programs. By sharing knowledge, you not only contribute to the development of others but also solidify your own understanding of the subject matter.

10. Seek external expertise: When faced with complex cybersecurity issues or the need for specialized knowledge, seek external expertise. Engage with cybersecurity consultants, trainers, or subject matter experts who can provide insights and guidance tailored to your specific needs.

By implementing these strategies, health and wellness professionals can ensure a continuous learning mindset and stay prepared to defend against evolving cyber threats.

Case Study: Cybersecurity Boot Camp

To illustrate the effectiveness of ongoing education, let's consider a case study of a cybersecurity boot camp for health and wellness professionals.

The boot camp is a week-long immersive program designed to provide a comprehensive overview of cybersecurity fundamentals and practical skills. It covers topics such as threat intelligence, network security, incident response, and secure coding practices.

Throughout the boot camp, participants engage in hands-on exercises, simulations, and real-world case studies. They learn how to identify and mitigate common cyber threats and gain practical experience with industry-standard tools and technologies.

In addition to the technical aspects of cybersecurity, the boot camp also addresses the human factor by emphasizing the importance of security awareness, social engineering prevention, and incident reporting.

At the end of the program, participants receive a certification, validating their knowledge and skills in cybersecurity. They also gain access to a network of alumni and industry experts, providing ongoing support and opportunities for collaboration.

The success of this boot camp lies in its ability to provide an intensive, immersive learning experience tailored to the needs of health and wellness professionals. By focusing on hands-on training and practical application, participants develop the necessary skills and confidence to tackle cybersecurity challenges in their organizations.

Additional Resources

To further support ongoing education and continuing professional development in cybersecurity, here are some additional resources:

- Online Learning Platforms: Platforms such as Coursera, Udemy, and edX offer a wide range of cybersecurity courses, many of which are self-paced and flexible to accommodate busy schedules.
- Webinars and Virtual Conferences: Stay updated with the latest cybersecurity trends and best practices by participating in webinars and virtual conferences offered by industry organizations and cybersecurity vendors.
- Professional Associations and Organizations: Join professional associations and organizations, such as the Healthcare Information and Management Systems Society (HIMSS) and the International Information System Security Certification Consortium (ISC^2), which offer resources, training opportunities, and networking events for cybersecurity professionals.
- Open-Source Tools and Communities: Explore open-source tools and communities, such as the Open Web Application Security Project (OWASP) and the National Institute of Standards and Technology (NIST), which provide a wealth of knowledge, tools, and guidance on cybersecurity practices.
- Podcasts and Blogs: Subscribe to cybersecurity podcasts and blogs to stay informed about the latest industry news and insights. Popular options include "Darknet Diaries" and "Schneier on Security."

Remember, ongoing education and continuing professional development are not one-time events but rather lifelong journeys. Stay curious, keep learning, and embrace the challenges and opportunities that cybersecurity presents in the health and wellness industry.

Training and Awareness for Non-Technical Employees and Patients

In today's digitally connected world, it is crucial for both non-technical employees and patients in the health and wellness industry to be aware of the risks and threats associated with cybersecurity. Training and awareness programs play a vital role in empowering individuals to protect their personal information and enhance their overall cybersecurity posture. This section will explore the importance of training and awareness, key topics to cover in training programs, effective strategies for delivering training, and resources available for non-technical employees and patients.

Importance of Training and Awareness

Training and awareness initiatives are essential for non-technical employees and patients to understand the potential cybersecurity risks they face and how to mitigate them. By providing education and guidance, organizations can empower individuals to make informed decisions and take proactive steps to protect themselves and their data.

For non-technical employees, training helps them recognize common cyber threats, understand their role in maintaining security, and develop good cybersecurity practices. It enables them to identify and report suspicious activities, such as phishing emails or social engineering attempts, reducing the risk of successful attacks. Additionally, training ensures that employees are aware of their legal and ethical responsibilities regarding patient privacy and data protection.

Patients, on the other hand, need to be aware of cybersecurity risks associated with their personal health information and digital interactions with healthcare providers. Training programs can help patients understand the importance of protecting their healthcare data, recognize potential threats, and practice safe online behaviors. This empowers them to actively participate in safeguarding their personal information.

Key Topics for Training Programs

Training programs for non-technical employees and patients should cover a range of topics to provide a comprehensive understanding of cybersecurity risks and best practices. Some key topics to include are:

1. Overview of Cybersecurity: Introduce the basic concepts of cybersecurity, including common threats, attack vectors, and risks associated with the health and wellness industry.

2. Phishing and Social Engineering: Explain the techniques used by attackers to deceive individuals and steal sensitive information through emails, phone calls, or other communication channels. Teach employees and patients how to recognize and respond to phishing attempts.

3. Password Security: Emphasize the importance of strong passwords and the use of multi-factor authentication. Provide guidelines for creating secure passwords and best practices for password management.

4. Protecting Personal Identifiable Information (PII): Educate employees and patients about the types of personally identifiable information that need to be protected and provide guidelines for secure handling and sharing of sensitive data.

5. Safe Internet Usage: Teach employees and patients how to browse the internet safely, recognize and avoid malicious websites, and practice responsible downloading and file sharing.

6. Mobile Device Security: Highlight the unique cybersecurity risks associated with mobile devices and educate individuals on best practices for securing smartphones and tablets, including the use of screen locks, encryption, and regular software updates.

7. Email and Messaging Security: Train employees and patients on secure email and messaging practices, including encrypting emails, avoiding suspicious attachments and links, and implementing email authentication protocols.

8. Social Media Awareness: Educate individuals on the risks associated with social media platforms, such as privacy breaches and social engineering attacks. Provide guidelines for secure social media usage, including setting privacy settings and avoiding sharing sensitive information.

9. Incident Reporting: Encourage employees and patients to report any suspicious activities or cybersecurity incidents promptly. Provide clear procedures for reporting and ensure individuals understand the importance of reporting promptly.

Effective Strategies for Training

To ensure the effectiveness of training programs for non-technical employees and patients, organizations should consider the following strategies:

1. Interactive Training: Implement interactive training methods, such as scenario-based exercises, quizzes, and simulations. This engages participants and helps reinforce key cybersecurity principles.

2. Role-Specific Training: Tailor training programs to the specific roles and responsibilities of employees and the needs of patients. For example, healthcare providers may require training on secure handling of electronic health records,

while patients may benefit from training on secure online communication with healthcare providers.

3. Continuous Education: Cybersecurity threats are ever-evolving, so it is crucial to provide regular updates and reminders to employees and patients. Continuous education programs, such as newsletters, webinars, or annual refresher courses, help reinforce good cybersecurity practices.

4. User-Friendly Materials: Develop training materials in a user-friendly language, avoiding technical jargon and complex explanations. Use visual aids, infographics, and real-world examples to enhance understanding and engagement.

5. Collaboration with IT Teams: IT teams play a vital role in supporting training initiatives. Collaborate with IT professionals to provide accurate and up-to-date information, guidance, and technical resources for training programs.

Resources for Non-Technical Employees and Patients

Several resources are available to support non-technical employees and patients in their cybersecurity training and awareness efforts. These include:

1. Online Training Platforms: Utilize online platforms that offer cybersecurity training courses specifically tailored for healthcare professionals and patients. These platforms provide convenient and accessible training modules that cover a range of cybersecurity topics.

2. Industry-specific Associations and Organizations: Many industry-specific associations and organizations offer resources and training materials to support cybersecurity awareness in the health and wellness sector. These resources often include guidelines, best practices, and educational materials.

3. Government Agencies: Government agencies, such as the Department of Health and Human Services (HHS) in the United States, provide cybersecurity resources and guidance for healthcare professionals and patients. These resources outline the latest regulations and best practices for protecting health information.

4. Educational Webinars and Workshops: Attend educational webinars and workshops conducted by cybersecurity experts in the healthcare industry. These events often cover current cybersecurity trends, practical tips, and real-world case studies.

5. Security Awareness Campaigns: Participate in industry-wide security awareness campaigns, such as National Cybersecurity Awareness Month (NCSAM), to stay updated on the latest cybersecurity trends and access resources for training and awareness.

Remember, cybersecurity is a collective responsibility, and by investing in training and awareness for non-technical employees and patients, organizations can create a culture of security and resilience in the health and wellness industry.

Evaluating the Effectiveness of Cybersecurity Training Programs

Evaluating the effectiveness of cybersecurity training programs is crucial in order to ensure that the intended outcomes are being achieved and that the training is having the desired impact on the target audience. This section explores the key elements of evaluating cybersecurity training programs, including the importance of assessment, metrics for evaluation, and methods for collecting feedback.

The Importance of Assessment

Assessment plays a critical role in evaluating the effectiveness of cybersecurity training programs. It helps to measure the knowledge, skills, and behaviors of the participants before and after the training, providing valuable insights into the impact of the training program.

There are several reasons why assessment is important:

- **Identifying gaps in knowledge and skills:** Assessment allows trainers to identify areas where participants lack the necessary knowledge or skills, helping to tailor the training content and delivery to address these gaps effectively.

- **Measuring knowledge retention:** By assessing participants' knowledge before and after the training, trainers can determine the level of knowledge retention and identify areas for improvement in both the training program and individual learning strategies.

- **Determining training effectiveness:** Assessment provides a means to measure the effectiveness of the training program by evaluating whether participants have acquired the intended knowledge and skills.

- **Demonstrating return on investment (ROI):** By evaluating the impact of the training program, organizations can demonstrate the value and ROI of their cybersecurity training investments to stakeholders and decision-makers.

Metrics for Evaluation

To effectively evaluate the effectiveness of cybersecurity training programs, a set of metrics should be established. These metrics should align with the defined learning outcomes and provide measurable indicators of the program's success. Here are some common metrics for evaluating cybersecurity training:

- **Knowledge assessment:** Assessing participants' knowledge through pre and post-training tests can determine the extent to which the training has improved their understanding of cybersecurity concepts, best practices, and regulations. This can be done using multiple-choice quizzes, scenario-based questions, or practical assessments.

- **Skills demonstration:** Hands-on assessments or simulations can evaluate participants' ability to apply cybersecurity skills in real-world scenarios. This can involve tasks such as identifying and mitigating security vulnerabilities, responding to incidents, or configuring secure systems.

- **Behavioral observation:** Observing participants' behavior and actions in simulated or real-world situations can provide insights into their adoption of cybersecurity practices. This can involve monitoring their adherence to security policies, use of secure communication channels, or ability to detect and report suspicious activities.

- **Training satisfaction and engagement:** Collecting feedback from participants on their satisfaction with the training program, its content, and delivery can provide insights into the training's effectiveness and its impact on their motivation to apply cybersecurity practices.

Methods for Collecting Feedback

Collecting feedback from participants is crucial for evaluating the effectiveness of cybersecurity training programs. This feedback can help identify areas for improvement and guide the development of future training programs. Here are some methods for collecting feedback:

- **Surveys and questionnaires:** Online surveys or questionnaires can be used to collect feedback from participants on various aspects of the training program, such as content relevance, material clarity, and training delivery. Open-ended questions can provide valuable qualitative feedback, while Likert scale or multiple-choice questions can provide quantitative data.

- **Focus groups:** Organizing focus groups with a representative sample of participants can engage them in a discussion about their training experience. This method allows for in-depth exploration of their opinions, insights, and suggestions for improvement.

- **One-on-one interviews:** Conducting individual interviews with selected participants can provide a deeper understanding of their training experience and challenges. This method allows for personalized feedback and can uncover additional insights that may not be captured through surveys or focus groups.

- **Observation and shadowing:** Observing participants during training sessions or their daily work activities can provide valuable insights into their application of cybersecurity practices. This method allows trainers to assess the translation of knowledge and skills into actual behavior and identify areas for improvement or additional support.

Data Analysis and Reporting

Once data from assessments and feedback collection methods are obtained, it is essential to analyze and interpret the findings to draw meaningful conclusions about the effectiveness of cybersecurity training programs. This analysis can involve statistical calculations, comparing pre and post-training scores, identifying patterns or trends in the data, and extracting key insights. The findings should be reported in a clear and concise manner, highlighting the strengths of the program, areas for improvement, and recommendations for future enhancements.

Continuous Improvement and Iteration

Evaluating the effectiveness of cybersecurity training programs is an ongoing process. As technology evolves and new cybersecurity threats emerge, training programs need to be regularly updated to address the changing landscape. Feedback from participants and evaluation metrics should be used to inform continuous improvement efforts and guide the iteration of training programs. Regular assessments can help track progress, identify gaps in knowledge and skills, and ensure that training remains aligned with the evolving needs of the organization and its workforce.

Conclusion

Evaluating the effectiveness of cybersecurity training programs is essential to ensure that the objectives of the training are being achieved and that participants are equipped with the necessary knowledge, skills, and behaviors to mitigate cybersecurity risks. Through effective assessment, the establishment of relevant metrics, the collection of feedback, and continuous improvement, organizations can enhance the impact and value of their cybersecurity training efforts. By investing in evaluation, organizations can stay proactive in protecting their information and maintaining a high level of cybersecurity in the health and wellness industry.

Employee Certification and Credentialing Programs

In today's fast-paced and ever-evolving digital landscape, it is imperative for health and wellness professionals to acquire the necessary skills and knowledge to mitigate cyber risks and protect sensitive information. One effective way to demonstrate competency in cybersecurity is through employee certification and credentialing programs. These programs validate the skills and expertise of individuals in the field of cybersecurity, ensuring that they are equipped to handle the challenges of the digital age.

Why Employee Certification and Credentialing Programs Matter

Employee certification and credentialing programs provide a structured framework for individuals to enhance their cybersecurity skills and knowledge. These programs offer several benefits, both for individuals and organizations:

- **Recognizing expertise:** Certification programs provide a standardized and recognized way to assess an individual's competency in cybersecurity. By earning a certification, professionals can demonstrate their expertise and commitment to the industry.

- **Enhancing career prospects:** Having a cybersecurity certification can significantly enhance career prospects. It can open doors to new job opportunities, increase earning potential, and provide a competitive edge in the job market.

- **Ensuring best practices:** Certification programs ensure that professionals are equipped with the knowledge of best practices in cybersecurity. This helps organizations establish and maintain robust cybersecurity protocols and procedures.

- **Compliance requirements:** Certification programs often cover specific regulatory and compliance requirements in the health and wellness industry. By ensuring employees are certified, organizations can meet these standards and reduce the risk of legal and regulatory penalties.
- **Continuing professional development:** Certification programs often require professionals to engage in ongoing education and stay up-to-date with the latest cybersecurity trends. This ensures that certified individuals are equipped with the knowledge and skills needed to address emerging cyber threats.

Certification and Credentialing Programs for Health and Wellness Professionals

Several certification and credentialing programs are available for health and wellness professionals looking to enhance their cybersecurity knowledge and skills. These programs encompass a wide range of cybersecurity domains and cater to different skill levels. Some of the popular certification programs include:

- **Certified Information Systems Security Professional** (CISSP): Offered by the International Information System Security Certification Consortium $(ISC)^2$, CISSP is a globally recognized certification for cybersecurity professionals. It covers various domains, including security and risk management, asset security, and security engineering.
- **Certified Ethical Hacker** (CEH): The CEH certification, provided by the International Council of E-Commerce Consultants (EC-Council), focuses on ethical hacking and penetration testing. It equips professionals with the skills to identify vulnerabilities and secure digital assets.
- **Certified Healthcare Information Security and Privacy Practitioner** (HCISPP): The HCISPP certification, offered by $(ISC)^2$, is specifically designed for individuals working in the healthcare industry. It focuses on the unique privacy and security challenges faced by healthcare organizations.
- **CompTIA Security+:** CompTIA Security+ is a vendor-neutral certification that covers foundational cybersecurity principles and skills. It is ideal for individuals starting their careers in cybersecurity or for those working in roles that require a broader understanding of cybersecurity.

- **Certified Cloud Security Professional** (CCSP): Offered by $(ISC)^2$, the CCSP certification focuses on cloud security and covers topics such as cloud concepts, architecture, and governance. It is suitable for professionals working in cloud environments in the health and wellness industry.

Choosing the Right Certification Program

With numerous certification programs available, it's essential to choose the one that aligns with your career goals and professional interests. Consider the following factors when selecting a certification program:

- **Relevance:** Ensure that the certification program covers the specific cybersecurity domains and skills relevant to your role in the health and wellness industry.
- **Recognition:** Look for certifications that are widely recognized and respected in the industry. Well-established organizations, such as $(ISC)^2$ and EC-Council, offer globally recognized certifications.
- **Prerequisites:** Some certifications have prerequisites, such as a certain number of years of experience in the field. Consider your current level of expertise and choose a program that suits your experience level.
- **Cost and maintenance:** Certification programs often require an initial investment in terms of examination fees and study materials. Additionally, some certifications require ongoing maintenance and continuing education to keep the certification valid. Consider the cost and maintenance requirements of the certification program.
- **Career goals:** Evaluate how the certification aligns with your long-term career goals. Some certifications may be more suitable for specific roles or industries, so choose accordingly.

Beyond Certifications: Additional Credentialing Programs

While certifications are valuable, they are not the only form of credentialing available for health and wellness professionals. Consider exploring other forms of credentialing that can complement certifications and further enhance your professional profile. Some examples include:

- **Digital badges:** Digital badges are micro-credentials that validate specific skills or achievements. They can be displayed on professional profiles or resumes, providing a more detailed view of an individual's capabilities.

- **Healthcare privacy and security certifications:** Organizations such as the Health Information and Management Systems Society (HIMSS) offer certifications specifically focused on healthcare privacy and security. These certifications validate expertise in managing privacy and security risks in healthcare settings.

- **Specialized training programs:** Consider specialized training programs that focus on specific areas of cybersecurity, such as incident response, risk management, or secure software development. These programs provide in-depth knowledge and practical skills beyond what certifications may cover.

Implementing Certification and Credentialing Programs

To implement employee certification and credentialing programs effectively, organizations should consider the following strategies:

- **Identify key roles:** Identify the key roles within the organization that require cybersecurity expertise. Determine the appropriate certifications and credentialing programs for each role based on the specific knowledge and skills required.

- **Establish a career progression framework:** Create a career progression framework that outlines the certifications and credentialing programs associated with each level. This framework will provide employees with a clear path for advancement and encourage professional development.

- **Provide financial support:** Certification exams and study materials can be costly. Consider providing financial assistance or reimbursement to employees who pursue certifications, demonstrating organizational support and commitment to professional growth.

- **Encourage ongoing learning:** Emphasize the importance of continuous learning by supporting employees' participation in conferences, workshops, and webinars related to cybersecurity. Encourage them to stay updated with the latest industry trends and emerging cyber threats.

- **Recognize achievements:** Celebrate employees who earn certifications or complete credentialing programs. Recognize their achievements publicly, provide opportunities for knowledge sharing, and consider tying certification achievements to performance evaluations or compensation incentives.

Conclusion

Employee certification and credentialing programs play a crucial role in equipping health and wellness professionals with the necessary skills and knowledge to protect sensitive information and mitigate cyber risks. By implementing these programs, organizations can ensure that their employees are well-prepared to navigate the complex world of cybersecurity. Remember, certifications are just one piece of the puzzle, and professionals should continuously strive for ongoing learning and development to stay ahead in the ever-changing cybersecurity landscape.

In the next section, we will delve into the importance of security awareness for patients and consumers in the health and wellness industry, exploring strategies to educate and empower them in protecting their personal information.

Security Awareness for Patients and Consumers

Educating Patients on Privacy and Security Considerations

In today's digital age, it is crucial for individuals to understand the importance of privacy and security when it comes to their personal health information. As technology continues to advance, the risk of cyber threats targeting healthcare data increases. Therefore, educating patients on privacy and security considerations is essential to ensure the safety and confidentiality of their sensitive information.

The Need for Patient Education

Many patients are unaware of the potential risks associated with sharing their health information in the digital realm. They may not realize that their personal data can be vulnerable to hacking, identity theft, or unauthorized access. By educating patients, we can empower them to take an active role in protecting their privacy and making informed decisions about how their health information is used and shared.

Principles of Privacy and Security

To effectively educate patients on privacy and security considerations, it is important to establish the foundational principles of privacy and security in the healthcare context. These principles include:

- **Confidentiality:** Ensuring that an individual's health information is kept private and is only accessible to authorized individuals. This principle emphasizes the need to protect personal health information from unauthorized disclosure.

- **Integrity:** Maintaining the accuracy and completeness of health information. Patients should be aware of the risks associated with the tampering or alteration of their health data and the potential consequences it can have on their care.

- **Availability:** Ensuring that health information is accessible to authorized individuals when needed. This principle emphasizes the importance of maintaining proper systems and safeguards to prevent disruptions in accessing healthcare data.

Patient's Role in Privacy and Security

Patients play a vital role in safeguarding their health information. By understanding and implementing certain practices, they can actively contribute to maintaining privacy and security. Here are some key considerations patients should keep in mind:

- **Strong Password Management:** Encouraging patients to create unique and strong passwords for their healthcare accounts. A strong password consists of a combination of lowercase and uppercase letters, numbers, and special characters. Patients should also be advised against sharing passwords or using the same password across multiple platforms.

- **Awareness of Phishing Attacks:** Educating patients about common types of cyber threats, such as phishing attacks. Patients should be cautious about clicking on suspicious links or providing personal information in response to unsolicited emails or messages. They should also be encouraged to verify the authenticity of requests before sharing any sensitive data.

- **Secure Use of Personal Devices:** Reminding patients to secure their personal devices, such as smartphones and laptops, by enabling passcodes or biometric authentication. Patients should also be advised to keep their devices up to date by installing security patches and updates regularly.
- **Careful Sharing of Health Information:** Patients should be cautious when sharing their health information on social media platforms or with third-party applications and websites. They should understand the potential risks and consequences of sharing sensitive information without proper safeguards.
- **Privacy Settings and Consent:** Educating patients on how to manage privacy settings on healthcare portals and apps. Patients should be empowered to make decisions about who can access their health information and under what circumstances. They should also be informed about their rights and options for providing informed consent.

Resources and Support for Patients

To further support patient education on privacy and security, healthcare providers can offer resources and tools to help patients navigate the digital landscape safely. These resources may include:

- **Educational Materials:** Providing brochures, pamphlets, or online resources that explain privacy and security practices in an easy-to-understand language. These materials can cover topics such as password management, recognizing phishing attempts, and securing personal devices.
- **Training Sessions and Workshops:** Conducting training sessions or workshops for patients to enhance their knowledge and skills in protecting their health information. These sessions can include demos on privacy settings management, safe browsing practices, and secure communication methods.
- **Patient Portals:** Offering patient portals that allow patients to access and manage their health information securely. It is important to provide clear instructions on how to use the portal, set up privacy preferences, and report any suspicious activities.
- **Helpdesk and Support Channels:** Establishing helpdesk services or support channels where patients can seek assistance or report any privacy or security concerns. Prompt and responsive support can help patients feel more secure and confident in their healthcare interactions.

Real-World Example: Protecting Your Health Information

Emily, a patient with a chronic medical condition, wants to learn more about protecting her health information online. She attends a workshop organized by her healthcare provider, where she learns about the importance of secure passwords and creating unique login credentials for her healthcare accounts. She also learns about phishing emails and how to identify suspicious links or requests for personal information.

After the workshop, Emily updates her passwords and enables multi-factor authentication for her patient portal. She checks the privacy settings on her social media profiles and adjusts them to limit the visibility of her health-related posts. Emily feels more confident in managing her health information securely and is more aware of the potential risks in the digital space.

Caveats and Considerations

While patient education is crucial for enhancing privacy and security, it is important to consider the diverse needs and demographics of the patient population. Healthcare providers should aim to provide education in a language and format that is accessible to all patients, including those with limited digital literacy or varying cultural backgrounds. Tailoring the educational content to different patient groups can help ensure that everyone receives the necessary information to protect their health information effectively.

Conclusion

Educating patients on privacy and security considerations is a necessary step towards creating a safer digital environment for healthcare. By empowering patients with the knowledge and tools to protect their health information, we can safeguard their privacy, maintain data integrity, and ensure the availability of healthcare data when needed. It is a shared responsibility between patients and healthcare providers to promote a culture of privacy and security in the digital age.

Safe Internet Usage and Social Media Awareness

In today's digitally connected world, the internet and social media platforms have become integral parts of our lives. From staying connected with friends and family to accessing information and entertainment, the internet offers a wide range of opportunities. However, it is crucial to be aware of the potential risks associated with online activities and understand how to use the internet safely and responsibly. This section focuses on safe internet usage and social media awareness, providing guidance on protecting oneself from online threats and ensuring privacy and security in the digital realm.

Understanding Online Risks

The internet is teeming with various risks that can compromise our privacy and security. Some of the common online risks include:

- **Identity theft:** Cybercriminals may attempt to steal personal information, such as social security numbers, credit card details, and login credentials, to commit fraud and financial crimes.
- **Phishing attacks:** Phishing is a technique used by hackers to trick individuals into revealing sensitive information by impersonating legitimate organizations or individuals through emails, text messages, or websites.
- **Malware infections:** Malicious software, such as viruses, worms, and ransomware, can infect our devices and compromise our data and privacy.
- **Cyberbullying:** Online harassment and bullying have become prevalent on social media platforms, leading to psychological and emotional distress for victims.
- **Fake news and misinformation:** The internet is filled with misinformation and fake news, which can have significant social and political consequences. It is crucial to critically evaluate the sources and credibility of information before sharing or relying on it.

By understanding these risks, we can take proactive measures to protect ourselves and mitigate the potential harm caused by online threats.

Social Media Privacy and Security

Social media platforms play a significant role in our lives, allowing us to connect with others, share experiences, and express ourselves. However, it is crucial to be mindful of the privacy and security settings on these platforms to protect our personal information. Here are some best practices for safeguarding your privacy on social media:

- **Review and adjust privacy settings:** Regularly review and update your privacy settings on social media platforms to control who can view your posts, photos, and personal information. Customize these settings based on your comfort level and the level of privacy you desire.
- **Be cautious with personal information:** Avoid sharing sensitive information, such as your full address, phone number, or financial details, on social media. Cybercriminals can abuse this information for fraudulent activities.
- **Manage friend requests and followers:** Be careful about accepting friend requests or followers from strangers. Verify the authenticity of their profiles before connecting with them, as fake profiles can be used for malicious purposes.
- **Use strong and unique passwords:** Ensure that you use strong and unique passwords for your social media accounts. Avoid using common phrases, personal information, or easily guessable passwords that can be cracked by attackers.
- **Beware of social engineering attacks:** Be cautious of unsolicited messages or emails from unknown individuals asking for personal information or initiating suspicious online interactions. These could be social engineering attempts to gain unauthorized access to your accounts or obtain sensitive information.
- **Think twice before sharing:** Before posting anything on social media, consider the potential consequences. Once something is posted online, it can be challenging to remove it entirely, and it may have a lasting impact on your personal and professional life.
- **Report and block abusive users:** If you encounter cyberbullying, harassment, or any abusive behavior on social media, report the user and, if necessary, block them to prevent further interactions.

By implementing these practices, you can enhance your social media privacy and reduce the risk of falling victim to online threats.

Safe Internet Browsing

Browsing the internet exposes us to various risks, including malware infections, phishing attacks, and drive-by downloads. To ensure safe internet browsing, consider the following measures:

- **Keep your software up to date:** Regularly update your operating system, web browsers, and other software to patch vulnerabilities and protect against known security exploits.

- **Use a reliable antivirus software:** Install reputable antivirus and anti-malware software on your devices and keep them updated. These tools can detect and prevent the installation of malicious software.

- **Be cautious of suspicious links and downloads:** Avoid clicking on links or downloading files from unfamiliar or untrusted sources. These may contain malware or lead to phishing websites.

- **Verify website authenticity:** When visiting websites, ensure that the connection is secure by looking for the padlock icon in the browser's address bar. Additionally, pay attention to the website's URL and ensure it matches the trusted source you intended to visit.

- **Enable browser security features:** Utilize built-in browser security features such as pop-up blockers, privacy settings, and safe browsing modes to protect against malicious scripts and unwanted ads.

- **Educate yourself about online scams:** Stay informed about common online scams, such as fake lottery winnings, fraudulent online marketplaces, and email phishing scams. Be skeptical and think critically before providing personal information or engaging in financial transactions.

By adopting these safe browsing practices, you can minimize the risk of falling victim to online threats and protect your personal and financial information.

Social Media Awareness

Social media platforms can be a double-edged sword. While they offer numerous benefits, they can also expose us to fake news, cyberbullying, and privacy breaches. To navigate social media safely, consider the following tips:

- **Verify the credibility of sources:** Before sharing news articles or information, verify the credibility of the sources. Rely on reputable news agencies and fact-checking organizations to ensure the accuracy of the information you consume and share.

- **Exercise critical thinking:** Be critical of the content you encounter on social media. Question the legitimacy and motives behind posts, images, and videos that seem sensational or inflammatory. Avoid spreading unverified information that can contribute to the spread of misinformation.

- **Respect others and practice digital etiquette:** Treat others on social media with respect and practice digital etiquette. Avoid engaging in online arguments or spreading hate speech. Be mindful of the impact your words and actions may have on others.

- **Protect the privacy of others:** Obtain consent before sharing someone else's personal information or media on social media. Respect others' privacy and refrain from posting sensitive or private content without their permission.

- **Be mindful of your digital footprint:** Regularly review your social media profiles and posts to understand the image you are projecting online. Think about how your social media activity may be interpreted by others, including future employers or educational institutions.

By being socially aware and responsible on these platforms, we can contribute to a safe and positive online environment for ourselves and others.

Further Resources

To delve deeper into safe internet usage and social media awareness, consider exploring the following resources:

- **Stay Safe Online** (https://staysafeonline.org): A comprehensive resource for individuals and organizations, providing tips and resources for staying safe online.

- **TechSafety** (https://www.techsafety.org): Offers resources for survivors of domestic violence, with guides on internet and social media safety.

- **WiredSafety** (https://www.wiredsafety.org): Provides information and resources for internet safety, including information on online scams and cyberbullying.

Remember, the internet can be a powerful tool when used wisely and with caution. By practicing safe internet usage and social media awareness, we can protect ourselves and promote a secure digital environment. Stay informed, stay vigilant, and stay safe online.

Exercise:

Imagine you come across a sensational news article on social media that aligns with your beliefs. What steps would you take to verify the credibility of the information before sharing it with others? Provide a detailed plan of action, including specific techniques or resources you would employ.

Solution:

When encountering a sensational news article on social media, it is essential to exercise critical thinking and verify the credibility of the information before sharing it. Here is a plan of action to determine the legitimacy of the content:

1. **Read beyond the headlines:** Avoid making judgments based solely on the article's headline, as they can often be misleading. Read the entire article to understand its content and context.

2. **Check the source:** Investigate the source of the news article. Is it a well-known and reputable news organization? Is the source known for unbiased reporting? Look for signs of credibility, such as proper citations, author bylines, and contact information.

3. **Cross-reference with other sources:** Compare the information provided in the article with other reputable sources. Check if other professional news organizations or fact-checking websites have reported on the same topic. Look for consistent reporting and corroboration from multiple sources.

4. **Consult fact-checking organizations:** Utilize fact-checking organizations such as Snopes, FactCheck.org, or Politifact to verify the accuracy of the claims made in the article. These organizations specialize in debunking false information and providing evidence-based assessments.

5. **Examine the author's expertise:** Assess the author's credentials and expertise in the subject matter. Is the author an expert in the field or a reputable journalist? Look for indications of their qualifications, such as their educational background or previous work.

6. **Identify potential bias:** Consider any potential bias in the article. Does it present a balanced viewpoint or lean heavily towards a particular perspective? Understanding the potential bias can help evaluate the objectivity and accuracy of the information.

7. **Evaluate supporting evidence:** Determine if the article provides credible evidence to support its claims. Look for references to research studies,

expert opinions, or verifiable data. Assess the quality and reliability of the evidence presented.

8. **Consider the article's tone and language:** Analyze the article's tone and language for signs of sensationalism, exaggeration, or emotional manipulation. Biased or unreliable news articles often employ such tactics to evoke strong emotional responses.

By following this plan of action, you can make an informed judgment and decide whether the news article is credible and worthy of sharing. Remember, promoting the spread of accurate and reliable information is crucial for fostering a trustworthy digital environment.

By prioritizing safe internet usage and adopting social media awareness, we can protect ourselves and others from online risks. Remember to regularly update your privacy settings, exercise caution while sharing personal information, and critically evaluate the content you encounter online. By applying these practices, we can safely navigate the digital landscape and preserve our privacy and security.

Recognizing and Reporting Cyber Threats

In today's digitally connected world, cyber threats are becoming increasingly prevalent and sophisticated. Health and wellness professionals, as well as individuals, must be aware of these threats to protect themselves and their sensitive information. This section will provide an overview of common cyber threats that target the health and wellness industry and outline best practices for recognizing and reporting these threats.

Types of Cyber Threats

Cyber threats can take various forms and have different objectives. It is essential to understand the different types of threats to effectively identify and respond to them. Here are some common cyber threats:

1. **Phishing Attacks:** Phishing attacks involve the use of deceptive emails, messages, or websites to trick individuals into revealing their sensitive information, such as usernames, passwords, or credit card details. These attacks often mimic legitimate organizations or individuals to gain the target's trust.

2. **Malware:** Malware, short for malicious software, is designed to gain unauthorized access to systems or cause damage. This includes viruses,

worms, Trojan horses, ransomware, and spyware. Malware can be delivered through email attachments, malicious websites, or infected software downloads.

3. **Social Engineering:** Social engineering attacks exploit human psychology to manipulate individuals into divulging sensitive information or granting unauthorized access. Examples include pretexting, baiting, tailgating, and quid pro quo.

4. **Insider Threats:** Insider threats refer to cyber threats that originate from within an organization. These can be malicious actions by disgruntled employees or accidental breaches caused by employee negligence or lack of awareness.

5. **Distributed Denial of Service (DDoS) Attacks:** DDoS attacks overwhelm a target system with a flood of traffic, rendering it inaccessible to legitimate users. These attacks are usually carried out by botnets, which are networks of compromised computers.

6. **Supply Chain Attacks:** Supply chain attacks target vulnerabilities in the supply chain, aiming to compromise the software or hardware before it reaches the end-user. This can lead to the installation of backdoors or other malicious code on devices.

Recognizing Cyber Threats

Recognizing cyber threats is vital for early detection and mitigation. Health and wellness professionals should be vigilant and look out for indicators of potential threats. Here are some signs to watch out for:

- **Unusual Emails or Messages:** Be cautious of unexpected or suspicious emails, messages, or requests for sensitive information. Look for grammatical errors, email addresses that differ slightly from legitimate sources, or requests for urgent action.

- **Unusual Network Activity:** Monitor your network for any unusual or suspicious activity, such as significant increases in data transfers, frequent login failures, or unexpected system crashes. These may indicate the presence of malware or an attacker attempting to gain unauthorized access.

- **Changes in System Settings:** Be aware of any unauthorized changes to your system settings, including configurations, installed software, or browser extensions. These changes could indicate a security compromise.
- **Unfamiliar Devices or Users:** Pay attention to the presence of unfamiliar devices or users on your network. Unauthorized devices connected to your network could be a sign of a security breach, as well as unauthorized users accessing sensitive information.
- **Suspicious URLs or Websites:** Exercise caution when visiting websites or clicking on links. Look for signs of suspicious URLs, such as misspellings, unusual domain extensions, or warnings from your web browser about potential security risks.

Reporting Cyber Threats

When you encounter a cyber threat or suspect that a security breach has occurred, it is crucial to report it promptly. Reporting cyber threats helps to prevent further damage and enables authorities to investigate and take appropriate action. Here are steps to follow when reporting cyber threats:

1. **Document the Incident:** Gather as much information as possible about the cyber threat or security breach. Take screenshots, record dates and times, and keep a detailed log of any suspicious activity.
2. **Contact Internal IT Support:** If you are part of an organization, report the incident to your IT support team or the designated security contact. Provide them with all relevant information and cooperate fully throughout the investigation process.
3. **Report to Law Enforcement:** If the incident involves a significant security breach or potential criminal activity, report it to your local law enforcement agency or the appropriate cybercrime unit. Provide them with a detailed account of the incident, including any evidence or documentation you have gathered.
4. **Notify Relevant Authorities and Organizations:** Depending on the nature of the incident, you may need to report it to other organizations or regulatory bodies. For example, if personal health information (PHI) or personally identifiable information (PII) is compromised, you may need to notify the affected individuals and relevant regulatory agencies.

5. **Share Information with Industry Groups:** Consider sharing information about the cyber threat or security breach with relevant industry groups or information sharing and analysis centers (ISACs). Sharing this information can help others protect themselves from similar attacks and contribute to collective defense efforts.

6. **Participate in Incident Response and Information Sharing:** Cooperate with incident response efforts and share any relevant information with your organization's cybersecurity team or external cybersecurity experts. This collaboration enables a quicker recovery and helps prevent future incidents.

Real-World Example

To illustrate the importance of recognizing and reporting cyber threats, consider the following real-world example:

A healthcare clinic receives an email that appears to be from a trusted vendor, requesting an update to their payment information. The email contains a link that directs the recipient to a website that looks identical to the vendor's website. The email uses urgent language, pressuring the clinic staff to act quickly.

One of the clinic employees recognizes the signs of a phishing attack. They notice that the email address is slightly different from the vendor's legitimate email address and hover over the link to reveal a suspicious URL. The employee reports the incident to their IT department, who confirms it as a phishing attempt.

By reporting the incident, the healthcare clinic's IT department can alert other employees to be cautious of similar phishing emails. They can also report the incident to the relevant authorities and share the information with industry groups to prevent other organizations from falling victim to the same attack.

Further Resources

To learn more about recognizing and reporting cyber threats, consider the following resources:

- U.S. Department of Homeland Security (DHS) Cybersecurity and Infrastructure Security Agency (CISA) - cisa.gov
- Federal Bureau of Investigation (FBI) - fbi.gov
- The National Cybersecurity Alliance (NCSA) - staysafeonline.org
- Information Sharing and Analysis Centers (ISACs) - isaccouncil.org

Exercises

1. Research the latest phishing techniques prevalent in the health and wellness industry. Create a short presentation highlighting the key characteristics of these phishing attacks and share it with your colleagues or classmates.

2. Conduct a cybersecurity awareness campaign in your organization or community. Develop creative materials such as posters, infographics, or short videos to educate others on recognizing and reporting cyber threats.

3. Evaluate your organization's incident reporting process. Identify any gaps or areas for improvement and propose solutions to enhance your reporting capabilities.

4. Familiarize yourself with the reporting requirements outlined by relevant regulatory bodies in the health and wellness industry. Develop a checklist to ensure compliance with these requirements in the event of a cybersecurity incident.

Remember, preventing and mitigating cyber threats requires a collective effort. By recognizing and reporting these threats, we can contribute to a safer and more secure digital landscape in the health and wellness industry. Stay vigilant and continue to educate yourself and others about the evolving cyber threat landscape.

Providing Resources and Support for Patient Cybersecurity

As technology continues to reshape the healthcare industry, patients find themselves increasingly reliant on digital platforms to manage their health information and communicate with healthcare providers. This digital shift brings about numerous benefits, including convenience and improved access to care. However, it also exposes patients to various cybersecurity risks, such as data breaches, identity theft, and unauthorized access to personal health information. To address these concerns, healthcare organizations must prioritize patient cybersecurity and provide resources and support to ensure their safety in the digital landscape.

Understanding Patient Cybersecurity Needs

Before healthcare organizations can effectively provide resources and support for patient cybersecurity, it is crucial to understand and address the specific needs and challenges patients face. Some key areas of concern include:

- Education: Many patients lack awareness and knowledge about cybersecurity best practices. They may not understand the risks associated with sharing personal health information online or using insecure devices or networks.
- Technology literacy: Patients of varying age groups and backgrounds may have different levels of comfort and familiarity with technology. It is essential to consider these differences when designing resources and support systems.
- Trust and confidence: Patients need to have confidence in the security measures implemented by healthcare organizations. They must trust that their personal health information will be safeguarded and that their cybersecurity concerns will be taken seriously.

By considering these needs, healthcare organizations can develop targeted resources and support programs to empower patients and enhance their cybersecurity.

Patient Cybersecurity Resources

Healthcare organizations should provide patients with a range of resources and tools to help them navigate the digital landscape safely. Some essential resources to consider include:

- Cybersecurity Awareness Materials: Develop informative brochures, fact sheets, and online resources that educate patients about common cybersecurity risks, such as phishing attacks, password security, and secure online communication.
- Secure Communication Platforms: Offer secure communication channels, such as patient portals or encrypted messaging apps, to enable patients to communicate securely with healthcare providers. Provide clear instructions on how to use these platforms effectively.
- Patient Education Programs: Conduct cybersecurity education programs or workshops to raise awareness among patients. These programs can cover topics such as password management, recognizing and reporting cyber threats, and safe internet usage.
- Risk Assessment Tools: Provide patients with user-friendly risk assessment tools to help them evaluate the security of their digital devices, networks, and online behaviors. These tools can identify potential vulnerabilities and suggest mitigation strategies.

- Privacy and Security Policies: Clearly communicate the organization's privacy and security policies to patients, detailing how their information will be protected and what measures are in place to ensure cybersecurity.

By offering these resources, healthcare organizations can empower patients to take an active role in protecting their personal health information and improving their overall cybersecurity resilience.

Supporting Patient Cybersecurity

In addition to providing resources, healthcare organizations should actively support patients in their journey towards better cybersecurity. Here are some ways to offer support:

- Helpdesks and Support Hotlines: Establish dedicated helpdesks or support hotlines where patients can seek assistance with cybersecurity-related issues. These channels should be staffed with knowledgeable professionals who can address patients' concerns promptly.

- Cybersecurity Training Sessions: Host regular training sessions or webinars where patients can learn about the latest cybersecurity threats and how to protect themselves. These sessions can also serve as forums for patients to ask questions and share their experiences.

- Security Incident Reporting: Implement a streamlined process for patients to report cybersecurity incidents or suspicious activities. Ensure that reported incidents are promptly investigated and appropriate actions are taken to mitigate risks.

- Collaborations with Patient Advocacy Groups: Partner with patient advocacy groups and organizations to raise awareness about cybersecurity among patients. Engage these groups in developing patient-centric cybersecurity initiatives and involving patients in the decision-making process.

By providing comprehensive support, healthcare organizations can build trust with patients and foster a collaborative approach to cybersecurity.

Case Study: Cybersecurity Resource Kit for Patients

To illustrate the practical application of patient cybersecurity resources, let's consider the development of a Cybersecurity Resource Kit for patients. The goal of this kit is to provide patients with the necessary tools and knowledge to protect their personal health information. The contents of the kit can include:

- Informational Pamphlets: Concise brochures outlining common cybersecurity risks, best practices for online security, and tips for protecting personal health information.
- Password Manager Guide: A step-by-step guide on using password managers to create and manage strong, unique passwords for online accounts.
- Secure Communication Guide: Instructions on how to safely communicate with healthcare providers through secure platforms, emphasizing the importance of end-to-end encryption.
- Mobile Device Security Tips: Tips for securing smartphones and tablets, including enabling encryption, installing security updates, and using reputable mobile antivirus software.
- Internet of Things (IoT) Security Checklist: A checklist to help patients secure their smart devices, such as wearables and home health monitoring systems, by changing default passwords, updating firmware, and disabling unnecessary features.
- Incident Reporting Card: A card detailing the process for reporting cybersecurity incidents, including contact information and step-by-step instructions.

By distributing this Cybersecurity Resource Kit to patients during clinic visits or making it available for download on the organization's website, healthcare providers can equip patients with practical tools and information to enhance their cybersecurity.

Conclusion

Protecting patient cybersecurity is a shared responsibility between healthcare organizations and patients themselves. By providing resources and support tailored to patient needs, healthcare organizations can empower patients to actively participate in their cybersecurity and safeguard their personal health information.

With continuous education, collaboration with patient advocacy groups, and the implementation of secure communication platforms, healthcare organizations can create a safer digital environment for patients and strengthen their overall cybersecurity posture. In the era of digital health, patient cybersecurity is vital for maintaining trust and ensuring the well-being of individuals and the healthcare industry as a whole.

Ethical and Legal Responsibilities in Cybersecurity

Legal and Regulatory Compliance in Cybersecurity

Ensuring legal and regulatory compliance is a crucial aspect of cybersecurity in the health and wellness industry. The increasing number of cyber threats and the potential impact of data breaches have prompted governments and regulatory bodies to enact laws and regulations to protect sensitive information, safeguard privacy, and maintain the integrity of digital systems. In this section, we will explore the key legal and regulatory requirements that organizations in the health and wellness sector need to adhere to in order to maintain cybersecurity.

Understanding the Legal Landscape

Before delving into specific regulations, it is important to have a broad understanding of the legal landscape related to cybersecurity in the health and wellness industry. Different countries have enacted various laws and regulations to address cybersecurity and safeguard personal information. It is essential for organizations to be aware of and comply with the relevant legal requirements in the jurisdictions they operate.

Some of the core legal principles that underpin cybersecurity regulations include:

1. **Data Protection and Privacy Laws:** These laws govern the collection, storage, and use of personal information and data. They typically require organizations to obtain consent for data collection, implement security measures to protect personal information, and provide individuals with the right to access and control their data.

2. **Intellectual Property Laws:** Intellectual property laws protect the rights of individuals and organizations regarding inventions, trademarks, copyrights, and trade secrets. Protecting proprietary cybersecurity technologies and strategies is crucial for organizations in the health and wellness industry.

3. **Contract Law:** Contracts play a significant role in determining the legal obligations and responsibilities of parties involved in cybersecurity. This includes agreements with vendors, customers, and partners that outline data protection measures and liability provisions.

4. **Tort Law:** Tort law covers civil wrongs and provides a legal basis for individuals and organizations to seek compensation for harm caused by

cybersecurity incidents. This can include negligence, breach of duty, or invasion of privacy.

5. **Criminal Law:** Criminal law addresses offenses against the state and society as a whole. In the context of cybersecurity, it includes activities such as hacking, cyber fraud, and identity theft. Criminal law provides the legal framework for charging and prosecuting cybercriminals.

Key Regulations in Cybersecurity

In addition to the general legal principles, several specific regulations have been introduced to address cybersecurity concerns in the health and wellness industry. These regulations aim to protect patient privacy, secure electronic health records, and promote the overall integrity and trustworthiness of healthcare systems. Let's now explore some of the key regulations that organizations need to comply with.

Health Insurance Portability and Accountability Act (HIPAA): HIPAA is a federal law in the United States that safeguards the privacy and security of protected health information (PHI). It applies to covered entities such as healthcare providers, health plans, and clearinghouses, as well as their business associates who have access to PHI. HIPAA requires organizations to implement administrative, physical, and technical safeguards to protect PHI and ensure compliance with privacy and security standards.

General Data Protection Regulation (GDPR): The GDPR is a regulation implemented by the European Union (EU) to protect the personal data and privacy of EU citizens. It applies to organizations that process personal data of individuals within the EU, irrespective of the organization's location. The GDPR imposes strict obligations on organizations, including the requirement to obtain consent for data processing, implement security controls, and uphold individuals' rights regarding their personal data.

California Consumer Privacy Act (CCPA): The CCPA is a state law in California, United States, aimed at enhancing consumer privacy rights and promoting transparency in data collection and usage. It grants California residents certain rights over their personal information and imposes obligations on businesses that collect, process, or sell consumer data. The CCPA requires organizations to provide notice of data collection, allow consumers to opt-out of data sales, and implement reasonable security measures to protect personal information.

Medical Device Regulation (MDR): The MDR is a regulation in the European Union that sets forth requirements for medical devices to ensure their safety and quality. It also includes provisions for cybersecurity, as medical devices are increasingly connected to networks and vulnerable to cyber attacks. The MDR requires manufacturers to implement appropriate cybersecurity measures to protect medical devices against unauthorized access, alteration, or loss of data.

These are just a few examples of the many regulations that exist globally to address cybersecurity in the health and wellness industry. Organizations must stay informed about the specific regulations applicable to their jurisdictions and understand the requirements and obligations imposed by these regulations.

Challenges in Regulatory Compliance

Complying with cybersecurity regulations can be challenging, particularly for organizations in the health and wellness industry that handle large amounts of sensitive personal information. Some of the common challenges organizations face include:

1. **Complexity and Variability of Regulations:** The legal and regulatory landscape surrounding cybersecurity is complex and constantly evolving. Organizations need to navigate through various regulations, each with its own set of requirements, which can be overwhelming and time-consuming.

2. **Resource Constraints:** Achieving compliance often requires significant financial, technological, and human resources. Many organizations, especially small and medium-sized enterprises, may struggle to allocate the necessary resources to implement robust cybersecurity measures and meet regulatory requirements.

3. **Interoperability and Standardization:** Organizations operating in multiple jurisdictions may encounter challenges in reconciling different regulatory standards and ensuring interoperability between systems. Harmonization of cybersecurity regulations can streamline compliance efforts across borders.

4. **Rapid Technological Advances:** The pace of technological advancements often outpaces the development of regulations. Organizations need to keep up with emerging technologies such as artificial intelligence, blockchain, and

Internet of Things to effectively secure their systems while complying with regulations.

5. **Third-Party Risk Management:** Many organizations rely on third-party vendors and service providers whose actions can impact their cybersecurity posture. Managing and monitoring third-party compliance with regulations presents a significant challenge, as organizations need to ensure that their partners also adhere to regulatory requirements.

Addressing these challenges requires a comprehensive approach, including establishing effective governance structures, conducting risk assessments, implementing technical security controls, and providing ongoing training and awareness programs for employees.

Tips for Successful Compliance

To successfully comply with legal and regulatory requirements in cybersecurity, organizations in the health and wellness industry can consider the following tips:

1. **Stay Informed:** Regularly monitor the legal and regulatory landscape to stay updated on changes and new requirements. Engage legal counsel and industry experts to interpret and understand the specific implications of regulations for your organization.

2. **Implement a Compliance Program:** Develop a comprehensive compliance program that includes clear policies, procedures, and guidelines. Assign roles and responsibilities, conduct training sessions, and establish mechanisms for monitoring and enforcement.

3. **Conduct Risk Assessments:** Perform regular risk assessments to identify vulnerabilities and potential non-compliance areas. Prioritize risks based on their impact and likelihood, and implement appropriate controls to mitigate these risks.

4. **Engage in Industry Collaboration:** Participate in industry associations and collaborate with peers to share best practices and insights. Engaging with industry experts can help organizations navigate complex compliance requirements more effectively.

5. **Establish Incident Response Plans:** Develop and test incident response plans to address cybersecurity incidents promptly and effectively. Include

processes for reporting, investigation, mitigation, and communication in the event of a breach or violation.

6. **Maintain Documentation:** Document all compliance efforts, including policies, procedures, risk assessments, and training records. Accurate and detailed documentation is crucial for demonstrating compliance during audits or investigations.

By following these tips, organizations can enhance their ability to meet legal and regulatory compliance requirements while strengthening their overall cybersecurity posture.

Case Study: GDPR Compliance in Healthcare

To better illustrate the practical implications of legal and regulatory compliance in cybersecurity, let's explore a case study on GDPR compliance in the healthcare industry.

Scenario: A healthcare organization based in Germany holds a large database of patient records and personal health information. They are subject to the GDPR and need to ensure compliance with the regulation's data protection requirements.

Solution: The organization takes the following steps to achieve GDPR compliance:

1. Conducts a thorough data inventory and mapping exercise to identify the personal data they hold, the purposes of processing, and the legal basis for processing.

2. Implements appropriate technical and organizational measures to protect personal data by encrypting sensitive information, regularly patching systems, and implementing access controls.

3. Obtains explicit consent from patients for processing their personal data and clearly explains the purposes of processing, data retention periods, and the rights of individuals.

4. Implements procedures to handle data subject requests, including providing access to personal data, rectifying inaccuracies, and erasing data upon request.

5. Establishes a data breach response plan, which includes processes for notifying the supervisory authority and affected individuals in case of a breach, and conducts regular security testing and monitoring to ensure the effectiveness of security controls.

6. Trains employees on the principles and requirements of the GDPR, emphasizing the importance of data protection and privacy in handling patient information.

7. Regularly reviews and updates their privacy policies and procedures to align with any changes in the regulatory landscape, ensuring ongoing compliance with the GDPR.

By implementing these measures and maintaining a proactive approach to compliance, the healthcare organization can mitigate the risk of data breaches, protect patient privacy, and demonstrate their commitment to GDPR compliance.

Summary

Legal and regulatory compliance is vital for organizations operating in the health and wellness industry to ensure the protection of personal information and maintain the trust of patients and consumers. Understanding the legal landscape, adhering to specific regulations, and addressing compliance challenges are key components of effective cybersecurity governance.

In this section, we explored some of the core legal principles relevant to cybersecurity, discussed key regulations such as HIPAA, GDPR, CCPA, and MDR, and examined the challenges organizations face in achieving regulatory compliance. We also provided tips for successful compliance and presented a case study on GDPR compliance in healthcare.

Complying with legal and regulatory requirements is an ongoing process that requires continuous monitoring, improvement, and adaptability. By prioritizing compliance, organizations can establish a strong foundation for cybersecurity and protect the sensitive information entrusted to them.

Liability and Accountability in Cybersecurity Incidents

In the ever-evolving landscape of cybersecurity, incidents are bound to occur despite the best preventive measures. When these incidents happen, it is crucial to understand the concepts of liability and accountability to effectively address the aftermath. This section focuses on exploring the legal and ethical aspects of cybersecurity incidents, including the responsibilities of various parties involved, the consequences they may face, and the frameworks that guide liability and accountability.

Understanding Liability in Cybersecurity Incidents

Liability refers to legal responsibility for one's actions or omissions that result in harm or damage to others. In the realm of cybersecurity, liability involves identifying the parties responsible for safeguarding information and preventing unauthorized access or breaches. The goal is to establish accountability and allocate responsibility for the consequences of cybersecurity incidents.

Primary Parties of Liability

Several key parties can be held liable in cybersecurity incidents:

- **Organizations:** Whether they are healthcare providers, wellness centers, or technology companies, organizations are generally held responsible for maintaining appropriate cybersecurity measures. They have a duty to protect sensitive information and prevent data breaches. Failure to fulfill this duty can result in legal liability.

- **Employees:** Individuals who work for an organization can also be held liable if their actions or negligence contribute to a cybersecurity incident. For example, an employee falling victim to a phishing attack or knowingly sharing sensitive information with unauthorized individuals may be held accountable.

- **Third-party Service Providers:** Organizations often rely on third-party service providers to handle certain aspects of their operations, such as cloud storage or IT support. If these providers fail to meet agreed-upon security standards or contribute to a breach, they may share liability for the incident.

- **Regulatory Bodies:** In some cases, regulatory bodies may be held accountable for cybersecurity incidents if they fail to enforce appropriate security standards or neglect their responsibility to oversee industry compliance.

Legal Framework for Liability

Liability in cybersecurity incidents is governed by various laws and regulations depending on the jurisdiction. Two primary legal concepts are relevant when determining liability:

1. **Negligence:** Negligence refers to the failure to exercise reasonable care to prevent harm to others. In the context of cybersecurity, negligence can be

established if an organization or individual breaches their duty of care by not implementing adequate security measures. To prove negligence, the following elements must be demonstrated:

- Duty of care: The defendant had a legal obligation to protect the information.
- Breach of duty: The defendant failed to meet the required standard of care.
- Causation: The breach of duty directly caused the cybersecurity incident.
- Damages: The incident resulted in harm or loss.

2. **Strict Liability:** Strict liability holds a party responsible for the consequences of an action or omission, regardless of fault or intent. While strict liability is less commonly applied in cybersecurity incidents, it may be invoked in cases where inherently dangerous activities or products, such as certain types of software, result in harm.

Accountability in Cybersecurity Incidents

Accountability refers to the expectation that individuals and organizations take responsibility for their actions and are answerable for their decisions and their consequences. In the context of cybersecurity incidents, accountability involves not only the determination of liability but also the actions taken to address the incident, mitigate its impact, and prevent future occurrences.

Responsibilities of the Parties

When a cybersecurity incident occurs, the various parties involved have specific responsibilities to fulfill, including:

- **Organizations:** The primary responsibility of organizations is to promptly detect, respond, and contain cybersecurity incidents. They must also notify affected individuals, regulatory bodies, and other stakeholders as required by applicable laws and regulations. Organizations should implement incident response plans, provide necessary resources, and conduct thorough investigations to determine the cause and extent of the incident.
- **Employees:** Employees have a crucial role in preventing and addressing cybersecurity incidents. They should be trained to recognize and report potential security threats, adhere to security protocols, and promptly report

any incidents or suspicious activities to the designated authority within the organization.

- **Third-party Service Providers:** Service providers should have robust security measures in place and regularly assess their systems to detect and respond to potential vulnerabilities. They should promptly inform their clients of any security breaches that may impact the shared systems or data.

- **Regulatory Bodies:** Regulatory bodies are responsible for enforcing cybersecurity regulations and standards. They should actively monitor compliance and take necessary actions to ensure organizations adhere to the prescribed security measures. In the event of a cybersecurity incident, regulatory bodies may conduct investigations, provide guidance, and impose penalties or sanctions where warranted.

Consequences and Remedies

The consequences of cybersecurity incidents can vary depending on the severity and impact of the breach. Some common consequences include financial loss, reputational damage, legal penalties, and regulatory sanctions. Remedies for the affected parties may include financial compensation for damages, identity theft protection services, and corrective actions to rectify security vulnerabilities or weaknesses.

Emerging Trends in Accountability

As the field of cybersecurity continues to evolve, new trends in accountability are emerging. Two notable trends are:

1. **Cyber Insurance:** Organizations are increasingly turning to cyber insurance policies to manage the financial risks associated with cybersecurity incidents. These policies provide coverage for various costs, including legal fees, investigation expenses, and customer notifications. Cyber insurance can help incentivize responsible cybersecurity practices and allocate liabilities.

2. **International Cooperation:** Cybersecurity incidents often transcend national boundaries, necessitating international collaboration. Cooperation between governments, regulatory bodies, and law enforcement agencies enhances accountability by enabling the sharing of knowledge, resources, and the pursuit of shared solutions to combat cyber threats.

Ethical Considerations in Cybersecurity Incidents

Cybersecurity incidents raise important ethical considerations, particularly when it comes to protecting individuals' privacy, maintaining trust, and upholding professional integrity. Ethical principles that guide proper conduct in cybersecurity incidents include:

- **Confidentiality:** Ensuring the privacy and confidentiality of individuals' personal information is crucial. Unauthorized access to sensitive data, intentional or accidental, can result in significant harm.
- **Transparency:** Organizations should maintain transparency in disclosing cybersecurity incidents to affected individuals, stakeholders, and regulatory bodies. Prompt and accurate communication helps build trust and enables individuals to take appropriate actions to protect themselves.
- **Integrity:** Professionals involved in incident response should act with integrity, transparency, and honesty. They should not attempt to conceal or downplay the severity of the incident or mislead stakeholders regarding its impact.
- **Equity:** Fairness and equity should be maintained in the allocation of responsibilities and consequences associated with cybersecurity incidents. Each party involved should be treated impartially and held accountable according to their level of involvement and responsibility.

Liability and Accountability Exercises

1. **Case Study: Hospital Data Breach**

A major hospital experiences a data breach due to a phishing attack, resulting in the unauthorized access of patients' personal and medical information. The incident leads to financial loss for affected individuals and a significant decline in the hospital's reputation.

a) Identify the primary parties that could be held liable in this case.

b) Discuss the legal framework that would determine liability.

c) Describe the responsibilities of each party in addressing the breach and mitigating its impact.

2. **Emerging Trends in Accountability**

Research and discuss other emerging trends in accountability and liability related to cybersecurity incidents, such as the role of artificial intelligence in attribution, the impact of international regulations on liability, or the use of bug bounty programs to incentivize responsible disclosure.

3. **Ethical Dilemma**

Consider a scenario where an organization becomes aware of a potential cybersecurity vulnerability that could result in a major breach. However, disclosing the vulnerability could have severe financial and reputational consequences for the organization. Discuss the ethical considerations involved in this dilemma and propose a course of action that upholds the principles of cybersecurity ethics.

Additional Resources

- "The Cybersecurity Handbook: A Practical Guide to Securing Your Information in the Digital Age" by Patricia L. Bellia, Paul M. Schwartz, and Daniel J. Solove. (Publisher: Oxford University Press, 2017)
- "Cybersecurity and Cyberwar: What Everyone Needs to Know" by P.W. Singer and Allan Friedman. (Publisher: Oxford University Press, 2014)
- National Institute of Standards and Technology (NIST) Cybersecurity Framework: `https://www.nist.gov/csframework`
- International Organization for Standardization (ISO) 27001:2013 - Information Security Management Systems

Conclusion

In the realm of cybersecurity, liability and accountability play vital roles in determining responsibility for incidents and addressing their consequences. Organizations, employees, service providers, and regulatory bodies all have roles to play in preventing and responding to incidents. Understanding the legal and ethical frameworks surrounding liability and accountability is essential for creating a safer and more secure digital landscape for health and wellness. By embracing proper accountability and effectively managing liability, individuals and organizations can protect personal information, maintain trust, and prevent cyber threats from compromising the health and well-being of individuals and communities.

Reporting and Whistleblowing in Cybersecurity

In the world of cybersecurity, reporting and whistleblowing play a critical role in identifying and addressing potential threats and vulnerabilities. They serve as essential mechanisms for individuals to disclose unethical or illegal activities, and they promote transparency and accountability within organizations. This section will explore the importance of reporting and whistleblowing in cybersecurity, the challenges and risks involved, and the necessary steps to support those who come forward.

Importance of Reporting

Reporting cybersecurity incidents and potential vulnerabilities is crucial for several reasons. First and foremost, it enables organizations to take prompt action to mitigate the impact of an attack or prevent future breaches. It allows professionals to identify weak points in their systems and develop solutions to bolster security measures.

Moreover, reporting helps in creating a comprehensive incident response plan, which enables organizations to effectively manage and recover from cybersecurity incidents. By gathering and analyzing incident data, organizations can identify patterns, trends, and root causes, thus improving their overall security posture.

Reporting also plays a vital role in regulatory compliance. Many cybersecurity regulations and frameworks, such as the General Data Protection Regulation (GDPR), Health Insurance Portability and Accountability Act (HIPAA), and Payment Card Industry Data Security Standard (PCI DSS), require organizations to report security incidents promptly.

Challenges and Risks

Reporting cybersecurity incidents and blowing the whistle on unethical or illegal activities can be challenging and risky for individuals. Several factors contribute to these challenges:

1. **Fear of Retaliation:** Whistleblowers may fear retaliation from their employers or colleagues. They may worry about negative consequences, such as termination, demotion, harassment, or blacklisting within the industry.

2. **Lack of Trust:** Whistleblowers may hesitate to report incidents due to a lack of trust in the organization's response. They may worry that their concerns will not be taken seriously or that their identities will be compromised, leading to further harm or victimization.

3. **Legal Implications:** Whistleblowers often face legal challenges, as some organizations may attempt to silence them through non-disclosure agreements or legal actions. Whistleblowers need to understand the legal protections available to them and navigate the potential risks involved.

4. **Ethical Dilemmas:** Whistleblowers may grapple with ethical dilemmas, questioning whether it is their responsibility to report and potentially harm their organization or colleagues. They may struggle with the potential consequences of their actions, weighing the greater good against personal and professional relationships.

Supporting Whistleblowers

Organizations must develop a culture of trust and support to encourage individuals to come forward with cybersecurity concerns. Here are some steps organizations can take to support and protect whistleblowers:

1. **Establish Clear Reporting Channels:** Organizations should provide clear guidelines and easy-to-use reporting channels for cybersecurity incidents. This includes both anonymous reporting mechanisms and a transparent process for investigating and responding to reports.

2. **Emphasize Confidentiality:** Organizations must prioritize protecting the confidentiality of whistleblowers. Implementing strict protocols and safeguards to prevent the disclosure of identities will help build trust and encourage individuals to report potential issues without fear of reprisal.

3. **Educate Employees:** Organizations should conduct regular training sessions to educate employees about the importance of reporting and whistleblowing. It is essential to emphasize the benefits of reporting incidents and reassure employees that their actions will be supported and rewarded.

4. **Establish Legal Protections:** Governments and regulatory authorities play a crucial role in providing legal protections for whistleblowers. Organizations should comply with relevant whistleblower protection laws and work towards creating a supportive legal framework that encourages reporting.

5. **Offer Whistleblower Support Programs:** Organizations can provide resources and support programs to assist whistleblowers. This may include legal assistance, counseling services, and career transition support, helping individuals navigate the challenges they may face after coming forward.

Real-World Example: Edward Snowden

One notable example of a whistleblower in the cybersecurity realm is Edward Snowden. In 2013, Snowden, a former National Security Agency (NSA) contractor, leaked classified information revealing the extent of global surveillance programs, including PRISM. Snowden's actions sparked a global debate on privacy and government surveillance.

Snowden's decision to blow the whistle came with tremendous personal consequences. He faced charges of espionage and theft of government property, forcing him to seek asylum in Russia. While opinions on Snowden's actions are divided, his case highlights the complex ethical and legal considerations whistleblowers navigate in the cybersecurity landscape.

Conclusion

Reporting and whistleblowing are essential components of a robust cybersecurity program. They empower individuals to come forward, disclose cybersecurity incidents, and expose unethical or illegal activities. Organizations must create a culture that supports and protects whistleblowers, fostering an environment where individuals feel safe to report incidents without fear of retaliation. Governments, regulatory bodies, and organizations must work together to develop legal protections and support programs that encourage responsible reporting and enable a safer and more secure cyber world for health and wellness.

Building a Cybersecurity Team and Incident Response Capability

Roles and Responsibilities in a Cybersecurity Team

In order to effectively manage cybersecurity, organizations need to establish a dedicated cybersecurity team. This team is responsible for developing and implementing strategies to protect the organization's information systems, data, and overall digital infrastructure. The roles and responsibilities within a cybersecurity team can vary depending on the size and nature of the organization, but there are some core roles that are typically found in most cybersecurity teams.

Chief Information Security Officer (CISO)

The Chief Information Security Officer (CISO) is a senior executive responsible for overseeing the organization's cybersecurity program. They are responsible for developing and implementing the organization's cybersecurity strategy, policies, and procedures. The CISO works closely with other executives to align cybersecurity initiatives with business objectives and ensure that cybersecurity measures are integrated into the organization's overall risk management strategy. They are also responsible for budgeting and resource allocation for cybersecurity activities, and for providing regular reports to senior management and the board of directors on the state of cybersecurity within the organization.

Security Architect

The security architect is responsible for designing and implementing the organization's cybersecurity infrastructure. They work closely with IT teams to ensure that security measures are integrated into the design and implementation of new systems and applications. The security architect also conducts regular security assessments to identify vulnerabilities and weaknesses in the organization's infrastructure, and works to develop and implement remediation plans. They are responsible for staying up to date with the latest security technologies and trends, and for conducting research and development to identify innovative approaches to cybersecurity.

Security Analyst

Security analysts play a key role in monitoring and analyzing the organization's security posture. They are responsible for identifying and investigating potential security incidents, and for analyzing security alerts and logs to detect and respond to threats. Security analysts also conduct vulnerability assessments and penetration tests to identify potential weaknesses in the organization's systems and applications. They work closely with the incident response team to develop and implement incident response plans, and provide support during security incidents and breaches. Security analysts are also responsible for maintaining and updating security tools and systems, and for staying up to date on the latest security threats and trends.

Network Security Engineer

The network security engineer is responsible for designing and implementing the organization's network security infrastructure. They work closely with the security architect to ensure that security measures are integrated into the design and deployment of network infrastructure. Network security engineers are responsible for configuring and managing firewalls, intrusion prevention systems, and other network security technologies. They also monitor network traffic for signs of potential security threats, and work to implement controls to mitigate risks.

Network security engineers collaborate with other IT teams to ensure that best practices in network security are followed throughout the organization.

Application Security Engineer

The application security engineer is responsible for ensuring the security of the organization's software applications. They work closely with software development teams to ensure that security measures are integrated into the application development process. Application security engineers conduct code reviews and vulnerability assessments to identify potential security risks in applications. They also work to implement secure coding practices and provide guidance and training to developers on application security. Application security engineers collaborate with other teams to ensure that proper security controls are in place throughout the software development lifecycle.

Security Operations Center (SOC) Analyst

The Security Operations Center (SOC) analyst is responsible for monitoring and responding to security incidents and threats in real-time. They work in the organization's SOC to monitor security alerts, analyze potential threats, and respond to security incidents. SOC analysts use a variety of tools and technologies to detect and investigate security incidents, and work closely with other teams to respond to and mitigate security threats. They are responsible for documenting incident response activities and lessons learned, and for providing recommendations for improving the organization's overall security posture. SOC analysts also conduct ongoing threat intelligence analysis to stay informed about the latest security threats and trends.

Cybersecurity Trainer and Awareness Specialist

The cybersecurity trainer and awareness specialist is responsible for developing and delivering cybersecurity training programs and initiatives within the organization. They develop training materials and resources to educate employees about cybersecurity best practices, policies, and procedures. The cybersecurity trainer and awareness specialist also conduct regular cybersecurity awareness campaigns to promote a culture of security within the organization. They work closely with other teams to ensure that cybersecurity training is integrated into employee onboarding programs and ongoing professional development initiatives. The cybersecurity trainer and awareness specialist also provide ongoing support and guidance to employees on cybersecurity matters.

Ethical Hacker and Penetration Tester

The ethical hacker and penetration tester is responsible for conducting authorized hacking and penetration testing activities to identify vulnerabilities in the organization's systems and applications. They work closely with the security analyst and network security engineer to ensure that potential vulnerabilities are identified and remediated. Ethical hackers and penetration testers use a variety of tools and techniques to simulate real-world attacks and identify potential areas of weakness. They provide detailed reports and recommendations to management and other teams on vulnerabilities discovered during testing. Ethical hackers and penetration testers also contribute to the ongoing improvement of the organization's overall security posture.

Vendor Risk Manager

The vendor risk manager is responsible for assessing and managing cybersecurity risks associated with third-party vendors and suppliers. They work closely with the procurement and legal teams to evaluate the cybersecurity posture of vendors and suppliers, and to ensure that appropriate security controls are in place. The vendor risk manager conducts vendor risk assessments and due diligence reviews, and works with vendors to remediate any identified security issues. They also monitor and audit vendor compliance with contractual security requirements, and work to ensure that vendors are meeting the organization's cybersecurity standards.

Legal and Compliance Specialist

The legal and compliance specialist is responsible for ensuring that the organization's cybersecurity practices and initiatives are in compliance with relevant laws, regulations, and industry standards. They provide legal guidance and support to the cybersecurity team, and work closely with other teams to develop and implement policies and procedures that are compliant with applicable regulations. The legal and compliance specialist also assists with incident response and breach notification activities, and represents the organization in legal and regulatory proceedings related to cybersecurity. They stay up to date on legal and regulatory developments in the cybersecurity field, and provide recommendations and guidance to management and other teams on compliance matters.

Privacy Officer

The privacy officer is responsible for ensuring the privacy and protection of personal data within the organization. They work closely with the cybersecurity team to ensure that appropriate privacy controls are in place to protect sensitive information. The privacy officer is responsible for developing and implementing privacy policies and procedures, and for providing guidance and training to employees on privacy matters. They also work closely with legal and compliance teams to ensure that privacy practices are compliant with applicable laws and regulations. The privacy officer monitors and audits the organization's privacy practices, and works to implement continuous improvement initiatives.

Conclusion

A well-structured and skilled cybersecurity team is essential for protecting an organization's digital assets and ensuring the confidentiality, integrity, and availability of information. The roles and responsibilities within a cybersecurity team are diverse and require a range of skills and expertise. By understanding these roles and responsibilities, organizations can build a strong cybersecurity team that can effectively identify, mitigate, and respond to security threats. Regular training, ongoing development, and collaboration with other teams within the organization are crucial for the success of the cybersecurity team.

Incident Response Planning and Execution

Incident response planning and execution is a critical aspect of effective cybersecurity management in the health and wellness industry. It involves the development and implementation of strategies and procedures to respond to and mitigate the impact of cybersecurity incidents. In this section, we will discuss the key components of incident response planning, the steps involved in executing an incident response plan, and provide practical guidance on incident response best practices.

Importance of Incident Response Planning

In today's digital landscape, cyber attacks are becoming increasingly sophisticated and prevalent. The healthcare sector, in particular, is a prime target for cybercriminals due to the sensitivity of the data it handles and its critical role in patient care. Incident response planning is crucial because it helps organizations reduce the impact of cyber incidents, minimize downtime, and protect sensitive data.

An effective incident response plan establishes a clear framework for identifying, responding to, and recovering from cybersecurity incidents promptly. It ensures that all stakeholders are aware of their roles and responsibilities, enabling a coordinated and effective response. By having a well-defined incident response plan in place, health and wellness organizations can minimize the potential damage caused by cyber attacks and protect the trust of their patients and stakeholders.

Components of Incident Response Planning

Developing a comprehensive incident response plan involves several essential components. These components provide guidance on different aspects of incident response and enable organizations to respond effectively to cyber attacks.

1. **Incident Response Team:** The first step in incident response planning is to establish an incident response team. This team comprises individuals responsible for coordinating and executing the incident response plan. Key roles within the incident response team include incident commander, technical experts, legal advisors, communication specialists, and representatives from relevant departments such as IT, legal, and human resources.

2. **Incident Response Plan Documentation:** It is vital to document the incident response plan. The plan should include clear guidelines and procedures for reporting incidents, classifying incident severity levels, coordinating response actions, and communicating with stakeholders. The documentation should also outline the roles and responsibilities of each team member and provide a step-by-step guide on incident handling.

3. **Incident Detection and Reporting:** Organizations need effective mechanisms for detecting and reporting incidents promptly. This involves implementing technologies such as intrusion detection systems, security information and event management (SIEM) solutions, and threat intelligence feeds. Employees should also be trained to recognize and report potential incidents to the incident response team.

4. **Incident Analysis and Response:** Once an incident is detected and reported, the incident response team performs a thorough analysis to understand the nature and extent of the incident. This analysis involves conducting forensic investigations, collecting evidence, and identifying the root cause of the incident. Based on the analysis, the team develops an appropriate response strategy to contain and mitigate the incident.

5. **Incident Containment and Mitigation:** The incident response team takes immediate actions to contain the incident and mitigate its impact. This may involve isolating compromised systems, disabling user accounts, applying software patches or updates, and taking other measures to prevent further damage. The team should prioritize the restoration of critical systems and services to minimize downtime and ensure continuity of operations.

6. **Communication and Stakeholder Management:** Effective communication is essential during incident response. The incident response team should establish clear lines of communication with internal stakeholders (e.g., senior management, employees) and external stakeholders (e.g., customers, regulatory bodies, law enforcement). Regular updates should be provided to keep stakeholders informed about the incident, response progress, and any necessary actions they should take.

7. **Lessons Learned and Continuous Improvement:** After the incident has been successfully resolved, it is important to conduct a post-incident review. This review helps identify any gaps in the incident response plan and provides insights into areas that need improvement. Lessons learned from the incident should be incorporated into future incident response planning and training programs to enhance the organization's overall cybersecurity posture.

Steps in Executing an Incident Response Plan

Executing an incident response plan involves a series of well-defined steps that help organizations effectively respond to and recover from cyber incidents. The following steps provide a general framework for incident response execution:

Step 1: Preparation - Ensure that the incident response team is ready to respond by verifying that all necessary resources, tools, and communication channels are in place. Review and update the incident response plan and documentation to reflect the latest threats and vulnerabilities.

Step 2: Incident Identification - Utilize monitoring tools and employee reports to detect and identify cyber incidents. It is crucial to maintain situational awareness and have mechanisms in place to promptly identify potential incidents.

Step 3: Incident Triage - Classify the incident based on severity and impact. Assess the potential risks and prioritize response actions accordingly. This step involves gathering initial information about the incident and communicating it to the incident response team.

Step 4: Incident Containment - Take immediate actions to contain the incident and prevent further damage. This may involve isolating affected systems, disconnecting from the network, or implementing temporary mitigations.

Step 5: Incident Investigation - Conduct a thorough investigation to determine the root cause and impact of the incident. Preserve evidence, perform forensic analysis, and identify any indicators of compromise (IOCs) that may help in understanding and preventing future incidents.

Step 6: Incident Eradication and Recovery - Remove the presence of the attacker from the affected systems and restore them to a trusted state. This step includes cleaning up infected systems, applying software patches, and restoring data from backups.

Step 7: Post-Incident Analysis - Evaluate the effectiveness of the incident response plan and identify areas for improvement. Document lessons learned and update incident response procedures and training programs accordingly.

Step 8: Reporting and Documentation - Prepare incident reports for stakeholders, including senior management, legal, regulatory bodies, and law enforcement if necessary. Maintain accurate documentation of the incident, response actions, and findings for future reference and compliance purposes.

Step 9: Continuous Improvement - Regularly review and update the incident response plan based on lessons learned from previous incidents and changes in the threat landscape. Conduct periodic training and drills to ensure that all team members are familiar with their roles and responsibilities.

Challenges and Best Practices

Implementing an effective incident response plan comes with its own set of challenges. Some common challenges include the evolving threat landscape, resource limitations, and the complexity of healthcare systems. However, by following best practices, organizations can overcome these challenges and enhance their incident response capabilities.

1. **Regular Training and Drills:** Conduct regular training sessions and simulated exercises to test the incident response plan. This helps identify any gaps or weaknesses in the plan and provides an opportunity for team members to practice their roles and responsibilities.

2. **Collaboration and Communication:** Foster collaboration and open communication within the incident response team and with relevant stakeholders. Ensure that everyone understands the importance of timely and accurate information sharing during incident response.

3. **Continuous Monitoring and Threat Intelligence:** Implement continuous monitoring solutions and leverage threat intelligence feeds to stay updated on emerging threats. Proactively identify potential incidents and respond swiftly before they escalate.

4. **Incident Coordination:** Assign a designated incident commander responsible for coordinating the incident response efforts. Clearly define the roles and responsibilities of each team member to ensure a coordinated response.

5. **Documentation and Knowledge Management:** Maintain detailed documentation of incidents, response actions, and lessons learned. Develop a centralized knowledge base to facilitate information sharing and ensure that incident response knowledge is retained even when team members change.

6. **External Collaboration:** Establish relationships with external partners such as cybersecurity vendors, law enforcement agencies, and industry groups. Leverage their expertise and resources during incident response and collaborate on threat intelligence sharing initiatives.

7. **Regular Plan Review and Updates:** Review and update the incident response plan periodically to reflect changes in the threat landscape, organizational structure, and technology. Conduct post-incident reviews and incorporate lessons learned into future planning.

Case Study: Healthcare Data Breach Incident Response

To illustrate the importance of incident response planning and execution, let's consider a case study of a healthcare data breach incident:

Scenario: A healthcare organization discovers that its patient database has been compromised, potentially exposing sensitive patient information such as medical records and personally identifiable information (PII).

Incident Response Steps:

Step 1: Preparation - The incident response team reviews the incident response plan, verifies that all necessary resources are available, and establishes secure communication channels for incident coordination.

Step 2: Incident Identification - An employee notices unusual system behavior and promptly reports it to the incident response team. The team confirms the incident and initiates the response process.

Step 3: Incident Triage - The incident is classified as a high-severity incident due to the potential impact on patient privacy and organization reputation. The team analyzes the scope of the breach and identifies affected systems.

Step 4: Incident Containment - The team isolates the compromised systems from the network to prevent further unauthorized access. It also disables compromised user accounts and restricts access to critical systems.

Step 5: Incident Investigation - The incident response team conducts a forensic analysis to determine the cause and extent of the breach. They identify the vulnerability that was exploited and collect evidence for further analysis.

Step 6: Incident Eradication and Recovery - The team removes the attacker's presence from the affected systems, patches the vulnerability, and restores the systems from clean backups. They also strengthen security measures to prevent future incidents.

Step 7: Post-Incident Analysis - The incident response team conducts a post-incident review to identify any shortcomings in the response process. They update the incident response plan to incorporate lessons learned from the incident.

Step 8: Reporting and Documentation - The team prepares an incident report, highlighting the breach's impact, response actions, and recommendations for preventing similar incidents. The report is shared with senior management and relevant stakeholders.

Step 9: Continuous Improvement - The incident response plan is updated to include additional preventive controls, employee training, and incident response drills. The organization invests in cybersecurity awareness programs to educate employees about potential threats and their role in incident response.

By effectively executing the incident response plan, the healthcare organization can minimize the impact of the data breach, prevent further unauthorized access, and enhance its overall cybersecurity posture.

Conclusion

Incident response planning and execution are critical components of a comprehensive cybersecurity strategy in the health and wellness industry. A well-defined incident response plan enables organizations to detect, respond, and recover from cyber incidents promptly and effectively. By following the best practices outlined in this section, health and wellness organizations can enhance their incident response capabilities, protect sensitive data, and maintain the trust of their patients and stakeholders. Remember, incident response is not just a reactive process; it is a proactive approach to cybersecurity that helps organizations in their efforts to create a safer and more secure digital environment.

Collaboration with Law Enforcement and Cybersecurity Agencies

In the constantly evolving landscape of cybersecurity threats, collaboration between organizations is crucial for combating cybercrime effectively. This extends beyond internal collaboration within an organization to include partnerships with external entities such as law enforcement agencies and cybersecurity organizations. Collaboration with law enforcement and cybersecurity agencies can provide valuable resources, expertise, and legal support in addressing cyber threats. This section delves into the importance of such collaborations and explores various aspects of working together to enhance cybersecurity efforts.

Understanding the Role of Law Enforcement and Cybersecurity Agencies

Law enforcement agencies, such as the FBI (Federal Bureau of Investigation) and Interpol, along with specialized cybersecurity agencies like CERT (Computer Emergency Response Team), play a pivotal role in combating cybercrime. These agencies have the jurisdiction and authority to investigate and prosecute cybercriminals, making them essential partners in the fight against cyber threats.

Law enforcement agencies bring their investigative capabilities, legal authority, and access to international law enforcement cooperation to cybersecurity collaborations. They can help identify cybercriminals, gather evidence, and facilitate prosecution, ensuring justice is served. On the other hand, cybersecurity agencies focus on providing technical expertise, threat intelligence, and incident response support to help organizations defend against and mitigate cyber threats effectively.

The Benefits of Collaboration

Collaboration between organizations and law enforcement/cybersecurity agencies offers several benefits in the realm of cybersecurity. Some of the key advantages include:

1. **Enhanced Investigation Capabilities:** By working with law enforcement agencies, organizations can tap into their specialized investigative resources and expertise. This collaboration can help gather crucial evidence, track down cybercriminals, and ultimately bring them to justice.

2. **Access to Threat Intelligence:** Cybersecurity agencies and law enforcement organizations have access to extensive threat intelligence networks. Collaborating with these entities enables organizations to stay informed about the latest cyber threats and trends. This knowledge can help organizations enhance their defensive strategies and proactively safeguard their systems and data.

3. **Legal Assistance and Expertise:** Cybersecurity incidents often involve complex legal issues, and organizations may require legal guidance and support. Law enforcement agencies can provide expert advice on navigating

the legal landscape, ensuring compliance with relevant regulations, and assisting in the prosecution of cybercriminals.

4. **Incident Response and Recovery:** Collaborating with cybersecurity agencies can significantly enhance an organization's incident response capabilities. These agencies can provide technical expertise and guidance during the critical phases of incident detection, response, and recovery. By leveraging their experience and knowledge, organizations can minimize the impact of cyber incidents and expedite the restoration of normal operations.

5. **Sharing Best Practices:** Collaboration fosters the exchange of knowledge, best practices, and lessons learned between organizations and law enforcement/cybersecurity agencies. This sharing of information enhances overall cybersecurity awareness and promotes effective strategies for preventing and mitigating cyber threats.

Establishing Collaborative Partnerships

Building effective collaborative partnerships with law enforcement and cybersecurity agencies requires a proactive and strategic approach. Here are some key considerations for establishing such partnerships:

1. **Identify Relevant Agencies:** Research and identify law enforcement and cybersecurity agencies that specialize in dealing with cybercrime. Local agencies, national bodies, and international organizations like Interpol should be considered based on the scope and nature of the organization's operations.

2. **Establish Contacts and Relationships:** Reach out to the identified agencies and establish contacts at different levels. Building relationships with key personnel helps foster effective communication and collaboration during cyber incidents.

3. **Define Roles and Responsibilities:** Clearly define the roles and responsibilities of each party involved in the collaboration. Understand the resources, support, and expertise that law enforcement and cybersecurity agencies can provide, while identifying the organization's obligations and responsibilities in the partnership.

4. **Maintain Regular Communication:** Effective collaboration requires ongoing communication and information sharing. Establish regular communication

channels and mechanisms for sharing threat intelligence, incident updates, and other relevant information.

5. **Participate in Joint Exercises and Training:** Joint exercises and training sessions provide an opportunity to test and enhance the collaborative framework. Engage in simulations or workshops conducted by law enforcement or cybersecurity agencies to improve incident response capabilities and strengthen the partnership.

6. **Ensure Legal and Privacy Compliance:** Cybersecurity collaborations must adhere to legal and privacy requirements. Understand the jurisdictional boundaries, legal frameworks, and data protection regulations that apply to the partnership. This ensures compliance with applicable laws and protects sensitive information throughout the collaboration process.

Case Study: Operation Bot Roast

One notable example of collaboration between law enforcement and cybersecurity agencies is Operation Bot Roast, led by the FBI in the United States. This operation, conducted between 2005 and 2007, targeted individuals responsible for infecting and controlling thousands of computers with botnet malware.

Through collaboration with various cybersecurity organizations and international partners, the FBI identified and pursued cybercriminals involved in the operation of botnets. Together, they disrupted multiple botnets, arrested several individuals, and raised awareness about the importance of securing computer systems.

Operation Bot Roast highlights the effectiveness of cross-sector collaboration in combating cyber threats and underscores the crucial role played by law enforcement agencies in investigating and prosecuting cybercriminals.

Conclusion

Collaboration with law enforcement and cybersecurity agencies is a valuable and necessary component of a comprehensive cybersecurity strategy. By forging partnerships and sharing resources, organizations can enhance their ability to detect, respond to, and recover from cyber incidents. The benefits of collaboration include enhanced investigation capabilities, access to threat intelligence, legal assistance, improved incident response, and the sharing of best practices.

To establish effective collaborative partnerships, organizations should identify relevant agencies, establish contacts, define roles and responsibilities, maintain regular communication, participate in joint exercises, and ensure legal and privacy compliance. The case study of Operation Bot Roast demonstrates the effectiveness of such collaborations in combating cyber threats on a large scale.

By working together, organizations and law enforcement/cybersecurity agencies can create a safer and more secure digital world for health and wellness. The next section explores the emerging technologies and security challenges that will shape the future of cybersecurity in this industry.

Performing Post-Incident Analysis and Remediation Strategies

After a cybersecurity incident occurs, it is crucial for organizations in the health and wellness industry to conduct a thorough post-incident analysis and implement effective remediation strategies. This section will delve into the steps involved in the post-incident analysis process, the importance of conducting such analysis, and the strategies for remediation.

Importance of Post-Incident Analysis

Post-incident analysis plays a vital role in enhancing cybersecurity practices and preventing future incidents. By conducting a detailed analysis, organizations can identify the root causes of the incident, assess the impact of the breach, and gather valuable insights for strengthening their security posture. The analysis also helps in identifying any existing vulnerabilities or weaknesses in the system, improving incident response capabilities, and ensuring compliance with regulatory requirements.

Furthermore, post-incident analysis provides organizations with an opportunity to learn from their mistakes and refine their incident response plans. It helps in enhancing the overall cybersecurity awareness and preparedness within the organization, enabling them to better protect sensitive data and ensure the privacy of their clients.

Steps in Post-Incident Analysis

The following steps outline a systematic approach to conducting a post-incident analysis:

1. **Documenting the Incident:** Start by documenting all the relevant details of the incident, including the timeline of events, actions taken during the incident, and any evidence collected. This documentation provides a

foundation for the analysis process and serves as a reference for future investigations.

2. **Gathering Forensic Evidence:** In order to understand the scope and impact of the incident, gather forensic evidence from affected systems and devices. This may involve capturing network traffic, analyzing log files, and preserving memory snapshots. The evidence should be collected in a forensically sound manner to ensure its admissibility in legal proceedings, if necessary.

3. **Performing Root Cause Analysis:** Identify the root causes that led to the incident. This involves a detailed examination of the vulnerability that was exploited, the attack vectors used, and any security lapses or misconfigurations. By understanding the root causes, organizations can take targeted steps to address the underlying issues and prevent similar incidents in the future.

4. **Assessing Impact and Damage:** Evaluate the impact of the incident on the organization, its stakeholders, and the affected individuals. This assessment includes determining the extent of data breaches, financial losses, reputational damage, and regulatory non-compliance. Understanding the full impact helps in prioritizing remediation efforts and allocating resources effectively.

5. **Identifying Lessons Learned:** Identify the key lessons learned from the incident. This involves analyzing the effectiveness of existing security controls, incident response procedures, and employee training programs. Organizations should consider factors such as incident detection and response time, communication and coordination during the incident, and the level of preparedness. These lessons will inform the development of more robust security strategies and incident response plans.

Remediation Strategies

Once the post-incident analysis is complete, organizations need to implement remediation strategies to address the identified vulnerabilities and prevent future incidents. The following strategies outline a comprehensive approach to remediation:

1. **Patch Management and System Updates:** Regularly update and patch all software, operating systems, and firmware to address known vulnerabilities. Implement an effective patch management process to ensure timely updates and minimize the risk of unpatched systems being exploited.

2. **Secure Configuration Management:** Review and enhance the system and network configurations to align with industry best practices and security standards. This includes disabling unnecessary services, enforcing strong access controls, and configuring firewalls and intrusion detection systems to monitor and protect the network.

3. **Employee Training and Awareness:** Provide regular cybersecurity training to employees to create a culture of security awareness. Educate employees on phishing attacks, social engineering techniques, and best practices for secure communication and data handling. Encourage reporting of suspicious activities and promote a proactive stance towards cybersecurity.

4. **Incident Response Plan Updates:** Revise and update the incident response plan based on the lessons learned from the incident. Ensure that the plan reflects the organization's current capabilities, technology landscape, and regulatory requirements. Regularly test and simulate incident response procedures to validate their effectiveness.

5. **Enhanced Monitoring and Detection:** Strengthen monitoring and detection capabilities by deploying advanced threat detection tools and security information and event management (SIEM) systems. Implement real-time monitoring of critical systems, network traffic, and user activities to identify any suspicious behavior or indicators of compromise.

6. **Continuous Vulnerability Scanning:** Implement an ongoing vulnerability scanning program to identify and remediate potential weaknesses in systems and networks. Regularly assess the security posture of critical assets and prioritize remediation efforts based on the risk level posed by each vulnerability.

Case Study: Post-Incident Analysis of a Ransomware Attack

A real-world example of a post-incident analysis is the analysis of a ransomware attack on a healthcare organization. In this case, the incident response team documented the incident timeline, gathered forensic evidence from affected systems, and identified the root cause as a phishing email that led to the initial compromise.

The analysis revealed that the organization lacked adequate email security controls and had not conducted regular employee training on identifying phishing emails. As a result, the ransomware was able to encrypt critical patient data and disrupt the organization's operations.

Based on this analysis, the organization implemented several remediation strategies, including:

- Strengthening email security controls, such as implementing email authentication protocols and spam filters.
- Conducting regular employee training on phishing awareness and safe email practices.
- Enhancing backup and recovery mechanisms to ensure the availability and integrity of critical data.
- Implementing advanced endpoint protection solutions to detect and prevent malware infections.

By conducting a thorough post-incident analysis and implementing these remediation strategies, the organization significantly improved its cybersecurity posture and reduced the risk of similar incidents in the future.

Conclusion

Performing a post-incident analysis is crucial for organizations in the health and wellness industry to learn from cybersecurity incidents, improve their incident response capabilities, and prevent future incidents. By following a systematic approach to analysis and implementing effective remediation strategies, organizations can strengthen their cybersecurity posture and ensure the protection of sensitive data. Continuous evaluation, learning, and adaptation are key to staying ahead of evolving cyber threats and maintaining a secure environment in the digital age.

Training and Development for Cybersecurity Professionals

In the rapidly evolving field of cybersecurity, continuous training and development are critical for professionals to stay up-to-date with the latest threats, tools, and techniques. This section will explore various aspects of training and development programs for cybersecurity professionals, including the importance of ongoing education, certification programs, and the need for a multidisciplinary approach.

Importance of Ongoing Education

Cybersecurity is a dynamic and ever-changing field where new vulnerabilities and attack vectors emerge regularly. Therefore, it is essential for cybersecurity professionals to engage in ongoing education to keep pace with these developments.

One approach to ongoing education is through industry conferences, seminars, and workshops. These events provide an opportunity to learn from experts in the field, gain insights into emerging trends, and network with peers. Additionally, professional organizations, such as the International Information System Security Certification Consortium $(ISC)^2$ and the Information Systems Audit and Control Association (ISACA), offer continuing education programs and resources for cybersecurity professionals.

Furthermore, staying informed about the latest cybersecurity news, research papers, and publications is crucial. This can be achieved through subscribing to industry-leading journals, following cybersecurity blogs and podcasts, and participating in online forums or communities. By actively engaging in these activities, professionals can strengthen their knowledge base and enhance their skills.

Certification Programs

Certification programs play a significant role in the training and development of cybersecurity professionals. They provide a standardized framework for assessing knowledge, skills, and abilities, and serve as a validation of expertise in specific cybersecurity domains.

One widely recognized certification for cybersecurity professionals is the Certified Information Systems Security Professional (CISSP) offered by $(ISC)^2$. The CISSP covers various topics, including security and risk management, asset security, security architecture and engineering, communication and network security, and more. Obtaining the CISSP certification demonstrates a comprehensive understanding of cybersecurity principles and best practices.

In addition to the CISSP, there are numerous other certifications available, such as Certified Ethical Hacker (CEH), Certified Information Security Manager (CISM), and Certified Cloud Security Professional (CCSP). These certifications focus on specific areas of cybersecurity, allowing professionals to specialize and demonstrate expertise in their chosen field.

While certifications are important, it is crucial to note that they should not be considered the sole measure of competence. Practical experience, critical thinking skills, and the ability to adapt to new challenges are equally important factors that contribute to a cybersecurity professional's effectiveness.

Multidisciplinary Approach

Cybersecurity is a multidisciplinary field that requires professionals to have a broad range of skills and knowledge. In addition to technical expertise, cybersecurity professionals should possess critical thinking, problem-solving, communication, and leadership skills.

Technical skills are fundamental and typically include areas such as network security, secure coding, system administration, and incident response. Professionals should continuously develop their technical skills through practical hands-on experience and by staying informed about the latest technologies and tools in the field.

However, cybersecurity is not solely a technical problem. It also involves understanding legal and regulatory frameworks, risk management, business continuity planning, and human factors. Therefore, professionals should cultivate a holistic understanding of cybersecurity by developing skills in areas such as risk assessment, policy and governance, security awareness training, and incident response planning.

Collaboration and effective communication are also critical aspects of cybersecurity. Professionals should be able to work well in teams, collaborate with colleagues from various disciplines, and effectively communicate complex technical concepts to non-technical stakeholders.

Hands-on Practical Exercises

To reinforce theoretical knowledge and develop practical skills, hands-on exercises are an essential component of cybersecurity training. These exercises provide an opportunity for professionals to apply their knowledge in real-world scenarios, test their problem-solving abilities, and learn from their mistakes in a controlled environment.

Capture the Flag (CTF) competitions are popular training exercises in the cybersecurity community. These competitions simulate real-world scenarios where participants solve a series of challenges, such as finding vulnerabilities, cracking passwords, and analyzing network traffic. CTF competitions encourage critical thinking, teamwork, and technical skills development.

Simulations and virtual labs are another effective way to provide hands-on training. These platforms allow professionals to practice skills such as penetration testing, incident response, and secure coding in a safe and controlled environment. By simulating real-world scenarios, professionals can gain practical experience without risking harm to actual systems and networks.

Promoting Diversity and Inclusion

To address the shortage of cybersecurity professionals and promote a more inclusive industry, efforts should be made to attract individuals from diverse backgrounds. Encouraging participation from underrepresented groups, such as women and racial minorities, can bring fresh perspectives and insights to the field.

Organizations should implement initiatives to bridge the gender and diversity gaps in cybersecurity. This can include scholarships, mentorship programs, and outreach activities aimed at inspiring and educating young individuals about cybersecurity career opportunities. Additionally, fostering an inclusive and diverse work environment is crucial for attracting and retaining talent from all backgrounds.

Conclusion

The field of cybersecurity requires continuous learning and development to stay ahead of evolving threats. Ongoing education, certification programs, and a multidisciplinary approach are all vital components of training and development for cybersecurity professionals. By investing in their knowledge and skills, professionals can contribute to building a safer and more secure digital ecosystem for health and wellness.

The Future of Cybersecurity in Health and Wellness

Emerging Technologies and Security Challenges

Artificial Intelligence and Machine Learning in Cybersecurity

Artificial Intelligence (AI) and Machine Learning (ML) are revolutionizing the field of cybersecurity. With the increasing complexity and sophistication of cyber threats, traditional security measures are becoming inadequate in dealing with the rapidly evolving landscape. AI and ML technologies offer the promise of identifying and mitigating emerging threats in real-time, enhancing the overall security posture of organizations and individuals. In this section, we will explore the applications, benefits, challenges, and future prospects of AI and ML in cybersecurity.

Introduction to Artificial Intelligence and Machine Learning

Artificial Intelligence refers to the simulation of human intelligence in machines that can perceive, learn, reason, and make decisions autonomously. Machine Learning, a subset of AI, involves the development of algorithms that enable computers to learn from data and improve their performance without being explicitly programmed. ML algorithms identify patterns, correlations, and anomalies in large datasets, empowering machines to make accurate predictions and take intelligent actions.

The application of AI and ML in cybersecurity leverages the enormous processing power and advanced algorithms to analyze vast amounts of data, detect anomalies, identify potential threats, and respond proactively. These technologies have the potential to revolutionize how we protect sensitive information and secure digital assets.

Applications of AI and ML in Cybersecurity

AI and ML are finding application in various areas of cybersecurity, providing innovative solutions to complex challenges. Some of the key areas where AI and ML are making a significant impact include:

Threat Detection and Prevention AI and ML algorithms have the capability to analyze massive amounts of data, including network traffic, system logs, user behavior, and threat intelligence feeds, to identify emerging threats. They can detect patterns and anomalies that are often missed by traditional security tools. By continuously learning from new data, these algorithms can adapt to evolving threats and update defenses in real-time. This enables organizations to detect and prevent attacks before they cause significant damage.

For example, ML algorithms can identify patterns of malicious behavior in network traffic and flag suspicious activities for further investigation. AI-powered systems can also scan emails, identify phishing attempts, and prevent malicious links and attachments from reaching users' inboxes.

Malware Analysis and Detection AI and ML algorithms can analyze malware samples and identify characteristics that distinguish them from legitimate software. By learning from vast malware databases, these algorithms can detect new and unknown malware variants, even if they have been disguised or obfuscated. ML techniques, such as anomaly detection and behavioral analysis, can detect previously unseen or zero-day attacks, providing proactive defense against evolving threats.

User and Entity Behavior Analytics (UEBA) AI and ML can analyze user behavior and identify anomalous activities that may indicate insider threats or compromised accounts. By establishing baseline behavior patterns, these algorithms can detect deviations, such as unauthorized access attempts or data exfiltration. UEBA systems powered by AI can also identify suspicious patterns in system logs and network traffic, enabling organizations to respond quickly to potential threats.

Automated Incident Response AI and ML technologies can automate various aspects of incident response, improving the efficiency and effectiveness of security operations. ML algorithms can triage and prioritize security alerts, reducing the workload of security analysts and enabling faster response times. These algorithms can also recommend remediation actions based on historical data and threat intelligence, allowing for more effective and consistent incident response.

Benefits and Challenges of AI and ML in Cybersecurity

The integration of AI and ML in cybersecurity brings several benefits, but it also presents certain challenges. Let's explore some of these benefits and challenges in detail:

Benefits

- **Improved Threat Detection:** AI and ML algorithms can detect complex and evolving threats that traditional security tools may miss. This enhances the overall security posture and helps organizations stay one step ahead of attackers.
- **Real-time Defense:** By analyzing data in real-time, AI and ML systems can respond quickly to emerging threats, preventing attacks before they cause significant damage.
- **Reduced False Positives:** ML algorithms, with their ability to learn from data, can reduce false positives by distinguishing between genuine threats and benign activities, reducing the burden on security analysts.
- **Automation and Efficiency:** AI and ML can automate repetitive and time-consuming tasks, freeing up security personnel to focus on more complex and strategic activities.
- **Threat Intelligence Enhancement:** ML algorithms can analyze vast amounts of threat intelligence data to provide actionable insights and enable proactive defense strategies.

Challenges

- **Adversarial Attacks:** AI and ML systems are vulnerable to adversarial attacks, where attackers manipulate input data to deceive or mislead the algorithms. Adversarial attacks can lead to false positives or negatives, undermining the effectiveness of AI and ML in cybersecurity.
- **Lack of Explainability:** AI and ML algorithms are often seen as black boxes since they make decisions based on complex models that are difficult to

interpret. The lack of explainability raises concerns about trust, accountability, and legal and ethical considerations.

- **Data Privacy:** The success of AI and ML heavily relies on access to large amounts of high-quality data. However, this raises concerns about data privacy and the potential misuse or mishandling of sensitive information.
- **Bias and Fairness:** AI and ML algorithms can inherit biases present in the data they are trained on, leading to discriminatory outcomes. Ensuring fairness and avoiding bias in AI-driven security systems is a critical challenge.

Future Prospects

The future of AI and ML in cybersecurity holds immense potential for further advancements and innovations. Some of the key areas that are likely to shape the future of AI and ML in cybersecurity include:

Intelligent Threat Hunting AI and ML algorithms can be utilized to proactively hunt for threats within an organization's network. By combining historical data, threat intelligence, and real-time monitoring, these algorithms can identify hidden threats and malicious activities that may have evaded traditional security measures.

Enhanced Privacy and Compliance AI and ML can play a crucial role in ensuring compliance with privacy regulations and industry standards. ML algorithms can assist in data anonymization and develop privacy-preserving techniques for secure data sharing and collaboration without compromising sensitive information.

Explainable AI The lack of explainability in AI and ML algorithms can hinder their adoption in critical security applications. Future research and development efforts aim to create explainable AI systems that can provide transparent justifications for their decisions, enabling better trust, understanding, and accountability.

Automated Threat Response The integration of AI and ML in threat response can lead to fully automated incident response systems. These systems can detect, investigate, and remediate security incidents without significant human intervention, reducing response times and minimizing the impact of attacks.

AI-Powered Cybersecurity Assistants AI-driven cybersecurity assistants can provide real-time threat intelligence, assist in security policy management, monitor system health, and help users adhere to security best practices. These assistants can also provide personalized security advice and educational resources, enhancing security awareness and behavior.

In conclusion, AI and ML technologies have the potential to revolutionize the field of cybersecurity by enhancing threat detection, automating incident response, and providing proactive defense against emerging threats. While there are challenges to overcome, the benefits of leveraging AI and ML in cybersecurity are immense. The future holds exciting prospects as AI and ML continue to evolve, enabling safer and more secure digital environments for individuals and organizations alike.

Resources and Further Reading

For more information on Artificial Intelligence and Machine Learning in Cybersecurity, you may refer to the following resources:

- Shackleford, D. (2019). AI in cybersecurity: Leveraging artificial intelligence and machine learning for cybersecurity defense. O'Reilly Media.
- Buczak, A. L., & Guven, E. (2016). A survey of data mining and machine learning methods for cybersecurity intrusion detection. IEEE Communications Surveys & Tutorials, 18(2), 1153-1176.
- Biggio, B., Corona, I., Maiorca, D., Nelson, B., & Srndic, N. (2018). Evasion attacks against machine learning at test time. In Proceedings of the European Symposium on Research in Computer Security (pp. 3-18). Springer.
- Wang, H., Du, Z., & Wang, H. (2019). Explainable artificial intelligence (XAI) for cybersecurity: A survey. arXiv preprint arXiv:1907.09136.
- Rauschecker, A. M., & Sahami, M. (2019). Securing the future of artificial intelligence and machine learning at the edge. In Proceedings of the ACM Workshop on Artificial Intelligence and Security (pp. 4-14).

Exercises

1. Explain the concept of adversarial attacks in the context of AI and ML in cybersecurity. Provide examples of how attackers can manipulate input data to deceive ML algorithms.

2. Discuss the ethical considerations and challenges associated with the use of AI and ML in cybersecurity. How can biases and fairness issues be addressed in AI-driven security systems?

3. Research and analyze a recent cybersecurity incident where AI or ML technologies played a significant role in threat detection or incident response. Summarize the incident and discuss how AI or ML enhanced the security capabilities.

Conclusion

AI and ML have the potential to revolutionize cybersecurity by enhancing threat detection, automating incident response, and providing proactive defense against emerging threats. While there are challenges to overcome, the benefits of leveraging AI and ML in cybersecurity are immense. By embracing these technologies, organizations can gain a competitive advantage in combating evolving cyber threats and protecting their digital assets. The future holds exciting prospects as AI and ML continue to evolve, enabling safer and more secure digital environments for individuals and organizations alike.

Blockchain Technology in Healthcare Security

Blockchain technology has gained significant attention in recent years for its potential impact on various industries, including healthcare. In the context of cybersecurity, blockchain offers a promising solution to enhance the security and privacy of healthcare data. This section explores the principles and applications of blockchain technology in healthcare security, discussing its benefits, challenges, and future prospects.

Introduction to Blockchain Technology

Blockchain is a distributed ledger technology that enables secure and transparent record-keeping of transactions or data. It is based on a decentralized network of nodes that collectively validate and store information in blocks, forming an immutable chain. Each block contains a cryptographic hash of the previous block, ensuring the integrity and continuity of the entire chain.

In healthcare, blockchain can be utilized to securely manage and share sensitive health data, mitigate data breaches, streamline administrative processes, and foster trust among stakeholders. The key features of blockchain technology that contribute to its potential in healthcare security are:

- **Decentralization:** Blockchain operates in a decentralized manner, where multiple participants have copies of the distributed ledger. This eliminates the need for a central authority and reduces the risk of a single point of failure.

- **Immutability:** Once data is recorded on the blockchain, it becomes nearly impossible to alter or tamper with. The use of cryptographic hashes and consensus mechanisms ensures the integrity and non-repudiation of the stored information.

- **Transparency:** The transparency of blockchain allows all participants to have visibility into the transactions and data stored on the network. This promotes trust and accountability in healthcare processes.

- **Security and Privacy:** Blockchain employs robust cryptographic techniques to secure data, providing protection against unauthorized access and data breaches. Additionally, it enables granular control over data sharing permissions, ensuring privacy compliance.

- **Smart Contracts:** Smart contracts are self-executing agreements coded into the blockchain. They enable automation and enforce predefined rules, facilitating secure and efficient execution of healthcare processes.

Applications of Blockchain in Healthcare Security

Blockchain technology offers various applications and use cases in healthcare security, addressing the vulnerabilities and challenges faced by the industry. Some notable applications include:

1. **Secure Health Data Exchange** Healthcare systems often struggle with interoperability and secure sharing of patient health records. Blockchain can provide a secure and decentralized platform for efficient and seamless data exchange among healthcare providers, patients, and other authorized entities. By using blockchain, patients have more control over their health data, deciding who can access and modify it. This enhances privacy and reduces the reliance on intermediaries for data exchange.

2. **Medical Identity Management** Identity theft and medical fraud remain significant concerns in the healthcare industry. Blockchain-based identity management systems can securely store and verify patient identities, reducing the

risk of fraudulent activities. Patients can have a unique, immutable digital identity on the blockchain, making it easier to authenticate their personal health information.

3. **Drug Supply Chain Management** Counterfeit drugs pose a severe risk to patient safety and public health. Blockchain can be employed to create an immutable record of the entire supply chain, from drug manufacturing to dispensing. This helps to detect and eliminate counterfeit medicines by ensuring transparency and traceability. Pharmacies and patients can verify the authenticity of drugs by scanning their unique blockchain-based identifiers.

4. **Clinical Trials and Research Integrity** Blockchain technology can address the challenges of data integrity, traceability, and reproducibility in clinical trials and research studies. By recording trial protocols, informed consent, and trial data on the blockchain, researchers can ensure the immutability and transparency of the research process. This enhances the trustworthiness of research findings and accelerates the development of new treatments and interventions.

5. **Medical Device Security** The increasing connectivity of medical devices presents significant cybersecurity risks. Blockchain can enhance the security and integrity of medical devices by creating an auditable and tamper-proof record of device data and transactions. It can enable secure firmware updates, identity management, and detection of unauthorized access or tampering.

Challenges and Future Directions

While blockchain holds immense potential for healthcare security, several challenges need to be addressed for its widespread adoption and effectiveness:

1. **Scalability and Performance** Blockchain networks face scalability and performance issues when dealing with a large volume of transactions and data. Enhancements in consensus mechanisms, such as Proof of Stake (PoS) and sharding, can help overcome these challenges and enable faster transaction processing.

2. **Data Privacy and Compliance** Ensuring compliance with data privacy regulations, such as the Health Insurance Portability and Accountability Act (HIPAA), is crucial in healthcare. Proper encryption, obfuscation techniques, and

selective data sharing protocols need to be integrated into the blockchain infrastructure to protect sensitive patient information.

3. Interoperability and Standardization Achieving interoperability between different blockchain platforms and existing healthcare systems is essential for seamless data exchange. Collaboration among stakeholders and the development of industry standards are necessary to overcome interoperability challenges.

4. User Adoption and Education Blockchain technology is still relatively new and complex for many healthcare professionals. Adequate training, education, and awareness programs are necessary to facilitate the adoption and understanding of blockchain in healthcare.

The future of blockchain in healthcare security is promising, with ongoing research and development in areas such as privacy-enhancing technologies, integration with emerging technologies like Internet of Things (IoT) and Artificial Intelligence (AI), and the establishment of regulatory frameworks. Blockchain has the potential to revolutionize healthcare security, facilitating secure data exchange, reducing fraud, and enhancing patient outcomes.

Conclusion

Blockchain technology offers unique capabilities to address the security and privacy challenges faced by the healthcare industry. Its decentralized nature, immutability, transparency, and cryptographic security measures make it a promising solution for enhancing the security of health data, ensuring patient privacy, and mitigating cyber threats. However, challenges such as scalability, data privacy compliance, and interoperability need to be overcome for the widespread adoption and effectiveness of blockchain in healthcare security. Despite these challenges, the future of blockchain in healthcare holds great potential, paving the way for a more secure and patient-centric healthcare ecosystem.

Biometrics and Authentication Methods

Biometrics and authentication methods play a crucial role in ensuring the security and integrity of personal information in the health and wellness industry. Biometrics refers to the identification and verification of individuals based on their unique physical or behavioral characteristics. Authentication methods, on the other hand, involve the verification of the identity of individuals before granting them access to sensitive data or resources. In this section, we will explore different biometric technologies and authentication methods commonly used in the health and wellness industry.

Biometric Technologies

1. **Fingerprint Recognition:** Fingerprint recognition is one of the oldest and most widely used biometric technologies. It involves capturing an individual's unique fingerprint pattern and matching it against a pre-existing database. Fingerprint recognition systems are highly accurate and have a low false acceptance rate, making them suitable for secure authentication in healthcare settings.

2. **Face Recognition:** Face recognition technology analyzes a person's facial features for identification purposes. With advancements in deep learning algorithms, face recognition systems have become more reliable, even in varying lighting conditions and pose variations. Face recognition can be used for access control to restricted areas and patient identification in healthcare facilities.

3. **Iris Recognition:** Iris recognition technology involves capturing high-resolution images of an individual's iris, which contains unique patterns that are stable over time. Iris recognition systems offer high accuracy and are resistant to fraud attempts. In the health and wellness industry, iris recognition can be used for secure access to sensitive medical records and facilities.

4. **Voice Recognition:** Voice recognition technology analyzes an individual's voice patterns for authentication purposes. It can be used to verify the identity of patients when accessing telehealth services or medical call centers. Voice recognition systems are convenient and non-intrusive, making them suitable for remote patient authentication.

5. **Behavioral Biometrics:** Behavioral biometrics analyze an individual's unique behavioral patterns, such as typing rhythm, mouse movement, or gait recognition. These patterns can be used to continuously authenticate a user during their interaction with digital systems. Behavioral biometrics offer continuous authentication without the need for explicit user intervention, enhancing the overall security of sensitive health and wellness data.

6. **Vein Pattern Recognition:** Vein pattern recognition technology captures the unique patterns of blood vessels under the skin. It requires a near-infrared light source to capture the vein patterns, making it highly secure and difficult to forge. Vein pattern recognition can be used for secure access control in healthcare facilities or for patient identification.

Authentication Methods

1. **Multi-Factor Authentication (MFA):** Multi-factor authentication combines two or more authentication factors to verify an individual's identity. Common factors include something the user knows (e.g., a password or PIN), something the user possesses (e.g., a smart card or token), and something the user is (e.g., biometric authentication). MFA provides an additional layer of security and reduces the risk of unauthorized access to sensitive health and wellness data.

2. **Token-based Authentication:** Token-based authentication involves the use of physical devices, such as smart cards or security tokens, to authenticate users. These tokens generate one-time passwords that are synchronized with the authentication server. Token-based authentication is widely used in the health and wellness industry to secure access to electronic health records and other sensitive information.

3. **Passwordless Authentication:** Passwordless authentication is an emerging authentication method that eliminates the need for traditional passwords. It relies on alternative factors, such as biometrics or possession of a trusted device, for authentication. Passwordless authentication offers convenience and enhanced security, as biometric traits are more difficult to fake or steal compared to passwords.

4. **Risk-based Authentication:** Risk-based authentication adapts the level of authentication required based on the risk associated with a particular transaction or user behavior. It analyzes various inputs, such as device type, geolocation, and user behavior patterns, to assess the risk level. This approach enhances both security and user experience by providing a seamless authentication process for low-risk transactions and applying stronger authentication methods for high-risk activities.

5. **Single Sign-On (SSO):** Single sign-on allows users to authenticate once and gain access to multiple systems or applications without the need to provide credentials again. SSO provides convenience to healthcare professionals who need to access multiple applications during their workflow, without compromising security.

6. **Adaptive Authentication:** Adaptive authentication uses risk-based assessment and user behavior analysis to dynamically adjust the authentication process. It can require additional authentication factors if a user's behavior or risk level deviates from the norm. Adaptive authentication provides a balance between security and user experience, ensuring that the appropriate level of authentication is applied based on the context.

Example: Secure Patient Access to Electronic Health Records

In a modern healthcare system, secure access to electronic health records (EHRs) is paramount to protect patient privacy and confidentiality. By implementing biometric technologies and authentication methods, healthcare organizations can enhance the security of patient data while providing convenient and seamless access for authorized individuals.

For example, a healthcare facility can implement fingerprint recognition as a biometric authentication method for healthcare professionals to access patient EHRs. When a healthcare professional needs to access a patient's record, they would submit their fingerprint for identification. The system would match the fingerprint against the stored template and grant access if the match is successful. This ensures that only authorized personnel can access sensitive patient information.

To further strengthen the security, a multi-factor authentication (MFA) approach can be used. In addition to fingerprint recognition, the healthcare professional may be required to provide a one-time password generated by a token-based authentication device or a trusted application on their mobile device. This combination of biometric and token-based authentication adds an extra layer of security to prevent unauthorized access to EHRs.

Moreover, adaptive authentication can be employed to analyze user behavior and adjust the authentication requirements accordingly. For example, if a healthcare professional tries to access patient records from an unfamiliar location or at an irregular time, the system may prompt for additional authentication factors to ensure the legitimacy of the access request.

By integrating biometric technologies and authentication methods, healthcare organizations can establish a robust and secure access control system for patient EHRs, protecting patient privacy and preventing unauthorized access.

Resources and Further Reading

1. Jain, A. K., Ross, A., & Prabhakar, S. (Eds.). (2016). *Handbook of Biometrics*. Springer.

2. Fierrez, J., Ortega-Garcia, J., & Bigun, J. (Eds.). (2019). *Biometric Recognition: Challenges and Opportunities*. Springer.

3. Sasse, M. A., & Flechais, I. (2017). *User-Centered Security: Making Users an Active Part of Your Security Strategy*. O'Reilly Media.

4. Madsen, C., Dhamija, R., & Kamvar, S. (2009). *Security Immersion: How to Protect Yourself from Phishing Scams, Identity Theft, and Other Online Security Threats.*

Stanford University Press.

Exercises

1. Research and compare the advantages and limitations of fingerprint recognition and face recognition for secure patient identification in healthcare settings.

2. Describe how behavioral biometrics can be used to continuously authenticate users during their interaction with digital healthcare systems. Discuss its advantages and potential privacy concerns.

3. Investigate the challenges and solutions for implementing biometric authentication methods in telehealth platforms. How can biometrics enhance the security and convenience of remote patient authentication?

4. Analyze the security implications of using passwordless authentication in health and wellness applications. What are the benefits and risks associated with this authentication method?

5. Reflect on the ethical considerations of collecting and storing biometric data in the health and wellness industry. What measures should be taken to ensure the responsible use of biometrics?

Quantum Computing and Cybersecurity Implications

As technology continues to advance rapidly, quantum computing is emerging as a powerful tool with the potential to revolutionize various fields, including cybersecurity. Quantum computing is a form of computation that utilizes the principles of quantum mechanics to manipulate quantum bits or qubits. Unlike classical computers, which use bits that can represent a 0 or a 1, qubits can represent both states simultaneously, thanks to a property called superposition.

The development of practical, large-scale quantum computers poses both opportunities and challenges for cybersecurity. On one hand, quantum computing has the capacity to solve complex mathematical problems significantly faster than classical computers. This could potentially undermine many cryptographic protocols that currently ensure the security of sensitive data and communication.

Overview of Quantum Computing

To understand the implications of quantum computing on cybersecurity, it is important to delve into the fundamental principles of quantum mechanics and how they relate to computation. In classical computing, information is encoded in a series of bits, which can be in a state of either 0 or 1. Quantum computing, on the other hand, leverages the principles of superposition, entanglement, and interference to perform computations in parallel.

Superposition allows qubits to exist in multiple states simultaneously. It is as if a qubit can represent a 0 and a 1 at the same time. Entanglement refers to the phenomenon where two or more qubits become correlated, such that the state of one qubit depends on the state of the others. Interference is the interaction between multiple quantum states, resulting in constructive or destructive interference, which can enhance or diminish specific outcomes.

Quantum computers employ quantum gates, which are analogous to logic gates in classical computers, to manipulate qubits and perform computations. By applying various quantum gates to superposed qubits, quantum algorithms can exploit parallelism to perform certain computations more efficiently than classical counterparts.

Shor's Algorithm and its Impact on Cryptography

One of the most significant implications of quantum computing for cybersecurity lies in its potential to break many of the cryptographic algorithms that currently ensure the confidentiality and integrity of sensitive information. Peter Shor's algorithm, developed in 1994, demonstrated the ability of a quantum computer to solve the factorization problem efficiently.

The factorization problem is at the core of one-way functions, which are widely used in modern encryption schemes such as the widely used RSA algorithm. One-way functions are relatively easy to compute in one direction (e.g., multiplying two large prime numbers) but computationally hard to reverse (i.e., factoring the result back into its prime factors). Shor's algorithm exploits the quantum parallelism and offers a way to factor large numbers exponentially faster than classical algorithms.

If large-scale, fault-tolerant quantum computers become a reality, these machines could break RSA and other public-key cryptography schemes used for secure communication, digital signatures, and key exchange. This could render much of the current cryptographic infrastructure vulnerable to attacks, potentially compromising the security of financial transactions, sensitive communications, and critical infrastructure systems.

Post-Quantum Cryptography

In light of the potential threats posed by quantum computing to existing cryptographic methods, researchers are actively working on developing a new generation of cryptographic algorithms called post-quantum cryptography (PQC) or quantum-resistant cryptography. These algorithms are designed to resist attacks from both classical and quantum computers, ensuring the long-term security of sensitive data.

Post-quantum cryptographic algorithms fall into different categories, including lattice-based, code-based, multivariate polynomial-based, hash-based, and isogeny-based schemes. These algorithms leverage mathematical problems that are believed to be hard for a quantum computer to solve efficiently.

Implementing post-quantum cryptography involves assessing the computational and network performance of new algorithms, addressing backward compatibility issues, and ensuring a smooth transition from existing cryptographic systems. While there are ongoing efforts to standardize post-quantum cryptographic algorithms, adopting them on a large scale will require collaboration between industry, academia, and standardization bodies.

Quantum Key Distribution

Another approach to mitigate the risks associated with quantum computing is quantum key distribution (QKD). QKD is a method of secure key exchange that leverages the principles of quantum mechanics to generate and distribute cryptographic keys.

QKD utilizes the ability to detect eavesdropping on quantum communication channels based on the principle of the "observer effect." Any attempt to intercept or measure quantum signals during transmission will disturb the quantum state, introducing detectable errors. As a result, QKD can provide a secure key exchange that is theoretically impossible to compromise without detection.

While QKD offers promising security properties, it is important to note that it is limited by factors such as distance and the requirement for dedicated quantum communication channels. Overcoming these limitations and building practical QKD systems suitable for widespread deployment is an ongoing research challenge.

Preparing for the Quantum Future

As quantum computing continues to advance, the cybersecurity community needs to proactively prepare for the post-quantum era. This involves a multi-faceted approach that encompasses research, standardization efforts, and infrastructure upgrades to protect critical systems.

Organizations must start evaluating their cryptographic systems and identifying those that are vulnerable to quantum attacks. This includes assessing the lifetime of sensitive data and systems, as quantum computers will be able to retroactively decrypt encrypted information once they become available.

Investments in research and development are crucial to advancing the field of quantum-resistant cryptography. This includes exploring new mathematical problems that are resistant to quantum algorithms and developing efficient algorithms based on these problems.

Additionally, the adoption of quantum-safe cryptographic algorithms in a manner that ensures compatibility and interoperability is vital. This requires close collaboration between academia, industry, and standardization bodies to establish a unified set of cryptographic standards that provide security in both classical and quantum computing environments.

Cybersecurity professionals should also stay informed about the latest advancements and potential threats in quantum computing. Ongoing education and training on quantum-resistant encryption methods and technologies will be necessary to adapt to the changing landscape of cybersecurity.

The future of quantum computing and its implications for cybersecurity is still unfolding. While quantum computing brings immense computational power, it also presents challenges that need to be addressed to maintain the security and privacy of digital systems and communication. By working together, researchers, practitioners, and policymakers can navigate the quantum revolution and ensure a safer and more secure cyber world for health and wellness.

Genetic and Biomarker-Based Cybersecurity Solutions

In recent years, advancements in genetic and biomarker-based technologies have revolutionized the health and wellness industry. These technologies have enabled personalized medicine, enhanced disease diagnosis, and facilitated the development of targeted therapies. However, the increased reliance on genetic and biomarker data has also introduced new cybersecurity challenges. Protecting this sensitive information is crucial to ensure the privacy and security of individuals' genetic and health-related data. In this section, we will explore the cybersecurity solutions that can be employed to safeguard genetic and biomarker-based data.

Understanding the Risks

Before delving into the cybersecurity solutions, it is important to understand the risks associated with genetic and biomarker data. Genetic data contains highly sensitive and personal information that can reveal an individual's susceptibility to diseases, genetic disorders, and even their ancestral heritage. Unauthorized access or exposure of this data could lead to various privacy and security risks, including identity theft, discrimination, and compromise of personal and family information. Moreover, the potential for unauthorized alteration or manipulation of biomarker data poses a significant risk to the accuracy and integrity of diagnostic tests and treatment plans.

Encryption and Access Control

One of the fundamental cybersecurity measures to protect genetic and biomarker-based data is encryption. Encryption algorithms can transform genetic and biomarker data into a form that can only be accessed or deciphered with a secret key. By encrypting the data at rest and in transit, the risk of unauthorized access and data breaches can be significantly mitigated. Additionally, access control mechanisms should be implemented to ensure that only authorized personnel can access and modify the genetic and biomarker data. This includes strong authentication and authorization processes, such as multi-factor authentication and role-based access control, to verify the identity and permissions of users accessing the data.

Secure Storage and Transmission

When it comes to genetic and biomarker data, secure storage and transmission are of utmost importance. Storage systems should be protected against physical and logical threats, such as theft, accidental loss, or unauthorized access. Protected storage facilities with advanced physical security measures, including biometric access controls and video surveillance, can help safeguard the genetic and biomarker data. Additionally, secure transmission protocols, such as secure socket layer (SSL) and transport layer security (TLS), should be used when transmitting the data over networks to prevent eavesdropping and unauthorized interception.

Data Anonymization and Pseudonymization

To further enhance privacy and security, data anonymization and pseudonymization techniques can be applied to genetic and biomarker data. Anonymization involves removing or altering identifiers that can link the data to a specific individual, while pseudonymization replaces identifying information with a pseudonym or token. These techniques can help protect the privacy of individuals while still allowing researchers and healthcare professionals to analyze and process the data for medical and research purposes. It is important to note that the level of anonymization or pseudonymization should be carefully evaluated to balance privacy protection and data utility.

Continuous Monitoring and Intrusion Detection

Genetic and biomarker-based data may be targeted by cybercriminals seeking to gain unauthorized access or manipulate the data. To detect and respond to such threats, continuous monitoring and intrusion detection systems should be implemented. These systems use advanced algorithms and machine learning techniques to analyze network traffic, detect anomalies, and identify potential cyber attacks. In the event of a security incident, rapid response and incident management protocols should be in place to minimize the impact and prevent further compromise of the data.

Ethical Considerations

In the realm of genetic and biomarker-based cybersecurity, ethical considerations play a vital role. Genetic and biomarker data is highly personal and can potentially reveal sensitive information about an individual's health, behavior, and genetic makeup. Therefore, the ethical collection, use, and storage of this data should be a priority. Transparency, informed consent, and clear communication about the purposes, risks, and limitations of data collection and usage are essential to establish trust between individuals and healthcare organizations. Additionally, ethical guidelines and professional codes of conduct should be developed and adhered to by healthcare professionals and researchers working with genetic and biomarker data.

Emerging Technologies and Challenges

As genetic and biomarker-based technologies continue to evolve, new challenges and emerging technologies will shape the field of cybersecurity. For example, the increasing use of machine learning algorithms and artificial intelligence in analyzing genetic data introduces new vulnerabilities and risks, such as adversarial attacks and model poisoning. Similarly, the integration of blockchain technology in healthcare can enhance the security and immutability of genetic and biomarker data, but it also brings unique challenges related to scalability and interoperability. Keeping pace with these advancements and addressing the associated cybersecurity challenges will be critical for safeguarding genetic and biomarker-based data.

In conclusion, protecting genetic and biomarker-based data requires a multi-faceted approach that combines encryption, access control, secure storage and transmission, data anonymization, continuous monitoring, and ethical considerations. As technology continues to advance, healthcare organizations and researchers must remain vigilant in their efforts to secure this sensitive data. By implementing robust cybersecurity solutions, we can harness the power of genetic and biomarker-based technologies while safeguarding the privacy and security of individuals' genetic and health-related information.

Cybersecurity Risk Management and Governance

Implementing a Risk Management Framework

Implementing a risk management framework is crucial for organizations in the health and wellness industry to effectively identify, assess, and mitigate cybersecurity risks. A risk management framework provides a structured approach to managing risks and ensures that appropriate measures are in place to protect sensitive information and systems. In this section, we will discuss the key components of a risk management framework and provide guidance on how to implement it effectively.

Understanding Risk Management

Risk management is the process of identifying, analyzing, and evaluating potential risks to an organization and taking the necessary steps to mitigate or eliminate those risks. In the context of cybersecurity, risk management involves identifying and assessing potential threats and vulnerabilities to information systems and determining the impact they may have on the confidentiality, integrity, and availability of data.

The main goal of risk management is to strike a balance between the potential benefits of implementing new technologies and the potential risks associated with them. By implementing a risk management framework, organizations can make informed decisions about cybersecurity investments and ensure that they align with their overall business objectives.

Components of a Risk Management Framework

A risk management framework typically consists of the following components:

1. **Risk Identification:** This involves identifying and documenting potential risks that could impact the organization's information systems. This can be done through a variety of methods, such as conducting risk assessments, reviewing historical data on security incidents, and consulting with subject matter experts.

2. **Risk Analysis:** Once the risks have been identified, an analysis is conducted to determine the likelihood and potential impact of each risk. This analysis takes into account factors such as the value of the information at risk, the vulnerability of the system, and the potential threats that could exploit those vulnerabilities.

3. **Risk Evaluation:** The next step is to evaluate the identified risks based on the analysis conducted in the previous step. This involves determining the level of risk associated with each identified risk and prioritizing them based on their potential impact on the organization. Risk evaluation helps organizations allocate resources effectively and prioritize risk mitigation efforts.

4. **Risk Treatment:** Risk treatment involves selecting and implementing appropriate controls or countermeasures to reduce or eliminate the identified risks. This can include technical controls such as implementing firewalls or encryption, as well as administrative controls such as developing policies and procedures. The chosen controls should be based on the organization's risk tolerance, budget constraints, and legal and regulatory requirements.

5. **Risk Monitoring and Review:** Once the risk treatment measures have been implemented, it is essential to continuously monitor and review the effectiveness of these measures. This involves conducting periodic risk assessments, monitoring security incidents, and analyzing trends to identify any new or emerging risks. Regular reviews ensure that the risk management framework remains up-to-date and effective in addressing the evolving cybersecurity landscape.

6. **Risk Communication and Reporting:** Effective communication and reporting are critical aspects of a risk management framework. Clear and concise communication of risks, both internally within the organization and externally to stakeholders, helps ensure that everyone understands their role in managing cybersecurity risks. Regular reporting on risk management activities and the status of risk mitigation efforts keeps stakeholders informed and fosters accountability.

Implementing a Risk Management Framework

Implementing a risk management framework requires a coordinated effort and commitment from all levels of the organization. Here are some key steps to consider when implementing a risk management framework:

1. **Top-Level Commitment:** Senior management must demonstrate a commitment to cybersecurity and provide the necessary resources and support for implementing a risk management framework. This includes establishing cybersecurity policies, assigning responsibilities, and allocating funding for risk management activities.

2. **Risk Assessment:** Conduct a comprehensive risk assessment to identify and analyze potential risks to the organization's information systems. This can involve reviewing existing security controls, conducting vulnerability assessments, and engaging with external experts, if needed. The risk assessment should consider both internal and external threats and vulnerabilities.

3. **Risk Mitigation:** Develop and implement risk mitigation strategies based on the findings of the risk assessment. This may involve a combination of technical and administrative controls, such as implementing firewalls, intrusion detection systems, access controls, and security awareness training for employees. The risk mitigation measures should align with the organization's risk appetite and legal and regulatory requirements.

4. **Monitoring and Review:** Continuously monitor and review the effectiveness of the implemented risk mitigation measures. This can include monitoring security logs, conducting penetration testing, and analyzing incident reports. Regular reviews should be conducted to identify any gaps in controls and address emerging risks.

5. **Training and Awareness:** Provide regular training and awareness programs to employees to ensure they understand their roles and responsibilities in managing cybersecurity risks. This can include general cybersecurity awareness training, specific training on the organization's policies and procedures, and targeted training for individuals in high-risk roles.

6. **Continuous Improvement:** Establish a process for continuous improvement of the risk management framework. This can involve soliciting feedback from employees and stakeholders, conducting lessons learned

exercises after security incidents, and staying abreast of emerging threats and best practices in cybersecurity. Regularly updating the risk management framework ensures its effectiveness in addressing new and evolving risks.

Example: Implementing a Risk Management Framework

To illustrate how a risk management framework can be implemented, let's consider the example of a telehealth startup. The startup provides online healthcare services and collects sensitive patient information through their web platform. Here's how they can implement a risk management framework:

1. **Risk Identification:** The startup begins by identifying potential risks to the confidentiality, integrity, and availability of patient data. This includes risks such as unauthorized access to patient records, data breaches, and service interruptions.

2. **Risk Analysis:** The identified risks are analyzed to determine their likelihood and potential impact on the business. For example, the startup assesses the probability of a data breach occurring and the potential financial and reputational damage it could cause.

3. **Risk Evaluation:** Based on the analysis, the startup evaluates and prioritizes the identified risks. They determine that the risk of a data breach is high and that it poses a significant impact on the business, while other risks, such as minor service interruptions, have a lower priority.

4. **Risk Treatment:** The startup implements risk mitigation measures to reduce the identified risks. This includes implementing strong access controls, encrypting patient data, conducting regular security audits, and training employees on secure handling of patient information.

5. **Risk Monitoring and Review:** The startup continuously monitors and reviews the effectiveness of the implemented risk mitigation measures. They regularly analyze security logs, conduct vulnerability assessments, and stay updated on emerging cybersecurity threats to ensure their risk management framework remains effective.

6. **Risk Communication and Reporting:** The startup maintains open communication channels with stakeholders regarding cybersecurity risks. They regularly report on the status of risk mitigation efforts and communicate any changes to policies or procedures. They also provide

training to patients on how to protect their personal information when using the telehealth platform.

By implementing a risk management framework, the telehealth startup can effectively manage cybersecurity risks and protect the sensitive information of their patients, while ensuring the continuity of their business operations.

Key Takeaways

Implementing a risk management framework is essential for organizations in the health and wellness industry to effectively manage cybersecurity risks. A risk management framework consists of risk identification, analysis, evaluation, treatment, monitoring, and communication and reporting. It involves a coordinated effort from all levels of the organization and requires regular risk assessments, implementation of risk mitigation measures, and continuous monitoring and improvement. By implementing a risk management framework, organizations can make informed decisions regarding cybersecurity investments and protect sensitive information from potential threats.

Auditing and Assessing Cybersecurity Controls

In order to maintain a strong cybersecurity posture, it is essential for organizations in the health and wellness industry to regularly audit and assess their cybersecurity controls. Auditing allows organizations to identify any weaknesses or vulnerabilities in their systems, while assessments help to evaluate the effectiveness of existing controls. This section will explore the key concepts and best practices for auditing and assessing cybersecurity controls in the context of health and wellness.

Importance of Auditing and Assessing Cybersecurity Controls

Auditing and assessing cybersecurity controls are crucial activities for organizations as they provide insights into the overall security posture and help identify areas of improvement. By conducting audits, organizations can identify potential risks, vulnerabilities, and gaps in their cybersecurity controls. This allows them to prioritize their efforts and allocate resources effectively to mitigate any identified risks.

Assessments, on the other hand, provide a comprehensive evaluation of existing controls and their effectiveness. They help organizations gauge if their controls are adequately designed, implemented, and maintained to address the specific risks associated with their operations. Assessments also help organizations identify any deviations from established policies, standards, and regulatory requirements.

Overall, auditing and assessing cybersecurity controls enable organizations to proactively identify weaknesses, improve their security measures, and make informed decisions to enhance their overall cybersecurity resilience.

Auditing Cybersecurity Controls

Auditing cybersecurity controls involves a systematic and independent examination of an organization's cybersecurity infrastructure, policies, and processes. The primary objective of a cybersecurity audit is to evaluate the effectiveness of controls and ensure compliance with industry standards, regulations, and best practices. Here are some key steps involved in auditing cybersecurity controls:

1. **Define the Audit Scope and Objectives:** Begin by clearly defining the scope and objectives of the audit. This includes identifying the systems, processes, and policies that will be audited, as well as the goals to be achieved.

2. **Gather Information:** Collect and review relevant documentation, including security policies, procedures, incident reports, and previous audit findings. Understanding the organization's security architecture and controls is critical for an effective audit.

3. **Identify Risks:** Conduct a risk assessment to identify potential threats and vulnerabilities. This involves analyzing the organization's assets, processes, and technologies that could be targeted by cyber attacks. It is crucial to consider both internal and external risks.

4. **Evaluate Controls:** Assess the effectiveness of existing controls in mitigating identified risks. This includes examining technical controls, such as firewalls, intrusion detection systems, and encryption, as well as administrative controls, such as policies, training programs, and incident response procedures.

5. **Test Controls:** Perform various testing techniques, including vulnerability assessments and penetration testing, to determine the effectiveness of controls in real-world scenarios. This helps identify any gaps or weaknesses that could be exploited by attackers.

6. **Analyze Findings:** Evaluate the audit findings and categorize them based on their severity and impact. This allows the organization to prioritize actions and allocate resources accordingly.

7. **Recommendations and Remediation:** Develop recommendations for improving cybersecurity controls based on the audit findings. These

recommendations should address any identified weaknesses or deficiencies and align with industry best practices and regulatory requirements.

8. **Reporting and Communication:** Prepare a comprehensive audit report summarizing the findings, recommendations, and remediation plans. Clearly communicate the results to key stakeholders, such as management and IT teams, and ensure understanding of the identified risks and the need for remediation.

Assessing Cybersecurity Controls

Assessing cybersecurity controls involves a systematic evaluation of the effectiveness of an organization's control environment. The assessment helps identify the strengths and weaknesses of controls, measure their performance against defined objectives, and assess the organization's compliance with security requirements. Here are some key steps involved in assessing cybersecurity controls:

1. **Establish Assessment Criteria:** Define the assessment criteria and objectives for evaluating cybersecurity controls. These criteria should be aligned with industry standards, regulatory requirements, and organizational policies.

2. **Evaluate Control Design:** Assess the adequacy of control design in addressing specific risks and meeting the desired control objectives. This involves reviewing control policies, procedures, and guidelines to ensure they are comprehensive and well-defined.

3. **Assess Control Implementation:** Verify the implementation and effectiveness of controls. This involves conducting interviews, reviewing documentation, and performing testing to determine if control activities are performed as intended.

4. **Measure Control Effectiveness:** Evaluate the effectiveness of controls in mitigating risks and achieving control objectives. This may involve analyzing historical incident data, conducting control testing, and comparing control performance against defined benchmarks.

5. **Identify Control Gaps:** Identify any gaps or weaknesses in control design, implementation, or effectiveness. This includes identifying control deficiencies, non-compliance with policies, and areas where controls can be further enhanced.

6. **Report and Communicate:** Prepare a comprehensive assessment report that summarizes the findings, including control strengths, weaknesses, and recommendations for improvement. Clearly communicate the assessment results to key stakeholders, such as management, IT teams, and auditors, and ensure understanding of the identified control gaps and the need for remediation.

Best Practices and Considerations

When auditing and assessing cybersecurity controls, it is important to follow industry best practices and consider specific factors relevant to the health and wellness industry. Here are some best practices and considerations to keep in mind:

1. **Stay Updated with Regulations and Standards:** Stay informed about the latest cybersecurity regulations, standards, and frameworks relevant to the health and wellness industry. This includes HIPAA, GDPR, NIST Cybersecurity Framework, and ISO 27001. Ensure that the audit and assessment activities align with the requirements of these regulations and standards.

2. **Engage Professionals:** Consider engaging external cybersecurity auditing and assessment professionals who have expertise in the health and wellness industry. Their knowledge and experience can provide valuable insights and unbiased perspectives.

3. **Continuous Monitoring:** Implement continuous monitoring of cybersecurity controls to identify any deviations or changes in the control environment. Regular monitoring allows organizations to detect emerging threats, address control gaps in a timely manner, and adapt to evolving cybersecurity risks.

4. **Collaboration and Communication:** Foster collaboration and communication between IT teams, management, and internal audit functions. This ensures that audit findings are effectively communicated, remediation plans are understood, and accountability for control weaknesses is established.

5. **Risk-Based Approach:** Adopt a risk-based approach when auditing and assessing cybersecurity controls. Prioritize controls based on their criticality and potential impact on the organization's operations. This allows limited resources to be allocated to areas with the highest risk.

6. **Continuous Improvement:** Treat audits and assessments as opportunities for continuous improvement. Regularly review and update cybersecurity policies, procedures, and controls based on audit findings and emerging threats.

In conclusion, auditing and assessing cybersecurity controls are essential components of maintaining a robust cybersecurity program in the health and wellness industry. By following best practices and considering specific industry factors, organizations can identify weaknesses, remediate vulnerabilities, and improve their overall cybersecurity posture. Regular audits and assessments not only help safeguard sensitive data and systems but also demonstrate a commitment to protecting the privacy and security of patients and customers.

Collaborative Governance for Cybersecurity in the Health and Wellness Industry

The health and wellness industry is increasingly relying on digital technologies to provide efficient and convenient services to patients and consumers. However, with increased reliance on technology comes the risk of cybersecurity threats and breaches. In order to effectively mitigate these risks and ensure the protection of sensitive data, collaborative governance for cybersecurity is essential in the health and wellness industry.

Collaborative governance refers to the coordinated efforts of multiple stakeholders, including government agencies, industry associations, healthcare providers, and technology vendors, to address common challenges and achieve common goals. In the context of cybersecurity, collaborative governance fosters cooperation, information sharing, and collective decision-making to protect the integrity, confidentiality, and availability of critical information and systems.

One of the key benefits of collaborative governance in cybersecurity is the ability to leverage the diverse expertise and resources of different stakeholders. The health and wellness industry is vast and complex, involving various organizations such as hospitals, clinics, insurance providers, pharmaceutical companies, and digital health startups. Each of these organizations has unique cybersecurity needs and challenges. By coming together and sharing knowledge and experiences, these stakeholders can collectively develop best practices, standards, and guidelines for cybersecurity in the industry.

Collaborative governance also enables the establishment of robust information-sharing mechanisms. Sharing information about cybersecurity threats, attacks, and vulnerabilities is crucial for early detection and effective response. In a collaborative governance framework, stakeholders can share threat intelligence, incident reports, and mitigation strategies, allowing them to proactively defend against emerging cyber threats. This information-sharing can be facilitated through secure communication channels, such as trusted platforms or information-sharing and analysis centers (ISACs).

In addition, collaborative governance promotes the development and adoption of industry-wide cybersecurity standards and certifications. These standards and certifications ensure that health and wellness organizations have a consistent and measurable approach to cybersecurity. They provide a common framework for risk assessment, security controls, incident response, and compliance with relevant regulations and laws. By adhering to these standards, organizations can demonstrate their commitment to cybersecurity and build trust with their stakeholders.

An example of collaborative governance in the health and wellness industry is the Health Information Sharing and Analysis Center (H-ISAC). H-ISAC is an industry-driven organization that facilitates the sharing of cybersecurity information and best practices among healthcare providers, health insurance companies, pharmaceutical manufacturers, and medical device manufacturers. H-ISAC enables its members to collaboratively identify and address cybersecurity threats, promote awareness and education, and improve the overall cybersecurity posture of the industry.

However, collaborative governance for cybersecurity in the health and wellness industry also faces challenges. One of the major challenges is the need to balance information sharing with the protection of sensitive and confidential data. Healthcare organizations handle a vast amount of personal and medical data, which must be protected from unauthorized access and disclosure. Therefore, collaborative governance frameworks must establish robust privacy and security protocols to ensure the confidentiality of shared information.

Another challenge is the coordination and alignment of different stakeholders with varying priorities and interests. Healthcare providers may prioritize patient care and clinical outcomes, while technology vendors may focus on product innovation and time-to-market. Effective collaborative governance requires clear communication, mutual understanding, and a shared vision for cybersecurity in the industry. Regular meetings, workshops, and forums can facilitate dialogue and foster collaboration among stakeholders.

To promote collaborative governance for cybersecurity in the health and wellness industry, it is important to invest in education and awareness programs. Stakeholders should be educated about the evolving cybersecurity landscape, the latest threats and attack vectors, and the potential impact of breaches on patients' privacy and safety. Training programs, workshops, and simulations can enhance the cybersecurity awareness and skills of employees across different organizations.

Furthermore, regulatory authorities play a crucial role in promoting collaborative governance for cybersecurity. They can establish regulations, guidelines, and incentives to encourage information sharing, standardization, and collaboration in the industry. By enforcing cybersecurity requirements, conducting audits, and imposing penalties for non-compliance, regulatory authorities can incentivize organizations to actively participate in collaborative governance initiatives.

In conclusion, collaborative governance is essential for addressing the cybersecurity challenges faced by the health and wellness industry. By bringing together multiple stakeholders, sharing information, developing standards, and promoting awareness, collaborative governance enables organizations to collectively protect critical information and systems. The health and wellness industry must embrace collaborative governance to ensure the security and privacy of patient and consumer data in an increasingly interconnected and digitized world.

Cybersecurity Metrics and Key Performance Indicators

In the field of cybersecurity, metrics and key performance indicators (KPIs) play a crucial role in assessing the effectiveness of security measures and identifying areas that need improvement. By measuring specific aspects of a cybersecurity program, organizations can track their progress, evaluate the impact of security controls, and make informed decisions to mitigate risks. In this section, we will explore the importance of cybersecurity metrics and KPIs, discuss various measurement techniques, and provide examples of commonly used metrics.

Why Cybersecurity Metrics Matter

Cybersecurity metrics provide valuable insights into the overall security posture of an organization. They help quantify the effectiveness of security controls and provide a basis for decision-making and resource allocation. Without accurate and relevant metrics, it is challenging to identify vulnerabilities, assess the impact of security incidents, or measure the return on investment in cybersecurity.

Metrics also serve as a communication tool between cybersecurity professionals and organizational stakeholders. By presenting key metrics in a meaningful and easily understandable way, cybersecurity professionals can effectively communicate the potential risks and the need for investment in security initiatives. This enables organizational leaders to make informed decisions about cybersecurity strategies and resource allocation.

Additionally, cybersecurity metrics contribute to regulatory compliance efforts. Many cybersecurity regulations and frameworks require organizations to establish and report on specific metrics to demonstrate compliance with security standards. By diligently monitoring and tracking these metrics, organizations can ensure compliance with applicable laws and regulations.

Types of Cybersecurity Metrics

Cybersecurity metrics can be broadly categorized into four types: preventative, detective, corrective, and directive.

- **Preventative Metrics:** These metrics focus on measuring the effectiveness of preventive security controls. They aim to assess the organization's ability to stop or mitigate potential security incidents. Examples of preventative metrics include the percentage of successfully blocked malicious emails, the number of vulnerabilities remediated within a specified timeframe, and the rate of successful firewall rule validations.

- **Detective Metrics:** Detective metrics measure the organization's ability to identify and detect security incidents and vulnerabilities. They provide insights into the effectiveness of security monitoring and detection mechanisms. Examples of detective metrics include the average time taken to detect a security incident, the number of false positives in intrusion detection systems, and the rate of successful identification of unauthorized access attempts.
- **Corrective Metrics:** Corrective metrics assess the organization's ability to respond to and remediate security incidents promptly. They measure the efficacy of incident response processes and the speed of incident resolution. Examples of corrective metrics include the average time taken to resolve a security incident, the percentage of security incidents with documented root cause analysis, and the time taken to apply security patches and updates.
- **Directive Metrics:** Directive metrics focus on measuring the organization's adherence to established security policies, procedures, and standards. They provide insights into compliance efforts and the effectiveness of security awareness programs. Examples of directive metrics include the percentage of employees who have completed cybersecurity training, the number of security policy violations, and the rate of compliance with security control requirements.

Key Performance Indicators (KPIs)

Key performance indicators (KPIs) are specific metrics used to evaluate the performance of an organization or individual in achieving strategic objectives. In the context of cybersecurity, KPIs help assess the effectiveness of security programs and initiatives. They provide a high-level view of the security program's overall performance and aid in identifying areas for improvement.

When defining KPIs, it is essential to consider the organization's unique goals and priorities. KPIs should be aligned with the organization's strategic objectives and reflect its risk appetite. Some common cybersecurity KPIs include:

- **Mean Time to Detect** (MTTD)**:** This KPI measures the average time taken to detect security incidents. A lower MTTD indicates a more efficient incident detection capability, reducing the potential impact of security breaches.

- **Mean Time to Respond (MTTR):** MTTR measures the average time taken to respond to and remediate security incidents once they are detected. A lower MTTR indicates a prompt response to incidents, minimizing the duration and impact of security breaches.

- **Security Awareness Training Completion Rate:** This KPI measures the percentage of employees who have completed mandatory security awareness training. It helps assess the effectiveness of security awareness initiatives and the organization's overall security culture.

- **Percentage of Critical Systems with Up-to-date Patches:** This KPI measures the proportion of critical systems that have the latest security patches installed. It reflects the organization's ability to address known vulnerabilities in a timely manner, reducing the risk of exploitation.

- **Number of Successful Phishing Simulation Campaigns:** This KPI tracks the number of employees who successfully identify and report simulated phishing emails. It helps assess the effectiveness of phishing awareness programs and the organization's resilience against real-world phishing attacks.

Challenges in Metric Selection and Implementation

Selecting and implementing cybersecurity metrics can be challenging due to various factors. Some common challenges include:

- **Data Availability and Quality:** Metrics rely on accurate and reliable data. Lack of access to relevant data or poor data quality can undermine the validity and usefulness of metrics. Organizations need robust data collection, storage, and analysis processes to ensure the availability of high-quality data.

- **Subjectivity in Measurement:** Some cybersecurity aspects, such as the effectiveness of security awareness programs, can be challenging to measure objectively. Subjectivity in measurement introduces ambiguity and may result in inconsistent or unreliable metrics. Organizations should strive to develop standardized measurement techniques to increase the objectivity of metrics.

- **Metric Overload:** Monitoring too many metrics can be overwhelming and counterproductive. It can divert attention from essential security concerns and dilute the focus on critical areas. Organizations should carefully select a limited set of meaningful metrics that align with their strategic objectives and risk appetite.

- **Causality and Interpretation:** Metrics may indicate trends or correlations, but they may not provide a clear causal relationship or immediate action points. Interpreting metrics requires a deep understanding of the organization's security landscape and the broader context in which the metrics are operating.

To address these challenges, organizations should establish a robust process for metric selection, measurement, and reporting. This involves defining clear measurement objectives, leveraging automation and analytics tools for data collection and analysis, periodically reviewing and revising metrics based on changing threat landscapes, and integrating metrics into regular reporting and decision-making processes.

Conclusion

Cybersecurity metrics and key performance indicators are essential tools for assessing the effectiveness of security programs, communicating security risks to stakeholders, and making informed decisions to strengthen an organization's security posture. By carefully selecting and implementing metrics, organizations can monitor their progress, identify areas for improvement, and allocate resources effectively. However, it is important to acknowledge the challenges in metric selection, data quality, and interpretation to ensure that the metrics chosen truly reflect the organization's security objectives. With a well-defined set of metrics, organizations can continuously adapt and enhance their cybersecurity practices to withstand evolving threats in the digital landscape.

References:

1. Finkle, J. H., The Manager's Handbook for Corporate Security: Establishing and Managing a Successful Assets Protection Program

2. ISACA, Measuring and Managing Information Security Risk: A FAIR Approach

3. NIST Special Publication 800-55 Revision 1, Performance Measurement Guide for Information Security

Exercise:

Consider an organization that wants to improve its incident response capabilities. Define three potential metrics or KPIs that the organization can use to measure its progress in this area. Explain why each metric is relevant and how it can help the organization assess its incident response effectiveness.

Privacy and Security in Genomic Data

Securing Personal Genomic Data

With the rapid advancement of technology, the field of genomics has seen significant growth in recent years. Personal genomic data, consisting of an individual's genetic information and associated medical records, holds immense value for both medical research and personalized healthcare. However, the sensitive nature of this data raises concerns about privacy and security.

Importance of Personal Genomic Data Security

Personal genomic data contains highly sensitive information about an individual's genetic makeup, susceptibility to certain diseases, and potential health risks. Protecting this data is crucial to ensure the privacy and confidentiality of individuals' genetic information.

The unauthorized access, use, or disclosure of personal genomic data can have serious consequences, including genetic discrimination, stigmatization, and privacy breaches. To maintain public trust and foster advancements in genomics, robust security measures must be in place to protect personal genomic data.

Key Challenges in Securing Personal Genomic Data

Securing personal genomic data poses unique challenges due to its complex and sensitive nature. These challenges include:

1. **Data Volume and Complexity:** Personal genomic data is vast and complex, consisting of billions of genetic variants. Managing and securing this large-scale data requires scalable storage and processing solutions.

2. **Data Interoperability:** Personal genomic data is often generated and stored by different entities, including healthcare providers, laboratories, and research institutions. Ensuring secure interoperability between these diverse data sources is essential.

3. **Data Integrity and Accuracy:** Genetic data can be prone to errors and inaccuracies during the sequencing and interpretation process. Implementing mechanisms to verify data integrity and accuracy is crucial to ensure the reliability of personal genomic data.

4. **Consent and Control:** Individuals should have control over their own genomic data, including the ability to provide informed consent for data sharing and specify the purposes for which their data can be used. Preserving the autonomy and privacy of individuals is essential in the management of personal genomic data.

5. **Data Sharing and Collaboration:** Genomic research often relies on large-scale data sharing and collaboration between multiple stakeholders. Balancing the needs for data sharing while maintaining data security and privacy is a significant challenge.

6. **Emerging Technologies:** Advancements in technologies such as cloud computing and artificial intelligence offer new opportunities for genomic research and healthcare. However, these technologies introduce additional security risks that must be addressed.

Best Practices for Securing Personal Genomic Data

To address the challenges in securing personal genomic data, several best practices should be followed:

1. **Data Encryption:** Personal genomic data should be encrypted both at rest and in transit to protect against unauthorized access. Encryption algorithms and key management practices should adhere to industry-standard protocols.

2. **Access Controls and Authentication:** Implementing strong access controls and authentication mechanisms is crucial in limiting data access to authorized individuals. Multi-factor authentication and role-based access control should be enforced to ensure data privacy.

3. **Pseudonymization and Anonymization:** Personal identifiable information (PII) within genomic data should be pseudonymized or anonymized to minimize the risk of re-identification. De-identification techniques should be employed in accordance with relevant privacy regulations.

4. **Data Minimization:** Only collect and retain the minimum necessary genomic data for research and healthcare purposes. Avoid collecting unnecessary personal information to reduce the risk of data breaches.

5. **Secure Data Storage and Transmission:** Genomic data should be stored in highly secure environments that meet industry-accepted standards. This includes using secure servers, employing regular backups, and encrypting data during transmission.

6. **Audit Trails and Logging:** Implement comprehensive audit trails and logging mechanisms to track data access, modification, and transmission. Regular monitoring and analysis of these logs can help detect and respond to security incidents promptly.

7. **Data Breach Response Plan:** Develop a robust data breach response plan that outlines the steps to be taken in the event of a security incident. This plan should include procedures for notification, containment, mitigation, and recovery.

Ethical Considerations in Securing Personal Genomic Data

Securing personal genomic data also raises important ethical considerations, including:

1. **Informed Consent:** Individuals should be provided with clear and understandable information about how their genomic data will be used, shared, and secured. Informed consent is crucial to respect the autonomy and privacy rights of individuals.

2. **Data Ownership:** Clarify the ownership and control of personal genomic data. Individuals should have a say in deciding how their data is used and shared, and they should retain ownership of their genetic information.

3. **Equitable Access:** Ensure equitable access to the benefits of genomic research and personalized healthcare. Efforts should be made to address potential biases and disparities in the collection, analysis, and utilization of personal genomic data.

4. **Research Ethics:** Ethical considerations should govern the conduct of genomic research, including data sharing, privacy protection, and the use of personal genomic data for research purposes.

Conclusion

Securing personal genomic data is of paramount importance to protect the privacy and confidentiality of individuals' genetic information. By following best practices, addressing the unique challenges, and considering ethical considerations, we can ensure the safe and responsible use of personal genomic data. As technology continues to advance, it is crucial to stay updated with the latest security measures and adapt them to the evolving landscape of genomics.

Privacy Issues in Genetic Testing and Research

Genetic testing and research have become increasingly popular in recent years, thanks to advancements in technology and our growing understanding of genetics. However, with these advancements come privacy concerns. The nature of genetic information makes it highly sensitive and personal, raising important ethical and legal considerations. In this section, we will explore the privacy issues associated with genetic testing and research and discuss the measures in place to protect individuals' privacy.

The Nature of Genetic Information

Before delving into privacy concerns, it is important to understand the nature of genetic information. Genetic information refers to data about an individual's genetic makeup or inherited characteristics. It includes information obtained through genetic testing, such as DNA sequencing or analysis, as well as information derived from research studies involving genetic data.

Unlike other types of health information, such as medical diagnoses or treatment records, genetic information is unique to an individual. It contains highly personal details about one's ancestry, biological relationships, predispositions to certain health conditions, and potential response to medications. This makes genetic information particularly sensitive and merits special protection.

Existing Privacy Regulations

To address the privacy challenges posed by genetic testing and research, several laws and regulations have been enacted to protect individuals' genetic privacy. One of the landmark legislations in this area is the Genetic Information Nondiscrimination Act (GINA), which was enacted in the United States in 2008. GINA prohibits discrimination by health insurers and employers based on an individual's genetic information. It also restricts the collection and use of genetic information in employment and health insurance decisions.

In addition to GINA, other privacy laws, such as the Health Insurance Portability and Accountability Act (HIPAA), offer some level of protection for genetic information. HIPAA regulates the use and disclosure of protected health information by covered entities, including healthcare providers, health plans, and healthcare clearinghouses. Genetic information is considered protected health information under HIPAA.

Beyond the United States, many countries have implemented similar regulations to protect individuals' genetic privacy. For instance, the European Union's General Data Protection Regulation (GDPR) includes genetic data as a special category of personal data, enacting strict requirements for its processing and ensuring individuals have control over their genetic information.

Privacy Risks in Genetic Testing and Research

Despite the existing regulatory frameworks, privacy risks still exist in the context of genetic testing and research. These risks arise from various sources and require attention to safeguard individuals' genetic privacy.

One significant privacy risk is the potential re-identification of genetic data. While de-identifying genetic information is crucial to protect privacy, it is not always a foolproof method. With the vast amounts of publicly available genetic data, combined with other data sources, it may be possible to re-identify individuals who were thought to be anonymous. This highlights the need for robust de-identification methods and safeguards to prevent re-identification.

Another privacy risk is the unauthorized access or disclosure of genetic information. This could occur through data breaches, cyberattacks, or insider threats. Genetic data can be highly valuable to malicious actors, such as insurance companies, employers, or even individuals seeking to harm their relatives. Protecting genetic data from unauthorized access is crucial to ensure individuals maintain control over their personal information.

Furthermore, the potential misuse of genetic information poses a significant risk to privacy. For example, insurance companies could use genetic data to discriminate against individuals, denying coverage or charging higher premiums based on an individual's genetic predisposition to certain health conditions. Similarly, employers could discriminate in hiring or promotion decisions based on genetic information. Strict regulations and safeguards are necessary to prevent such potential abuses.

Protecting Genetic Privacy

To protect individuals' privacy in the context of genetic testing and research, various measures can be implemented.

First and foremost, organizations collecting and processing genetic data should prioritize data security. This includes implementing robust encryption methods, secure storage systems, access controls, and regular monitoring for any unauthorized activity. Additionally, organizations should conduct regular risk assessments and ensure they have incident response plans in place to address any privacy breaches effectively.

Transparency and informed consent are also crucial to protect genetic privacy. Individuals should be fully informed about the nature of the genetic testing or research, the potential privacy risks, and how their data will be used. Informed consent should be obtained before any data collection occurs, and individuals should have the option to revoke consent or limit the use of their genetic information at any time.

Data anonymization is another key principle in protecting genetic privacy. Prior to sharing or disseminating genetic data, all personal identifying information should be removed or de-identified to prevent re-identification. Organizations should adhere to best practices and guidelines for anonymization techniques to reduce the risk of re-identification.

Interdisciplinary collaborations between privacy experts, geneticists, and policymakers are instrumental in developing privacy-preserving approaches in genetic testing and research. This collaboration can help identify and address privacy concerns from the early stages of research design, ensuring that privacy is considered throughout the entire process.

Case Study: The Golden State Killer

The case of the Golden State Killer illustrates the privacy risks associated with genetic testing. The Golden State Killer was a notorious serial killer and rapist who committed crimes in California between 1974 and 1986. He remained unidentified for decades until he was apprehended in 2018, thanks to the use of genetic genealogy.

Investigators used genetic data from a crime scene to create a DNA profile of the suspect. This profile was then uploaded to a publicly accessible genealogy database, leading them to distant relatives of the suspect. Through careful research and reverse genealogy techniques, they were able to identify the Golden State Killer.

While this case demonstrated the power of genetic genealogy in solving crimes, it also raised concerns about the privacy of genetic data. The genetic information used to identify the suspect was not directly acquired from him but from relatives who had willingly uploaded their data to a genealogy database. The incident sparked a broader discussion about the potential risks and implications of genetic data sharing.

Conclusion

Privacy is a significant concern when it comes to genetic testing and research. The sensitive and personal nature of genetic information requires robust privacy measures to protect individuals' rights and prevent potential abuses. By adhering to existing regulations, implementing strong data security practices, obtaining informed consent, and prioritizing data anonymization, we can strike a balance between the benefits of genetic testing and research and the protection of individuals' privacy. Ultimately, safeguarding genetic privacy is crucial to ensure trust and promote the responsible use of genetic information for the betterment of health and wellness.

Ethical Considerations in Genomic Data Privacy

Genomic data privacy is a critical concern in the field of health and wellness. With the advancement of technology and the availability of genomic testing, individuals can now access detailed information about their genetic makeup. This data provides valuable insights into their health risks, potential diseases, and even ancestry. However, the sensitive nature of genomic data raises important ethical considerations that must be addressed to protect individual privacy and ensure responsible use of this information.

Importance of Genomic Data Privacy

Genomic data contains highly personal and sensitive information. It can reveal information about an individual's propensity for certain diseases, genetic conditions, and even their relatedness to others. Additionally, genomic data can carry significant implications for family members, as it unveils shared genetic traits and potential health risks. As a result, protecting the privacy of genomic data is paramount to safeguarding an individual's autonomy, confidentiality, and overall well-being.

Informed Consent and Ownership

In the context of genomic data privacy, obtaining informed consent from individuals is essential. This means that individuals must fully understand the implications and potential risks associated with genetic testing before providing their data. Informed consent should include clear explanations of how the data will be used, stored, and shared, as well as the potential benefits and limitations of genomic testing.

Furthermore, the issue of data ownership arises when it comes to genomic data. Should individuals retain ownership of their genomic data, or should it be considered a shared resource? Establishing clear guidelines on data ownership is crucial to address ethical concerns and ensure that individuals have the right to control the use and dissemination of their genetic information.

Data Sharing and Access Control

Genomic data privacy requires careful management of data sharing and access control. It is essential to have robust policies and procedures in place to regulate who can access and use genomic data. This includes defining clear criteria for granting access to researchers, healthcare providers, and other relevant stakeholders, while also ensuring that appropriate security measures are in place to protect against unauthorized access.

Additionally, data sharing practices should be transparent and subject to appropriate oversight. Institutions and organizations involved in genomic research or genetic testing should provide clear information on how genomic data will be shared, ensuring that individuals have the opportunity to opt-out of sharing their data if they wish. This promotes transparency and empowers individuals to make informed decisions about the use of their genetic information.

Data De-identification and Anonymization

One approach to enhancing genomic data privacy is through data de-identification and anonymization. De-identification involves removing or altering identifiable information from the data to eliminate the possibility of re-identification. Anonymization takes this a step further by irreversibly transforming the data, ensuring that it cannot be linked back to an individual.

While data de-identification and anonymization techniques can provide some level of privacy protection, it is important to note that complete de-identification may not always be foolproof. Advances in technology and the availability of public datasets can potentially be used to re-identify individuals from seemingly anonymized genomic data. Therefore, it is crucial to continuously evaluate and update de-identification and anonymization techniques to stay ahead of potential privacy breaches.

Genetic Discrimination and Stigmatization

Ethical considerations in genomic data privacy also extend to issues of genetic discrimination and stigmatization. Genetic information can be used to discriminate against individuals in various contexts, including employment, insurance coverage, and social relationships. Policies and laws should be in place to protect individuals from such forms of discrimination, ensuring that genomic data is not used to deny opportunities or perpetuate biases.

Moreover, stigmatization related to genetic conditions can severely impact an individual's mental and emotional well-being. Healthcare professionals, researchers, and policymakers must promote awareness and education to reduce stigma surrounding genetic conditions and ensure that individuals are not unfairly marginalized or judged based on their genetic information.

Public Education and Awareness

Promoting public education and awareness is pivotal in addressing ethical considerations in genomic data privacy. It is crucial to educate individuals about the risks, benefits, and limitations of genomic testing and the importance of protecting their genetic information. This includes informing individuals about their rights regarding data privacy, emphasizing the need for informed consent, and explaining how their data will be used and shared.

Additionally, fostering a culture of responsible data sharing and research collaboration is essential. Public awareness campaigns can highlight the importance of responsible data stewardship and the potential benefits of sharing genomic data for research purposes. Empowering individuals to actively participate in decisions regarding the use of their genetic information can help build trust and mitigate ethical concerns.

Case Study: The Henrietta Lacks Story

The story of Henrietta Lacks provides a compelling example of the ethical considerations surrounding genomic data privacy. Henrietta Lacks was an African American woman whose cancer cells were taken without her consent in 1951 and used for medical research. These cells, known as HeLa cells, have played a crucial role in numerous scientific discoveries and advancements.

The case of Henrietta Lacks raises questions about informed consent, data ownership, and the commercialization of genetic material. It highlights the need for ethical frameworks and policies that protect individuals' rights and ensure equitable access to the benefits derived from the use of genomic data.

Resources and Guidelines

Several organizations and guidelines contribute to the ethical considerations in genomic data privacy. The World Medical Association's Declaration of Helsinki provides ethical guidelines for medical research involving human subjects, including informed consent and privacy protection. The Global Alliance for Genomics and Health promotes responsible data sharing practices and patient-centered approaches to genomics.

Furthermore, regulatory bodies like the U.S. Health Insurance Portability and Accountability Act (HIPAA) and the European General Data Protection Regulation (GDPR) have specific provisions addressing the privacy and security of genomic data. Adhering to these guidelines and regulations can help ensure ethical and responsible use of genomic data.

Conclusion

Ethical considerations in genomic data privacy play a vital role in safeguarding individual rights and promoting responsible use of genetic information. Informed consent, data sharing practices, data de-identification, and awareness campaigns all contribute to building a framework that addresses the ethical challenges associated with genomic data privacy. By prioritizing these considerations, we can unlock the potential of genomics while protecting individual privacy and societal well-being.

Towards a Safer and More Secure Cyber World for Health and Wellness

Cybersecurity Awareness Campaigns and Advocacy

In today's digital age, where cyber threats and attacks are becoming increasingly sophisticated and prevalent, cybersecurity awareness has never been more important. It is crucial for individuals, organizations, and governments to understand the risks and take proactive measures to protect themselves and their valuable information. Cybersecurity awareness campaigns and advocacy play a significant role in spreading knowledge, promoting best practices, and encouraging a security-conscious mindset across all sectors, including health and wellness.

Importance of Cybersecurity Awareness

Cybersecurity awareness is the foundation of a robust and resilient cybersecurity posture. It involves educating individuals about the potential threats they face, equipping them with the knowledge and skills to identify and respond to these threats effectively, and fostering a culture of cybersecurity within organizations and communities. By raising awareness, we can empower individuals to make informed decisions, protect their personal information, and contribute to a safer digital environment.

In the context of health and wellness, cybersecurity awareness becomes even more critical. The sensitive nature of personal health information and the increasing reliance on digital health technologies make this industry a prime target for cybercriminals. Medical identity theft, unauthorized access to electronic health records, and ransomware attacks on healthcare institutions can have severe consequences for individuals' privacy, well-being, and even their lives. Therefore, promoting cybersecurity awareness in the health and wellness sector is of utmost importance to safeguard patient information and ensure the integrity of healthcare services.

Objectives of Cybersecurity Awareness Campaigns

Cybersecurity awareness campaigns aim to achieve several key objectives:

1. **Education and Training:** The primary objective is to educate individuals about cybersecurity risks, best practices, and preventive measures. This includes raising awareness about common threats such as phishing, malware, and social engineering attacks, as well as providing practical guidance on password security, software updates, and safe online behavior.

2. **Promotion of Good Cyber Hygiene:** Cyber hygiene refers to the adoption of habits and practices that enhance security and protect against cyber threats. Awareness campaigns focus on promoting good cyber hygiene practices such as regular data backups, strong passwords, multi-factor authentication, and software patching.

3. **Behavioral Change:** The ultimate goal of cybersecurity awareness campaigns is to bring about a behavioral shift. By informing and

empowering individuals, campaigns aim to encourage the adoption of secure behaviors in both personal and professional contexts. This includes being cautious when sharing personal information online, verifying the authenticity of requests for sensitive data, and reporting suspicious activities.

4. **Targeted Messaging:** Effective campaigns tailor their messages to specific audiences. In the health and wellness sector, campaigns may focus on healthcare professionals, patients, or both. Different messages may be created for different age groups, educational backgrounds, or levels of technical expertise to ensure maximum impact and relevance.

5. **Partnerships and Collaboration:** Cybersecurity awareness campaigns often involve collaborations between government agencies, industry associations, non-profit organizations, and private sector stakeholders. By working together, these entities can pool resources, share expertise, and reach a broader audience.

6. **Monitoring and Evaluation:** It is essential to track the effectiveness of awareness campaigns and their impact on behavior change. This can be done through surveys, assessments, and metrics to evaluate knowledge retention, perception of risks, and the adoption of secure practices.

Effective Strategies and Tactics

To ensure the success of cybersecurity awareness campaigns and advocacy efforts, various strategies and tactics should be employed. Here are some effective approaches:

1. **Multi-Channel Communication:** Campaigns should leverage multiple communication channels to reach diverse target audiences. These channels may include websites, social media platforms, mobile apps, email newsletters, posters, brochures, workshops, webinars, and public service announcements. By utilizing various mediums, campaigns can effectively convey their messages and engage individuals through their preferred channels.

2. **Engaging and Interactive Content:** Static and lengthy content is less likely to capture the attention of the target audience. Instead, campaigns should focus on creating engaging and interactive content that can hold individuals' interest. This can include videos, infographics, quizzes, gamified learning

platforms, and real-life case studies to make the content relatable and practical.

3. **Role-Modeling and Peer Influence:** Humans are social creatures, and we tend to seek validation from peers and role models. Awareness campaigns can leverage this by showcasing real-life stories of individuals who have fallen victim to cyber attacks or have successfully mitigated threats. These stories can inspire others to adopt safe cybersecurity practices and create a sense of community resilience.

4. **Continuous Updates and Reminders:** Cybersecurity threats and best practices evolve constantly. Therefore, campaigns should provide regular updates, reminders, and refresher content to ensure that individuals stay informed and up to date. This can be done using newsletters, social media posts, and periodic training sessions.

5. **Incentives and Rewards:** Incentives can be an effective way to motivate individuals to actively participate in cybersecurity initiatives. This may include rewards for completing online training modules, reporting potential vulnerabilities, or suggesting improvements to existing cybersecurity practices. By gamifying the learning experience and offering tangible benefits, campaigns can increase engagement and knowledge retention.

6. **Partnerships with Influencers and Experts:** Collaborating with influencers, subject matter experts, and respected figures in the health and wellness industry can lend credibility and widen the reach of cybersecurity awareness campaigns. These individuals can help deliver messages effectively, engage their followers, and provide expert advice and insights.

7. **Community Engagement and Grassroots Efforts:** Cybersecurity is a collective responsibility, and campaigns should encourage community engagement. This can involve organizing local events, workshops, and community forums to raise awareness, share knowledge, and facilitate discussions on cybersecurity challenges specific to the health and wellness sector. Grassroots efforts can empower individuals to take ownership of their cybersecurity and become advocates within their communities.

Addressing Challenges and Pitfalls

While cybersecurity awareness campaigns have the potential to make a significant impact, there are challenges and pitfalls to be mindful of. Here are a few key considerations:

1. **Content Overload:** Information overload can overwhelm individuals, leading to disengagement and limited knowledge retention. Campaigns should strike a balance between providing comprehensive information and keeping the content concise, relevant, and easy to understand.

2. **Language and Accessibility:** Effective campaigns should consider the diverse audience they aim to reach. Content should be presented in plain language, free from technical jargon, and should accommodate individuals with varying levels of digital literacy and disabilities. Providing translated materials, closed captions, and audio versions can enhance accessibility.

3. **Changing Threat Landscape:** Cyber threats evolve rapidly, and new attack vectors emerge regularly. Awareness campaigns need to be adaptable and capable of addressing emerging threats in real-time. This requires continuous monitoring of the threat landscape and agile communication strategies to keep individuals well-informed and prepared.

4. **Sustainability and Long-Term Commitment:** Cybersecurity awareness is an ongoing process, and campaigns need to sustain their efforts beyond initial launches. It is crucial to secure long-term funding and commitment from stakeholders to ensure consistent messaging, continuous updates, and regular training opportunities.

5. **Measurement and Evaluation:** Establishing metrics and evaluation methods is vital to assess the effectiveness and impact of awareness campaigns. Regular assessments and feedback loops enable campaigns to identify areas for improvement and adjust strategies accordingly.

Resources and Collaborative Initiatives

Creating effective cybersecurity awareness campaigns requires access to reliable resources and collaborative initiatives. Various organizations and initiatives can provide valuable support, including:

- **National Cybersecurity Agencies:** Many countries have dedicated agencies responsible for promoting cybersecurity awareness at a national level. These agencies often provide guidance, best practices, and training materials that can be integrated into awareness campaigns.

- **International Organizations:** International organizations such as the World Health Organization (WHO) and the International Telecommunication Union (ITU) have initiatives and resources focused on cybersecurity in the health and wellness sector. These resources can serve as a valuable reference for awareness campaigns.

- **Industry Associations and Non-Profit Organizations:** Industry associations and non-profit organizations, such as the American Health Information Management Association (AHIMA) and the Health Information Trust Alliance (HITRUST), offer resources, guidelines, and collaborative platforms to promote cybersecurity awareness and best practices within the health and wellness industry.

- **Public-Private Partnerships:** Public-private partnerships can facilitate the exchange of knowledge, expertise, and resources to develop effective cybersecurity awareness campaigns. These partnerships leverage industry insights while collaborating with government agencies and academia to address cybersecurity challenges collectively.

- **Open-Source Projects:** Open-source projects, such as the Cybersecurity Awareness Framework (CSAF), provide comprehensive resources, templates, and toolkits that organizations can use to develop customized awareness campaigns. These projects often involve collaboration from cybersecurity experts worldwide.

Case Study: "Stop. Think. Connect." Campaign

One notable cybersecurity awareness campaign is the "Stop. Think. Connect." campaign, a global initiative aimed at promoting safe and responsible online behavior. The campaign addresses a wide range of cybersecurity issues and provides practical tips for individuals and organizations to protect themselves in the digital realm.

The "Stop. Think. Connect." campaign focuses on four core principles:

- **Be Vigilant:** Individuals are encouraged to be cautious and think critically before sharing personal information online. The campaign emphasizes the importance of verifying the authenticity of websites, emails, and messages before providing sensitive information.

- **Protect Personal Information:** This principle emphasizes the need to safeguard personal data by using strong passwords, enabling multi-factor authentication, and being aware of privacy settings on social media platforms. The campaign educates individuals about the risks of oversharing personal information online and highlights the importance of maintaining privacy.

- **Connect with Care:** The "Connect with Care" principle advises individuals to exercise caution when interacting with others online. It includes guidelines on safe social media usage, identifying potential scams, and recognizing the signs of social engineering attacks.
- **Be a Good Online Citizen:** This principle emphasizes responsible digital citizenship and encourages individuals to report cybercrimes and suspicious activities. It promotes ethical behavior, respect for others' privacy, and the importance of contributing to a safe and secure online environment.

The "Stop. Think. Connect." campaign provides a wide range of resources, including posters, tip sheets, infographics, and videos that can be utilized in cybersecurity awareness campaigns. Collaborative events, online training sessions, and public-private partnerships are also established to extend the reach and impact of the campaign.

Conclusion

Cybersecurity awareness campaigns and advocacy efforts play a crucial role in equipping individuals, organizations, and communities with the knowledge and skills necessary to navigate the ever-evolving cybersecurity landscape. In the health and wellness industry, where sensitive personal information and critical healthcare systems are at stake, promoting cybersecurity awareness is paramount to protecting patient privacy, ensuring the integrity of healthcare services, and fostering a culture of cybersecurity across all stakeholders.

By harnessing effective strategies, leveraging available resources, and collaborating with industry experts and organizations, cybersecurity awareness campaigns can make a meaningful impact in promoting safe and secure practices. It is through continuous education, training, and behavior change that we can collectively build a safer and more secure cyber world for health and wellness.

International Collaboration in Cybersecurity

In today's interconnected world, cyber threats know no national borders. The global nature of cyber attacks necessitates international collaboration and cooperation in the field of cybersecurity. By joining forces, countries can share information, resources, and expertise to combat cyber threats effectively. In this section, we will explore the importance of international collaboration in cybersecurity and discuss various initiatives and organizations working towards a safer and more secure cyber world.

The Need for International Collaboration

Cybersecurity threats are not limited to a single country or region. Adversaries can launch attacks from anywhere in the world, targeting individuals, organizations, and even critical infrastructure systems. To effectively defend against these threats, it is essential for countries to collaborate and work together. Some key reasons for international collaboration in cybersecurity include:

- **Information Sharing:** Collaboration allows countries to share real-time threat intelligence, tactics, techniques, and procedures (TTPs) used by cybercriminals. By exchanging information, countries can enhance their situational awareness and stay ahead of emerging threats.
- **Capacity Building:** Developing countries often face challenges in building robust cybersecurity capabilities due to limited resources and expertise. International collaboration can help bridge this gap by providing technical assistance, training programs, and knowledge sharing.
- **Global Governance:** Cybersecurity requires consistent standards and policies at a global level. Collaboration among nations allows for the development of internationally recognized frameworks and regulations, ensuring a cohesive and unified approach to cybersecurity.
- **Promoting Trust and Stability:** International collaboration helps build trust among nations by fostering cooperation and transparency. By working together, countries can establish a secure and stable cyberspace for economic growth, trade, and innovation.

Initiatives and Organizations

Several initiatives and organizations are actively involved in promoting international collaboration in cybersecurity. Let's explore some of the key players in this field:

1. **United Nations (UN):** The UN plays a vital role in facilitating international cooperation and dialogue on cybersecurity. The UN Group of Governmental Experts (UN GGE) provides a platform for member states to discuss and address cybersecurity challenges at a global level. The UN also promotes capacity building through various training programs and workshops.

2. **International Telecommunication Union (ITU):** As an agency of the UN, the ITU focuses on information and communication technologies (ICTs) and their impact on society. The ITU's Global Cybersecurity Index (GCI) assesses countries' cybersecurity preparedness and promotes international collaboration in this domain.

3. **Organization for Economic Cooperation and Development (OECD):** The OECD facilitates discussions among member countries on cybersecurity policy frameworks, best practices, and risk management. It also conducts research and analysis on emerging cybersecurity issues.

4. **Forum of Incident Response and Security Teams (FIRST):** FIRST is a global organization that brings together incident response teams from around the world. It enables member teams to collaborate, share information, and coordinate responses to cyber incidents.

5. **International Multilateral Partnership Against Cyber Threats (IMPACT):** IMPACT, based in Malaysia, aims to enhance the global community's capacity to prevent and respond to cyber threats. It provides training programs, cybersecurity awareness campaigns, and assists member countries in developing their cybersecurity strategies.

6. **Cybersecurity and Infrastructure Security Agency (CISA):** CISA, a part of the United States Department of Homeland Security, works with international partners to strengthen global cybersecurity. It focuses on sharing threat intelligence and coordinating incident response efforts.

Challenges in International Collaboration

While international collaboration is crucial for effective cybersecurity, it comes with its own set of challenges. Some of these challenges include:

- **Differing Priorities and Interests:** Countries often have diverse priorities and varying levels of cybersecurity maturity. Aligning these interests and coordinating efforts can be challenging but is necessary for effective collaboration.

- **Legal and Regulatory Hurdles:** Differences in legal frameworks and regulatory environments can impede information sharing and cooperation. Harmonizing laws and regulations can facilitate smoother collaboration between countries.

- **Language and Cultural Barriers:** Effective collaboration requires clear communication and understanding among countries. Language and cultural barriers can hinder information sharing and coordination efforts. Efforts should be made to bridge these gaps through translation services and cultural awareness programs.

- **Cyber Sovereignty Concerns:** Some countries prioritize national sovereignty in cyberspace, which can create challenges in information sharing and coordination. Striking the right balance between sovereignty and collaboration is crucial to address shared security concerns effectively.

Case Study: The Budapest Convention

The Budapest Convention on Cybercrime, also known as the Council of Europe Convention on Cybercrime, is an international treaty aimed at combating cybercrime. It serves as a framework for international cooperation among countries in investigating and prosecuting cybercriminal activities. The convention addresses various forms of cybercrime, including offenses related to computer systems, data, and network security. It also facilitates the exchange of information and provides a legal basis for international cooperation by establishing measures for mutual assistance and extradition.

The Budapest Convention is an excellent example of international collaboration in cybersecurity. It currently has 65 member states, including countries from Europe, the Americas, and Asia. The convention has been instrumental in promoting cooperation, harmonizing legislation, and facilitating joint investigations and prosecutions of cybercriminals.

Conclusion

International collaboration is crucial in the ever-evolving field of cybersecurity. By working together, countries can effectively combat cyber threats, share valuable information, and build robust cybersecurity capabilities globally. Initiatives and organizations play a vital role in facilitating this collaboration and promoting trust and stability in cyberspace. While challenges exist, efforts must continue to overcome these hurdles and foster a safer and more secure cyber world for health and wellness.

Resources:

- The Budapest Convention on Cybercrime: `https://www.coe.int/en/web/cybercrime/the-budapest-convention`

- United Nations Group of Governmental Experts (UN GGE) on Cybersecurity: `https://www.un.org/disarmament/topics/cybersecurity/un-gge/`

Promoting Cyber Wellness in the Digital Age

In today's digitally connected world, where technology plays a crucial role in our daily lives, promoting cyber wellness is of utmost importance. Cyber wellness refers to the state of well-being and security individuals experience in the digital realm. It encompasses not only the protection of personal information and prevention of cyber threats but also the development of healthy digital habits and responsible online behavior.

As the health and wellness industry becomes increasingly digitized, it is vital for individuals, organizations, and governments to work together to promote cyber wellness. This section explores various strategies and initiatives that can be undertaken to ensure a safer and more secure digital environment for all.

Educating the Public on Cybersecurity

One of the key steps in promoting cyber wellness is to educate the public on the significance of cybersecurity. This includes raising awareness about the potential risks and threats associated with the use of digital technologies and providing practical tips on how to stay safe online.

Educational campaigns and initiatives should target individuals of all ages and backgrounds. By providing accessible and engaging materials, such as videos, infographics, and interactive workshops, people can learn about topics like password hygiene, identifying phishing attempts, and using secure communication channels.

Furthermore, it is essential to emphasize the importance of regularly updating software and devices to safeguard against vulnerabilities, as well as the significance of strong passwords and multi-factor authentication in protecting personal information.

Promoting Digital Citizenship and Ethical Behavior

Promoting cyber wellness also involves encouraging digital citizenship and ethical behavior online. Digital citizenship refers to the responsible and ethical use of technology, with a focus on respecting others' rights, privacy, and intellectual property.

Schools and educational institutions should incorporate digital citizenship into their curriculum, helping students develop a strong foundation in online ethics. This includes teaching them about online etiquette, responsible social media usage, and the potential consequences of cyberbullying and online harassment.

Moreover, organizations and industry leaders have a role to play in setting ethical standards for digital practices. By promoting transparency, data privacy, and fair use of information, they can create a culture of digital responsibility and integrity.

Collaboration with Technology Companies

Promoting cyber wellness requires collaboration between various stakeholders, including technology companies. These companies are at the forefront of digital innovation and can significantly influence the security and privacy of their users' data.

To promote cyber wellness, it is crucial for technology companies to prioritize user security and privacy in the design and development of their products and services. This includes implementing robust security measures, providing clear privacy policies, and offering user-friendly security features.

Additionally, collaboration between technology companies and cybersecurity experts can lead to the development of more secure and resilient digital systems. By sharing knowledge and best practices, these collaborations can drive innovation in cyber defense and help safeguard individuals' digital well-being.

Government Regulations and Policies

Government regulations and policies play a vital role in promoting cyber wellness. They provide a framework for organizations to adhere to cybersecurity standards and ensure the protection of individuals' digital rights.

Governments should enact legislation that addresses issues such as data privacy, cybercrime, and digital literacy. They should also establish regulatory bodies to enforce compliance and hold organizations accountable for cybersecurity breaches.

Furthermore, governments can support initiatives aimed at promoting cyber wellness, such as funding research and development in cybersecurity, providing resources for public awareness campaigns, and offering incentives for organizations that prioritize cybersecurity.

Building Resilience and Recovery Strategies

Despite the best preventive measures, cyber incidents may still occur. Therefore, promoting cyber wellness also involves building resilience and recovery strategies. This includes the establishment of incident response teams and the development of comprehensive incident response plans.

Organizations should conduct regular cybersecurity assessments, identify vulnerabilities, and implement appropriate controls to mitigate risks. They should also ensure the availability of regular backups and disaster recovery plans to minimize the impact of cyber incidents.

Moreover, organizations should provide training and resources to empower individuals to respond effectively to cyber incidents. This includes educating employees on reporting procedures, providing incident response training, and conducting simulated exercises to test the effectiveness of response plans.

Public-Private Partnerships

Promoting cyber wellness requires the collective effort of both public and private sectors. Public-private partnerships can foster collaboration, knowledge sharing, and resource mobilization to address the multifaceted challenges of cybersecurity.

These partnerships can involve government agencies, technology companies, industry associations, academic institutions, and non-profit organizations. By pooling their expertise and resources, they can develop joint initiatives, awareness campaigns, and capacity-building programs to promote cyber wellness.

Public-private partnerships can also facilitate information sharing and collaboration on threat intelligence, ensuring a more coordinated and effective response to emerging cyber threats.

Conclusion

Promoting cyber wellness in the digital age is essential to ensure the protection of personal information and the overall well-being of individuals. By educating the public on cybersecurity, promoting digital citizenship, collaborating with technology companies, implementing government regulations, building resilience, and fostering public-private partnerships, we can create a safer and more secure cyber world for all.

Remember, cybersecurity is a constantly evolving field, and staying informed and proactive is key to maintaining cyber wellness. By adopting the principles outlined in this section and continuously updating our knowledge and practices, we can navigate the digital landscape with confidence and security.

Research and Development in Cybersecurity Solutions

Research and development play a crucial role in the ever-evolving field of cybersecurity. As cyber threats continue to advance in sophistication, it is essential to stay ahead of attackers by continually exploring and implementing innovative solutions. This section explores current research trends and key areas of development in cybersecurity, providing insights into the future of safeguarding health and wellness information.

1. Artificial Intelligence and Machine Learning

Artificial intelligence (AI) and machine learning (ML) techniques have become powerful tools in the fight against cyber threats. AI algorithms can analyze vast amounts of data, identify patterns, and detect anomalies that may indicate a cyber attack. ML models can be trained to make accurate predictions and decisions in real-time, enabling proactive defense mechanisms. For example, anomaly detection algorithms can identify unusual behavior in network traffic or user activity, alerting system administrators to potential security breaches.

One key research focus is developing AI and ML models that can automatically adapt and learn from new threats. This involves using techniques such as deep learning to enable systems to detect and respond to emerging attack vectors. Moreover, researchers are exploring ways to enhance the interpretability and explainability of AI models to ensure transparency and accountability in cybersecurity decision-making.

Example Problem:

Develop an AI-based system that uses machine learning to detect and prevent phishing attacks targeted at healthcare providers. The system should analyze email content, attachments, and user behavior to identify suspicious indicators and provide real-time warnings to potential victims.

2. Blockchain Technology in Cybersecurity

Blockchain technology has gained significant attention in recent years, primarily due to its association with cryptocurrencies like Bitcoin. However, its potential in cybersecurity extends beyond cryptocurrency applications. Blockchain's decentralized and immutable nature can provide a secure and tamper-proof environment for storing healthcare data and ensuring data integrity.

Research efforts are focused on exploring ways to leverage blockchain to enhance security in areas such as electronic health records (EHRs), supply chain management, and identity verification. For instance, blockchain-based EHR systems can provide patients with control over their health data, ensuring privacy while allowing secure access to authorized healthcare providers.

Example Problem:

Design a blockchain-based system to secure medical device data, ensuring the integrity and authenticity of readings stored in electronic health records. Develop a proof-of-concept implementation that demonstrates the benefits of blockchain technology in preventing tampering and unauthorized access.

3. Biometrics and Authentication Methods

Traditional authentication methods, such as passwords and PINs, are increasingly susceptible to security breaches. Biometric-based authentication, which uses unique physical or behavioral characteristics, offers a more secure alternative. Biometrics, such as fingerprints, facial recognition, and voice recognition, can provide a robust means of verifying user identity.

Ongoing research focuses on developing advanced biometric systems that are resistant to spoofing attacks and can handle large-scale deployments. Additionally, researchers are exploring multi-modal biometrics, which combine multiple biometric traits to achieve higher levels of accuracy and security. These efforts aim to enhance user authentication in healthcare systems, protecting sensitive information from unauthorized access.

Example Problem:

Develop an AI-powered biometric recognition system that incorporates facial, voice, and fingerprint authentication for secure access to electronic health records. The system should be resistant to spoofing attacks, capable of handling diverse user populations, and provide fast and accurate authentication.

4. Quantum Computing and Cybersecurity Implications

Quantum computing holds great promise for solving complex problems that are currently intractable for classical computers. However, it also presents significant challenges for conventional cryptographic algorithms used to secure data. Quantum computers have the potential to break many commonly used encryption algorithms, threatening the confidentiality and integrity of sensitive information.

Researchers are working on post-quantum cryptography, which aims to develop encryption algorithms resistant to attacks by quantum computers. These new cryptographic techniques leverage mathematical problems that are difficult for both classical and quantum computers to solve. Furthermore, research efforts involve investigating quantum-safe protocols for secure communication and key exchange in a future where quantum computers are prevalent.

Example Problem:

Design and implement a quantum-resistant encryption algorithm that can be used in healthcare systems to protect sensitive patient data even in the presence of powerful quantum computers. Evaluate the algorithm's security, efficiency, and compatibility with existing systems.

5. Genetic and Biomarker-Based Cybersecurity Solutions

With advancements in genomics and personalized healthcare, genetic and biomarker-based data are becoming increasingly valuable. Protecting this sensitive information from a cybersecurity perspective is critical. Researchers are exploring innovative techniques to secure genetic and biomarker data, ensuring privacy and confidentiality.

One area of research focus involves developing encryption schemes specifically designed for genomic data. These schemes aim to preserve data utility while guaranteeing privacy. Additionally, there are efforts to explore techniques such as homomorphic encryption and secure computation to allow secure analysis of encrypted genomic data.

Example Problem:

Design a secure and privacy-preserving framework for sharing genetic and biomarker data among healthcare providers for research purposes. The framework should protect the confidentiality of individual genomic information while allowing aggregation and analysis of large-scale datasets.

Resources and Future Directions

Research and development in cybersecurity solutions continue to accelerate, driven by the growing threats and challenges in the health and wellness industry. Academic institutions, government organizations, and industry collaborations play a vital role in advancing cybersecurity research.

Researchers can benefit from participating in conferences, workshops, and collaborative projects dedicated to cybersecurity in the health and wellness sector. Peer-reviewed journals and technical reports also provide valuable resources for staying updated on the latest advancements.

The future of cybersecurity in health and wellness holds great promise for enhancing information protection and safeguarding personal wellbeing. Continued research and development efforts will be essential to address emerging threats, develop robust defense mechanisms, and foster a culture of cybersecurity awareness across all stakeholders.

Summary

This section highlighted key research and development trends in cybersecurity solutions for health and wellness. Advancements in artificial intelligence, blockchain technology, biometrics, quantum computing, and genomic data security are shaping the future of cybersecurity in this field. Engaging in research activities, collaborating with industry professionals, and staying informed about the latest advancements are crucial for tackling emerging threats and securing personal information in a digitally connected world.

Public-Private Partnerships for Cybersecurity in Health and Wellness

In today's digitally connected world, the importance of cybersecurity in the health and wellness industry cannot be overstated. Cyber attacks and data breaches can have severe consequences on personal wellbeing, as sensitive healthcare information can be misused and exploited. To combat these threats, it is crucial for public and private entities to come together and form partnerships that focus on cybersecurity in the health and wellness sector.

The Need for Public-Private Partnerships

Cybersecurity is a complex and ever-evolving field, requiring expertise from various stakeholders. Public-private partnerships bring together the resources, knowledge, and capabilities of both sectors to create a collaborative and comprehensive approach to cybersecurity. In the context of health and wellness, such partnerships are essential due to the highly sensitive nature of the data involved.

Goals and Objectives

The primary goal of public-private partnerships in cybersecurity for health and wellness is to protect the privacy and security of personal health information. This includes securing electronic health records, health monitoring devices, and communication platforms. These partnerships aim to establish robust cybersecurity frameworks and best practices, facilitate information sharing, and create a culture of cybersecurity awareness among healthcare professionals and consumers.

Roles and Responsibilities

Public-private partnerships allocate specific roles and responsibilities to each sector involved. The public sector, comprising government agencies and regulatory bodies, plays a crucial role in creating and enforcing cybersecurity regulations and standards. They also provide guidance, oversight, and coordination in establishing partnership frameworks.

The private sector, including healthcare organizations, technology companies, and cybersecurity firms, brings their industry expertise and technical capabilities to the table. They collaborate with the public sector to develop innovative cybersecurity solutions, implement best practices, and improve the resilience of health and wellness systems.

Collaboration and Information Sharing

Public-private partnerships foster collaboration and information sharing among stakeholders. By working together, organizations can share threat intelligence, vulnerabilities, and best practices, contributing to a collective defense against cyber threats. Collaboration may occur through regular forums, working groups, and joint initiatives aimed at addressing cybersecurity challenges specific to the health and wellness sector.

By sharing information, public and private entities can learn from each other's experiences, identify emerging threats, and collectively develop effective strategies. This collaborative environment enables faster response times, more efficient incident management, and continuous improvement in cybersecurity capabilities.

Funding and Resource Allocation

Financial resources are critical for implementing cybersecurity measures effectively. Public-private partnerships may involve funding arrangements where both sectors contribute to the financial requirements. While the government provides financial support through grants, subsidies, and investments, the private sector contributes its resources, expertise, and financial commitments to cybersecurity initiatives.

Proper resource allocation ensures that cybersecurity programs receive adequate funding, enabling research and development, cybersecurity education and training, and the implementation of cutting-edge technologies to strengthen the health and wellness sector's cybersecurity defenses.

Benefits and Challenges

Public-private partnerships offer several benefits for cybersecurity in health and wellness. These partnerships leverage the diverse skills and perspectives of both sectors, leading to more comprehensive and effective cybersecurity strategies. Collaboration facilitates faster knowledge sharing and enables coordinated response to cyber threats. Moreover, public-private partnerships promote a culture of cybersecurity awareness and responsibility across the sector.

However, challenges may arise in establishing and maintaining these partnerships. Differences in organizational culture, legal frameworks, and business interests between the public and private sectors can create complexities. Finding a balance between information sharing and protecting proprietary data can also be challenging. Effective governance, strong leadership, and clear communication channels are crucial for overcoming these challenges and ensuring the success of such partnerships.

Case Study: Health Information Sharing and Analysis Center (H-ISAC)

One example of a successful public-private partnership in the health and wellness sector is the Health Information Sharing and Analysis Center (H-ISAC). H-ISAC is a global, non-profit organization that brings together healthcare stakeholders, including government agencies, private sector companies, and industry associations, to share cybersecurity threat intelligence and best practices.

H-ISAC facilitates collaboration through information sharing, incident response coordination, and education. Its members exchange cybersecurity information in real-time, enabling proactive threat mitigation and response. H-ISAC also provides training and conducts tabletop exercises to enhance the sector's cybersecurity preparedness.

The success of H-ISAC demonstrates the value of public-private partnerships in improving cybersecurity in the health and wellness industry. By pooling resources and expertise, H-ISAC enables its members to stay ahead of evolving cyber threats and protect critical healthcare systems and data.

Conclusion

Public-private partnerships are integral to enhancing cybersecurity in the health and wellness sector. These partnerships offer a collaborative approach that combines the strengths of both sectors to protect personal health information and ensure the overall wellbeing of individuals. By working together, public and private entities can establish robust cybersecurity frameworks, share critical information, and develop innovative solutions to combat cyber threats effectively. Through these partnerships, we can achieve a safer digital ecosystem for health and wellness.

Index

9 781779 610935

Printed by
Libri Plureos GmbH · Friedensallee 273
22763 Hamburg · Germany